The New Inflation

THE NEW INFLATION

The Collapse of Free Markets

W. David Slawson

Princeton University Press
Princeton, New Jersey

Published by Princeton University Press, Princeton, New Jersey In the United Kingdom; Princeton University Press, Guildford, Surrey

Library of Congress Cataloging in Publication Data will be found on the last printed page of this book

Clothbound editions of Princeton University Press books are printed on acid-free paper, and binding materials are chosen for strength and durability

Printed in the United States of America by Princeton University Press, Princeton, New Jersey

FOR MY FATHER AND MOTHER

Donald G. Slawson and

Virginia B. Slawson

CONTENTS

ACKNOWLEDGMENTS vii

INTRODUCTION 3

PART I The New Inflation 25

1. The Inflationary Forms of Competition 30
2. Inflationary Markets 46
3. Pricing Institutions 65
4. Sellers' Uncertainties 108
5. Competitive Inflation 126
6. Demand-Pull / Cost-Push / Wage-Push 155

PART II The Need for a New Economics 179

7. The Sources of Economic Determinism 184
8. The Costs of Economic Determinism 223
9. The New Economics 267

PART III Controlling Inflation 303

10 The Shape of the Program 310

11. Some Specific Directions for the Program 350

INDEX 415

ACKNOWLEDGMENTS

My interest in inflation began in 1970, when I wrote an article for a law journal on price controls,[1] but it did not really become focused until I became general counsel to the Price Commission in the 1971 Economic Stabilization Program. The day-to-day tasks of the Price Commission job kept me fully occupied, but when I left I already had the nucleus of the ideas that came to compose the book. On the strength of the job and the article and a preliminary exposition of the ideas, I obtained a grant from the Social Sciences Division of the National Science Foundation that enabled me to interview business people, labor union officials, and government officials, and to employ assistants to do library research and additional interviewing. I would like to thank the foundation and the one-time director of its Social Sciences Division, Walter Probert, in particular. Professor Probert displayed an intuitive understanding of my ideas, without which, I think, the grant would not have been obtained. I also want to thank my former colleague, Louis M. Brown, for his encouragement and support at this critical stage of the project.

I have learned from the writings of too many economists to be able to acknowledge them all individually, but there are three whose ideas or insights I found to be especially helpful: John Kenneth Galbraith, Robert L. Heilbroner, and Peter Wiles. The principal shaping influence on the book, however, was provided by the historian Thomas S. Kuhn. His book, *The Structure of Scientific Revolutions,*[2] assured me that my ideas could be right although almost no economists understood them, and it provided me with a strategy for getting my ideas across. I am indebted to the philosopher Hannah Arendt and the historians Isaiah Berlin and John Lukacs for their different but mutually supportive analyses of why human actions

[1] W. David Slawson, "Price Controls for a Peacetime Economy," *Harvard Law Rev.* 84 (March 1971), 1090–1107.

[2] 2d ed. (Chicago: University of Chicago Press, 1970).

are never just the results of events. I am also indebted to Hannah Arendt for her analysis of judgment, which was so unfortunately cut short by her death. I am indebted to the historian Eric Voegelin for his profound exposition of history as a search for meaning. It helped me to understand the development of economic thought. All these people helped me to see that economics, like any body of thought, distorts the understanding of life, and life itself, when it pictures human behavior as objectively determined.

I wish to thank my colleagues at the University of Southern California Law Center, in particular Michael H. Shapiro, Jeff Strnad, Stephen J. Morse, and Scott H. Bice, and my occasional colleague, Allan Axelrod, for their contributions to my thinking, their help on parts of the manuscript, and their moral support. I also want to thank Professor Louis B. Schwartz of the University of Pennsylvania Law School for his support and scholarly assistance. I thank Dorothy W. Nelson, the former dean of the University of Southern California Law Center, and again, Scott H. Bice, the present dean, for their official support.

I thank Vernon White and Lee Nemcheck, both of whom willingly gave me secretarial assistance far beyond the requirements of their job. I am grateful to the staff of the library of the law school, which helped me immeasurably and with unfailing good humor throughout, in particular Fannie Fishlyn, Jill Mubarak, Will Vinet, and Robert Rich. I benefited from the efforts of many good research assistants, two of whom, Joel Fishman and Michael Cane, gave outstanding help.

I thank my friends, Betty Ann Kevles and Daniel J. Kevles, for their help on parts of the manuscript and their advice on publishing and publishers.

I thank the many business and professional persons, labor union officials, and civil servants who talked with me or my assistants, sometimes at great length. There are too many to be named, and some of them asked not to have their names disclosed. Many of them used the occasion to ask me my views, and we frequently disagreed. Nevertheless, I never felt that any of them told me anything they did not believe or held back anything significant. The chief source of my long interest in economics is the thrill I have always felt in participating in, observing, or contemplating the world's work. These interviews were a pleasure from first to last.

I acknowledge my indebtedness to the excellent business reporting of the *Wall Street Journal* and *Fortune* magazine, both of which are cited numerous times. A book of this kind would hardly be possible without journalistic sources upon which it could depend. Scholarly sources are generally available only for information that has been shown to be relevant by theoretical work, and they generally lag years behind.

Most of all I thank Kaaren Tofft Slawson, my wife, for her long though imperfect tolerance of my shifting moods, her emotional support, her invaluable and utterly comprehensive editorial assistance, and her help in working out my ideas.

The New Inflation

INTRODUCTION

The ability of free markets to keep prices down has collapsed. This is the cause of the new inflation—not too much money or too few goods. What is more, free markets will never again be able to keep prices down. Advances in technology and changes in societal conditions have seen to this. The advances and changes cannot be reversed, and most of us would not want them to be if they could. There will therefore have to be wage and price controls if the inflation is to be stopped, although these controls should not be like those we have had in the past. Those require a large bureaucracy, they inhibit competition, and they interfere with free market's ability to allocate resources, which has not collapsed. But different kinds of controls would work. There will also have to be a new economics, to enable us to understand the new inflation and how it could be stopped. The economics we have is obsolete, among other reasons because it is still premised on the ability of free markets to keep prices down.

This is the second time in our history that a failure of economic understanding has led to a major economic collapse. The first was the Great Depression. Cycles of "boom and bust" had plagued the market economies of the world since they began, and had never been understood. The Great Depression was only the most recent and one of the worst. The English economist John Maynard Keynes provided the key to understanding business cycles in 1936, but it came too late to be of immediate help.[1] The Great Depression was eventually overcome fortuitously, by the economic stimulation provided by the Second World War.[2]

This time, however, the failures of economic understanding

[1] John Maynard Keynes, *The General Theory of Employment Interest and Money* (New York: Harcourt, Brace, Jovanovich, 1936). See generally, Robert Lekachman, *The Age of Keynes* (New York: Vintage Books, 1966).

[2] Lekachman, *Age of Keynes*, pp. 188–91.

are more fundamental and their consequences are less likely to be overcome fortuitously. Any war or similar emergency is only likely to make inflation worse. The measures that will have to be adopted to overcome the present crisis are likely to change the market economies of the world much more than they were changed by the Keynesian measures that were adopted to control business cycles. As the title of this work indicates, the very basis of a market economy, the markets themselves, have ceased to function as they should, and there is nothing that we could feasibly do that would restore their efficacy so long as they remain "free"—that is, so long as sellers remain unconstrained in setting prices. Capitalism is not fated to disappear, but if we choose to have it survive it will have to be changed substantially.

There are currently two schools of opinion about contemporary inflation. The more influential holds that contemporary inflation is caused by excess aggregate demand and that this excess aggregate demand is caused either by too large a deficit between government expenditures and receipts, or by too rapid an expansion of the money supply. The influence of this school is manifest in the policies of both the present administration and the administration that preceded it. They both sought to reduce federal spending and to restrict the expansion of the money supply. The Carter administration also resisted tax decreases. The Reagan administration has sought tax decreases, but is intent on reducing federal spending even more. The members of this school tend to be politically conservative.[3]

The second school is more diffuse, which partly accounts for its being less influential. In essence it claims that contemporary inflation is caused by certain economic structual characteristics. Those most commonly identified are large business enterprises; labor unions; minimum wage laws; limits on agricultural production and agricultural price supports; high

[3] Robert D. Hershey, Jr., "Inflation at 13.3%: What Is This Rapacious Thing?" *New York Times,* February 3, 1980, sec. 3, pp. 1, 8, 9.

levels of unemployment compensation; high costs of antipollution, safety, and health regulation; changes in the composition of the labor force; the spread of egalitarian attitudes; and the tide of economic progress that allows an affluent population to spend more and work less. The members of this school tend to be politically liberal.[4]

The liberals, or structuralists, as they are also called, probably have also had less influence than they might because the conservatives' prescriptions have been more appealing. The temper of the seventies was conservative. It appears that the eighties will be the same. Conservative opinion favors less government spending because it favors less government. It is also inclined to view government spending other than that which goes to support the military or the police as morally blameworthy: most such spending supposedly results from the demands of people who want to be paid but do not want to work. Again, the structuralists have been less influential because government spending, monetary policy, or even taxes are generally much easier to change than are structural characteristics. We would all like to think that there was an easy way to make inflation go away.

But despite their differences in influence and appeal, the two current schools of opinion about inflation are ultimately the same, and they are wrong. They both at bottom blame excess demand. The structuralists disagree with the conservatives only on how they think the excess demand is produced. The conservatives think it is produced directly by excessive government spending or excessive rates of increase in the money supply. The structuralists think it comes from one or more structual characteristics. The minimum wage laws, for example, are thought to increase demand by increasing the income of low-paid workers and to decrease supply by making these workers too expensive to hire. Both effects tend to make demand exceed supply.

John Kenneth Galbraith, himself a leading structuralist,

[4] Ibid.

has made the similarity between the two schools even clearer. Presumably referring to the structural characteristic I called "the spread of egalitarian attitudes," he has said,

> The son or daughter of a working class family is assumed to have a right to go to university. Except by a clothing expert their jeans are not distinguishable from those of the children of the boss. Even in the United States there is now a persistent feeling . . . that the poor should have access to a doctor. . . . The economic effect of this release of consumption from occupational and class restraint is to put a strong, even relentless, pressure on the supply of both private and public goods and services.[5]

The "strong, even relentless, pressure" to which Mr. Galbraith refers is of course increased demand.

Robert Lekachman, also a leading structuralist, expressed the similarity as follows:

> If depression were a politically viable policy, even our friendly oligopolists and health-care supporters would in time respond to the shrinking markets for their products and services by trimming their definitions of acceptable prices and wages. But since the citizenry will not—and should not—wait for the 10% and 15% unemployment to cure inflation, the course of events is predictable: Strong unions obtain wage improvements that come close to the rate of inflation, which their employers in turn pass on in the shape of higher prices, while everyone else struggles as best he can to catch up.[6]

Mr. Lekachman apparently believes that reducing demand would indeed eliminate inflation, but that the amount of demand reduction that would be required makes this morally wrong and politically impractical.

Some of the structural characteristics that supposedly cause

[5] Ibid., p. 8.

[6] Robert Lekachman, "The Desperate Need for Wage-price Curbs," *Los Angeles Times,* February 1, 1980, pt. 2, p. 5.

inflation are said to do so by reducing competition. This claim is indirectly tantamount to the conservatives' claim that the cause is excess demand. For, according to traditional economics, increases or decreases in demand work, respectively, to increase or decrease prices through the mechanism of competition, and decreases or increases in competition work, respectively, in the same way. Thus, if excess demand were indeed causing contemporary inflation, it would be because prices are being pulled up by what is in effect a decrease in competition: the same numbers of sellers are offering the same quantity of goods in a market in which selling is being made easier by increasing demand. Likewise, if reducing demand (or increasing supply) really would reduce contemporary inflation, it would, by this theory, be because prices would be forced down by the increased competition that would result from the same numbers of sellers offering the same quantity of goods for sale in markets in which selling had been made more difficult by decreased demand.[7] So, although the schools are not identical, their differences are more a matter of political temperament than of understanding. The conservatives tend to blame government spending or easy money. The liberals tend to blame rising affluence, big business, or powerful labor unions. But both place the ultimate responsibility on the same condition that these factors, which they consider immediate, supposedly create: excess aggregate demand.

The new theory brought into national prominence by the Reagan administration, "supply-side economics," cuts across both of the established schools. The underlying rationale is that by cutting tax rates, especially on high incomes, economic activity can be stimulated so much that tax revenues will rise, and the increased economic activity will also benefit the econ-

[7] The statements in the text are logical conclusions drawn from elementary economic theory on how and why prices supposedly respond to changes in competition and changes in demand levels. A reduction in demand level will lower a demand curve in its entirety, and an increase in competition will lower the left side of the kind of rightward-sloping demand curve that represents less-than-perfect competition, and in each case vice versa. Paul A. Samuelson, *Economics,* 9th ed. (New York: McGraw-Hill, 1973).

omy by increasing economic growth and decreasing inflation. Lower tax rates and increased economic growth are the principal benefits expected from supply-side economics, but decreased inflation is expected too, because the increased economic growth is supposed to reduce excess demand by increasing supply.[8]

But contemporary inflation has nothing to do with excess demand. If our government persists in its various demand-reducing measures, the result will eventually be increased unemployment and decreased economic growth but no enduring slackening of inflation. This will be the case even if unemployment reaches the depression levels of 10 to 15 percent hypothesized by Mr. Lekachman. The drastic reductions in demand that would be required to reach such large unemployment percentages would cause some temporary price reductions, and so some temporary slowing in inflation, but if nothing else were changed, inflation would resume at its previous pace, or faster. Very large or sudden reductions in demand will always catch some producers with commitments to produce more than they can sell without reducing prices, and they will always catch some producers and some retailers with larger inventories than they can sell without reducing prices. But after the surplus production commitments or inventories had been exhausted, the same forces that had been causing the inflation would be effective again.

Exactly this has happened on a small scale several times already. In late 1979 and 1980, large and unexpected reductions in the demand for automobiles, caused by sharp increases in the prices of gasoline—which were caused, in turn, by the Iranian crisis—coupled with the business difficulties of the Chrysler Corporation, caught the American automobile industry with larger production commitments and inventories than it could sell without reducing prices. So some automobile prices were reduced. But automobile production volumes were quickly reduced even more, and it is practically certain

[8] Arthur B. Laffer and Jan P. Seymour, *The Economics of Tax Revolt: A Reader* (New York: Harcourt, Brace, Jovanovich, 1979), pp. 5–44.

that the prices will go back up and resume rising after the surplus supplies are gone.[9] The automobile industry experienced the same thing for essentially the same reasons in 1974 and 1975, following the first sudden oil price increase. Some price reductions were made then, but automobile prices went back up again and resumed their inflationary spiral.[10] A very steep wage inflation occurred in the late 1960s and early 1970s in the construction industry, despite concurrent unemployment rates of 5 to 10 percent or more—and these rates failed to take into account the large numbers of men who were unemployed in construction because they were denied entry into an apprentice-training program.[11] I will give other examples later.

Large demand reductions may also temporarily reduce inflation by decreasing the prices (including wages) of those sellers whose prices are still largely determined by the forces of supply and demand—sellers of commodities, for example. Although these sellers are very much in the minority, there are still some of them. If we are willing, we can reduce inflation by placing most of the burden on them. This reduction would also only be temporary, however, because prices that are largely set by supply and demand will go right up again when demand is permitted to rise, and demand will have to rise again if people are to be employed and the economy is to grow.

Finally, large demand reductions may also temporarily slow inflation by reducing inflationary expectations. Anything that reduces sellers' expectations of inflation will reduce the inflation that ensues by reducing the amount that sellers think they ought to increase their prices in order to achieve the in-

[9] J. L. Sheler, "Detroit's Hard Sell to Lure Back Customers," *U.S. News & World Report,* February 25, 1980, pp. 71–72; Edward Meadows, "How Detoit Got Stuck with All Those Cars," *Fortune 100* (October 23, 1979), 54–56; "Chrysler Running out of Road," *The Economist,* August 4, 1979, p. 51.

[10] "Autos: Chrysler's Crisis," *Newsweek,* January 13, 1975, pp. 61–62; "Autos: A Bold Bid for Sales," *Newsweek,* January 20, 1975, p. 63: Autos: Get Out There—and Sell," *Newsweek,* January 27, 1975, pp. 47–48; *Statistical Abstract of the United States* (1979), pp. 479, 484.

[11] Daniel Q. Mills, *Industrial Relations and Manpower in Construction* (Cambridge: MIT Press, 1972), pp. 89–92, 229–30.

come or profits to which they aspire. Large demand reductions may reduce these expectations simply because people believe they will slow inflation. They may also reduce them by actually reducing inflation, albeit only temporarily, thereby convincing people that they have worked. But reductions in inflation achieved by reductions in inflationary expectations will only be temporary, too, because they can last only as long as the expectations stay low; and if the real underlying causes of the inflation are not removed or controlled, the inflation will again increase and the expectations will increase with it. Inflation seemed to be slowing down for exactly these reasons in 1981, shortly before this book went to press. Observers were also noting that the kinds of price increases that fueled inflation over the long term were showing no signs of slowing.[12]

If I deny that contemporary inflation is being caused by excess demand, I must logically also deny that it is being caused by lessened competition. I do. The evidence in support of this denial is even more overwhelming than the evidence against the direct causal role of excess demand. There are simply no data showing that there has been any lessening of competition since 1973 or thereabouts, when inflation substantially increased. All that the structuralists have been able to do is to assert that the inflation indicates that there must have been a decline in competition, which of course begs the question. Comparative measurements of competition over time for an economy as a whole are extremely difficult to make. Such measurements are at best only approximately accurate, even for very long periods. They seem to show that competition in the American economy has not changed much in recent decades, or, indeed, since the turn of the century.[13]

This book is divided into three parts. Part I identifies the causes of contemporary inflation. Part II identifies and cor-

[12] "A Guide to Understanding the Supply-Siders," *Newsweek,* December 22, 1980, pp. 76–78; Tom Redburn, "Economists Say Inflation Will Lessen," *Los Angeles Times,* March 29, 1981, pp. 1, 10–11.

[13] Phillip Areeda, *Antitrust Analysis,* 2d. ed. (Boston: Little, Brown, 1974), pp. 658–65.

rects the misconceptions of contemporary economics that have prevented our ascertaining these causes and bringing the inflation under control. Part III suggests some measures by which we could control inflation. The reasoning is unorthodox. If the reader is not well versed in economics he need not hesitate on that account. If he is, he will not find that his background will make the going much easier. In any event I will outline my argument in this introduction, so as to ease his task. The unorthodoxy of my reasoning also enables me to avoid jargon. When I have had to find words for new concepts, I have tried to use words that connote what I mean. I have also tried to write clearly. If the reader disagrees with me, he will at least know that he does.

In Part I, I will show that contemporary inflation results from changes in the nature of competition that have made competition less effective than it once was for holding prices down. I have deliberately used the phrase "results from" rather than "is caused by." The connection between inflation and the changes that I will identify is sometimes causative, but usually it is not. When it is not, it is permissive: the changes in the nature of competition have allowed sellers (or others who control prices, such as governmental administrators) to raise prices, although the changes do not compel or even necessarily encourage them to. In these cases, additional reasons why the prices rise, and why they rise as much as they do, must be sought; prominent among these is, of course, simple greed.

To explain these changes in the nature of competition, I have had to invent what I think is a new, or at least a very uncommon, concept: the effectiveness of competition for particular ends. The end with which I will be most concerned, of course, is holding down prices. Economists since Adam Smith have generally conceived of competition as homogeneous. It supposedly differs from situation to situation only in "strength," "vigor," "intensity," or some other synonym for amount. For example, a "perfectly competitive market" is said to be a market that meets certain conditions such that competition in it exists to the maximum possible extent. "Imperfect markets," on the other hand, are said to differ from the ideal in various ways that reduce the amount of competition or—what comes to the same thing—increase the amount of "monopoly power." "Workable competition" is commonly defined as enough competition to keep prices and profits reasonably in line.[14] The antitrust laws rest upon the same quantitative simplifications. Certain practices are prohibited because they "lessen competition" or, what the antitrust laws also conceive to be the same thing, because they "create monopoly power."[15] In fact, however, competition can also vary from situation to situation in nature or in kind, and some kinds can be more or less effective for certain ends than are others. Thus, it is quite possible that the amount of competition in the American (or any other) economy has not changed, but that the nature of competition has evolved so as to make competition less effective in holding down prices. I shall show that this has happened.

I shall also show in Part I that these changes are generally irreversible. They derive from technological advances and societal developments that could not feasibly be changed, and that most of us would not want changed. These advances and developments were generally slow in coming about. Yet inflation throughout the modern world increased dramatically in 1973. The explanation is that the effects of the advances and developments were cumulative and did not reach a "flashpoint" in most countries until about 1970. 1973 just happened to be the year in which the "spark" set off the "fire." The spark, of course, was the first round of OPEC oil price increases. But if these had not served the purpose, something else would have. Moreover, the higher rates of inflation that began in 1973 themselves contributed substantially to the even higher rates that followed, by demonstrating to sellers their power to raise prices without regard to demand. In its effects on economic behavior, the awareness of power is generally at least as important as the extent of power.

Contemporary inflation has also brought with it a new form

[14] Samuelson, *Economics,* pp. 482, 483, 529.

[15] For example, Clayton Act, §§3, 7, 38 Stat. 730 (1914), as amended, 15 U.S.C.A. §§14, 21 (1973).

of competition, which I call "competitive inflation." Competitive inflation occurs when groups (whether or not they are formally organized) compete with one another to raise the prices of the goods or services that their members sell. The groups are competing for real income gains. Each strives to raise its prices before the inflation caused by the price increases of other groups can take away the value of its previous price increases. Since inflation generally raises costs as well as prices, the real income gains that are sought are frequently intended to offset what would otherwise be real income losses. Like the other kinds of price increases that have become common, competitive inflation is not appreciably restrained by reductions in the size of the federal deficit, by limitations on the rate of growth of the money supply, or by other devices for reducing demand. Nor would it be appreciably restrained by increases in the strength or vigor of the usual kinds of competition, since the nature of these has been changed.

Competitive inflation has a propensity to spread and to accelerate. Groups are newly formed for the purpose of raising their members' incomes, and already existing groups are used for the first time to raise their members' incomes—in both cases because their members have been frightened by the reductions that inflation has caused in their real incomes, or angered by seeing other persons' incomes rise more rapidly. Thus, for example, teachers, hospital workers, policemen, firemen, and other government workers have organized and engaged in strikes for higher incomes during the last decade, in almost every case thereby breaking a long-standing tradition.[16] Each group's contribution to competitive inflation tends to accelerate, because as the pace of the inflation increases, the group must obtain greater monetary gains in order to make the same gains in real income. More than anything else, competitive inflation is responsible for the generally accelerating pace of contemporary inflation.

[16] Compare *Statistical Abstract of the United States* (1970), p. 239, with *Statistical Abstract of the United States* (1978), p. 431; Jack Stieber, *Public Employee Unionism: Structure, Growth, Policy* (Washington, D.C.: Brookings Institution, 1973), pp. 114–27.

Competitive inflation also threatens to make our government's supposedly anti-inflationary fiscal and monetary measures actually promote inflation. By reducing demand, these policies also reduce incomes and thereby intensify the angers and anxieties that give competitive inflation its impetus. Competitive inflation is disruptive and chaotic. It is my principal justification for characterizing contemporary inflation as the collapse of free markets. Finally, it is competitive inflation that makes indexing only an expedient. To the extent that the indexing allows people to keep up with inflation who otherwise could not, it increases the pace of inflation. This requires any group that wishes to make a real income gain to increase its prices even more rapidly, which still further increases the pace of inflation. Countries that have maintained widespread indexing for substantial periods have found their inflation rates eventually "going through the roof."

What I call competitive inflation differs from what others have called the wage-price spiral, cost-push inflation, or wage-push inflation in several respects. First, it is much more widespread. It is not confined to oligopolistic industries or to industries with powerful and aggressive labor unions. It includes the large majority of all prices, including wages, salaries, and other forms of personal compensation. It includes most farm prices, the prices of almost all consumer goods at retail, and the salaries of almost all white-collar workers even though they are not union members, for example. Second, competitive inflation does not occur just because rising wages or other rising costs "push" up the prices charged by corporations or other business entities. It also works by emulation, custom, tacit agreement, secret agreement, and by the simple desire of the groups concerned to increase their members' real incomes or to maintain them despite inflation. Third, competitive inflation would not be significantly slowed by the kinds of measures advocated by those who write about the wage-price spiral. As I said earlier, it would not be significantly slowed by reductions in aggregate demand or by increases in the usual kinds of competition. Although it would be significantly slowed by the abolition of labor unions, since labor unions do contribute significantly to it, even this drastic step would not bring it to a halt.

The changes in the nature of competition and the competitive inflation that has ensued have worked a fundamental change in the nature of the economic world. New kinds of government measures will be needed to quell the inflation, and a new kind of economics is needed to help us decide what the new measures should be. In the present economic world, prices and other results of economic behavior are no longer closely determined. It is now not even approximately correct to say, for example—as is still commonly asserted in textbooks—that prices are determined by the intersections of marginal revenue and marginal cost curves or by supply and demand curves.[17] Rather, prices and other results of economic behavior today are generally discretionary: they are the results of people's decisions, which within a wide range are no longer compelled by considerations of marginal analysis, of supply and demand, or of anything else. They are free. Prices, like other choices that people make when they are not coerced, are results of the exercise of free will.

This is one aspect of what I meant earlier when I said that the connection between the changes in the nature of competition and inflation is largely permissive rather than causative. Traditional economics conceives of competition as generating "forces"—usually called "market forces" or "economic forces"—that "push" or "pull" prices up or down, or hold prices where they are. These "forces" can be conceived of as pushing at a price from the high side and the low side in opposite directions, the price being like an object pressed between two coiled springs, the one above pushing it down, the other pushing it up. Following this conception still further, the changes in the nature of competition that have occurred can be pictured as creating "gaps" between the coiled springs, within which prices are free to move either up or down a cer-

[17] Samuelson, *Economics*, pp. 454–57, 495.

tain distance without encountering a contrary push from a market force. Thus, within these gaps, people can, but are not compelled to, raise prices.

The sizes of the gaps vary, of course, but for most personal services they are now so large as to make the pricing of the services in effect entirely free from market determination. Most wages and salaries in the United States have come to be set virtually without regard for market forces. The gaps that exist for the sellers of ordinary goods are generally much smaller, but they still permit a steep inflation because price levels can be raised by activities elsewhere—by the price increases of other sellers in the same industry, by the price increases of other industries, or by wage and salary increases. The amount of inflation that exists in an economy at any given time, therefore, *is hardly affected by market forces*—which explains why neither excess demand nor lessened competition is the cause of inflation, and why neither demand-reducing measures nor efforts to increase competition will ever significantly reduce the inflation.

So at least for the purpose of understanding contemporary inflation and designing measures for controlling it, economics as it has existed since Adam Smith is obsolete. Its basic premise is that prices and all other significant aspects of economic behavior are determined by market forces. Economics textbooks are still almost entirely devoted to identifying and explaining these supposed "determinants." Research economists still devote most of their efforts to trying to discover them, or to testing the claimed discoveries of others. The "determinative" relationships, when they are "discovered," used to be called "economic laws." Today it is more common to call them "models." Their basic character has not changed, however. They were and still are mathematical formulations of how some economic variables (prices, for example) are supposedly determined by others (supply and demand, for example).

A second basic premise of contemporary economics that has been rendered obsolete is its positivism. Like economic determinism, economic positivism has philosophical roots going back into the eighteenth century, but as applied today it means simply that only "positive," as contrasted with "normative," or only "objective," as contrasted with "subjective," statements, reports, or other forms of data should be taken into account in the formulations of economic models or laws. Only such data, it is supposed, can be unambiguously true.[18] The price at which some goods were sold would be a "positive" or "objective" item of data. The seller's reasons for setting his price or the purposes he was pursuing, on the other hand, would be "normative" or "subjective." A "positive" economics is an economics without reasons or purposes. It is also an economics without values, which of course are invariably "normative" or "subjective."[19] In practice, even the most doctrinaire economist is likely to take into account "subjective" or "normative" information, just as in practice a lawyer, no matter how firmly he believes in the rule of law, is likely to consider the temperament or political persuasion of a judge. The practical effect of economic positivism is nevertheless substantial. It leads economists to consider only "positive" or "objective" data when making long-range predictions, when making decisions, and when applying economic laws or models. Members of some schools of economic opinion deny that they are positivists, but their denials are inconsistent with their other opinions.[20] Economic positivism is a logical corollary to economic determinism. With rare exceptions, economists today differ only in the extent of their awareness of their own positivism.

Economic positivism is obsolete because the "gaps" in the determinative effects of market forces that have been opened

[18] See, for example, Milton Friedman, "The Methodology of Positive Economics," in *Essays in Positive Economics* (Chicago: University of Chicago Press, 1953), pp. 3–43; Lawrence A. Boland, "A Critique of Friedman's Critics," *Journal of Economic Literature* 17 (June 1979), 503–22.

[19] See also Robert Aaron Gordon, "Rigor and Relevance in a Changed Institutional Setting," *Amer. Econ. Rev.* 66 (March 1976), 1, 2, and passim.

[20] Phyllis Deane, *The Evolution of Economic Ideas* (Cambridge: Cambridge University Press, 1978), pp. 216–20.

are filled, so to speak, with precisely those normative and subjective influences that positivism ignores. There is no way of understanding the movements of prices within these gaps without understanding the reasons why the people who move the prices do so, and these price movements *are* the inflation. The price-setters' reasons have to do with custom, politics, status, envy, morality, ambition, fear, insecurity, generosity, patriotism, greed—all the "soft," impossible-to-measure aspects of the real world that positivists choose to ignore. Normative and subjective knowledge has also become essential for understanding the price and income relationships that exist in our society, especially the relationships among the prices of personal services and the incomes of those who provide them. Such considerations now provide much more insight into the relationships among the incomes of physicians, lawyers, police, teachers, and plumbers, for example, than do the supplies of and demands for the services of these professions or occupations—which, according to positivist economics, supposedly determine all such relationships. A modern economy can no more be understood merely from a knowledge of its prices, supplies, demands, unemployment rates, and so on, than the American Revolution can be understood from a listing of the dates, places, and numbers of men engaged in its battles.

Normative and subjective knowledge will also be essential for designing the measures to eliminate the inflation. The measures will have to include legal rules and systems of arbitration and regulation. These will have no chance of success unless they are designed to take into account what people want and how people feel about their jobs, incomes, and status.

The obsolescence of economic positivism is nowhere more clearly demonstrated than in the confusion it has wrought among economists about the causative role of rising demand in contemporary inflation. Aggregate demand has indeed been rising in the United States at especially rapid rates since inflation rates have risen. This correlation holds true in other countries as well. That demand is rising does not prove that it is rising excessively, however. In a healthily growing economy demand ought to be rising. Nor, even if the rise is excessive, does the correlation with inflation by itself prove the causation or its direction. If *A* and *B* are generally observed to happen together, it may be *A* that is causing *B,* it may be *B* that is causing *A,* or there may be some other cause or causes behind both of them. One way of solving the causative puzzle is to ascertain which happens first, but this is not possible with rising demand and inflation because they have both been rising continuously over long periods. If *A* and *B* are both the results of people's decisions, in general the next easiest way of solving the causative puzzle is to ascertain why people make these decisions. If people do *B* or something that results in *B* because of *A* or of something that results from *A,* then it is reasonable to say that *A* causes *B.* Similar deductions can be made for the other two logical possibilities. But as obvious and as straightforward as this procedure is, it has never been applied to solving the causative puzzle of rising demand and inflation, so far as I am aware, until I applied it—presumably because the positivist philosophy that economists have adopted tells them that people's reasons are inherently irrelevant and unscientific. People's reasons are "subjective."

As one might expect when there are large numbers of people making decisions in widely varying situations, their reasons do not compose uniform patterns, but the actual causative relationship can nevertheless be discerned, and it is the opposite of that which traditional economists postulate. When prices go up, fewer goods are sold unless more money is made available for buying them (that is, unless demand rises). If fewer goods are sold, fewer people are employed to produce, distribute, and sell them. When there is inflation, therefore, the government has to take steps to cause demand to rise, or refrain from taking the steps that would prevent it from rising, if it is to prevent employment from going down. So it is inflation that causes the demand to rise, rather than vice versa, by compelling the government to choose between rising demand and falling employment. When, as occasionally happens, the urgings of conservative economists persuade the government, and demand is restricted despite the awareness that it will permit rising unemployment, unemployment has indeed risen—but the pace of the inflation has not significantly slowed for long.

Economic determinism and economic positivism are among the fundamental misconceptions incorporated in contemporary economics to which I referred in describing the contents of Part II. In that part I shall show that these and other misconceptions are indeed incorporated in contemporary economics; I shall identify their historical and ideological sources; and I shall describe the harm they have done, in addition to preventing our understanding contemporary inflation. Part II will also give the outlines of a new economics, one that would be neither deterministic nor positivistic, and that could enable us to bring contemporary inflation under control.

Part III will use the new economics that was explained in Part II and the understanding of the new inflation that was gained from Part I to design and explain some new kinds of wage and price controls. There are those who claim that we are doomed to lose our freedoms if we rely on wage and price controls,[21] but the claim rests upon an outmoded conception of wage and price controls that bears no significant resemblance to the kinds I will suggest. Moreover, we have no alternative but to try them despite the risks. Markets no longer generally work to prevent inflation and are no longer generally capable of being made to so work.

A well-designed system of wage and price controls would make an economy run *more* efficiently. It would eliminate most strikes, for example, and substantially reduce the even more costly and difficult-to-identify slowdowns and sabotage that result from workers' fear of producing themselves out of work or their resentment at their working conditions. The full costs of strikes, slowdowns, and industrial sabotage are incalculable. The statistics of work days lost through strikes do not

[21] For example, Michael Polanyi, *The Logic of Liberty* (Chicago: University of Chicago Press, 1969), pp. 111–37.

begin to measure the costs; for one thing, they ignore the costs that strikes impose on everyone but the striking workers. A well-designed system of wage and price controls would also facilitate business planning and stimulate economic growth.

Traffic laws provide an analogy. A well-designed set of traffic lights, stop signs, and rules of the road makes traffic run more rapidly and with fewer accidents than it would under either poorly designed controls or no controls at all. Wage and price controls of the kind we have had in the past are like an extremely crude set of traffic regulations. Wage and price "freezes," which we have also had in the past, are like a single, all-encompassing traffic rule that forbids any driver to change his speed or direction. Wage and price controls as they are conjured up by some of their fervid opponents are like a traffic-control system in which a policeman would personally instruct every driver when and how far to turn his steering wheel or to press or let up on his brake or gas pedal. None of these would be useful for combatting contemporary inflation. It will be the first task of a new economics to design a good set of "rules of the road" for wages and prices.

A well-designed system of wage and price controls would also make allowance for the operation of market forces insofar as they are still effective and the effects are desirable. This means, among other things, that wage and price controls would not need to be entirely comprehensive. There are some sectors of our economy in which competition is still effective for holding down prices—more precisely, in which competition would be effective for holding down prices if prices elsewhere were not continually rising. The continued though only partial efficacy of market forces also means that even where the wage and price controls would apply, they would not need to set or limit every single wage or price.

A well-designed set of wage and price controls would also make our economy more just. Considerations of economic justice already enter into the setting of prices, but they are all too frequently entirely subjective. Thus, for example, the members of a labor union may believe that they deserve as much or more than the members of another labor union, and will strike to get it if their employers do not agree with them. The workers' sense of economic justice is operative in determining both the wages they want and in whether they will strike. The problem is that there does not as yet exist any system for weighing the arguments of the workers in such a situation against the arguments of the employers and the arguments that ought to be made in the interests of consumers and the economy at large, and then for coming to an authoritative decision.

Economic justice would not only be desirable in a wage and price control program, it would be essential for the purpose of ending contemporary inflation, because, as I will show, widespread perceptions of economic injustice are one of the chief causes of inflation. This is especially the case for competitive inflation. The members of the groups that compete to stay equal with, or to outstrip, the members of other groups with respect to their real incomes are often motivated by a belief that their real incomes are not, or otherwise would not be, what they justly deserve. A system of wage and price controls that failed to give the appearance of at least trying to make just allocations of incomes would ultimately lose the widespread support that it would need in order to be obeyed, and it would not give this appearance in the long run, at least, if the appearance were not the fact.

Designing the wage and price controls to be just will be doubly difficult because the problem is both to restore the economic justice that inflation has destroyed and to build a more just economic order than existed before the inflation. Inflation has aggravated inequalities among organized workers and has increased the gap between those who are organized and those who are not.[22] It has enriched some professions and impoverished others.[23] Retired persons have suffered from the dimin-

[22] A. H. Raskin, "Jim Crow, Union Member," *New York Times Book Review*, June 12, 1977, p. 12.

[23] Paul Blumberg, "White-Collar Status Panic," *New Republic*, December 1, 1979, p. 21.

ished real values of savings and pensions. Owners of real estate purchased at pre-inflation prices with mortgages at pre-inflation interest rates have profited. Even before the inflation, wealth and income were distributed very unequally in the United States, and the inequalities were not generally closely related to need or merit.[24] Both the inflation and the economic injustice and uncertainties that preceded the inflation have contributed to the high levels of anxiety, loneliness, and alienation in our population.[25]

Part III will offer the outlines of a wage and price control program that aspires to the high standards set here. I have sufficiently explained, I think, why if a program does not come close to meeting these standards, it will not work. More important than whether I have hit upon the right answers, however, is whether the measures I propose will succeed in beginning a public discussion that is already late. Perhaps the worst affliction resulting from our having a deterministic and positivistic economics is that we have failed to think about how to create a just, humane, and efficient economic system

[24] A survey has shown that a small fraction of 1 percent of the population holds 65 to 70 percent of the marketable corporate stock, for example, and the authors of the survey concluded that their results probably erred substantially on the side of underestimating the true concentration. John Keith Butters, Lawrence E. Thompson, and Lynn L. Bollinger, *Effects of Taxation: Investments by Individuals* (Boston: Harvard University Graduate School of Business Administration, 1953).

The best evidence that wealth and income distribution in a market economy are not according to merit or need is the fact that markets serve to distribute wealth and income according to supply and demand, which bear no necessary connection to merit or need. Even the most competent and industrious plasterers commonly found themselves unemployed when construction preferences turned from plastering to "dry walls," for example. Samuelson, *Economics,* pp. 43–48, 90–93.

[25] The classic study of the American character that finds these characteristics is David Riesman, *The Lonely Crowd* (New Haven: Yale University Press, 1953). See also Joyce Carol Oates, "A Taut Novel of Disorder," *New York Times Book Review,* April 3, 1977, pp. 3, 34–35; Paul Jonas, "Home Thoughts from Abroad," *Harpers* 254 (April 1977), 20–21; John Leonard, "Falling off the Train," *New York Times Book Review,"* April 3, 1977, pp. 3, 31; Robert Nisbet, "Public Unions and the Decline of Public Trust," in A. Lawrence Chickering, ed., *Public Employee Unions* (San Francisco: Institute for Contemporary Studies, 1976), pp. 13–33.

until the system we have—which with all its faults is still among the world's best—has come close to collapse. There are some bad times ahead. But with the fundamental rethinking of economic questions that this inflation will ultimately compel, the benefits in the long run ought to be great.

PART I

The New Inflation

When competition is working as in theory it should, and aggregate demand is not increasing at an excessive rate, there is *no* inflation.[1] Sellers are deterred from raising prices by the fear of being undersold. Competition in this country did work substantially in this way until about fifteen years ago. Prior to 1966, except during wartime, inflation never exceeded 2 percent and was usually only half that.[2] During the 1930s depression, there was deflation.[3] Yet, since the 1930s competition has not decreased in strength; if anything, it has become stronger.[4] In this part I will explain how competition has changed, so that now, even when competition is strong, sellers can generally raise their prices either without fear of being underpriced or, if they are underpriced, without fear of being undersold. Each of the first four chapters describes such a change. The fifth chapter describes "competitive inflation," the new process that is a form of competition and inflation at the same time, and that is a result of the changes in the nature of competition described in Chapters 1 through 4. The sixth and last chapter in this part addresses the question of the extent to which classical demand-pull inflation—inflation that is truly a result of excess aggregate demand—still is, or could become, a problem in our time.

Contemporary inflation is a new kind of inflation, which is to say that it is a result of conditions that did not heretofore exist, and it is not caused by excess aggregate demand, which prior to the end of the Second World War was essentially the

[1] When it works as in theory it should, competition produces a price equilibrium. Paul A. Samuelson, *Economics,* 9th ed. (New York: McGraw-Hill, 1973).

[2] *Statistical Abstract of the United States* (1978), p. 490.

[3] *Historical Statistics of the United States, Colonial Times to 1957* (Washington, D.C.: U.S. Govt. Printing Office, 1960), p. 125.

[4] Phillip Areeda, *Antitrust Analysis,* 2d. ed. (Boston: Little, Brown, 1974), pp. 658–65.

only cause of inflation. Contemporary inflation is not really caused at all. The conditions from which it results rather permit it, by making what I metaphorically described in the introduction as "gaps" in the market forces by which prices would otherwise be determined. Its immediate causes are the undetermined, discretionary acts of people—the people in business and government who are in positions of authority to set prices. From now on I will usually refer to this new kind of inflation as "indeterminate inflation" rather than as "contemporary inflation." Obviously, I need a name that is not time-referent if I am going to address such questions as are addressed in Chapter 6: whether this new kind of inflation and classical demand-pull inflation do, or can, coexist.

When traditional economists describe different kinds of competition, they generally describe them by the kinds of markets in which they occur. Thus, one speaks of "perfectly competitive markets" instead of "perfect competition."[5] Or by "oligopolistic competition" one means the competition that occurs in an "oligopolistic market," which is a market that meets certain conditions.[6] The kinds of markets that supposedly determine the kinds of competition that will occur in them are themselves described in objective terms.[7] I do not take this approach, because I do not believe that objective market conditions determine economic behavior, and different kinds of competition are of course different kinds of economic behavior. Contemporary forms of competition, at least, amply support this belief. They exist in a literally uncountable profusion. They are changing all the time. Of course they are *influenced* by objective conditions—by the nature of the product, whether the product is expensive or cheap, unique or uniform, for example. But it would be quite impossible to connect all these different forms of competition with different objective market conditions in a way that would even begin to explain their profusion and their continuous processes of

[5] Samuelson, *Economics,* p. 43.
[6] Ibid., pp. 116, 484, 487–98.
[7] See ibid., pp. 43, 116, 484, 487–98.

change. Moreover, it is impossible to talk to the men and women who engage in business competition today without realizing that the choices they make are not determined for them by objective conditions. The element of creativity and innovation is much too high for this to be true. The focus of the descriptions and explanations that follow is, therefore, competition itself. The conditions, both objective and nonobjective, that presumably influence it are described too, but competition, in the last analysis, is accepted for what it is. No attempt is made to explain it as a "determined" result of something else.

CHAPTER 1

The Inflationary Forms of Competition

Competition holds prices down, when it does, by threatening sellers with lowered sales if they increase their prices. It does not hold prices down, therefore, when sellers have means of increasing their prices without lowering their sales or increasing their sales without lowering their prices. In a modern economy like ours, sellers increasingly do have such means, which I will call "nonprice forms of competition." The name will serve to distinguish these forms of competition from price competition, in which a seller engages to the extent he relies upon his prices to maintain or increase his sales. Price competition, of course, does hold prices down, or at least tends to.

Not only do nonprice forms of competition not hold prices down; if they are costly, as they generally are, they tend to drive prices up at least to the extent of covering their costs. This must be so: if a form of competition did not increase receipts from sales more than enough to cover its costs, it would not be profitable and sellers would not engage in it; and although it is logically possible for increased sales to reduce *unit* costs enough to more than compensate for the added costs of obtaining the increased sales, under normal conditions in an economy like ours this rarely happens.[1] Most producers in the United States are already producing at volumes well above those that are required to maximize their efficiencies, and there is no persuasive evidence that it is nonprice forms of competition that make it possible for them to do so.[2] Most

[1] Lester G. Telser, "Advertising and the Consumer," in Yale Brozen, ed., *Advertising and Society* (New York: New York University Press, 1974), pp. 25–41.

[2] Phillip Areeda, *Antitrust Analysis,* 2d. ed. (Boston: Little, Brown, 1974), pp. 27–34.

competition is mutually canceling anyway, in its effects on sales. Generally, the sales that any seller gains he gains at other sellers' expense, since all sellers' sales together are limited by what people want to or can afford to buy.

Traditional economic theory agrees that nonprice forms of competition do not hold prices down but rather drive them up, although the agreement is not always avowed.[3] What I call nonprice forms of competition are in traditional theory regarded as practices that obtain "monopoly power" or that are evidence of "monopoly power" which sellers already have, and "monopoly power" is the traditional term for the power to increase profits by increasing prices.[4] Moreover, in the traditional view, a power to increase profits is invariably exercised. Simple observation also confirms that nonprice forms of competition lead to higher prices. The most common nonprice form of competition is advertising. A glance at almost any supermarket shelf is enough to demonstrate that the heavily advertised brands of foods and beverages sell at substantially higher prices than the less-advertised or unadvertised brands. Surveys confirm that this is the case, at least in general.[5] Advertising whose primary purpose is to convey information about the sellers' (truly) lower prices *may* reduce prices, either by reducing sellers' profits or by permanently increasing the sales of some sellers enough to reduce their unit costs, but this situation is rare, and in any event it is a form of price rather than nonprice competition.[6]

Although nonprice forms of competition do tend to raise prices by raising costs, this tendency is not an immediate cause of indeterminate inflation. It can serve to initiate the in-

[3] See Telser, "Advertising and the Consumer." For a summary of the traditional literature on the subject of advertising, see Peter Doyle, "Economic Aspects of Advertising: A Survey," *Economic Journal* 78 (September 1968), 570–602.

[4] Areeda, *Antitrust Analysis,* pp. 16–17, 21–22, 195–96.

[5] A. Kent MacDougall, "Battle of Brands: 70% of Those 'New' Items Really Aren't," *Los Angeles Times,* May 27, 1979, pt. 7, pp. 1–3, 18.

[6] John M. Scheidell, *Advertising Prices and Consumer Reaction* (Washington, D.C.: American Enterprise Institute for Public Policy Research, 1978), pp. 24, 53.

flation, as we will see, but the tendency is not to continue to increase prices indefinitely, in real terms. A producer may spend, say, 10 percent of his gross receipts on advertising his products. His costs and prices are presumably both increased thereby. But if there is inflation, his advertising costs, his other costs, his profits, and therefore also his prices will presumably all rise apace. The advertising costs will not cause, or even permit, his prices to go up any faster than they otherwise would. The significance of nonprice forms of competition for inflation is rather that they serve to free sellers from the market forces that would otherwise determine their prices for them. They contribute to the creation of the "gaps."

The profitability of nonprice forms of competition such as advertising is ordinarily impossible to predict with precision. A seller can usually be sure that advertising, for example, will increase his sales somewhat, but he cannot ordinarily be sure how much, so he also cannot be sure whether or to what extent the increased sales will more than offset the expense of the advertising. Precise predictions of such matters are impossible for several reasons. Advertising is available in a wide variety of kinds and amounts, each of which will have different effects on different people. The effects of advertising are on people, and people's reactions inherently cannot be predicted precisely. Advertising ordinarily must be planned well in advance of its presentation to the public, which in turn is ordinarily well before its effects on sales will be felt, and the advertiser has no control over events (including his competitors' advertising) that may intervene between his commitment to the plans and his hoped-for sales. All these uncertainties are equally true of other nonprice forms of competition. And when, as is usually the case, a seller has available a wide variety of different forms of nonprice competition, the uncertainties of choosing are compounded. Moreover, the uncertainties of predicting what combinations of forms of competition—what "selling strategy"—a seller will choose generally exceed even the seller's own uncertainties as to which combinations will be the most profitable for him. For it will often be the case that so far as he can tell, several different combinations would be equally profitable. In that case, he will have to make his choices among them on some basis other than their expected profitability, and an outsider, such as an economist seeking to ascertain how to predict the propensities for inflation in the situation, will have no way of knowing which combination the seller will actually choose without getting inside the seller's mind, so to speak.

All this contributes to the creation of a "gap" in the market determination of a seller's prices, because every combination of nonprice and price forms of competition implies a particular set of prices, and the objectively ascertainable market conditions do not alone determine which combination the seller will choose from the number available to him. For example, a soft-drink manufacturer choosing a selling strategy for his products might have these three strategies (among hundreds of others) available to him: simply selling the drinks for a very low price, without any advertising or other promotion, in the expectation that people will buy them to try them out because they are so low-priced, and then continue buying them because they like them; an initial and very expensive advertising blitz, coupled with very low introductory prices, to persuade large numbers of people to try his drinks, followed by higher prices that would more than recoup the high initial expenses of advertising and the high initial losses from the very low introductory prices; or a long-range advertising campaign of moderate dimensions, designed both to persuade people to buy the drinks initially and to keep them buying, coupled with prices high enough to cover the costs of the advertising and to return a good profit. The price consequences of these strategies differ. To the extent that they differ, there is a gap in the market determination of the prices.

If, on the other hand, the only way open for a seller to sell his soft drinks is through price competition, his prices will generally be predictable, and they will be largely determined by the objective conditions of the market. If he succeeds in surviving against the competition of his competitors, his prices will eventually be the same as theirs for their comparable products. This price, which is by definition the "market price," will tend to be just high enough to keep the least profitable seller from giving up and withdrawing from the market.[7] The availability of nonprice forms of competition tends, however, to create gaps in the market determination of sellers' prices, within which sellers are free, both individually and as a group, to increase their prices.

It might seem that even if sellers engaged in nonprice forms of competition they would have to engage in price competition too, if only because at least one seller in every market would be likely to do so and thereby compel the others to follow, and that the price competition would keep prices down despite being mixed with other forms. But nothing compels a seller to respond to another seller's competition in the same form, except in the rare case in which there is only one form available to him. Ordinarily, a lower price by one seller can be offset or more than offset by another seller's greater advertising, for example. The exception exists in the markets for those commodities in which the only form of competition available is price competition, because all the sellers' goods possess identical qualities.[8]

It might also seem that at least the "competition" to lower costs would tend to lower prices, and this is seemingly a nonprice form of competition. But cost reduction is not really a form of competition. To the extent a business can achieve what it wants at lower costs, it is rewarded with higher profits whether or not it is in competition. It is probably true that a seller whose receipts are only slightly above his costs has a very strong incentive to lower his costs, and competition, of course, may thus squeeze a sellers' profit margins, but neither the competition that has this effect nor the competition by which the seller responds needs to be price competition. Any form of competition is capable of squeezing a seller's profit margin.

Finally, it might seem that although nonprice forms of competition would raise prices, they could not be a source of

[7] Paul A. Samuelson, *Economics*, 9th ed. (New York: McGraw-Hill, 1973), pp. 68–70.

[8] Ibid., pp. 487–88, 512–14.

inflation because they could not keep prices rising. Once every seller had increased his prices to the full extent permitted by his gaps, it would seem, the price-increasing and so the inflation would stop. I cannot fully explain why this limit is never in fact reached until I explain competitive inflation, but, very briefly and incompletely, the explanation is this. Once gaps come to exist for enough sellers in enough markets, for the reasons to be dealt with in the present chapter and Chapters 2 through 4, and once enough of the sellers for whom the gaps exist make use of them to raise their prices, not only will prices rise but costs will rise too. If goods are sold that are not consumer goods, those prices constitute a part of some other seller's costs. The prices of steel constitute a part of the costs of manufacturing automobiles, for example. And as costs rise, so do the price levels at which the gaps exist. A soft-drink manufacturer who is permitted by the conditions of his industry to vary his prices 20 percent up or down by varying his advertising expenditures, for example, will ordinarily find that if inflation (caused by other sellers' price increases within their gaps) raises his costs, it will have raised the costs of his competitors in the soft-drink industry by about the same amounts, and that his gap—and their gaps—will all now exist at higher price levels than they did before. So he is now given more space, so to speak, within which to raise his prices still more. If he does raise his prices still more, his doing so will of course contribute to still more inflation; other sellers doing the same will presumably raise his costs and other sellers' costs still more; and the gaps will all rise again, and so on without limit. No seller's gap-limit, ordinarily, will ever be reached, at least not for long.

Sellers Generally Prefer Nonprice Forms of Competition

Economic investigations indicate that many—perhaps most—sellers prefer nonprice to price competition, even if price competition would be more profitable in the short term.[9]

[9] Areeda, *Antitrust Analysis,* pp. 229, 500–504.

Price competition runs a greater risk of getting out of control, with the result of drastically reducing the profits of all concerned. Price competition fails to erect what economists call "barriers to entry" against new sellers entering a market, thus increasing the competition when they do. If a seller can build up strong buyer loyalty to his products by advertising or by distinctive attributes, for example, a new seller will generally have to make large expenditures in advertising or otherwise before he can expect to persuade many buyers to buy his products instead; whereas if buyers have been in the habit of buying the goods primarily on the basis of price, a new seller can enter the market without any additional initial expense, simply by offering his products at the same or a slightly lower price. Nonprice forms of competition can also be more difficult for competitors to counteract than price reductions. A clever advertising campaign can increase sales for months or years, while competitors are trying to devise ones as clever for themselves. Price reductions, on the other hand, can be matched or exceeded almost overnight. In the course of my interviews with businessmen I never met one whose firm sold consumer products who did not express a preference for nonprice forms of competition. One told me proudly that his firm had *never* engaged in price competition during his entire tenure as vice president in charge of sales, some twenty years.

Additional evidence of manufacturers' preference for nonprice competition is provided by the long history of "resale price maintenance"—the practice by which a manufacturer dictates to those to whom he sells the minimum prices at which they can resell the products. The practice goes back at least to 1911, when its legality under the federal antitrust laws was first decided (in the affirmative) by the United States Supreme Court.[10] Its legality under both federal and state laws has had a checkered history, and it is currently illegal everywhere except to the extent that a manufacturer is able to enforce it simply by refusing to sell to those who fail to resell at or above the

[10] Dr. Miles Medical Co. v. John D. Park and Sons Co., 220 U.S. 373 (1911).

resale prices he sets.[11] But the economic effects of the practice have managed largely to survive its (perhaps only temporary) legal demise. It remains legal for manufacturers merely to suggest the prices at which their goods should be resold, and in most cases suggestions are enough. Suggested resale prices are frequently printed on the goods or on the packages in which the goods come wrapped. Resale price maintenance of course eliminates price competition among retailers of the same manufacturer's goods.

Investigations have revealed that manufacturers of consumer goods like resale price maintenance because it protects the public image of a product against retail price cutting, which can make the product appear cheap; because it can guarantee retailers sufficiently high profits from a product to be able to offer services in connection with the product before or after sale (demonstrations of the product before sale and free warranty service after sale, for example); because it can guarantee retailers sufficiently high profits per sale to encourage them to carry the product even when sales volume is low; because it can force retailers to engage in nonprice forms of competition when the manufacturer believes that such forms are more effective for the product concerned; because it encourages a retailer to sell the manufacturer's products in preference to other manufacturers' products of the same kind; and because it prevents retail price competition, which can spread back to the manufacturers' level.[12]

Retailers also generally prefer nonprice forms of competition, although it is generally more difficult for them than for manufacturers to act on their preferences. Retailers have in the past joined with manufacturers in lobbying legislatures to make mandatory resale price maintenance legal,[13] and the current systems of suggested resale prices work only because retailers generally join them voluntarily. It is not uncommon

[11] Areeda, *Antitrust Analysis,* pp. 500, 516–17; Phillip Areeda, *Antitrust Analysis, 1978 Supplement* (Boston: Little, Brown, 1978), p. 13.

[12] Areeda, *Antitrust Analysis,* pp. 500–504.

[13] Andreas George Papandreou and John T. Wheeler, *Competition and Its Regulation* (Englewood Cliffs, N.J.: Prentice-Hall, 1954), p. 448.

for retailers to show their distaste for price competition by declining to engage in it even if a manufacturer tries to force them. They will price the products higher than the manufacturer wants, or fail to reduce their prices to the public when the manufacturer reduces its prices to them.[14] Retailers' preferences rest on substantially the same considerations as do those of manufacturers. The forms of nonprice competition generally available to retailers differ from those available to manufacturers, of course. A retailer's decision to emphasize nonprice forms of competition usually takes the form of offering a wide selection of goods of a kind, displaying them in an attractive setting, providing knowledgeable sales personnel, and locating outlets in convenient places.[15] The existence of retail stores that offer one or more of these services while charging higher prices than do discount stores demonstrates that nonprice forms of competition can succeed at retail.

Even when retailers do engage in price competition, the manufacturers of the goods concerned are often not compelled to do so, and if the manufacturers do not engage in price competition the retailers are helpless to prevent the manufacturers' prices, and so also their own, from going steadily up. Retail automobile dealers generally engage in vigorous price competition, for example, but automobile manufacturers only rarely do. As a result, automobile retail prices rise regularly year after year.[16] Finally, investigations, including my own, indicate that manufacturers of goods that are not consumer goods also prefer nonprice forms of competition and manage to engage in them in lieu of price competition to a great extent.[17] My own investigations led me to conclude that price competition among such manufacturers, when it

[14] See Albrecht v. The Herald Co., 390 U.S. 145 (1968); Kiefer-Stewart Co. v. Joseph E. Seagram and Sons, 340 U.S. 211 (1951); Anheuser-Busch, Inc. v. Federal Trade Commission, 289 F. 2d 835 (7th Cir. 1961).

[15] Areeda, *Antitrust Analysis*, p. 500, 516–17; Areeda, *1978 Supplement*, p. 13.

[16] *Statistical Abstract of the United States* (1977), p. 479.

[17] Areeda, *Antitrust Analysis*, p. 229.

occurs at all, is largely confined to secret discounts for favored buyers—usually very large buyers.

Except in the relatively few markets—such as the markets for commodities at wholesale—in which price competition is the norm, price competition now generally occurs only as a result of miscalculation. A manufacturer has overestimated how much he will be able to sell and so has manufactured too much, or a retailer has overestimated how much he will be able to sell and so has purchased too much. The best way out in either case may be to sell the surplus at distress prices, which will ordinarily be substantially below the prices of one's competitors.[18] But although miscalculations will always occur, in reasonably normal times, at least, they will not be characteristic of an economy.

Nonprice Forms of Competition Are Increasingly Effective and Increasingly Being Employed

The principal nonprice form of competition is advertising, which is actually a large number of different forms. The varieties and effectiveness of advertising have increased as technological advances have made more means available to advertisers (television, for example) and improved the effectiveness of existing means (mass reproduction of full-color photographs, for example). The varieties and effectiveness of advertising have also increased as sellers and professional advertising advisers have devised new means and improved existing ones. Some advertising tells people what is good about a product, but most aims at nothing so obvious. The principal purpose of most consumer advertising today is to familiarize people with a product's name or "image." The image can include anything from a bottle's characteristic shape (such as the Coca-Cola bottle), to a picture of something that connotes

[18] See, for example, Lawrence Ingrassia, "Pinchpenny Shoppers Stir Retailers' Worries and Force Price Cuts," *Wall Street Journal,* August 1, 1979, pp. 1, 26.

an attitude the seller wants to associate with its products (such as the Rock of Gibraltar, which presumably connotes security and reliability), to an attitude engendered by repeating the same words in the advertisements over and over again for years (such as that Texaco service station attendants are friendly). Name or image advertising sells products in at least two ways. It leads people to think automatically of the seller's product when they think about the category of products to which it belongs. And it leads people to associate the desirable aspects of the image with the product, however irrationally.

Still other advertising is merely informative. The product is described and the buyer is told where to buy it (or perhaps how to buy it—by mail, for example) and how much it will cost; no claim is made that the product is superior. This kind of advertising frequently appears in catalogs or newspapers. Another form of advertising is by association. Sports stars are paid to eat a particular brand of breakfast cereal; a cigarette brand advertised to be especially for women sponsors a major woman's tennis tournament. Some advertising tells the public that the sellers' profits are low or nonexistent. An impression is thereby created that more of what a buyer pays goes into making a better product or into permitting lower prices. "Mutual" (that is, without shareholders) savings and loan associations, retail stores, and insurance companies frequently advertise this way. Much advertising also seeks to tell the public what nice people the sellers are. For example, during the last several years advertising has pointed out that the seller hires Blacks or women or, in the case of drug companies, that the seller is "dedicated" to research for better drugs or to maintaining and improving the health of the public.

The form of advertising varies significantly, depending on the media. Television has a uniquely powerful nonverbal impact, as we all know, and reaches very large numbers of people; it is also very expensive. Radio is better for some products. There are several varieties of printed publications, some national, some local, some appealing to a general readership, but most appealing to a highly specialized readership, which makes them attractive to the sellers of products associated with those specialties (yachting magazines to yacht sellers, and so on).

The structure of a sales organization is also a form of competition. Some manufacturers in the United States have their own retail sales organizations; this is true of the major automobile manufacturers. Others sell their goods to independent retailers; this is the rule in the food industry. Still others sell directly by mail. There are many variations on each of these, especially on the ways of selling to independent retailers. The sales can be outright, leaving the retailers free to resell the goods as they wish. Or they can be not strictly sales at all, but consignments; the goods are owned by the manufacturer even while they are being offered for sale by the retailer, and the retailer earns his profit by taking a commission, bonus, or fee out of the proceeds of whatever he sells. Consignment arrangements are ordinarily coupled with controls by the manufacturer over how the retailer sells, and even what prices he will charge. There are also different types of consignment. Sometimes the retailer-consignees are given exclusive territorial rights, sometimes not. Sometimes they are given exclusive access to certain classes of buyers, or denied such access. The automobile manufacturers have traditionally kept so-called "fleet sales"—sales to big buyers such as car rental agencies—to themselves, for example, in effect if not in theory denying them to their car dealers.

Another nonprice form of competition that has become common is product innovation. The automobile industry and the high-fidelity sound reproduction industries engage prominently in this form. New model automobiles are introduced every year. New sound reproduction systems are introduced by one manufacturer or another about once a week. Sometimes the models are truly new, sometimes they are new only in appearance or gimmick. For our purposes it is all the same. The sellers use the newness as a means of selling their products; the newness has an appeal that is independent of any price reductions that may or may not be offered concurrently.

Still another common nonprice type of competition by manufacturers of consumer products takes the form of offering incentives to the retailer or to the retailer's sales employees for selling its products. One refrigerator manufacturer, for example, has for years sent its retailers' sales employees and their husbands or wives on expense-paid tours to exotic places abroad as a reward for meeting the sales quotas it sets. In other cases the rewards consist of advertising subsidies for reduced-price sales of the manufacturer's products in the retailers' stores. The retailer profits from the sale, which the subsidy enables him to carry on at little or no extra cost, and he also profits from the additional sales of his other products to the people whom the sale attracts. There are many other kinds of rewards, too—as many as there are ways of pleasing people or of encouraging them to work.

Still another method of selling a product is to tie it to another—a buyer who wants the "tying" product cannot have it without also taking, or promising to take, the "tied." Although so-called "tying arrangements" are generally prohibited by the antitrust laws, there are numerous exceptions. Lending institutions commonly offer lower rates on loans if the borrower agrees to take other services being offered, for example; and manufacturers design their products so that it is difficult to use any but their own related products in conjunction with them, although it is never said that the related products are required.[19] Another only marginally legal but still common form of nonprice form of competition is the prize contest. State antigambling laws generally prohibit them if a buyer has anything to lose other than the cost of his postage, but sellers manage to use them to sell their products anyway by making it embarrassing as well as inconvenient for a person to enter them without buying.[20] An extremely common form of nonprice competition is simply to claim—by advertising, by de-

[19] Richard A. Posner, *Antitrust: Cases, Economic Notes and Other Materials* (St. Paul, Minn.: West Publishing Co., 1974), pp. 612–87.

[20] For example, California Penal Code §§319–27 makes "lotteries" illegal and defines them as something in which the participants can lose. The California courts are kept reasonably busy deciding whether selling schemes are "lotteries" or not. See, for example, Finster v. Keller, 18 Calif. App. 3d 836 (4th Dist. Ct. of Appeals, 1971).

signing one's stores to look shabby, or otherwise—that one's prices are "low," "lower," or "lowest," without necessarily making them so.

All the examples I have taken so far have been from retail selling. The same kinds of competition are also used for selling to other businesses—as, for example, when a steel company sells steel to an automobile company—but the emphases in these cases are different. Generally, since a business is more likely than the public to be informed about the product it buys, the efforts to convince another business to buy one's own product are more likely to appeal to logic than to emotions or instincts. When the business that does the buying is a retailer and the goods it is buying are intended for resale to the public, the competition also differs from that described so far in that the seller's major purpose is to persuade the buyer not that the goods would be useful or a bargain but that he, the buyer, will make a good profit by reselling them. The effect is that price competition becomes even less important. For the buyer cares essentially only about the difference between what he pays and what he can expect to get on resale, and this depends almost entirely on how effectively the seller (usually a manufacturer) has engaged in nonprice forms of competition aimed "through" or "over" the retailer to the public.

Some parts of the economy have their own special forms of competition. Most professions restrict the extent to which their members can engage in advertising or salesmanship, for example, and the result is not generally to encourage price competition. Buyers of the services that professions provide typically find it difficult to judge either the quality of the services they receive or the appropriateness of the prices they are charged for them. The result is generally a very subdued, "underground" form of competition, if there is any competition whatever. New professionals entering the field typically practice in subordinate relationships with those already established rather than compete with them. The new professionals may pay the established ones for the privilege of practicing with them, or they may provide their own services through the established professionals' outlets and under their supervision, and, in return, hand over a portion of the fees they earn.

Nonprice forms of competition are not only increasingly available, effective, and desired. In comparison to price competition, they are also increasingly employed.[21] The Supreme Court has recently taken account of the power of advertising and promotion to override price competition as it has fashioned rules for distinguishing legal from illegal corporate mergers and acquisitions under the federal antitrust laws.[22] In many industries, if one or two sellers achieve a dominant position by advertising or other nonprice methods, other sellers must either emulate their methods or withdraw.[23] If they emulate their methods, their prices of course also go up. Thus, nonprice forms of competition do not just permit or encourage higher prices, they sometimes require them. Basically, however, price competition has become much less common than nonprice forms of competition in our economy, and promises to remain so, because modern economic conditions make price competition both difficult (this will be dealt with in Chapter 2) and harmful, especially to sellers (this will be dealt with in Chapter 3). A fitting conclusion to this chapter is

[21] See, for example, MacDougall, "Battle of Brands"; Paul Ingrassia, "Whopper War: Burger King Begins Big Hamburger Fight against McDonald's," *Wall Street Journal,* April 5, 1978, p. 1; Walter Kiechel, III, "The Soggy Case against the Cereal Industry," *Fortune,* April 10, 1978, pp. 49–51; Frank J. Prial, "The Titans of Beer Head to Head: A Battle Full of Foam and Fury," *New York Times,* April 29, 1979, p. 20E; Bill Abrams and John Koten, "Soft-Drink Companies Prime Their Weapons in Market-Share Battle," *Wall Street Journal,* April 26, 1979, p. 1.

[22] See Federal Trade Commission v. Proctor & Gamble Co. (Clorox), 386 U.S. 568 (1967); United States v. Falstaff Brewing Corp., 410 U.S. 526 (1973).

[23] The proposition in the text is usually approached from the other side, that is, that advertising and other forms of nonprice competition make it more difficult for a new firm to enter an industry, by requiring it to incur the same heavy selling costs or, because it is new, even heavier ones. See Joe S. Bain, *Barriers to New Competition* (Cambridge: Harvard University Press, 1956); Joe S. Bain, *Industrial Organization* (New York: John Wiley & Sons, 1968), ch. 8; James F. Mongoven, "Advertising as a Barrier to Entry: Structure and Performance in the Soft-Drink Industry," *Antitrust Law & Economics Review* 8:1 (1976), 93–101.

supplied by the *Wall Street Journal,* which reported in 1979 that the liquor industry, after having "vainly tried to stimulate demand through price discounts," became the *last* major consumer-products industry to abandon price competition in favor of what the *Journal* called the new form of "planning, budgeting and marketing" designed to raise prices and increase sales.[24] Sometime in 1979, it seems, an era of competition that had existed in the United States since the nation began came to an end.

[24] Bill Abrams, "Liquor Firms, Turning to Modern Marketing, Lift Prices, and Outlays," *Wall Street Journal,* August 22, 1979, pp. 1, 31.

CHAPTER 2

Inflationary Markets

What Makes a Market Inflationary

A "market" in the economic sense is not necessarily a particular place, such as the Chicago Grain Exchange, or a particular retail establishment, such as a supermarket. It is the whole set of conditions and circumstances under which goods that are in competition with one another are bought and sold. In this sense one can thus speak of "the market for steel in the United States" or "the market for pay television in Poughkeepsie."[1] In this chapter, I shall deal with a kind of market that makes it generally profitable for sellers to charge higher and higher prices—one that encourages inflation. This kind of market has become the rule in the United States, at least for consumer goods, and is destined to remain so. I call it an "inflationary market."

Markets in which the goods differ despite being sold in competition with one another, or in which, although the goods do not really differ, the buyers generally think they do, have traditionally been termed "monopolistic markets."[2] The term derives from the fact that because of the goods' differences (whether real or apparent), an only slightly lower price will not substantially increase sales, and an only slightly higher price will not substantially reduce sales. Some buyers, to be sure, will be attracted by an only slightly lower price or deterred by an only slightly higher price, but more, in general, will not be. Those who will not presumably believe that the

[1] Paul A. Samuelson, *Economics*, 9th ed. (New York: McGraw-Hill, 1973), pp. 17–19.

[2] Ibid., pp. 483 n.2, 482–85; J. Fred Weston and Steven H. Lustgarten, "Concentration and Wage—Price Changes," in Harvey J. Goldschmid, H. Michael Mann, and J. Fred Weston, eds., *Industrial Concentration: The New Learning* (Boston: Little, Brown, 1974), pp. 307–22.

goods whose prices have been lowered are still not worth buying despite their lower prices, or the goods whose prices have been raised are still worth buying despite their higher prices. This fact gives to each seller some "monopoly power," which is, by definition, a power to increase or decrease his prices without substantially affecting his sales. Monopoly power is obviously a matter of degree. The degree to which a market is monopolistic is likewise a matter of degree. An inflationary market is a monopolistic market that, in addition, possesses at least one of the following characteristics: 1. buyers generally do not understand the differences among the goods; 2. buyers generally cannot assign dollar values to the differences among the goods; 3. buyers generally regard the differences among the goods as so much more important than the price differences as effectively to ignore the latter. If any of these additional characteristics is present, small price differences have especially small effects on sales, and the effects are especially unpredictable. The significance of this is that price competition is generally unprofitable, whereas increasing prices is generally profitable.

Take the case of a manufacturer of men's suits, for example. Men's suits sell at retail for about $100 to well above $500, with almost every price within this range occupied by some suits, some place. Although most buyers of men's suits at retail could tell the difference between two suits, one selling for $250 and the other for $150, and know that the latter was worth less, most buyers could not be sure of such a difference in value if the price difference was only about $20 in the lower price range or as much as $100 in the upper price range. So if the manufacturer is selling its suits currently in the $200 price range, it could probably raise the prices of most of them by $20 without appreciably affecting its sales. If the manufacturer is typical in this respect, its profits are less than 10 percent of receipts from sales.[3] A 10 percent increase in price that had no effect on sales would therefore increase its profits 100 percent. Moreover, it could achieve the same increased profits

[3] *Statistical Abstract of the United States* (1977), p. 550.

by making small or hidden reductions in the quality of its suits, which would reduce their cost but, since buyers would be generally unaware of them, would not appreciably reduce sales. It could sew on buttons with cheap thread that breaks easily, for example, as many clothing manufacturers currently do. Buyers would not become aware of what had been done until a week or so after they had purchased a suit, which would be too late to affect sales. Product degradations are economically tantamount to price increases in every respect, including their ability to contribute to inflation. Price increases in an inflationary market are also not likely to decrease sales appreciably because, since many buyers are unable to assess product differences in relation to price, these days they resort to assessing product differences *by* price. They assume that a product is better *because* it has a higher price.[4] Even if the market is not composed entirely of such buyers, their presence in substantial numbers offsets any decrease in sales that a price increase would otherwise cause. Thus, if either of the first two characteristics of an inflationary market is present, a seller will generally find it profitable to raise his prices slightly—by amounts that do not result in appreciable reductions in sales. The more that either of these two characteristics is present, the greater this margin of profitable price increasing will be. It should be apparent that the presence of the third characteristic has the same effect, so I will not go through the trouble of explaining it.

Inflationary markets therefore do not just permit inflation, as do the other economic conditions treated in Chapters 1 through 4, they also encourage it. They permit it, as do the

[4] Philip Revzin, "Feeling Flush: Affluent Consumers Turn Optimistic, Buy More-Expensive Goods," *Wall Street Journal,* July 23, 1976, p. 1; Lindley H. Clark, Jr., "Inflation's Hot Spot: Medical, Repair Bills, Costs of Other Services Keep Rising Rapidly," *Wall Street Journal,* June 23, 1977, p. 1; Paul Ingrassia, "Changed Picture: In a Color-TV Market Roiled by Price Wars, Sony Takes a Pounding," *Wall Street Journal,* March 16, 1978, pp. 1, 26. See also Phillip Areeda, *Antitrust Analysis,* 2d. ed. (Boston: Little, Brown, 1974), pp. 16–17, 20–21 (many manufacturers of consumer products shun price competition because they believe that consumers associate low prices with low quality).

other conditions, by creating gaps in the market determination of prices within which sellers can, but are not compelled to, raise their prices. The gaps created by inflationary markets are the variations in a seller's prices that can be made without significantly affecting his sales. Inflationary markets encourage inflation by making it profitable for sellers to raise their prices to the full extent of their gaps. A seller who declined to take full advantage of the gaps available to him would be refusing the opportunity to make an effortless, costless profit. The kind of gaps treated in Chapter 1 did not possess this characteristic. For example, a seller who was in a position to increase or decrease his prices a certain extent depending on how much advertising he employed would not necessarily be in a position to increase (or decrease) his profits by doing so. Since his advertising would cost him something, if he increased it he would raise his costs, and his higher prices might not yield him more profits after all. And vice versa, of course, if he reduced his advertising and tried to compensate by cutting his prices.

If only one seller in an inflationary market were to increase his prices, his ability to do so without appreciably reducing his sales would end as soon as the *differences* between his prices and his competitors' prices became large enough to influence buyers to buy his competitors' goods in preference to his, despite the market's inflationary characteristics. But if all or almost all the sellers in the market increase their prices by small amounts continually, each being careful not to open up such wide price differences, there will be no limit to the progressively higher prices that all of them can charge. Thus inflationary markets permit and encourage a "creeping" inflation—an inflation that proceeds by small steps. There is no necessity that the pace with which the steps are taken be slow, however, so a creeping inflation can be indefinitely rapid.

How rapid a creeping inflation will be in a particular market depends upon how inflationary the market is in terms of the characteristics described earlier, because these determine how profitable it will be for a seller in the market to raise his prices, and how alert all the sellers are to exploit their opportunities to raise prices. Inflation in the economy at large, whether it results from the presence of inflationary markets or from other causes, intensifies both factors. It makes it all the more difficult for buyers to assign dollar values to the differences between goods, because it makes it necessary also to assign, and continually reassign, real-dollar values to the dollars; and it teaches sellers to exploit profitably their opportunities to raise prices. When there is inflation in the economy at large, price increasing is easier for everyone, for a host of reasons. The techniques learned then, like the techniques learned in skiing, tennis, swimming, or anything else by doing it first under easy conditions, can be employed later when inflation in the economy at large has slowed down. Thus, here as elsewhere, inflation begets inflation.

Creeping inflation is the precise opposite of price competition, which consists, ordinarily, of sellers slowly lowering their prices in an attempt thereby to increase their profits by increasing their sales. Inflationary markets also contribute to inflation by making price competition generally unprofitable, for precisely the same reasons as they make upward price-creeping generally profitable—the difference in price is unlikely to affect sales. It remains true even in an inflationary market that a *large* price decrease would appreciably augment sales, just as a large price increase would still induce an appreciable decline in sales; but price competition can rarely consist of large price decreases, because these are rarely profitable under any market conditions. In order to be profitable, a price decrease must improve sales enough to more than compensate for the decrease in profit per item sold, and this becomes more and more unlikely as the decrease becomes larger. If the price is less than unit cost, obviously, no quantity of sales would be sufficient to make a price decrease profitable. Moreover, experience seems to demonstrate that even when price competition does prove to be profitable in an inflationary market for some sellers, the result is usually not to make price competition the rule for the market as a whole, but to split the market into two parts, neither of which thereafter engages in much price competition. The market splits into a "discount" part and a "regular" part, and each again becomes inflationary, at their generally different price levels. This result is supported by economic theory, which teaches that price competition is never profitable for sellers in the long run.[5]

There have been innumerable examples of creeping inflation in recent years, but that which occurred with candy bars is perhaps the easiest to follow. Until the 1950s candy bars normally sold for a nickel. But over the years their prices were increased by increments of five cents until the normal price is now 35 cents. Each increase was disguised by making the bar larger at the same time—the size of the bar having been gradually decreased since the time of the previous price rise. People generally choose candy bars on the basis of taste and size, neither of which encourages them to make close distinctions on the basis of price. Moreover, the manufacturers, one assumes deliberately, make the size difficult to assess by making wrappers larger than the bars inside, and by using a wide variety of shapes of both bars and wrappers. The only thing not typical in the history of candy bars is the size of the direct price increases, which were uncharacteristically large in relation to the prices. Obviously, however, most buyers are not strongly influenced by price in such a low-priced item.

The traditional analyses of monopolistic markets fail to point out that they are inflationary when the characteristics that I have identified are present, presumably because they have not identified these characteristics or have not realized their significance. It is traditionally said that monopolistic markets reach price equilibria no differently from any other kind of market. This belief rests on the assumption that the sellers in a monopolistic market, like sellers generally, supposedly maximize their profit, and on the assumption that the sellers can all find prices at which their profits will all be maximized simultaneously.[6] Economists are not unaware of the fact that people often do not understand the differences

[5] Areeda, *Antitrust Analysis,* pp. 16–17, 20–21.

[6] See Samuelson, *Economics,* pp. 17–19; Weston and Lustgarten, "Concentration and Wage," pp. 307–22.

among competing goods in monopolistic markets,[7] but they have seen the significance of this fact only for monopoly power. The less people understand about product differences, the more monopolistic the market is said to be, but from this the only conclusions drawn to date are that nonprice forms of competition are more likely to be preferred and that prices are likely to be higher—although still stable.[8]

There is another way of explaining the operations of inflationary markets which, although less clear to the layman, is perhaps clearer to the economist because it uses more of his technical concepts. The *demand* for some particular goods, in the technical economic sense, is the volume of the goods that buyers will buy (or, equivalently, that sellers will sell) at a particular price level. It is useful to distinguish two kinds of demand for our purposes. Overall demand will be taken to mean the total volume of goods that will be sold by all the sellers in a market at a set of particular price levels. Individual demand will be taken to mean the volume of goods that a particular seller will sell at a particular price level for his goods. Now, it should be clear that the individual demand for the goods of any particular seller in a market will depend upon the other seller's prices. The higher the other sellers' prices, the higher the individual demand for the goods of the one seller, and vise versa. This follows because buyers, to the extent they are influenced by price differences among competing goods at all, are influenced in the direction of buying the goods with the lower prices relative to the goods' perceived dollar values. One other orthodox conclusion that needs to be taken into account is that, other things remaining the same, the higher the individual demand for a sellers' goods, the higher will be the sellers' prices. This conclusion follows from application of the

[7] See, for example, the many consumer surveys and other empirical studies referenced in "Guidelines for Extending Implied Warranties to Service Markets, *Univ. of Pa. Law Rev.* 125 (1976), 365, 367–69, 371–72, and passim.

[8] See, for example, Tibor Scitovsky, "Ignorance as a Source of Oligopoly Power," *Amer. Econ. Rev.* 40 (1950), 48; Phillip Nelson, "Information and Consumer Behavior," *Journal of Political Economy* 78 (March/April 1970), 311.

profit-maximization principle; it also follows even if sellers are assumed merely to want profits, without necessarily maximizing them. So creeping inflation can also be explained as a condition in which the sellers in a market are generally raising their prices because their individual demands are rising, and each of their individual demands is rising because others are generally raising their prices. This condition can occur even if the overall demand for the goods in the market as a whole is not rising, if at least one of the characteristics of an inflationary market described earlier is present. This way of explaining the operation of an inflationary market also has the advantage of emphasizing the self-supporting, circular nature of the process.

This explanation of inflationary markets also helps to identify a fourth characteristic that, although not sufficient by itself to make a market inflationary, makes a market more inflationary if at least one of the other three characteristics is also present. Although creeping inflation can occur even if the overall demand for the goods in a market is not increasing, it should be clear that the price-creeping of which the inflation consists will be all the more profitable if the overall demand does not fall very sharply as the prices rise. For if this is the case, each seller is likely to find not only that his share of the market's total sales is not appreciably decreased by a small price increase, but also that the market's total sales are not appreciably decreased as his and the other sellers' prices all creep upward together. In fact, this characteristic—what in technical terms would be called "a generally flat overall demand curve"— is very common in a modern economy. It results either from a condition of necessity or from what Adolph Lowe has called the "disappearance of conditions of undersatiation,"[9] but which I will call a condition of satiety. A condition of necessity means that people will not appreciably reduce their purchases of something even if its price is raised substantially, because they think they need it. A condition of

[9] *On Economic Knowledge* (New York: Harper and Row, 1965), pp. 203–10.

satiety means that people will not appreciably increase their purchases of something even if the price is reduced substantially, because they think they already have enough of it. For example, the fourfold rise in oil prices has not substantailly reduced oil sales worldwide, apparently because people think they need about as much oil as they are using (a condition of necessity), and the 50 percent or so drop in coffee prices a few years ago (which followed an even larger rise) did not substantially increase coffee sales,[10] apparently because people thought they were already buying enough of it (a condition of satiety). Necessity and satiety are in practice hardly distinguishable in a modern economy. Sales of a necessity will not increase substantially if its price is dropped, because people will already have been buying as much of it as they think they need. Conversely, if people are buying as much as they want of something, sales will not generally decrease if its price goes up, because people are presumably not limiting their purchases by the price but because they think they have enough of it. Oil and coffee make convenient illustrations, but they would be misleading if they were taken to mean either that necessity or satiety needs to be as powerfully operative as it was in their cases in order to make a significant contribution to creeping inflation. It is sufficient for this purpose if overall demand remains essentially constant despite only a 10 percent increase in price. Prices in particular markets can probably rise only 10 percent over prices in other markets throughout the economy before the other prices rise, too. Necessity and satiety will be taken up again in the next chapter, where it will be shown that they contribute to inflation even more through

[10] Crude oil prices have increased much more than tenfold since 1973, yet it was not until 1980 that demand for crude oil in the United States began to fall, and even now the annual rate of decrease is only between 5 and 10 percent. *Statistical Abstract of the United States,* 1979 (Washington, D.C.: U.S. Printing Office), p. 602; *The Economist* (November 29 to December 5, 1980), pp. 13–14; and April 11 to 17, 1981, pp. 71–72. It is doubtful that even this rate of decrease will continue after the old "gas guzzling" automobiles have all worn out and been replaced by energy-efficient models. "Prices: Coffee Simmers Down," *Time,* June 27, 1977, p. 63; John Valentine, "Some Retail Prices of Coffee Drop, Further Reductions Are Expected," *Wall Street Journal,* June 21, 1977, p. 32.

"pricing institutions" than they do through their effects on inflationary markets.

It still might seem that although prices in inflationary markets would never reach equilibrium, they still would not contribute to inflation over the long term, because after every sellers' prices got high enough, at least one seller would find it profitable to cut his prices by large amounts—large enough to be widely noticed and to be influential on buyers' choices, despite the market's inflationary characteristics. This lone price cutter would seemingly gain such a substantial increase in sales at the others' expense that the others would quickly have to lower their prices to remain competitive. Prices over the long term, therefore, would theoretically not increase. The pattern would rather be a sawtooth: gradual rises followed by precipitous falls, alternating around a nonincreasing, long-term level. Something like this would indeed be likely if it were not for the additional fact of general inflation. When inflation is general—that is, when prices are rising almost everywhere rather than just in a particular inflationary market—prices are not likely ever to get high enough in relation to costs in any market to make it profitable for a seller to make a drastic price cut. General inflation drives costs up just as rapidly as it does prices, because what is a price for one person is generally a part of some other person's costs. Since costs generally rise as rapidly or almost as rapidly as prices, the point at which it would become profitable for a seller to cut his prices by large amounts is never reached. In effect, by raising costs, inflation makes it practically essential that sellers everywhere participate in creeping inflation in their own markets, whether or not they might otherwise have chosen to do so.

It would be a misinterpretation of my thesis for the reader to conclude, however, that inflationary markets necessarily produce inflation, even if conditions of necessity or satiety are also present. My thesis is only that such markets *encourage* inflation, by making small price increases generally profitable. The belief that economic conditions lead necessarily to certain results, such as inflation, is economic determinism in the sense that I defined and condemned earlier. Indeed, economists probably would have discovered inflationary markets long ago had their economic determinism not blinded them, since such markets have surely existed in our economy since long before they produced noticeable amounts of inflation. People must have had difficulty in understanding the differences among competing goods or in attaching dollar values to their differences long before indeterminate inflation became a serious problem in the United States, which was about 1973 or 1974. But inflationary markets presumably did not produce noticeable amounts of inflation earlier because sellers did not generally realize their profitable potentialities. Certainly one gains the impression from reading reports in the *Wall Street Journal* or *Fortune* magazine on pricing activities that since 1974 sellers have frequently been surprised—and pleased—at how much easier it is to increase profits by increasing prices than they had previously thought possible.[11] Moreover, there surely was some actual inflation from inflationary markets prior to the early seventies, although, being minor, it was mostly hidden by increases in productivity.[12] If it were not for concurrent inflation, an increase in productivity would produce deflation of exactly the same percentage.

Why the Markets for Consumer Goods Have Become Generally Inflationary

Inflationary markets have become the rule for consumer products. The basic reason is the advance of technology, which has intensified each of the three characteristics that make markets inflationary.

Technological advance has increased job specialization. As a result, a job today typically involves its occupant in only a narrow segment of the economy, and teaches its occupant

[11] See Chapter 3 at notes 22–26. See also Chapter 1 at note 21 (sellers increasingly prefer nonprice forms of competition).

[12] *Statistical Abstract of the United States* (1977), p. 405.

very little that would be useful to him as a buyer even in that narrow segment. Today, for example, only about 4 percent of Americans farm for a living,[13] whereas a century or two ago the vast majority did. And farming today typically involves a farmer in a few "cash" crops, whereas formerly a farmer grew many of the same foods that he and his neighbors ate.[14]

Technological advance has increased both the variety of products and the complication of the individual product. The variety of products has been increased by technological advances in transportation in particular, which have made the products of almost any part of the world available for sale almost everywhere. Technological advances in food preservation have had the same effect, and, in addition, have made almost all foods available at all times, regardless of season. An illustration of the vast increase in variety is provided by cleaning compounds. Formerly, there was only one cleaning compound—soap. Today there are chemically distinct cleaning compounds for bodies, hair, automobiles, floors, sinks, toilets, carpets, clothes, dishes, pets, swimming pools, driveways, automobile engines, and almost anything else that ever needs cleaning, and frequently the cleaning compounds for each of these have variations. Those for hair generally vary depending upon whether one's hair is dry, oily, regular, especially prone to dandruff, or "baby," for example, and shampoos are also sold for use with particular hair colors. Finally, it is also frequently the case that cleaning compounds sold for exactly the same uses nevertheless have varying chemical compositions, depending on their brand. The qualities of products generally have come to depend upon chemical, metallurgical, electronic, and mechanical properties that no one except an expert can adequately comprehend.[15] Products' qualities are generally more difficult to assess in themselves,

[13] *Statistical Abstract of the United States* (1977), p. 673.

[14] Clinton Rossiter, *The First American Revolution* (New York: Harcourt, Brace & Co., 1956), pp. 34–36.

[15] See Roger Smith, "For the Good Life, We Pay the Plumber," *Los Angeles Times,* December 15, 1978, pp. 1, 16, for a description of the vastly increased complexities of home repair services and legal services.

and there are generally more significant qualities per product. Many products today threaten the user's health or bodily safety, for example. So this threat and the protections, if any, against it (warranties or government-inspection certificates, for example) also constitute qualities of the product that need to be assessed or evaluated like any other.

Products have also become more complicated by being sold along with standard forms. Businessmen and their legal advisers have learned from decades of experience the many things that might go wrong with a loan, mortgage, installment purchase, or insurance, for example, and as a result have drafted the standard forms that accompany products so as to deal with every such contingency. The result, with insurance at least, is that the standard forms (the "policies") have become so complicated that even judges have difficulty understanding them.[16] One reason that standard forms have become complicated is that the arrangements that they define are complicated. Health insurance policies are perhaps the outstanding illustration of this. Not one of my colleagues whom I questioned had so much as read the health insurance policy that currently covered him—and my colleagues are law professors. Surveys show that people have generally given up the attempt to understand standard forms of almost any kind, and usually sign them without reading them.[17]

Technological advance has lured people into buying without much understanding by making buying seductively easy. People buy or, what comes to the same thing, take actions that commit them to buying, with little thought about the economic consequences. Few people calculate when they switch on an electric light what the light will cost them for a certain number of minutes and what its worth will be, compared to the price and worth of other things they might do with the same amount of money, for example. The same absence of thought ordinarily accompanies the buying of water by turn-

[16] Lon L. Fuller and Melvin A. Eisenberg, *Basic Contract Law*, 3rd. ed. (St. Paul, Minn.: West Publishing Co., 1972), p. 558.

[17] See, for example, William C. Whitford, "Strict Products Liability and the Automobile Industry: Much Ado about Nothing," *Wisconsin Law Rev.*, 1968, pp. 83, 141–50.

ing on a faucet or flushing a toilet, the buying of natural gas by turning on a stove, the buying of heating oil by letting the thermostat automatically turn on the heat, the buying of telephone services by dialing a call, the buying of gasoline by starting a car, and so on. For some people, credit cards and charge accounts have lent a measure of this seductive ease to all buying.

Technological advance has multiplied the situations that commit people to buying before they could feasibly gain a good understanding, even if they were willing to take the trouble to do so. Frequently this happens because the purchase of one product effectively commits the purchaser to buying related products later. When a person buys a product that comes with a warranty, for example, he takes the warranty without having any way of evaluating at the time the seller's later performance under its terms. A person's choice of an internist effectively commits him to a host of other medical services that he will not receive until later—the specialists to whom the internist may refer him, the hospitals to which either the internist or the specialists may commit him, the medical technicians whom the internist, the specialists, or the hospitals may employ or otherwise make use of, and the kinds or brands of drugs that any of the physicians may prescribe for him. The choice of a gas range commits a person to buying gas in the future even if electricity for heating purposes should in the meantime become relatively cheaper. And so on.

Since people today understand less about the products they buy, they are also less able to repair and maintain them, and it has become more important that a product be sufficiently durable not to need frequent or unusually expensive repairs or maintenance. Since modern products can pose serious risks of bodily harm (poison, accident, and so on), it has also become more important that a product possess qualities that ensure its safety. Compared with products' qualities, therefore, price has generally become less important.[18] It has been reported that

[18] "Out of Order: Repair People Struggle to Keep up with Glut of Breaking Products," *Wall Street Journal,* January 5, 1981, pp. 1, 10; Thomas Petzinger, Jr., "Out of Order: Avoiding Plant Failure Grows More Difficult for Many Industries," *Wall Street Journal,* January 8,

people increasingly wish to buy the higher priced brands and the higher priced products in a line of products.[19] Another indication of the greater importance that people attach to qualities is the increased importance of advertising. Since heavily advertised products generally sell for higher prices, the advertising would not be successful if it were not convincing people that the products' qualities were important enough to compensate for the higher prices.

On the other hand, nonprice forms of competition, such as advertising, also make it more difficult for people to understand the qualities of the products. A person would find it impossible to assign a dollar value to the images and fantasies about a product that advertising creates, even if he could in some way buy those images with the product, and in most cases he cannot do so. It is unlikely that most people actually feel younger and more lively from drinking a particular soft drink, for example.

Indications That Markets Possess the Characteristics That Make Them Inflationary, Gained from Sellers' Testimony and Conduct

All the executives whom I interviewed who worked for firms that manufactured consumer products took it for granted that the people who bought their firms' products did not understand them. Unless they were engineers, they generally did not understand them themselves. All but one of these executives also told me that in their opinion relatively small price differences had, or would have, no significant effect on sales. Research by others indicates that the usual response of a manufacturer of consumer products to a perceived need for lower prices is to redesign the product so that it costs

1981, pp. 1, 17; Roger B. May, "Out of Control: Compulsive Spenders Are Helped to Repay by Credit Counselors," *Wall Street Journal,* August 1, 1977, p. 1.

[19] See Revzin, "Feeling Flush"; Clark, "Inflation's Hot Spot"; Ingrassia, "Changed Picture"; Areeda, *Antitrust Analysis,* pp. 16–17, 20–21.

less to produce, after which the price is reduced.[20] Such a "price reduction" is really not one, of course.

Some common selling techniques rely specifically on the buyer's inability to understand the product. One such technique is selling a "product line" instead of a single product. Automobile manufacturers ordinarily sell not just one kind of automobile under a brand label but several, for example, with widely varying prices, styles, and qualities. One advantage thereby gained is additional buyer confusion. Some Chevrolets are priced higher, and so are presumably of higher quality than some Oldsmobiles, for example, although "everybody knows" that Oldsmobiles are generally of higher quality than Chevrolets. The lowest priced model in a line is usually intended for use as a price "come on." It enables the seller to advertise, truthfully, that a Ford, Chevrolet, or whatever can be purchased "for as little as *X*." The seller does not expect to sell many of them, however, and generally does not. The idea is rather that once a potential buyer has been attracted by the prospect of a low price, he will see by comparison how much better a product he can get in the same line, and buy a more expensive model instead. For one brand of vacuum cleaner, the cheapest model differs from the others in the line *only* in having a drab and apparently thin cover. The most expensive models in a line are not ordinarily intended for large numbers of sales either, but to add prestige or glamor. They are frequently pictured in advertisements for the whole line. The buyer of a model in the middle of the price range presumably can feel that he is participating in the glamor or prestige that he saw in the advertisements, or the glamor that comes from the fact that others whom he admires or envies are using the most expensive models.

It has become a common form of consumer fraud, at least in the Northeast, for food retailers to advertise "specials" on particular items and to sell them for *more* than their usual prices. It is currently common practice the country over for

[20] Neil W. Chamberlain, *The Firm* (New York: McGraw-Hill, 1962), pp. 191–95, 204, 339–51.

butchers to cut meats in odd ways, give the cuts fancy names, and sell the same meats—that is, meats from the same parts of the animal—at widely varying prices. Consumers buy their round steaks labeled, say, "Polynesian roast," and come back for more.[21] They presumably cannot tell that there is no real difference in quality, even when they eat it. Stores that advertise themselves as "discount" and that are careful to give themselves a "low-price look" (articles jumbled on shelves, pipes overhead, shabby storefronts, and just a few, always too-busy clerks) nevertheless often price many of their items higher than the same items in nearby, ordinary stores. Again, the deception could not work if buyers had any idea of what prices were usual or appropriate, or of what particular products were really worth to them.

Product degradation was pointed out earlier as a common means of raising prices indirectly and usually secretly. The fact that it can be kept secret for long periods is additional evidence that buyers do not understand what they are getting. Most product degradation is only partial. As technological advance permits products to be improved in some ways, they are simultaneously degraded, usually in order to reduce costs, in others.[22] This seems to have been the case with automobiles, which were allowed to become easier to damage and more expensive to repair during the sixties and early seventies, at the same time as they were being made more economical in their use of gasoline, and safer.[23] This also seems to have been the case with refrigerators, which in the sixties were lined with plastic that flows and bends rather than with metal, because plastic costs less.[24] At other times the degradations and the improvements are technological trade-offs. Tomatoes, for example, were allowed to become pale and nearly tasteless inside

[21] John Keats, "Rip-Off at the Supermarket," *Atlantic Monthly* 237 (March 1976), 27–34.

[22] "Hidden Costs, Consumers Find Firms Are Paring Quantities to Avoid Price Rises," *Wall Street Journal,* February 15, 1977, p. 1.

[23] William P. Henderson, "Dilemma: High Auto Repair Costs; Solution: Realistic Rates," *National Underwriter,* May 28, 1976, pp. 19–21.

[24] Interview with design engineer, Los Angeles.

while they were selectively hybridized to be firmer, harder-skinned, and of more uniform size—qualities that made them easier to pick, handle, and ship to market.[25] On the other hand, product degradation is sometimes unmitigated and done simply in order to decrease costs secretly. In at least one well-known case, that of reducing the proofs of liquor, the product degradations were unmitigated and not kept secret, because government labeling laws required that the proof be disclosed on the product (although not necessarily conspicuously); yet people continued to buy the products in substantially the same volumes.[26]

A single manufacturer generally cannot degrade a product very far before the differences between his product and the products of his competitors become widely noticed, at which point, presumably, his sales will decline. This eventuality can be avoided if all the manufacturers of the same product engage in substantially the same kinds of degradations at the same time. But even if the products of an entire industry are uniformly degraded, the degree of degradation has limits. Presumably at some point the products would cease to be functional and people would cease buying them even if they had no alternatives. This is avoided, however, either by simply ceasing the degradation, leaving the product just short of being dysfunctional, or by erasing a past series of degradations by one large, deliberately noticeable improvement, which is used to justify a large price increase, thereby opening the way for more degradations of the same kind in the future. Tomatoes, for example, have simply been left less tasty, although still with (just) enough taste and color to convince people to continue buying them. An example of the cyclic method is candy bars. Six times, so far, their gradually shrunken sizes

[25] See, for example, Charles M. Rich, "The Tomato," *Scientific American* 239 (August 1978), 82: "*In terms of tomatoes grown for processing* the changes did not degrade the quality" (emphasis added).

[26] Charles G. Burck, "Changing Habits in American Drinking," *Fortune* 94 (October 1976), 158; "A Revolution in Drinking Reshapes the Liquor Industry," *U.S. News and World Report,* March 21, 1977, pp. 17–73.

have been noticeably increased simultaneously with five-cent increases in the price of a bar. A product that has been degraded to a point just short of unacceptability can be degraded still more later, if in the meantime people's standards of acceptance have been lowered. The degraded product itself is usually the means of lowering the standards. It probably took people a long time to learn to like bread so lacking in substance and taste as it generally is today, for example. And radio and television commercials have been increased over the years in both number and offensiveness, the increases alternating with periods in which they were not changed while, presumably, listeners and viewers got used to the new levels of intrusion.[27]

Government Programs to Educate Consumers

Government programs to educate people about products might be valuable for any number of reasons, but for preventing inflation they could never be more than the proverbial drop in a bucket. People would have to understand an enormous amount in order to make the very close dollar-value comparisons that could engender enough price competition to have a measurable impact on inflation. Moreover, the subtle and subjective aspects of products—style, color, texture, sound, and so on—influence people the most, and these are the most difficult aspects to test and to educate people about. Very few people, surely, would want to spend any large amount of time studying in order to save what would probably be only pennies per purchase in most cases, even if such educational programs were offered free of charge. Fortunately, there are easier ways of preventing creeping inflation.

[27] Miles David and Kenneth Costa, "Since 1895, Radio Finds Its Niche in Modern World," *Advertising Age,* April 19, 1976, pp. 100–105.

CHAPTER 3

Pricing Institutions

A third development that has decreased the ability of competition to hold prices down is the emergence of what I call "pricing institutions." A "pricing institution" is a set of laws, customs, or practices (or what I call simply "rules") applicable to a group of sellers or buyers that enables or requires the sellers to set prices different from those they otherwise would. That is, to the extent that the conditions described in Chapters 1 and 2 do not also intervene, the prices are different from what they would be under a condition of unrestricted price competition. Most pricing institutions immediately affect only the sellers' pricing behavior. A labor union, for example, immediately affects its members' wages (and since a worker sells his labor, a union member's wages are his prices as a seller). Labor unions are also typical of pricing institutions, however, in having important effects on supply as well: they frequently restrict supply by imposing high initiation fees or long apprenticeship requirements, for example. A small but important minority of pricing institutions operate by directly affecting only supply. The United States Department of Agriculture's programs for supporting crop prices by restricting the amounts of a crop that farmers may grow are pricing institutions of this kind. The characteristic that many sellers are affected in the same way, through rules, distinguishes a pricing institution from the conditions described in Chapters 1 and 2, which operate on buyers or sellers individually.

The typical pricing institution contributes to indeterminate inflation in two ways. In the first place, its rules are designed to eliminate—not just reduce, but eliminate—price competition among its members. When some price competition occurs despite the presence of a typical pricing institution, it occurs in violation of the institution's rules. There is typically *some* price competition that occurs for this reason when the pricing institution is not government-sponsored, so that its rules are not laws; but pricing institutions cannot be understood unless it is understood how fundamentally antipathetic they are, in conception at least, to price competition. Again, a labor union makes a convenient illustration: the members of a labor union ordinarily do not compete with one another by offering their labor at lower wages. The rules of the typical pricing institution do not seek to eliminate or even reduce nonprice forms of competition among its members, but these, as we have seen, generally do not prevent indeterminate inflation. Second, the typical pricing institution was either designed for, or is used for, the purpose of raising its members' prices. In other words, it is not content merely to eliminate price competition; it also takes affirmative steps to raise prices. Labor unions are also typical in this respect. As everyone knows, they are not content to eliminate their members' price competition; they also take steps to raise their members' wages. Even the minority of pricing institutions that directly affect only supply contribute to indeterminate inflation in this second fashion. They typically seek to raise their members' prices by reducing the supply of the goods the members sell—a means of raising prices that does not require the simultaneous elimination or reduction of price competition.

It would be an exaggeration to imply, however, that because of the characteristics just described pricing institutions or their members are typically impervious to the price-limiting effects of either price competition or supply and demand. No institution, in a free society at least, is ever entirely impervious to the forces and influences arising from the broader societal context, and pricing institutions are no exception. Even the strongest labor unions are threatened occasionally by price competition from nonunion labor, for example, and even the strongest labor unions sometimes ameliorate their wage demands when the demand for the kind of labor they can supply has fallen far enough to leave a substantial portion of their members unemployed. But labor unions and other kinds of pricing institutions in the United States have generally become effective enough so that, where they exist, it is they rather than either competition or supply and demand that are chiefly responsible for the prices. And in the United States and other countries with modern economies, effective pricing institutions have come to exist for almost all the economically significant prices.

Traditional economics has largely ignored pricing institutions. To the extent that it treats them, it does so under the rubric of "monopoly power"—the power that a seller has to control prices despite competition. The traditional conception of monopoly power is that it is an "imperfection" present in what would otherwise be a perfectly competitive market, a presence that, as its name implies, ought to be reduced to as little as possible and that, if an economy is functioning "workably," is not large in fact.[1] A pricing institution indeed possesses monopoly power—and more. It has monopoly power in an *institutionalized* form: it is an enduring, legitimate, and on the whole valuable part of its economy, and needs to be understood at least as much as competitive markets if one is to understand the economy. This chapter will describe the most important kinds of pricing institutions that have come to exist in the United States, describe some of the factors that influence their behavior, and explain why they are unavoidable and on the whole desirable even though they have undoubtedly been the chief cause of our inflation.

The Major Kinds of Pricing Institutions in the United States

A common kind of pricing institution is regulated industry. A government commission sets the prices. This is the case for nearly all sellers of electricity, natural gas, telephone services, and public transportation, whether freight or passenger. Regulated industries constitute about 12 percent of the national

[1] Paul A. Samuelson, *Economics,* 9th ed. (New York: McGraw-Hill, 1973), pp. 482–83, 592; Phillip Areeda, *Antitrust Analysis,* 2d. ed. (Boston: Little, Brown, 1974), pp. 37–40.

economy measured by gross receipts.[2] For public transportation, with the possible exception of railroads, regulation is not economically inevitable; price competition would be *more* feasible in these industries than it generally is elsewhere. They are nevertheless regulated because their members long ago sought regulation as a protection against price competition.[3] Airlines subject to federal regulation are currently in the process of being deregulated, however.[4]

The United States Department of Agriculture operates pricing institutions for many crops, although the methods of operation differ from crop to crop and have changed over the years. With an eye toward maintaining what is sometimes called "price parity" between the prices a farmer obtains for a crop and the prices he pays for the things he needs, the department buys quantities of the crop and places them in storage, gives farmers loans that are collectible only against the crops they have grown and pays them to keep their harvested crops in storage, restricts the acreage that can be used for growing a crop, pays farmers acreage fees for not growing a crop, restricts imports of the crop, arranges sales of the crop abroad, and in other ways maintains or increases what farmers receive for their crops and what the public pays for them.[5]

[2] *Statistical Abstract of the United States* (1976), p. 395, no. 633.

[3] See, for example, Thomas G. Moore, *Freight Transportation Regulation* (Washington, D.C.: American Enterprise Institute for Public Policy Research, 1972), pp. 3–6.

[4] Airline Deregulation Act of 1978, P.L. 95–504.

[5] See "Commodity Programs and Related Legislation through the Years," *ASCS Background Information,* BI No. 11 (Agriculture Stabilization and Conservation Service, U.S. Dept. of Agriculture, May 1976); Luther Tweeten, *Foundations of Farm Policy* (Lincoln: University of Nebraska Press, 1970); for international aspects in particular, see Edward M. Leonard, "Commodity Price Fixing: The International Grains Arrangement of 1967," *Stanford Law Rev.* 23 (1971), 306; Ronald B. Schram, "International Repercussions of National Farm Policies: A Look at American Wheat Programs," *Law and Pol. Int'l. Bus.* 3 (1971), 239; Emma Rothschild, "Is It Time to End Food for Peace?" *New York Times Magazine,* March 13, 1977, p. 15; Geoffrey Barraclough, "Wealth and Power: The Politics of Food and Oil," *New York Review,* August 7, 1975, p. 23. About a tenth of the *Economic Report of the President* (1975)

In addition, the department oversees agricultural cooperatives, which are also pricing institutions. Federal law expressly exempts farmers from the antitrust laws' prohibitions against agreeing with one another on pricing and using common marketing facilities to the extent that they join cooperatives. Cooperatives do not in all cases include all the farmers who produce the same product, but they generally include very large numbers of farmers. Almost all the orange growers in California are members of one orange cooperative, for example, and almost all the orange growers in Florida are members of another. Agricultural cooperatives permit their members to sell their crops through the cooperative at whatever common prices they choose.[6]

An even more far-reaching government-administered pricing institution is the institution (strictly speaking, group of related institutions) that sets the prices of money. A price of money is the rate of interest or other earnings rate at which money can be obtained for spending for consumption or for investment. Money is bought and sold like any other kind of goods, but it is unique in being at the same time the medium of exchange by which it and other kinds of goods are bought and sold and the measure of their prices. This makes economic analyses of it more complicated, but its prices contribute to inflation in much the same way as do the prices of any other kinds of goods. Mortage interest is a part of the cost of living of which everyone is aware, for example. The single most important member of the money-pricing institution is the Board of Governors of the Federal Reserve System, but the institution also includes other agencies, departments, and particular government officials. The two most important members after the board are probably the Federal Open Market

was devoted to food prices and production, all of it assuming the continued responsibility of the government for both factors. See *Economic Report of the President,* Transmitted to the Congress, February 1975 (Washington, D.C.: U.S. Govt. Printing Office, 1975), pp. 160–86.

[6] Hal Lancaster, "Sweet, Sour Success," *Wall Street Journal,* July 24, 1978, p. 1.

Committee and the Controller of the Currency.[7] The institution exists as a loose confederation of which the board is the head but not the dictator.

Although they are aware that they are influencing the prices of money, the members of the money-pricing institution do not regard this as their principal function. They see as their principal function the formulation and implementation of monetary policy. Monetary policy and fiscal policy are the two means by which the government seeks to pursue one or the other of what are conceived to be the mutually contradictory goals of reducing inflation and increasing economic activity. Both means supposedly serve both goals through raising or lowering aggregate demand. Monetary policy raises or lowers aggregate demand by, respectively, increasing or decreasing the supply of money. Fiscal policy, on the other hand, raises or lowers aggregate demand by, respectively, increasing or decreasing the size of the government deficit. Influencing the prices of money can be viewed either as a means or as an incidental effect of the implementation of monetary policy. One means of decreasing the supply of money is to increase its price. People will then "buy" less of it, which is to say they will borrow or otherwise obtain less of it. And higher prices of money are an incidental effect of decreasing its supply, however the decrease is brought about, through the usual workings of the law of supply and demand. Likewise, lowering the price of money is associated with increasing its supply, also both as a means and as an incidental effect.[8]

[7] For a description of how the Treasury Department and the Controller of Currency fit into the money pricing institution, see Allan Sproul, "The 'Accord'—A Landmark in the First Fifty Years of the Federal Reserve System," in *Essays in Domestic and International Finance* (New York: Federal Reserve Bank of New York, 1969), pp. 15–24. For a description of the organization of the Federal Reserve System and of the Federal Open Market Committee, see *United States Government Manual* (1980–1981) (Washington, D.C.: Offices of the Federal Register, 1980), pp. 564–69.

[8] Samuelson, *Economics*, pp. 269–353. A more up-to-date account of this rapidly changing governmental mechanism can be found in Paul A. Samuelson, *Economics*, 11th ed. (New York: McGraw-Hill, 1980), pp. 274–312.

The odd result is thus that when the money-pricing institution acts in the way that is supposed to reduce inflation, it raises the prices of money and thereby increases inflation. This does *not* prove, however, that the attempt to reduce inflation in this manner is bound to be unsuccessful. Measures can have counterproductive side effects and still produce their intended effects overall. That the attempt is bound to be unsuccessful under current conditions in the United States, when demand is not really excessive, however, is one of the important things that Chapters 1 through 6 are seeking to demonstrate. Assuming what I have not yet finished demonstrating, therefore—that contemporary inflation does not result from excess demand, so that attempts to reduce it by reducing demand by monetary means among others are bound not to succeed—the incidental effect of such attempts, by raising the price of money, are *unmitigatedly inflationary.* Despite its presumably good intentions, the money-pricing institution has actually been aggravating inflation, and aggravating it seriously.

At the same time and by the same actions, the money-pricing institution has been effecting a massive income redistribution in favor of the wealthy. It is the wealthy, of course, who are typically the sellers of money, so it is typically they who profit when its prices are increased. However, it would be wrong to conclude from this alone that their profit is either unfair or unnecessary. It may be fair, because as holders of money they have also been losing as inflation depreciates money's value. It may be necessary, among other reasons because unless investment profits increase during inflationary times, there may not be enough funds available to make the reinvestments that are continually necessary to replace equipment as it wears out. I will not attempt to pass judgment on this very complex issue except to observe that whatever its merits, we are certainly not going about deciding it in the most intelligent way. The money-pricing institution has been increasing the prices of money practically without regard to considerations of income or wealth distribution, because it has been concentrating instead on trying to reduce inflation—a goal toward which, in fact, the raising of money prices is neither an effective means nor an unavoidable effect.

The increases in the prices of money that the money-pricing institution has effected have carried far beyond interest rates. The effects have already been felt in many other kinds of investment, and will eventually be felt in virtually all of them. How this happens can be explained by beginning with common stocks, which are another form in which investment money is bought and sold. Since common stocks in general carry more risk of loss than do bonds or other forms of indebtedness, they also in general provide a higher rate of return. Investors insist upon it before they will invest their money in them. So if the money-pricing institution raises interest rates, the prices of common stocks will generally fall.[9] (A lower price of a common stock represents a higher rate of return on it.) Not only do the lower prices of stocks in themselves mean higher rates of return on investment for shareholders; in addition, they ultimately influence higher rates of profits for the corporations that issued the stock or that will issue stock in the future. When stock prices are lower and interest rates are higher, a corporation that needs to obtain money in order to expand will have no choice but to limit its expansion to those areas in which it can expect to earn at least the higher rates that it will have to pay in order to obtain the necessary funds. If it cannot expect to earn at least this much, it probably will not be able to borrow the money or to sell the necessary number of shares of stock, and if it does manage to, it will have violated its fiduciary duties to its existing shareholders by diluting their shares' values. The latter result would also be the case if the corporation were to expand by using funds that it had generated internally. So in the long run, as the corporate part of the economy expands, corporate profit rates rise along with interest rates and rates of return on common stocks. The opposite happens, of course, if interest rates fall. Thus, the

[9] See, for example, "Economics and Votes, Interest Rates and the Boom," *New York Times,* September 4, 1966, p. E-1; James Tobin, "Check the Boom," *New Republic,* September 3, 1966, p. 10.

control over the prices of money that the money-pricing institution exercises is ultimately felt in every kind of rate of return on investment—and, in addition, in the costs of borrowing for consumption rather than investment, which I have not bothered to describe in detail.[10] Interest (including that on loans both for consumption and for investment) constitutes about 11 percent of national personal income.[11] Business earnings other than interest rates constitute about 15 percent of the gross national product.[12]

Governments are also the administrators of pricing institutions for the services they provide their citizens, since they either set these prices or charge for them indirectly through taxation. Taxes and other fees and charges imposed by governments constitute about a fourth of the gross national product.[13] The federal government also sets the minimum wage, which is a pricing institution. The minimum wage law covers almost all employees, but of course makes a difference only for a fraction of them.[14] No reliable figures exist for how many people are affected, but it is surely in the millions.

If prizes were awarded for the most complicated pricing institutions, however, the one that governs money pricing would not get first prize. That would undoubtedly go to one of the pricing institutions that exist for medical services. These are both privately operated (Blue Cross, Blue Shield, commercial insurance companies, hospitals, and medical professional or-

[10] W. David Slawson, "Taxing as Ordinary Income the Appreciation of Publicly Held Stock," *Yale Law Journal* 76 (1967), 623, 669.

[11] Personal interest income (that is, interest from investments) was 9.3 percent of personal income in 1978. Interest paid by consumers (that is, interest on loans for consumption) was 2 percent of personal income the same year. *Statistical Abstract of the United States* (1979), p. 443.

[12] Business net profits in 1977 were $283 billion *Statistical Abstract of the United States* (1980), p. 556. The gross national product that year was $1,900 billion (p. 437). The share of business net profits was therefore about 15 percent.

[13] Total taxes collected in 1977 were $722 billion (ibid., p. 290). This is about 38 percent of the gross national product of $1,900 billion for the same year (p. 437).

[14] *Statistical Abstract of the United States* (1978), p. 425.

ganizations) and government-operated (Medicare, Medicaid, and various other welfare programs). Hospitals control prices simply by setting them, since their services are generally sold in noncompetitive contexts. Private and government insurance programs control prices through "reimbursement schedules"—schedules dictating what a physician, hospital, or other provider of medical services will be paid by the insurance program.[15] Medical services constituted about 10 percent of personal consumption expenditures at last reckoning, and the percentage has been growing steadily for years.[16]

Labor unions are pricing institutions for the price of their members' labor (that is, wages). A powerful labor union is a pricing institution unto itself, whereas a less powerful union shares its power with employers. About a fourth of the nonfarm working population of the United States is composed of labor union members, although the portion may be shrinking.[17] But the influence of a labor union on wages and salaries extends far beyond its members. It has become common for a company to raise all its employees' wages or salaries in proportion to the raises it gives to union members.[18] Companies with no unionized employees commonly raise wages or salaries in proportion to the raises that are won by labor union

[15] Research on medical services pricing was done for me by Jane Stonecipher. A copy of her report, "Medical Costs," September 16, 1975, includes much additional information pertinent to third-party pay or plans. The Stonecipher paper is on file at the Asa V. Call Law Library, The Law Center, University of Southern California, Los Angeles, California 90007. And see generally Rita Ricardo Campbell, *Economics of Health and Public Policy* (Washington, D.C.: American Enterprise Institute for Public Policy Research, 1971), pp. 27–39; Robert Stevens and Rosemary Stevens, *Welfare Medicine in America: A Case Study for Medicaid* (New York: Free Press, 1974); A. F. Ehrbar, "A Radical Prescription for Medical Care," *Fortune* 95 (February 1977), 164–72.

[16] *Statistical Abstract of the United States* (1979), p. 440. See also *The Problem of Rising Health Care Costs,* Executive Office of the President, U.S. Council on Wage and Price Stability, Staff Report (Washington, D.C.: U.S. Govt. Printing Office, April 1976), p. ii.

[17] *Statistical Abstract of the United States* (1977), p. 418.

[18] Peter F. Drucker, "Managing the Knowledge Worker," *Wall Street Journal,* November 7, 1975, p. 12.

members doing similar work in other companies, even if the nonunion companies keep their wages or salaries lower.[19] On the other hand, labor unions benefit some workers much more than they do others,[20] and they probably make many workers worse off through the inflation to which they contribute.

Unregulated industries that sell at wholesale commonly use what I call an "industrial pricing institution." The prices being charged for the industry's products by its members at any moment constitute the industry's or institution's "price pattern"—the pattern of price *differences* that buyers and sellers alike have come to accept as normal and as reflecting the qualitative differences among the industry's different products. The two basic rules of an industrial pricing institution are that the price pattern be observed by all sellers in all their sales, and that it be maintained through all price changes. If prices go up, every seller's prices on every product it sells should go up by an amount that is required in order to preserve the pattern. The result is to eliminate price competition. Prices are increased without affording buyers any reason for changing their buying habits. If, for example, Buyer *A* was buying from Seller *B* because Seller *B*'s prices were just enough lower than the prices of other sellers to more than compensate, in *A*'s opinion, for the lower quality of *B*'s products, a price increase by all the sellers that maintains the price pattern will leave *A* just as likely to buy from *B* in preference to the other sellers as he was before. A price pattern may include lower prices for favored buyers or classes of buyers. A buyer that regularly receives a lower price normally gets it in the form of a discount. The price he pays is computed by taking the "list price" and subtracting a percentage.

When a member of an industrial pricing institution wants to raise its prices (an action that it knows will require all the other sellers to raise their prices too, in order to maintain the

[19] Interviews with business executives.

[20] Philip Shabecoff, "Unions also Are Split into Rich and Poor," *New York Times,* December 31, 1978, sec. 3, p. E-4; A. H. Raskin, "Jim Crow, Union Member," *New York Times Book Review,* June 12, 1977, p. 12.

price pattern), it publicly announces the higher prices it will charge, generally but not invariably in advance of the date upon which it announces that it will begin charging them. If the announced price increases are substantial, the announcement is usually accompanied by a statement of why they are necessary (higher wages being paid to the industry's employees, higher prices for the industry's supplies, and so on). The other members of the industry then make public announcements of their new and higher prices. If the industry follows the rules of announcing price changes in advance, the other members will generally choose the same future date as was chosen by the first member. If, but only if, the differences among the announced prices are sufficiently changed from the differences among existing prices to effect a significant change in the price pattern, the companies with the *higher* announced prices will retract them and announce prices enough lower to avoid changing the price pattern. It sometimes requires several retractions and new announcements by every company in an industry to raise prices without changing the price pattern, and sometimes, of course, the effort fails, in which cases prices generally remain as they have been. The industries that follow a rule of announcing price changes in advance are generally those whose products are identical or nearly so, such as the steel industry. A member of such an industry dares not charge more for a product than the other members are charging, since buyers will generally refuse to buy *any* of them at higher prices.[21] The reader can find the price announcements in any industry trade journal or, if the industry is a large one, in any financial or business publication with comprehensive coverage.

When a price pattern occurs in an inflationary market (as defined in the previous chapter), the sellers' price changes need not be announced in advance, because no seller is likely to incur significant losses—indeed, he may profit—if his prices are temporarily slightly higher than the other sellers'. In an inflationary market, therefore, institutional inflation (inflation from the operation of a pricing institution or institutions) may

[21] Interviews. See also Areeda, *Antitrust Analysis,* pp. 229–33.

be hardly distinguishable from creeping inflation (inflation from the individual encouragement to raise prices that sellers receive from an inflationary market). It hardly matters, since both processes lead to the same result, but some distinctions can nevertheless be drawn. Creeping inflation, from its nature, tends to be continual, without striking stops or starts. The number of sellers raising prices within a period of time tends to remain the same. Institutional inflation, on the other hand, proceeds by alternating periods of little or no inflation (in the particular market concerned) and sharp leaps, when all or almost all the sellers raise their prices by the amounts dictated by the price pattern at about the same time. The two processes can also be distinguished on the basis of the sellers' motivations. In creeping inflation the motivation is to have one's prices always a little, but only a little, higher than the rest. In institutional inflation the motivation is to keep one's place, as the whole price pattern moves up. There is no reason why the two processes cannot occur in the same market at the same time. In this case, prices are almost always rising at least slowly, and there are also sudden bursts in which they all rise substantially at about the same time.

It is impossible to trace the beginnings of industrial pricing institutions in the United States. They probably began as soon as competing firms began watching each others' prices and setting their own accordingly. But it is clear that their use has been increasing. Inflation itself has presumably been the principal teacher. *Fortune* magazine reports that the paper industry learned how to use the technique effectively in 1974 and that the aluminum industry learned the technique in 1975, for example—both dates shortly after the 1973–1974 burst of inflation.[22] Gardiner Means discovered the steel industry using it in the fifties.[23] I am aware of no cases prior to the 1950s in

[22] Paul H. Weaver, "The Papermakers Are Growing Less and Enjoying It More," *Fortune* 93 (May 1976), 197–98. Edmund Faltermayer, "Homely Metals Are Becoming Precious Again," *Fortune* 93 (May 1976), 197–98. See also Amal Nag, "Aluminum Price Rises Reverse Old Strategy and Anger Big Users," *Wall Street Journal,* May 7, 1979, pp. 1, 26.

[23] Gardiner C. Means, "Pricing Power and the Public Interest," in *Administered Prices: A Compendium on Public Policy,* Subcommittee on Antitrust and Monopoly of the Committee of the Judiciary, United States

which an industry was able to raise prices in the face of low or falling demand, except through explicit and therefore illegal price-fixing; but there were many situations prior to the fifties in which industries were able to prevent their prices from falling, or falling as far as perfect competition would have allowed. It was this condition, sometimes known as "price stickiness," that contributed importantly to the failure of "Say's Law" to work to cure the Great Depression as the traditional theory of the time said it would. (Say's Law predicted that depressions would never occur or, if they did, they would be cured automatically by the encouragement that falling wages gave employers to hire more workers and that falling prices gave consumers to buy more goods.)[24] By 1980, however, as far as I can ascertain, *every* major industry has proven itself capable of effectively using an industrial pricing institution.[25] I will explain later why in my opinion traditional economists have either been blind to this development or misinterpreted it (along with underestimating it) as "monopoly power" or "illegal collusion" (that is, explicit price-fixing).[26]

What I call the "retailers' percentage markup institution," or some variant of it, exists in virtually every industry of whatever size that sells at retail. Each retailer, for each kind of goods he sells, has a standard "percentage markup." A department store, for example, may have a standard percentage markup for men's pants of 100 percent. Whatever the whole-

---

Senate, 88th Congress, 1st Session (Washington, D.C.: U.S. Govt. Printing Office, 1963), pp. 223–30.

24 Areeda, *Antitrust Analysis*, p. 15; John Kenneth Galbraith, *Money: Whence It Came, Where It Went* (New York: Houghton-Mifflin, 1974), pp. 21–20.

25 See, for example, "Inflationary Threat; Prices Rise in Spite of Spare Capacity," *Business Week*, March 21, 1977, p. 120; Areeda, *Antitrust Analysis*, pp. 224–41. The principal support for the statement in the text, however, is my own interviews with business executives and sales persons.

26 See, for example, Joe S. Bain, *Price Theory* (New York: John Wiley & Sons, 1952), pp. 261–83; Joe S. Bain, *Industrial Organization*, 2d. ed. (New York: John Wiley & Sons, 1968), pp. 120–21; William James Adams, "Market Structure and Corporate Power: The Horizontal Dominance," *Columbia Law Rev.* 74 (1974), 1276, 1278–86.

sale price for pants, the price it charges is double this. It is *not* necessary that every retailer in the same institution, that is, selling the same kinds of goods to the same classes of people in the same area, have the same standard markups. Price patterns do not necessarily require uniform prices, as we have seen. The goods that retailers sell commonly differ enough so that price uniformity would not be meaningful anyway. With the markup system just described, when wholesale prices rise, so do the retail prices and by amounts that are exactly what they shold be to preserve the price pattern. An industrywide rise in prices is thus brought about smoothly and legally, without engendering any price competition.

What happens if some manufacturers raise their wholesale prices but others, manufacturing the same kinds of goods, do not? The retailers' percentage markup institution operates in the same way. The retail prices of only those goods whose wholesale prices have gone up also go up; the other retail prices stay where they were. When this happens, and it does frequently, it provides a striking contradiction of traditional economics, which predicts that the retailers would generally either reduce their markups on the goods whose wholesale prices had gone up or increase their markups on the other goods, or both, in order to maintain "profit-maximizing prices" on them all.[27] The reason, presumably, that the markup system works as it does rather than as traditional economics says it should is buyers' general lack of understanding of product differences, which prevents their attaching enough significance to price differences to force retailers to change their markups in order to avoid substantial losses of sales, as was explained in Chapter 2. If the sales of the goods whose prices are raised do fall off appreciably, the retailers' usual response is to stop carrying them. This may or may not be sufficient to convice the manufacturers to rescind the price increases. But retailers only rarely decrease their markups in order to avoid losing sales of goods whose wholesale prices

[27] Lawrence Abbott, *Economics and the Modern World,* 2d ed. (New York: Harcourt, Brace & World, 1967), pp. 94–96.

have increased more than those of other goods of the kind.[28]

The retailers' percentage markup institution amplifies any inflation that occurs at the wholesale level. With a markup of 50 percent, a dollar price increase at wholesale becomes a dollar fifty at retail, for example. Traditional economic analysis predicts quite a different result. According to the traditional analysis, a profit-maximizing retailer will raise his prices by a *smaller absolute amount* than is made in the wholesale prices that he pays, if other retailers with whom he is in competition have been required to pay the same wholesale increases. If the other retailers have not been required to pay the same wholesale increase, according to the traditional analysis the first retailer will simply "swallow" his and maintain the same retail prices. Every observation of which I am aware confirms the pricing-institutional analysis and contradicts the traditional analysis, but standard economics texts continue to offer the traditional analysis and nothing more.[29]

The amplification inherent in retailer's markup institutions also means that inflation is generally profitable for retailers. The dollar amounts of their markups generally increase more rapidly than the dollar amounts of their costs—either their costs of goods at wholesale or their other costs such as clerks' salaries. As a result, retailers do not as a rule resist price increases initiated at the wholesale level. On the contrary, they generally welcome them. This too is contrary to the teachings of traditional economics, which assumes that everyone resists a price increase that would increase his costs. When the Anheuser-Busch Company raised its wholesale beer prices fifteen cents a case in the 1960s, distributor and retailer markups

[28] Interviews with manufacturers and with retailers. Three cases involving the federal antitrust laws in which retailers refused to reduce their prices even though wholesale or manufacturers reduced theirs, or in which retailers raised their prices even though wholesalers or manufacturers did not raise theirs, are: Albrecht v. The Herald Co., 390 U.S. 145 (1968); Kiefer-Stewart Co. v. Joseph E. Seagrams and Sons, Inc., 340 U.S. 211 (1951); Anheuser-Busch, Inc. v. Federal Trade Commission, 198 F.2d 835 (7th Cir. 1961).

[29] See Abbott, *Economics and the Modern World,* pp. 94–96; Samuelson, *Economics,* 9th ed., pp. 593–42.

multiplied this to a dollar twenty cents at retail, which cost Anheuser-Busch substantially in lost sales. But when it sought to rescind the retail price increases by rescinding its wholesale increase, the distributors and retailers pocketed the fifteen cents and kept their retail prices the same. The lesson Anheuser-Busch took away from the experience was to avoid trying to sell beer through price competition and to use increased advertising and promotion instead.[30]

Although the percentage markup kind of pricing institution is not the only one that is used in retail industries, it seems to be the most common, and some kind of markup method seems to be used almost universally. A markup method is presumably preferred to a method that would require separate judgments to be made for every kind of product, because of its savings in administrative costs. Sometimes retailers' markups are suggested by manufacturers, either by placing printed retail prices on the products or their packages, or by distributing lists of suggested retail prices. I found that such lists were distributed by wholesalers who were not themselves manufacturers in the hardware industry. The conclusions drawn for the percentage markup kind of institution obviously also apply to these other kinds of retail institutions, with insignificant variations.

The pricing institutions that exist for the sale of services vary widely, depending on the kinds of service. (Medical services, which we treated earlier, are a special case, primarily because of the extent of government participation in their pricing.) Institutional control of the pricing of services seems not to be as firm, in general, as is the control of tangible products, probably because this is not necessary to avoid price competition. Lack of buyer understanding is generally at its greatest with respect to services.[31] The usual person whose automobile is repaired at a garage, for example, lacks any un-

[30] See Anheuser-Busch, Inc. v. Federal Trade Commission, 298 F.2d 835 (7th Cir. 1961).

[31] See, for example, Roger Smith, "For the Good Life, We Pay the Plumber," *Los Angeles Times,* December 15, 1978, pp. 1, 16 (home repair services and legal services).

derstanding of the repairs. He often lacks knowledge even of what the repairs will be until after he is committed to paying for them. Insurance services provide special problems for inflation by encouraging buyers to buy the best goods or services their insurance will pay for, regardless of its price, and by encouraging sellers to charge higher prices, in the knowledge that they will be paid by an insurance company.

Some pricing institutions are controlled by the buyers of the goods rather than by the sellers. This is the case with employers whose employees are not organized into labor unions, for example, or with employers whose employees' labor unions are too weak to be regarded as participants in the setting of the employees' wages. Such control by employers over employees' wages and salaries is generally firm and not substantially influenced by competition.[32] Employer pricing institutions are usually not an inflationary problem, because the

[32] That an employer whose employees are not members of an effective labor union generally has firm control of the employees' wages or salaries is so widely acknowledged to be the case, apparently, that no one has thought either to dispute it or to affirm it in print. See, for example, Graef S. Crystal, "Manager's Journal: Pay for Performance—Even If It's Just Luck," *Wall Street Journal,* March 2, 1981, p. 16, in which the author simply takes for granted that corporations are free from contraints from market forces to pay their executive employees whatever, and however, they choose. The responses to my questions to business executives about how they exercised this control were invariably to the effect that their companies checked with other companies of a similar nature to learn what the others were paying, and then made up their own minds, without feeling compelled to pay the same or more than the others were paying. In every case, moreover, the expressed motive for checking with other companies was fairness, not competition. Price competition generally seems to enter the nonunion employment picture only at two points: for extraordinarily skilled employees (outstanding sales executives, for example) and for initial hirings. And for initial hirings, although an employer would undoubtedly suffer if it were to offer substantially less than its competitors, the "going rate"—that is, the pay that all employers of a kind are offering at any particular time—is generally not set by competition but by a price-announcement process (here, a "beginning salary announcement" process) substantially identical in all relevant respects to that which was described earlier in the text and given the name of "industrial pricing institutions." One of the very few occasions upon which my confidential interviews disclosed what was probably an illegal price-fixing conspiracy was an agreement among employers not to pay secretaries more than particular amounts.

employers' interest is generally to prevent wages or salaries from rising. However, the highest-paid employees frequently control the organizations that employ them or, what comes to the same thing, are part of a social class or "old boy network" that controls organizational employers generally. These salaries and the pricing institutions by which they are set are very much of an inflationary problem.[33]

Finally, some pricing institutions work primarily through controlling supplies rather than prices. Prices in the short term are permitted to rise or fall with the ups and downs of demand, but in the long term supplies are controlled, essentially just as prices are controlled by members of an industrial pricing institution, for the purpose of maintaining or increasing prices. Supply pricing institutions generally operate with commodites. The prices of copper are apparently controlled over the long term in this manner, for example. Although aluminum prices apparently used to be, they are now controlled by the more usual kind of industrial institution.[34] The Department of Agriculture controls the prices of some crops over the long term by controlling supplies, as was mentioned earlier.

In Chapters 1 and 2 the conditions that give rise to indeterminate inflation were pictured as creating gaps in the market determination of prices, within which prices are free to rise. It is difficult to fit pricing institutions into this picture, because the gaps that they can create are so big. In the presence of a powerful pricing institution market forces have practically no effect. Senior airline pilots were being paid $100,000 a year plus generous amenities in the middle seventies. What they would have been paid in the absence of a powerful labor union is impossible to say, but it surely would have been less

[33] Graef S. Crystal, "Pay Watchers Beware," *Wall Street Journal,* January 22, 1979, p. 20; Charles G. Burck, "A Group Profile of the Fortune 500 Chief Executive," *Fortune* 93 (May 1976), 172, 176–77; Peter F. Drucker, "Is Executive Pay Excessive?" *Wall Street Journal,* May 23, 1977, p. 18; Isadore Barmash, "More Pay at the Top of the Ladder," *New York Times,* January 16, 1977, sec. 3, p. 1.

[34] See Faltermayer, "Homely Metals," and Nag, "Aluminum Price Rises."

than half of this, and probably less than that. So even under the assumption that the labor union in this case had exploited the gap to the fullest—and there is no reason to think that it had—the gap would have to be counted as being as large as the price itself. The Department of Agriculture has an even greater potential effect on the prices of the agricultural products that have been placed under its control. There is no discernible limit short of mass starvation on how high it could raise these prices, if it so chose. Not all pricing institutions are as powerful as these, of course, but they do characteristically possess a much greater gap-creating power, so to speak, than do the conditions treated in either Chapters 1 and 2 or the conditions to be treated in Chapter 4.

The Factors That Influence Pricing Institutions to Change Their Members' Prices

Traditional economics assumes that sellers always want higher profits, so that the only reason prices are not higher than they are is that competition prevents sellers from making more profits by raising them. But since the effect of a pricing institution is to eliminate this restraining effect of price competition, and since the other forms of competition generally do not prevent prices from rising, the traditional analysis cannot hold for prices governed by pricing institutions. If it did, these prices would always be rising, indefinitely rapidly. Although pricing institutions characteristically do not maximize the profits of their members, they do increase them.[35] A *general* reason that pricing institutions raise prices is that they thereby increase the profits of their members, but precisely because this reason is general it is not very interesting. Of more interest are the special reasons that might explain why the prices governed by pricing institutions rise at some times and not at others, and rise at some times more rapidly than at others. For convenience of analysis I have separated the special reasons

[35] See Chapter 4.

into explanations of why pricing-institutional prices rise and explanations of why they do not rise.

First, pricing institutions characteristically raise prices when they are created, since they are created for this purpose. The clearest recent example was the creation of the Organization of Petroleum Producing States (OPEC) in 1973 and the fourfold increase in the world price of oil that OPEC put into effect immediately afterward. OPEC is not an American pricing institution, of course, but its high visibility makes it a useful illustration, and its formation and operation are symptomatic of what will surely happen elsewhere whenever conditions are favorable.[36] The Interstate Commerce Commission was formed for the express purpose, among others, of preventing price competition in railroad rates in 1888, and was amended to do the same for trucking and bus rates in 1935.[37] Although the data are not readily available to show whether rates in either case rose immediately, both railroads and truckers have fought ever since to maintain the commission's protection.[38] The Department of Agriculture's pricing institutions for farmers were formed at various times beginning in the 1920s. There was never any question but that a crop's prices would be raised as soon as it came under the control of the department. The National Labor Relations Act was enacted in 1935.[39] Although labor unions had been legal before, the laws had made it difficult to organize and maintain them. The NLRA made the laws much more favorable to labor unions. It took some time for new labor unions to be organized and existing ones to strengthen themselves, and shortly after 1935

[36] See, for example, James C. Tanner, Neil Ulman, and Ray Vicker, "Divided Cartel: Oil-Price Rise Likely, but Discord in OPEC May Hold down Level," *Wall Street Journal,* September 23, 1975, p. 1; Everett G. Martin, "Protecting Prices: Tin Pact May Emerge as a Model for Future Raw Materials Groups," *Wall Street Journal,* April 21, 1976, p. 1.

[37] Interstate Commerce Act, February 4, 1887, Ch. 104, 24 Stat. 379; Motor Carrier Act of 1935, August 9, 1935, Ch. 498, 49 Stat. 543.

[38] See, for example, Albert R. Karr, "Truck Firms Gear up Major Lobbying Effort to Fight Deregulation," *Wall Street Journal,* July 5, 1979, p. 1.

[39] National Labor Relations Act, July 5, 1935, Ch. 372, 49 Stat. 449.

the Second World War began to involve the United States, but almost immediately after the war ended there was the worst period of labor strife and "wage push" inflation the United States has ever seen.[40] The late sixties and seventies have been a period of rapid formation of labor unions among farm workers and public employees, two labor categories that were not generally helped by the NLRA.[41] The wages concerned have risen much more rapidly than they had in the past. In the fifties, the formation of the pricing institutions for medical services got underway. The prices of medical services have risen at about twice the general inflation rate ever since.[42] The repercussions of the formation of particular industrial pricing institutions have already been noted.

Once it has become established, a pricing institution does not necessarily stop raising prices, of course. A relatively few have gone on to engender unceasingly large price increases. The government and private insurance programs for medical services are an example. Physicians and other service providers are paid virtually all of whatever they care to charge, and of course they choose to charge a lot and to increase their charges frequently. The private programs have been reluctant to impose any restraints, presumably because they have been dominated by the persons whose fees and charges they have been paying. These same people have managed to keep Congress from giving effective restraining powers to the administrators of the government programs. Similarly, some labor unions, most notably those for construction workers, airline

[40] U.S. Bureau of the Census, *The Statistical History of the United States, Colonial Times to the Present* (New York: Basic Books, 1976), p. 179.

[41] See, for example, Jeff L. Lewin, " 'Representatives of Their Own Choosing,' Practical Considerations in the Selection of Bargaining Representatives for Seasonal Farmworkers," *California Law Rev.* 64 (1976), 732–37; Leon Bornstein, "Industrial Relations in 1976: Highlights of Key Settlements," *Monthly Labor Rev.* 100 (January 1977), p. 35; Agricultural Labor Relations Act of 1975, California Labor Code §1140 et seq. (St. Paul, Minn.: West Supp., 1977).

[42] *The Problem of Rising Health Care Costs,* pp. ii, 7.

pilots, and longshoremen, have also been both powerful and irresponsible enough to get large increases for their members almost without cease.[43] The pricing institutions that exist for setting the pay of top executives of large organizations have also been more than ordinarily active and successful, despite their relative informality. The rates of price increases of institutions like these seem eventually to level off, however, presumably after the members' incomes have been raised sufficiently in relation to incomes in the rest of the economy to satisfy the members. Senior airline pilots, for example, obtained $100,000 a year plus travel privileges in exchange for only a few days' flying a month in 1977, but have not markedly increased their pay or decreased their working time since.

The norm for an established pricing institution appears to be to increase prices when, but only when, a convincing justification arises. The justification must be convincing to the members, to the portions of the public whose opinions the members value, or to the public generally. Easily the most frequently used justification is the need to raise prices in order to maintain past or current rates of profit or income. When the

[43] That electricians in 1976 were regularly earning $30,000 to $40,000 a year was told to me by contractors in a California area who did not want their identities disclosed. The wage rates for union plumbers in the New York City area in 1974 were such as would yield $60,000 a year for 40 hours a week for 52 weeks. See David R. Francis, "Business Booms for Nonunion Construction Firms," *Christian Science Monitor,* December 22, 1974, p. 10. For the official figures for organized construction workers, see *News,* U.S. Dept. of Labor, Bureau of Labor Statistics, May 21, 1975, p. 5, table 2.

June Kronholz, "Long Haul, for Pilot Jack Sallee, a 1,700 Mile-Commute Is All Part of the Job," *Wall Street Journal,* May 27, 1976, p. 1; Todd E. Fandell, "Flying High: New Pilot-Pay Pact at Delta Air Lines Has the Industry Agog," *Wall Street Journal,* September 19, 1974, p. 1; and see George E. Hopkins, *The Airlines Pilots—A Study in Elite Unionization* (Cambridge: Harvard University Press, 1971).

See "Automation Deal," *Business Week* March 25, 1961, pp. 56–57; "Sharing Automation Savings," *Business Week,* October 29, 1960, p. 86; "Dockers Vote . . . To Use $1.5 Million Indemnity against Loss of Work through Mechanization To Maintain Average Earnings," *Business Week,* April 23, 1960, pp. 64–66; Max D. Kossoris, "Working Rules in West Coast Longshoring," *Monthly Labor Rev.* 84 (January 1961), 5–7.

members of an industrial pricing institution have increased their employees' wages, for example, they are almost sure to justify their ensuing price increases by pointing to the need to cover the cost of the increased wages.[44] The retailers' markup pricing institution works automatically to increase retail prices only when wholesale prices, which are the retailers' costs, have risen. A consumer who inquires of a retailer will of course be told that this is the reason why retail prices have risen. Practically all government regulation of prices *requires* that the prices concerned be increased sufficiently to maintain the sellers' profits, should the sellers' costs increase. The Department of Agriculture's programs also work in this manner, although the requirement in this case is flexible.

Inflation itself is probably the next most commonly used justification. Not by coincidence, it is also commonly described as a rising cost—the "rising cost of living." Almost all across-the-board pay increases have come to be justified as needed to cover the "cost of living." A third common sort of justification is "catch-up." The sellers concerned declare their "need" or "right" to make more money in relation to what others make because, they claim, their previous incomes were unfairly small by comparison.[45] The pay increases won for agricultural workers in the sixties and seventies were generally thus justified, for example. No courts exist to decide whether a justification is entirely truthful, so there is a tendency for in-

[44] Leroy H. Mantell and Francis P. Sing, *Economics for Business Decisions* (New York: McGraw-Hill, 1972), pp. 239–48; Neil W. Chamberlain, *The Firm* (New York: McGraw-Hill, 1962), pp. 193–95; "Profit Pinch: Firms' Earnings Drop in 2nd Quarter Eased from 1st Period Slump," *Wall Street Journal,* August 1, 1975, p. 1; Ralph E. Winter, "Heading Higher: At Many Companies, the Order of the Day Is To Move Prices Up," *Wall Street Journal,* December 7, 1976, p. 1.

[45] John Sheahan, *The Wage-Price Guideposts* (Washington, D.C.: Brookings Institution, 1967), p. 27; Adrian W. Throop, "The Union-Nonunion Wage Differential and Cost-Push Inflation," *Amer. Econ. Rev.* 58 (1968), 79–80; Thomas Gale Moore, "Incomes Policy, Its Rationale and Development," in Phillip Cagan, Marten Estey, William Fellner, Charles E. McClure, Jr., and Thomas Gale Moore, *Economic Policy and Inflation in the Sixties* (Washington, D.C.: American Enterprise Institute for Public Policy Research, 1972), pp. 217–19.

flation, once started, to justify more and more inflation in an accelerating spiral.

An odd sort of justification for higher wages is a substantial reduction or threatened reduction in the number of employed workers. Traditional economics would predict exactly the opposite. Supposedly, when the demand for labor exceeds the supply wages should rise, whereas when the demand falls or threatens to fall, wages should fall with it. But, in fact, a large surplus or threatened surplus of workers seems to operate as a justification for a large wage increase, at least when a labor union is present. The workers seemingly want to make as much as they can while they can, and feel justified in doing so. The employers seem to feel that it is easier to pay more if they have or will soon have many fewer workers. And where unemployment or threatened unemployment is the result of the introduction of labor-saving technology, the union can trade its acceptance of the technology for higher wages. Typographers got higher and higher wages throughout the fifties and sixties while the demand for their services was declining or threatening to decline as a result of the introduction of labor-saving methods of typesetting.[46] Production workers in the American movie industry got higher and higher wages as the need for their services declined to practically nothing in the mid-sixties.[47] "Containerization"—a packaging process that drastically reduces the number of men needed to load or unload a ship—was introduced in the early sixties. Longshoremen's wages rose drastically.[48] Labor-saving machinery was widely introduced in the coal-mining industry shortly after the Second World War. Most coal miners were thereby unemployed, but those who retained their jobs were given sub-

[46] Harry Kelber and Carl Schlesinger, *Union Printers and Controlled Automation* (New York: Free Press, 1967); *Statistical Abstract of the United States* (1976), p. 383, table 616; p. 369, table 597.

[47] Garth Jowett, *Film, the Democratic Art* (Boston: Little, Brown, 1976), pp. 430–32.

[48] "Automation Deal"; "Sharing Automation Savings"; "Dockers Vote . . . To Use $1.5 Million Indemnity"; Kossoris, "Working Rules in West Coast Longshoring."

stantial pay increases.[49] The history of the American merchant marine has been one of steady pay increases accompanied by steady reductions in the number of workers for at least forty years.[50]

A justification rarely offered for increased prices is rising demand. The reason is presumably not that it would fail to impress the appropriate people, since it is fully in accord with traditional economic theory, but that it is simply not the real reason. If it is not the real reason the facts will ordinarily make this clear. If rising demand were really sufficient to cause prices to rise, a pricing institution would not need to raise them; if the sellers did not raise their own prices rapidly enough, buyers would bid them up. Moreover, rising demand as a justification for rising prices is contrary to the general tenor of the other common justifications, which, as we have seen, relate to rising costs. When demand is rising, sales are almost invariably rising too, and rising sales ordinarily mean lower unit costs. When prices seem to be rising because of rising demand, a pricing institution can usually be found to be the underlying cause after all. Occasionally a particular model of automobile will prove to be unexpectedly popular, for example, and as a result its retail prices will be strictly "list"—no discounts or bargain prices on trade-ins—or above list. The immediate cause will have been demand unexpectedly exceeding supply—but the manufacturer, of course, set the supply. The manufacturer will also have set the wholesale price,

[49] "Job Fill You How?" *Business Week,* June 4, 1949, pp. 94–97; "Coal: When Machines Took Over," *U.S. News & World Report,* April 29, 1963, pp. 69–72; *Statistical Abstract of the United States* (1976), p. 705, table 1200; p. 706, table 1202.

[50] Samuel A. Lawrence, *United States Merchant Marine Shipping Policies and Politics* (Washington, D.C.: Brookings Institution, 1966), pp. 91–94. Dudley Jackson, H. A. Turner, and Frank Wilkinson, *Do Trade Unions Cause Inflation?* 2d ed. (Cambridge: Cambridge University Press, 1974), reports the same general experience in England, that substantial increases in productivity, whether or not they put people out of work, stimulated wage inflation. And see Ronald L. Soble, "Jury still Out on Socialism in British Columbia," *Los Angeles Times,* March 7, 1976, pt. 5, p. 1, which reported the same in British Columbia. *Statistical Abstract of the United States* (1976), p. 624, table 1055.

through the industry's pricing institution, and this price will not rise, any more than this price would have fallen if demand had been unexpectedly low. When agriculture prices rise, the underlying reason, again, is ordinarily a pricing institution, in this case the Department of Agriculture. The department will deliberately have set the supply low enough that demand would cause prices to rise.

The principal reason why a pricing institution would not raise its members' prices is simply the absence of any convincing justification for doing so. It is extremely rare to read of a general price increase in an industry that is not simultaneously justified in public by reference to rising costs, for example. There are also some important "inertial" restraints on the rise of institutional prices—restraints on the frequency with which they can rise that therefore have the effect of maintaining the status quo. To the extent that the Department of Agriculture works through acreage restrictions, for example, its decisions about crop prices cannot practicably be changed more than once a year. Government regulatory commissions are not normally restricted by law as to how frequently they can change their minds about the prices they control, but the slowness of their procedures places a substantial practical restraint on how frequently regulated prices can change. Other inertial restraints are merely traditional. Medical services reimbursement schedules are traditionally not revised more than once a year. Most labor union contracts are traditionally made to last three years. Many industries (the automobile industry, for example) traditionally revise prices only once a year.

Some restraints on price increases are political. Every federal administration since John F. Kennedy's has established some kind of formal means of monitoring, giving publicity to, and making official comments on the wage or price increases of industries or labor unions.[51] President Johnson spoke by

[51] George P. Shultz and Robert Z. Aliber, eds., "Introduction," in *Guidelines: Informal Controls and the Market Place* (Chicago: University of Chicago Press, 1966), pp. 2–5. In addition, the Nixon-Ford administration had actual wage and price controls and, later, a Council on Wage

telephone with industry and labor leaders, urging them to keep prices or wages down.[52] When a government is giving a pay or price increase to some of its own employees, the political restraint sometimes works very quickly. In San Francisco, for example, a referendum rescinded most of a pay increase that the city had given some of its employees.[53]

Political restraints are presumably important because institutions realize that in the long run, at least, their power to increase prices depends upon the public's confidence that they will use the power responsibly. Governments also play upon their desire to appear, at least, to act responsibly in restraining institutional price increases in the short run. Strikes are frequently not settled until a government has sent in a mediator, sometimes the mayor or governor himself. Whose side this mediator takes, or whose side the government takes even if it does not send in a mediator, is probably the single most important factor for determining who wins in the final settlement.[54] In addition, the federal government can bring an antitrust prosecution against an industry that it concludes is abusing its pricing powers. At the very least, it can carry out an investigation that is costly and embarrassing to the industry. Congress can give or withhold tax favors or favorable tariff or import-quota legislation. State legislators are sometimes in a position to do likewise on tax matters for particular industries.

I unexpectedly uncovered another kind of political restraint while investigating a $4.00-an-hour wage increase that an electrician's union won in 1975 in a California city. Construc-

---

and Price Stability. The Council on Wage and Price Stability Act of August 24, 1974 (88 Stat. 750, 12 U.S.C. 1904 note), as amended by Act of August 9, 1975 (89 Stat. 411).

[52] Joseph Califano told me in 1966 that President Johnson had been on the telephone an average of more than once a day for about a year with business or labor officials about wages or prices.

[53] Leon Bornstein, "Industrial Relations in 1976: Highlights of Key Settlements," *Monthly Labor Rev.* 100 (January 1977), 33.

[54] Albert Rees, *The Economics of Trade Unions* (Chicago: University of Chicago Press, 1962), pp. 37–39.

tion unions do not usually bargain with employers directly but with an employer's association, in this case the Area Contractors' Association. I asked an association member whether he and the other association members thought that the higher wages they had been paying the past several years had cost them anything. He replied that they had not. Since every contractor had to pay the same wages, their job bids were all commensurately higher, and they all felt that they were making just as high profits as they would have been had the wages remained lower. I then asked why the association bothered to resist the unions' demands. (This association had resisted the unions' demands seemingly as best it could, although not very successfully. The electricians had had to go on strike for seven weeks to win their additional $4.00.) The member's reply was that he and his fellow members believed they were representing the public interest in keeping construction costs down. If they did not faithfully represent the public interest in this respect, he said, the federal government would eventually find it necessary to regulate the construction industry, which the contractors definitely did not want.

There are also restraints of a purely economic nature. An industry whose members' profits are uncommonly high attracts new firms, whose entry into the industry will probably reduce profits for several reasons. An entering firm may offer its products at especially low prices, at least for a while, to lure customers away from the old members. The addition of a firm also makes the effective operation of a pricing institution more difficult. The public-announcement process takes longer when there are more members; at some number, presumably, the process would take so long that it would not work. The more members there are, the more likely it is that one of them will cheat on the price pattern, and the less likely it is that its cheating will be detected and terminated before it severely damages the price pattern. If the entering firm is affiliated with one or more of the industry's customers, its effect on profits is likely to be especially substantial. The industry will then be left selling only to those buyers who have not built or purchased the facilities for manufacturing their own products, and will probably have to keep its prices low in order to keep its buyers in business.[55]

The major restraint on a labor union is the economic loss that it and its members will incur if there is a strike. Such losses are probably more of a restraint by virtue of being uncertain. The duration of a strike and the extent of the bitterness and resentment that it may engender in the employer or the public are difficult to predict before it has begun.[56] If a pricing institution does not include all the sellers who compete, or if some of its members are markedly less cooperative than others in refraining from price competition, the outsiders' or uncooperative members' price competition of course operates as a restraint upon the institution's ability to raise the prices of its members. All industrial and all retail pricing institutions confront this restraint at least potentially, and most of them confront it actually from time to time or even continuously. The antitrust laws and the strong tradition of business competition in our country combine to prevent industrial and retail pricing institutions from eliminating price competition entirely; they can only reduce it, although they can and often do reduce it substantially. Labor unions also confront this restraint, although generally to a lesser extent, from the competition of nonunion labor.

Pricing institutions also restrain themselves out of a sense of propriety, decency, or fairness. Their high incomes notwithstanding, physicians, for example, are still generally not charging nearly as much as they could if they were to exercise their institutional powers fully. They are undoubtedly restrained in part by the political factors mentioned previously, but their own sense of propriety is certainly also a restraining factor. Self-restraint may, in fact, be operating too powerfully on industry currently. Industry's profits are probably not high enough in general to provide either the funds or the profit in-

[55] George J. Stigler, *The Theory of Price,* 3rd ed. (New York: Macmillan, 1966), pp. 216–19.

[56] Rees, *Economics of Trade Unions,* pp. 31–37. See, for example, John R. Emshwiller, "Strike Is Traumatic for a Quiet Village in Michigan Woods," *Wall Street Journal,* June 30, 1977, p. 1.

centives for attracting the funds to finance a sufficiently rapid rate of investment at today's higher capital goods prices.[57]

None of the factors that influence pricing institutions either to raise or not to raise their members' prices even approaches in its efficacy the power attributed by traditional economics to the forces of competition. Moreover, it would be a mistake to assume that the prices governed by pricing institutions are subject to any other force of an analogous kind. Pricing institutions are essentially political entities. They can be understood, but their particular actions are no more predictable than the particular actions of governments, electorates, lobbying organizations, or legislatures. For no pricing institutions, any more than for other kinds of political entities, is there ever likely to be discovered an "invisible hand."

The Inevitability and Desirability of Pricing Institutions

Pricing institutions are desirable, for one thing, for preventing wide price fluctuations, which would otherwise be especially prevalent and especially harmful under modern economic conditions. When prices are fully responsive to supply and demand, an imbalance of supply over demand causes prices to fall until supply falls or demand rises (or both) sufficiently to right the balance. The falling price causes supply to fall by discouraging producers from producing. And it causes demand to rise by encouraging people to buy.[58] But because of the conditions of necessity and satiety described in Chapter 2, people in a modern economy generally do not buy in appreciably larger volumes merely because prices are lower. Therefore, in order to right an imbalance of supply over de-

[57] "Where Will the Growth Come From? *Business Week,* December 14, 1974, pp. 70–71; John O'Riley, "The Outlook: Review of Current Trends in Business and Finance," *Wall Street Journal,* January 20, 1975, p. 1; George Leland Bach, *The New Inflation: Causes, Effects, Cures* (Englewood Cliffs, N.J.: Prentice-Hall, 1973), pp. 20–21, 31.

[58] Samuelson, *Economics,* 9th ed., pp. 482–532.

mand in a modern economy, a price ordinarily has to fall until producers are sufficiently discouraged to lower supply enough to right the balance, while people continue to buy no more than before. A price would ordinarily, therefore, have to fall very, very far before its effects on supply alone would bring supply and demand back into balance.

Necessity and satiety operate especially in the case of manufactured products—for which, not coincidentally, pricing institutions are also especially prevalent and powerful. Take plumbing facilities, for example. Except for short-term inventory buying by retailers, a price change for sinks, faucets, toilets, and so on would have practically no effect on sales, because the uses of these things are almost entirely determined by considerations that do not include their prices. The number of sinks in a new residence, for example, depends upon the size of the residence, the number of bedrooms, the relative locations and distances from one another of the bedrooms and other rooms, the prices of lumber, plasterboard, concrete, brick, and other building materials, the price of construction labor, the interest rates and availability of mortgage money, and a host of other factors unrelated to the price of sinks. And since the price of sinks is only a small portion of the total price of a new residence, a price change in sinks would not appreciably change the number of new residences. So if the prices of plumbing facilities were not restrained from falling by pricing institutions, even slight overproductions would trigger massive price decreases, which would periodically drive plumbing producers out of business until the overproduction had been corrected. Massive price decreases today, with rare exceptions, in fact occur only for goods produced principally in underdeveloped countries and sold principally in developed countries, so that their producers do not have the benefit of effective pricing institutions although their sales are subject to conditions of necessity and satiety.[59] The last time that agricultural

[59] Robert Prinsky, "Ghana Moves To Stay No. 1 in Cocoa while Striving to Diversify," *Wall Street Journal,* May 14, 1976, p. 1; H. J. Maidenberg, "Misadventures of Cocoa Trade," *New York Times,* February 25, 1979, sec. 3, p. 1; H. J. Maidenberg, "Commodities: As Volatile as the

goods produced in the United States suffered massive price decreases was during the Great Depression, before government pricing institutions were established for them.[60] Economic theory, however, still regards price changes as the appropriate and beneficial means of righting an imbalance between supply and demand, presumably because the theory was formulated at a time when most goods were not sold under conditions of necessity and satiety. In Adam Smith's time, even basic foods were generally not available in sufficient quantities to satisfy most people, for example.[61]

Since necessity and satiety work about equally well in both directions, it might seem that what producers would lose from occasional overproduction they would gain from occasional underproduction, which would seemingly increase prices just as massively as overproduction would reduce them, and unrestrained price competition would not be harmful over the long term after all. But the gains and losses would not generally even themselves out, for a number of reasons. Under price competition, each seller is generally producing at full capacity, and both prices and profits are low.[62] As a result, when there are surpluses, many sellers quickly fail. Not having accumulated large profits, they have little staying power. Those who go under during a time of surplus do not survive to profit from a shortage, of course, no matter how profitable for the survivors a subsequent shortage may turn out to be. Shortages, moreover, will not generally be deliberately contrived. A seller who deliberately restricted his production in order to cause prices to rise would not be engaging in price competition. A shortage that is not deliberately contrived must result either from a natural condition that cuts production or pre-

Dollar," *New York Times,* February 4, 1979, International Economic Survey, p. 36.

[60] Arthur Meier Schlesinger, Jr., *The Crisis of the Old Order* (New York: Houghton-Mifflin, 1957), pp. 174–76.

[61] See generally Richard H. Tawney, *The Acquisitive Society* (New York: Harcourt, Brace, 1920), pp. 1–32; Karl Polanyi, *The Great Transformation* (Boston: Beacon Press, 1957), pp. 56–76, 90–104, 115.

[62] Samuelson, *Economics,* 9th ed., pp. 453–56.

vents distribution—a drought, in the case of crops, for example—or from some man-made condition beyond the sellers' control—a widespread strike of railroad workers, for example. A shortage from either cause will both aid and harm the sellers at the same time, and the harm is likely to exceed the aid for some producers and may exceed it for all. A drought will obviously hurt farmers by reducing or eliminating their crops at the same time as it increases the prices of the crops that are left, for example. A transportation stoppage will prevent some or all sellers from selling their goods at the same time as it increases the prices of those who can. Surpluses, on the other hand, generally only hurt; sellers have no offsetting benefits in the way of increased sales. Sales do not generally increase merely because prices fall, for the reasons given previously. Sellers generally could not take advantage of increased demand caused by the falling prices, because under price competition sellers are already selling at full capacity.

The relatively unrestrained price competition that would exist in the absence of pricing institutions would also be inefficient and unfair. The generally low profits would inhibit capital accumulation, which would reduce technological research and investment in new production facilities. The wide price fluctuations would make effort or investment in anything except speculation seem hardly worthwhile. The prices of crops grown in underdeveloped countries have recently fluctuated as much as 100 percent up and 50 percent down in six months, for example.[63] Such fluctuations make a crop worthless or double its value in less time than the crop needs to grow. Technological advance, by comparison, typically requires large capital expenditures and sustained effort, and still proceeds at a rate of only a few percent per year.[64] Resources thrown out of production because their owners have been financially ruined are generally expensive to restore. Price fluctuations hurt or help sellers without regard to how efficiently or wisely they have conducted their affairs, in relation either to one another or to others in the society as a whole. Wide-

[63] See the articles cited in n. 59.

[64] *Statistical Abstract of the United States* (1977), p. 405.

spread natural or man-made conditions that cause the fluctuations have a similarly arbitrary effect.

Despite their propensities for inflation, therefore, pricing institutions are needed to avoid the harshness, inefficiency, and unfairness of price competition whenever price competition would be vigorous without them. They are also probably needed as a "second line of defense" when, in their absence, price competition would only occasionally be vigorous, as would be the case in inflationary markets (see Chapter 2). When vigorous price competition does break out in inflationary markets, it is likely to be especially arbitrary and inefficient, because the characteristics of these markets prevent the competition from selecting the best-at-the-price products for survival from among the rest. There was intense price competition in the national market for smoke detectors during 1978 and 1979, for example, a market that possesses the characteristics for being inflationary. Some brands were reportedly selling for less than the manufacturers' costs.[65] Whatever manufacturers survived will *not* necessarily have been those who made the best smoke detectors at the least cost, since the people who buy smoke detectors have no practical way of knowing what brands or models these would be. The survivors are likely to have been the manufacturers with the most assets or who were cleverest at using nonprice forms of competition. There is therefore no reason to expect that this uncharacteristic outburst of price competition will have improved the industry's products or benefited the public in any other enduring way.

Even if unrestrained price competition were truly beneficial and pricing institutions were an unmitigated harm, substantial political obstacles would lie in the way of eliminating them. For one thing, they are generally profitable for their members, or at least they are perceived to be, and their elimination would surely result in bankruptcies for some sellers and lower profits for all in many, if not most, industries. Profits in the av-

[65] "Angry because You Think Prices Only Go Up, Not Down?" *Wall Street Journal,* January 17, 1979, p. 1.

erage American industry are only slightly more than 5 percent of sales.[66] It would take only a few percentage points' decline in prices, if it were more than temporary, to cut average profits in half and force a sizable portion of almost every industry to operate in the red indefinitely. When a high rate of inflation has become general, as it has in the United States, an effective pricing institution can be a matter of business survival. The creeping inflation described in Chapter 2 may then be inadequate to protect an industry's profits against sudden, large increases in its costs—against the loss of profits resulting from a large industrywide wage increase, for example. And some sellers, of course, do not sell in inflationary markets and so lack even the protections of "price creeping."

Efforts have been made to prosecute sellers for the kinds of practices that I have identified as following the rules of an industrial pricing institution, on the grounds that the practices violate the antitrust laws' prohibitions against fixing prices by agreement. But although the prosecutions were assisted by the extremely broad definition that the United States Supreme Court has given to "price-fixing agreement," they failed to prove that there had been any such agreements.[67] The fact is that the only kinds of pricing institutions whose members need to reach agreements with one another have been exempted from the antitrust laws. Farmers' cooperatives and labor unions are examples. Even if sellers were to use agreements to establish and maintain an industrial pricing institution, and they were prosecuted and convicted for doing so, they could presumably resume their institution without further agreement, and therefore legally. This has been the course of events in some industries.[68] It is so obvious that the

[66] *Statistical Abstract of the United States* (1977), p. 550.

[67] United States v. Socony-Vacuum Oil Co., 310 U.S. 150 (1940). For evidence of the difficulty of proving the existence of agreements among sellers who are nevertheless acting in unison, see Theatre Enterprises, Inc. v. Paramount Film Distibuting Co., 346 U.S. 537 (1954), and see generally Donald Arthur Washburn, "Price Leadership," *Virginia Law Rev.* 64 (1978), 691.

[68] See, for example, Areeda, *Antitrust Analysis,* pp. 307–18 (cement and portions of steel-fabrication industries); and Washburn, "Price Leader-

retailers' markup pricing institution can and presumably ordinarily does operate without agreement that, so far as I can ascertain, the federal antitrust prosecutors have never brought prosecutions against their members.

A glance back at the earlier pages in this chapter will show that there is one kind of industry in which a private pricing institution probably cannot exist—at least the sellers would have great difficulty in creating or maintaining a pricing institution without government help. This is an industry in which there are a very large number of sellers, no seller has a significant share of the market, and the products are identical or nearly so. The third characteristic ensures that price competition would not be precluded by the conditions described in Chapter 2. If the products are identical or nearly so, buyers *could* make meaningful price comparisons in order to determine which were the best to buy. The very large number of sellers would make it unlikely that a substantially unanimous agreement on prices would ever be reached by the public price announcement process, and it would guarantee that the process would at least take a very long time. These two characteristics would also greatly increase the chances that some sellers would "cheat" on the price pattern by engaging in price competition, so that even if a price pattern were established, it would not be likely to last. Price competition sufficient to prevent inflation could therefore presumably be engendered in an industry that had identical or substantially identical products, by breaking up its existing firms into a very large number of smaller units—say, until the total number was fifty or sixty firms of about equal size. This could be achieved under the existing antitrust laws if the Supreme Court were willing to interpret them broadly enough, and of course it could be achieved by government civil actions brought under new legislation.

ship," pp. 701–76. After a large number of real estate brokers in Rutland, Vermont, had been convicted in a *criminal* prosecution of conspiring to raise commissions from 6 percent to 7 percent, commissions nevertheless generally remained at 7 percent thereafter (interview with Mr. Jay Ashman, March 7, 1979).

But if industries of this nature (the steel industry, for example) were broken up into fifty or sixty units, efficiencies of scale would be lost. And once the pricing institutions were eliminated, the vigorous price competition that ensued would presumably have all the bad consequences described earlier, including the bankruptcies of the weaker firms. Thus, the industries would have to be continually refragmented in order to prevent the numbers of firms from decreasing to the point at which pricing institutions were again feasible. In any event, the Supreme Court has given no indication that it is prepared to give the antitrust laws such a broad interpretation, and Congress has not made the slightest move toward enacting any such new legislation. And it is *only* in industries whose products are nearly identical that fragmenting the firms into smaller units would achieve even these mixed and temporary results. In all other industries, the conditions described in Chapter 2 would ensure that pricing institutions could survive anyway, or, in many cases, would prevent effective price competition even in the absence of pricing institutions. The only way in which it would appear to be possible to eliminate pricing institutions without fragmenting industries with substantially identical products, or to eliminate them at all in other industries, would be to forbid sellers to publicize price information; but this would be neither politically possible nor economically desirable. It would contravene the guarantee of freedom of speech, and it would eliminate *all* price competition. Price competition cannot occur unless buyers know sellers' prices.

It might be hoped that business buyers, because they have generally greater economic power and greater access to relevant information than do consumers, could be counted on to destroy or at least control the actions of the pricing institutions that sold to them. One might think that the large automobile companies would be willing and able to destroy the pricing institution for the steel industry, for example, or at least use their considerable economic powers to keep steel prices down. John Kenneth Galbraith made essentially this suggestion some years ago with respect to labor unions. He hoped that they would prove to be a "countervailing power" to keep industrial profits and prices down.[69] The hope proved of no avail, for several reasons. Business buyers, if they have individual monopoly power or are members of pricing institutions of their own, generally find it easier to raise their own prices than to push or keep down the prices they pay. Raising one's own prices is almost always easier, for all the reasons set forth in Chapters 1 and 2. It is especially easy when one's own prices are on goods being sold to consumers, whereas the prices that one might try to force down are the prices of another powerful monopolist or pricing-institution member.

Moreover, business buyers normally do not care to reduce the general prices of the goods they buy. Rather, they want discounts—prices that are lower by some set amount than the prices their competitors are paying for the same or similar goods. A discount gives a buyer either extra profits or a competitive edge in the markets in which he sells. Lower prices that everyone pays, on the other hand, normally make no difference at all, since all buyers then have to pass the savings on in the form of lower prices on their goods to about the same extent.[70] Business buyers are also inclined to like pricing institutions among those from whom they buy because wide price fluctuations would interefere with business planning.[71] The desire for discounts and the dislike of price fluctuations are frequently combined to produce the "fixed" or "traditional" discount—a discount that, once negotiated, becomes a part of the price pattern and so only rarely needs to be renegotiated. Where wide price fluctuations are unavoidable, as they sometimes are with commodities or when free-floating foreign-currency exchange rates are involved, businesses often resort to "futures options" or other institutional devices to

[69] John Kenneth Galbraith, "Countervailing Power," *Amer. Econ. Rev.* 44 (1954), p. 1.

[70] Interviews.

[71] Areeda, *Antitrust Analysis,* pp. 293–301; John Kenneth Galbraith, *The New Industrial State* (New York: Houghton-Mifflin, 1971), pp. 194–95.

protect themselves from planning disruptions.[72] Finally, businesses are unlikely ever to be a major force for destroying or taming pricing institutions in other businesses because businessmen do not generally believe in "cut-throat" or "ruinous" competition for themselves.[73] Their sense of fairness would inhibit, at least, their attempts to enforce it on others.

History demonstrates beyond any possibility of a doubt that people do not like price competition. Labor, farmers, and the providers of transportation services each waged long and often bitter political battles to obtain government protection from price competition.[74] It was not so difficult for the members of other economic sectors, because the nature of their industries permitted them to establish pricing institutions without government assistance. Today, with or without government assistance, virtually everyone enjoys the protections of a pricing institution for the prices that constitute his principal source of profits or income. This is generally the case even when it would superficially appear otherwise. Stock brokers, for example, who deal in the buying and selling of stocks in nearly perfectly competitive markets, nevertheless earn their own profits from commissions that are substantially the same whether stock prices are high or low or rising or falling. Most of the outspoken proponents of price competition seem to be executives of big businesses or university professors. It is extremely unlikely that any of the former, and virtually impossible that any of the latter, has actually had to experience price competition for his own profits or income.

[72] Jonathan R. Laing, "New Game in Town? Commodity Markets May Soon be Trading in Options on Futures," *Wall Street Journal,* May 13, 1976, p. 1; Samuelson, *Economics,* 9th ed., pp. 194–95.

[73] See, for example, Chamberlain, *The Firm,* pp. 193–95, 203–94, 360–65.

[74] Moore, *Freight Transportation Regulation,* pp. 3–6 (surface transportation); Rees, *Economics of Trade Unions,* pp. 3–21 (labor); Arthur Meier Schlesinger, Jr., *The Coming of the New Deal* (New York: Houghton-Mifflin, 1958), pp. 64–67; Arthur Meier Schlesinger, Jr., *The New Deal in Action, 1933-39* (New York: Macmillan, 1940), pp. 54–56 (farmers). See also, Barbara Bry, "Less State Regulation? Businesses Just Won't Allow It," *Los Angeles Times,* June 10, 1979, pt. 6, pp. 1, 10.

All economic competition sets people against one another. Seller is set against buyer. One seller is set against other sellers of similar products. Cooperation is viewed suspiciously and frequently prohibited by law even if it is motivated by generosity or altruism. One result is that people in market societies like ours are characteristically insecure, anxious, and tense and are rarely capable of establishing deep or long-lasting personal relationships.[75] Some observers have used the word "atomistic" to describe the kind of person who is characteristic of a market society—which, significantly, is the same word formerly used by economists to describe a nearly "perfect" state of economic competition.[76] Although all competition tends to alienate, price competition does so especially strongly because its effects are in general more drastic.

The alienating or atomizing effects of competition are particularly harmful in the way they affect relationships among persons in the same industries or occupations, which would otherwise be especially friendly and cooperative. Members of the same profession, for example, traditionally prefer each other's company to that of outsiders, cooperate with one another to further professional goals, and contribute money and effort to educate and introduce younger people to the profession. My experience is that businessmen act in a similar fashion, except that they must do so in a less organized manner because they lack a common educational background, a formal association, or a formal set of goals held in common. Farmers have a tradition of solidarity. Solidarity is the essence of the tradition of the labor movement.

The vast majority of Americans who work outside the home

[75] Hannah Arendt, *The Origins of Totalitarianism* (New York: Harvest/HBJ Book, 1973), pp. 123–57, 314–16, 334–35, 382–84, 430–32; Joyce Carol Oates, "A Taut Novel of Disorder," *New York Times Book Review,* April 3, 1977, pp. 3, 34–35; Paul Jonas, "Home Thoughts from Abroad," *Harpers* 254 (April 1977), 20–21; John Leonard, "Falling off the Train," *New York Times Book Review,* April 3, 1977, p. 3, 31; Robert Nisbet, "Public Unions and the Decline of Public Trust," in A. Lawrence Chickering, ed., *Public Employee Unions* (San Francisco: Institute for Contemporary Studies, 1976), pp. 13–33.

[76] Samuelson, *Economics,* 9th ed., p. 482.

are employees. Probably the most accurate measure of how people in our country really feel about economic competition is therefore the amount and character of competition that is commonly found in the employment relationship. Much white-collar and most blue-collar employment in the United States has come to be structured so as to eliminate *all* competition among employees. This has usually been accomplished at the employees' insistence, often through labor unions, over the opposition of the employers. Where significant competition among employees remains, it is generally not price competition. An individual's salary is ordinarily considered a confidential matter between him and his employer, not to be disclosed to other employees, and especially not to other employees who would be considered to be in competition with him. Some highly prestigious employers, the Harvard Law School and the Princeton Institute of Advanced Study among them, make it a point to pay their professional employees entirely without regard to merit; pay rates are set simply by reference to seniority, or they are kept uniform for everybody. Throughout American industry, senior employees are generally paid more merely for being senior, although age is a neutral factor at best in determining an employee's value to his employer: when older people are unfortunate enough to have to compete for a job, they usually lose, and it is notoriously difficult for a person past fifty to get a new job even if he has an exemplary work record. Price competition is so foreign to our ideas of employment that it is difficult to conceive of how it would work in many cases. Would a teacher have to offer a lesson plan and lecture notes at a price to each potential student? Would anyone who liked be free to gather around a businessman's desk to take notes on his dictation, later to offer a letter to him at a price lower than all the others? Labor was once really bought and sold like a commodity. Those who were laborers then regarded the experience with horror.[77]

[77] Orville Schell, *In the People's Republic* (New York: Vintage Books, 1978), pp. 99–101.

Conclusion

Pricing institutions are ubiquitous, generally powerful, unavoidable, and on the whole desirable, although they surely constitute the principal source of indeterminate inflation. Like other socioeconomic institutions, however, their characteristics are amenable to change, and their behavior is capable of being restrained and channeled. The measures that will be proposed in Part III for controlling inflation are designed not to eliminate pricing institutions but to control them. For the control of inflation, it turns out, pricing institutions provide an enormous political and administrative advantage. Indeed, the problem of indeterminate inflation would be insoluble without them. They are the lesser political and administrative entities through which the policy decisions of the federal government can be effected. Without them, the federal government would have no choice but to decide directly the appropriateness of every price, and in an economy as large and complex as ours the central direction of all pricing would be a political and administrative nightmare.

CHAPTER 4

Sellers' Uncertainties

Contemporary competition also fails to hold prices down because sellers are uncertain what prices they *should* charge. As was explained in Chapter 1, prices are only one of the means by which sellers pursue their goals of profits, sales, market shares, prestige, economic power, or whatever else they may be seeking. A seller will therefore be uncertain about what prices he should charge to the extent that he is uncertain about the goals he is pursuing or about how he ought to pursue them. The uncertainty permits inflation by constituting another kind of "gap" within which sellers are free to raise prices. Market forces can determine prices only to the extent that sellers are capable of predicting the effects that their prices will have on profits, sales, and so on, that the markets are supposed to determine for them. So to the extent that sellers are uncertain, markets cannot determine their prices. The uncertainty also aggravates inflation, because sellers are inclined to resolve their uncertainties in favor of higher prices—especially during times of inflation. It is generally easier to lower a price that turns out to have been too high than it is to raise one that turns out to have been too low. A too-high price can be lowered and the lowering advertised as a "sale," for example. During times of inflation a too-high price may not even need to be lowered. The seller can keep it where it is and let the inflation gradually make it right for him.

I will estimate the size of the gap caused by uncertainty by estimating the extent of the inaccuracies in the so-called profit-maximization principle. This is the assumption that sellers always make the most profits they can.[1] It is almost

[1] See John Kenneth Galbraith, *The New Industrial State* (New York: Houghton-Mifflin Co., 1971), pp. 112–14 (description of the extent to which economists currently endorse the profit-maximization principle,

invariably applied in traditional economic analysis, where it is usually coupled with two other assumptions, or "principles"—that sellers act rationally, and that they possess all the information they need.[2] Frequently, no differentiation is made among the three assumptions: the profit-maximization principle is deemed to include the other two as well; it is not very useful to assume that sellers seek to maximize their profits if it is not also assumed that they know how.[3] I shall in general follow this same practice.

If the profit-maximization principle were a correct description of sellers' pricing behavior, there would be no gap caused by uncertainties about what goal or goals are being pursued. The principle establishes just the one goal: maximization of profits. With the help of the rationality and full-information assumptions, it also eliminates any uncertainties about how the goal of maximum profits should be pursued. A seller supposedly wants to achieve only one thing by his prices, and he supposedly knows precisely what prices will achieve this goal

---

with citations). See also Graham Keith Shaw, *An Introduction to the Theory of Macro-Economic Policy,* 2d. ed. (New York: Barnes and Noble, 1973), pp. 39–42; and Joan Robinson, *Economic Philosophy* (Garden City: Doubleday, 1962), p. 21. Even Galbraith felt constrained to accept it in his younger days; see Henry W. Briefs, *Pricing Power and "Administrative" Inflation* (Washington, D.C.: American Enterprise Institute for Public Policy Research, 1962), pp. 37–38, on Galbraith's attempts to fit the steel industry's 1950s price increases into the principle as delayed realization of "unliquidated short-run monopoly gains." According to the contemporary economist George Stigler, "profit is the strongest, the most universal, and the most persistent of the forces governing entrepreneurial behavior. This is a judgment based upon wide observation of entrepreneurs under innumerable sets of conditions." "The Theory of Price," in Robert Lekachman, ed., *The Varieties of Economics,* rev. ed. (Mountain View, Ca: World Pub. Co., 1962), p. 169. The principle goes back as far as Adam Smith. See Adam Smith, *The Wealth of Nations,* ed. Andrew Skinner (Harmondsworth: Penguin Books, 1974), pp. 118–19.

[2] For example, Phillip Areeda, *Antitrust Analysis,* 2d. ed. (Boston: Little, Brown, 1974), p. 7 at n. 17 (rationality), pp. 6–7 (full information).

[3] For example, Paul A. Samuelson, *Economics,* 9th ed. (New York: McGraw-Hill, 1973), pp. 488–89, uses the profit-maximization principle without mentioning either the rationality or full-information assumptions, although the conclusion drawn from use of the principle would not be warranted if both assumptions were not being made.

in every instance. This obviously does not coincide with the facts, and an uncertainty gap exists. The analysis of the size of this gap will be taken in two steps. The first will be to ascertain what the profit-maximization principle would require of sellers if it were to be a correct description of their pricing behavior. The second will be to ascertain how far short of this theoretical ideal an economy like ours falls.

The Requirements of the Profit-Maximization Principle

Although it is phrased as though it were an empirical observation, the profit-maximization principle serves an essential theoretical function. It enables economists to think logically about laws and theories of economic behavior that possess a deterministic form—the same form, that is, as the laws and theories of physics, astronomy, chemistry, and the other natural sciences.[4] The principle performs this function by eliminating all economically significant differences in motivation among persons. All kinds of persons—corporations, labor unions, partnerships, individuals, or whatever—supposedly seek only one thing, profits; and none of them, supposedly, is ever satisfied with the profits obtained. They always want more, no matter how profitable or wealthy they already are. Thus there are also no economically significant differences in motivation between profitable and unprofitable businesses or between wealthy and impoverished persons. Eliminating such differences enables the economist to think about economic behavior as if it were determined by the objective conditions under which it occurs. If he were to allow himself to acknowledge that people have different motiva-

[4] Robert Lekachman, in the same passage from which the Stigler quote is taken, comments, "There is no question that the precision of economic analysis, often envied by other social scientists, is the result in part of the maximizing assumptions which are here defended. Should they be destroyed, economics would require substantial revision." Lekachman, *The Varieties of Economics,* p. 170. See also Paul A. Samuelson, *Foundations of Economic Analysis* (New York: Atheneum, 1947), pp. 21–29.

tions, he would have to admit that they could behave in different ways even under identical objective conditions, since they might want different things. A physicist would be equally helpless to construct laws or theories of physics in deterministic form if he allowed himself to believe that electrons, say, were free to decide sometimes to pursue positive electric charges, sometimes to pursue negative electric charges, and sometimes just to stay where they were—in other words, if electrons had free will. The profit-maximization principle is a means of denying free will for economic behavior. It is for this reason, presumably, rather than for its dubious empirical values, that the principle has been embraced so universally and continuously by economists since Adam Smith.

How much leeway the principle leaves for free will depends upon the way that the individual uses it, but in the minds of a rigorous theoretical economist it leaves no room at all. Some thinkers, on the other hand, affirm the principle's general accuracy, but regard persons as still free to choose what kind of profits they will maximize. Conceived in this way, the principle leaves a person free to pursue power or prestige rather than monetary profits, for example, or even to pursue goals so far removed from maximum monetary profits as a quiet life, the admiration of one's customers, or the furtherance of the causes of one's nation or church.[5] Profit maximization in this sense means simply doing what you want to do, which of course leaves the profit-maximization principle with no meaning whatever.

Another common way of thinking of profit maximization is to limit the idea of profits to monetary profits but to allow the person seeking them to be completely free to consider when the profits should be aimed for, what factors might affect them, and what discounts for risk, delays, and other uncertainties should be employed. In this view, for example, a corporation is maximizing profits even when it voluntarily ac-

[5] For example, Amartya Sen, "Rational Fools: A Critique of the Behavioral Foundation of Economic Theory," *Philosophy and Public Affairs* 6 (1977), 317, seems to conceive of the profit-maximization principle as including any motive that is selfish.

cepts lower profits because it calculates that higher profits would present an unacceptable risk of triggering government action that would be costly to it in the future. Or a corporation is maximizing profits if it reduces its profits by large contributions to public causes, out of a similar calculation of long-range political benefits. The implications of this view are just as meaningless as those of the first. It logically regards even a regulated public utility as setting its prices at profit-maximizing levels, for example. Since any higher prices would violate the law and therefore presumably result in the assessment of fines and lower prices in the future, even regulated prices must be considered profit-maximizing. Indeed, *any* prices and *any* profits can be rationalized to be profit-maximizing in this view, just as in the first view described.

But when the principle is put to the theoretical uses for which it was designed, the results are different. To illustrate, I will use the basic theory that a profit-maximizing seller sets his prices so that his marginal revenues equal his marginal costs.[6] Marginal revenues are the extra revenues obtained by selling one more item. Marginal costs are the extra costs incurred from producing or otherwise obtaining one more item. Since profits are revenues less costs, marginal profits are marginal revenues less marginal costs, and marginal profits are the profits obtained from producing or otherwise obtaining and selling one more item. The theory, therefore, can also be phrased as that a profit-maximizing seller sets his prices so as to make his marginal profits nil. He does this because this yields him, by definition, the largest total profits, which he wants by virtue of being a profit-maximizer. Zero marginal profits mean maximum total profits because selling any fewer items would still leave some more marginal profits to be made, and selling any more items would make marginal profits negative and thus bring total profits down. The theory is commonly phrased in terms of prices, although its explanation requires reference to numbers of items sold, on the assumption

[6] Samuelson, *Economics,* pp. 492–95.

that the price a seller sets determines the number of items he will sell.

In order for the theory to make sense, prices, marginal profits, marginal revenues, and marginal costs must all be measurable in the same terms. If they are not, they cannot be equated in the ways the theory requires. For example, to conceive of profits as including the prestige or satisfaction obtained from selling high-quality products, as some economic thinkers do, requires that the theory be phrased as a seller setting his prices (a dollar measure) so that his marginal profits (a prestige measure) are zero, and it requires that marginal profits (a prestige measure) equal marginal revenues less marginal costs (both dollar measures). But how can a unit of prestige equal the difference between two dollar measures? It logically cannot, any more than a number of apples can equal the difference between two numbers of oranges. Moreover, it is also quite artificial to postulate that people in real life think of such highly subjective and difficult-to-measure things as prestige in marginal terms—so much more or less per extra item sold. Thus, the theory practically compels the theorist who uses it to conceive of profits in strictly monetary terms, and it compels him to think of profits only in precisely measurable, marginal terms. The future profits to be gained or losses to be avoided by making contributions to public causes or by keeping current profits low, although they are indeed conceivable in monetary terms, can hardly be reduced to marginal units of so many more or less per extra item sold. These difficulties hold for virtually all the theories or laws of economics in which the profit-maximization principle is employed.

Economic thinkers who prefer to think of the profit-maximization principle in vague, broadly inclusive terms, but at the same time purport to rely on the laws and theories of economics that require that the principle be conceived in measurable, monetary terms are thinking inconsistently. They cannot have it both ways. More important for our purposes, prices are in fact economically determined only to the extent that they are the results of economic behavior that follows the dictates of profit maximization as that principle is strictly conceived. Prices are *not,* in fact, economically determined to the extent that they do not result in the maximization of the sellers' *current* profits, measured in *monetary* terms.

The Extent to Which a Real Economy Deviates from the Profit-Maximization Ideal

The Common Necessity of Having to Choose Whose Profits to Pursue

The profit-maximization principle does not apply when one or more people make decisions that affect the profits of more than one person if the profits thus affected in any way conflict, because the principle cannot possibly apply in such a situation. If a decision has to be made as to whose profits will be increased at whose expense, it is impossible to maximize the profits of all of them—impossible even to maximize the profits of more than one of them. Such situations of conflict are unavoidable when the individuals who make the decisions for a profit-making organization are not the owners of the organization and therefore not entitled to all of its profits. They are unavoidable even when those individuals do own the organization and so are entitled to all of its profits if their decisions influence the shares of the profits each will receive. A moment's reflection should be enough to convince oneself that the organizational situations just described are typical of corporations, partnerships, and every other form of business organization in the United States. John Kenneth Galbraith is the first, to my knowledge, to have pointed this out, although he did so only for "public issue corporations,"[7] the stock of which is so widely dispersed among holders of small amounts that it is effectively controlled by its management.[8] If the profit-maximization principle is inapplicable to the decisions

[7] Galbraith, *New Industrial State,* pp. 115–27.

[8] Adolph A. Berle and Gardiner C. Means, *The Modern Corporation and Private Property* (New York: Macmillan, 1940).

by which business organizations are controlled, it hardly applies to the American economy at all, since the American economy consists overwhelmingly of business organizations.[9]

When the decision as to whose profits will be favored is made by a person whose own profits are included, there is a conflict of interest in the ethical and legal sense.[10] One obvious conflict of interest in a business organization arises when high-level executives set their own rates of pay. The higher they set the rates, the higher their own profits but the lower the profits of the organization that they control. The corporation laws of most states place obstacles in the way of corporate executives setting their own rates of pay, but the obstacles are easily surmounted. The easiest and probably most commonly used device is to permit the executives to vote on the boards or committees that set the rates of pay for everyone except themselves.[11] In the resulting community of interest, experience proves that most do very well.[12] Another conflict of interest arises when an executive must choose whether his corporation should expand its sales at the expense of its profits or its profits at the expense of its sales. The executive's own profits are maximized, generally, if he chooses to maximize the corporation's sales, which is to say, if he chooses not to maximize the corporation's profits. Executives are almost always paid more for managing a larger corporation than they are for managing a smaller corporation that is more profitable.[13] Indeed, very

[9] *Statistical Abstract of the United States* (1977), p. 550.

[10] For example, William L. Cary, *Cases and Materials on Corporations* (St. Paul, Minn.: Foundation Press, 1969), p. 552.

[11] See ibid., pp. 565–66.

[12] Graef S. Crystal, "Pay Watchers Beware," *Wall Street Journal,* January 22, 1979, p. 20; Charles G. Burck, "A Group Profile of the Fortune 500 Chief Executive," *Fortune* 93 (May 1976), 172, 176–77; Peter F. Drucker, "Is Executive Pay Excessive?" *Wall Street Journal,* May 23, 1977, p. 18: Isadore Barmash, "More Pay at the Top of the Ladder," *New York Times,* January 16, 1977, sec. 3, p. 1.

[13] The truth of the statement in the text is implicit in all the articles cited in the previous note, since size rather than profitability was the basis of selection of the business enterprises. See especially Barmash, "More Pay," who notes that the compensation of top executives kept rising right through the recession of the early seventies, when business profits fell substantially.

large corporations have been known to run in the red for years and still continue to pay their top executives very handsome salaries. The Penn Central Railroad paid its top executives higher and higher compensations right into bankruptcy.[14]

Still another conflict occurs when high-level executives choose how much of their corporation's profits to distribute to shareholders as dividends and how much to retain in the corporation for reinvestment. Money retained for reinvestment expands the corporation's assets and sales and so profits the executives. Whether it also profits the shareholders depends upon whether it would be more profitable for the shareholders to have the value of their stock increased than to have the money as dividends to spend or invest for themselves. *Fortune* magazine recently demonstrated that the shareholders of steel manufacturing corporations are almost certainly earning less on the profits retained and reinvested in their corporations than they could have made by reinvesting the money themselves, even after allowing for the taxes they would have to pay upon receiving the dividends.[15] When executives must choose whether to expand their corporations and their corporations' sales, they also confront a conflict between the corporation's profits and their own business goals in a broader sense. If we count the power, prestige, and plain fun that many executives enjoy from their positions, then the maximization of these, by enlarging the corporation or its sales, also frequently conflicts with the goal of maximizing the profits of the corporation.

There are also conflicts among the profits or other goals of the different executives within the same corporation, between the lower-level employees of the corporation and the corporation's shareholders, and so on. Other kinds of artificial eco-

[14] *The Penn Central Failure and the Role of the Financial Institutions: Staff Report of the Committee on Banking and Currency,* House of Representatives, 92d Congress, First Session, January 3, 1972 (Washington, D.C.: U.S. Govt. Printing Office, 1972), pp. 272–85.

[15] Carol J. Loomis, "Steel's Not-So-Solid Expansion Plans," *Fortune* 93 (January 1976), 196–97.

nomic entities are rife with similar conflicts.[16] A labor leader must continually choose between furthering his own profits and furthering the profits of his union's members, for example.[17]

Those who make the decisions for economic organizations also commonly face conflicts of interest even when their own profits are not at stake. This kind of conflict is confronted when a decision is made whether to curtail production and lay off workers, for example, or whether to continue to employ an old, loyal employee after his efficiency has declined. A labor leader confronts so many choices of this kind that it is hopeless to try to fit a labor union's actions into the mold of profit maximization.[18] A labor union typically includes members in many different kinds of jobs, of widely varying ages (and hence different interests in wages versus pensions, for example), of varying seniority on the job, with all sorts of different attitudes toward their work, with various ambitions or expectations of career advancement, and so on. Yet, somehow, the leader has to put all these together into a single set of demands on the employer when it comes time to renegotiate the contract. Which members' profits is he then supposed to maximize? And what particular interests of the members are to be regarded as their profits, to be maximized at the expense of other interests?

[16] See, for example, Nicholas Wolfson, *Conflict of Interest: Investment Banking,* Report to the Twentieth Century Fund Steering Committee on Conflict of Interests in the Securities Market (New York: Twentieth Century Fund, 1976).

[17] Derek C. Bok and John T. Dunlop, *Labor and the American Community* (New York: Simon and Schuster, 1970), p. 925.

[18] For a list and description of failed attempts to fit labor unions into the profit-maximization or some other maximization mold, see Wallace N. Atherton, *Theory of Union Bargaining Goals* (Princeton: Princeton University Press, 1973), pp. 3–30. One of the attempts cited is a book by John T. Dunlop, *Wage and Determination under Trade Unions* (New York: A. M. Kelley Pubs., 1944). Mr. Dunlop was deeply involved in labor matters in the Nixon and Ford administrations, eventually becoming secretary of labor. He is co-author with Derek C. Bok of *Labor and the American Community,* in which his earlier book is apparently not even mentioned, although this later book does treat union bargaining goals. Mr. Dunlop has apparently himself concluded that his earlier endeavor was a failure.

For corporations and other business organizations, the existence of pricing institutions adds another layer of conflicting choices among profits. Once the institution's price pattern has been established, each corporation must choose between maximizing its own profits by, possibly, "cheating" on the price pattern whenever it can or maximizing the long-run profits of the industry as a whole and presumably its own, too, by complying with the price pattern and helping to enforce it against other "cheaters." A similar set of choices must be made when a corporation participates in the round of public price announcements that precede a change in the price pattern. An executive's own profits are also involved here. If he puts the weight of his corporation on the side of a high price pattern, for example, he will be discouraging his industry's overall rate of expansion, which works against his own profits; but it presumably works in favor of his corporation's profits, as well as the profits of the other members of the pricing institution.

It is amazing that traditional economics has persisted as long as it has in assuming the general correctness of the profit-maximization principle without realizing the impossiblity of applying the principle to corporations and to people at the same time. The reason, if not the justification, is presumably that Adam Smith badly miscalculated the importance of corporations. They had already made their appearance when he wrote *The Wealth of Nations,* but he concluded that they were only of passing importance and proceeded to work out his economic principles deliberately ignoring them.[19] Smith also failed to take into account labor unions, with perhaps more justification: they did not become an important economic factor until considerably later than corporations. Traditional economics became aware of the impossibility of applying the profit-maximization principle to labor unions sometime in the 1940s or 1950s,[20] but it never seemed to apply

[19] Skinner, *Adam Smith,* pp. 164, 222–32, 240.

[20] Bok and Dunlop, *Labor and the American Community,* p. 925; Atherton, *Theory of Union Bargaining Goals,* pp. 3–30; Dunlop, *Wage Determination.*

this awareness to macroeconomics in general or to theories of inflation in particular.

The Difficulties Encountered in Deciding What Actions Will Maximize Profits

Even if we ignore the impossibility for a price setter simultaneously to maximize the profits of all the individuals or organizations he might have to consider, we are still left with the practical difficulties of his knowing what he ought to do in order to maximize them. These difficulties undermine the applicability of the principle by rendering it meaningless. To the extent that a price setter does not know what to do to maximize profits, we gain no insight into what his prices will be by asserting that he does. We might as well assert that he prices so as to maximize weekends.

One practical difficulty, for example, is whether to decide to go for immediate profits at the expense of higher profits later, or vice versa. Corporation executives seeking to maximize their corporations' profits confront this difficulty all the time. Offering a lower price to a particular buyer in order to take business away from a competitor will gain higher immediate profits, for example, but will it eliminate higher profits in the future by causing the same competitor to offer even lower prices to get the same buyer back, or by breaking the industry's pricing pattern? Every time an executive has to decide whether to try to sell in a new geographical area or whether to sell a new kind of product, he has to decide whether the losses his corporation is almost sure to suffer in the short term will be more than balanced by the profits he can hope it will make over the long term. Accounting theory dictates that expected future profits be "discounted" both by an interest factor and a risk factor to ascertain their present value. The risk factor is obviously subjective. The interest factor is too, although not so obviously. There are market interest rates of various kinds in effect at all times, but these do not reflect the rates at which any particular business can borrow, and they are likely to change many times between the present and the times when the future profits are expected to occur.

If, as is typically the case today, the price setter is deciding on price and nonprice forms of competition at the same time, the profit-maximization principle will be rendered meaningless, at least as a guide to the prices he will set, simply because there will be so many factors to take into account. Added to the difficulties of estimating what prices will prove to yield the highest profits, for what lengths of time, and so on, will be the many more and generally even more complex questions of what nonprice forms of competition—what kinds of advertising, in what amounts, in what kinds of media, for how long, for example—in combination with which particular prices or price changes will yield the most profits. One can gain an idea of the slight help the profit-maximization principle is likely to be in predicting or determining what prices will be by imagining the reaction of a corporation sales executive to a suggestion that he set prices so as to maximize profits. Would he consider the suggestion valuable, or would he regard it as meaningless? Another whole set of complications arises if the price setter also takes into account the justifications for price increases that typically influence and accompany increases in the price patterns of pricing institutions. Although justifications are not typically considered when prices are not part of, and will not substantially influence, a price pattern, the prices set by very large business enterprises constitute an exception. The impact of these prices may be sufficient to require justifications even if no other enterprises' prices are influenced by them. And of course justifications are pertinent to most pricing decisions that are widespread enough to contribute significantly to inflation, because most such price increases are parts of increases in price patterns.

Pricing Institutions

To the extent that prices are parts of or otherwise influenced by price patterns, price changes are almost entirely unrelated to the profit-maximization principle. Pricing institutions are not intended to maximize any particular seller's profits or profits in general. The government commissions that regulate utilities' prices are supposed to *limit* utilities' profits. The Department of Agriculture is supposed to provide farmers with "reasonable," "fair," or "parity," not maximal profits. When retail prices are raised by a percentage equal to the percentage increase in wholesale prices, as they generally are by a retailers' markup pricing institution, there is no possible way of ascertaining whether this is profit-maximizing either for the retailers as a whole or for any retailer in particular. The same kinds of difficulties are encountered in understanding the setting or changing of a price pattern by an industrial pricing institution. The prices of medical services are set by the interactions of a wide variety of mixed public and private pricing institutions, the effects of which are difficult either to unravel or to predict, but it is certain that they cannot simply be characterized as profit-maximizing. It is also certain that it would be impossible to say whose profits—the physicians', the insurance companies', some physicians' but not others', and so on—were being maximized, if any were. Private pricing institutions are by their nature difficult to fit into the profit-maximizing mold because they work largely by custom or practice, whereas the profit-maximization principle implicitly assumes a rationally calculated decision for each price.

Prices that are set by pricing institutions also fail to fit the profit-maximization principle because the profits that would be obtainable by that principle are generally so high that the actual prices rarely come even near maximizing them. The American steel industry has shown that it can raise its members' prices by more than 50 percent in less than two years, for example.[21] It could more than *quadruple* its members' profits if it were to raise its members' prices only 20 percent more, which its history demonstrates it clearly has the power to do. (Its profits vary between 3 and 5 percent of its sales.)[22] Presumably, if the Japanese and European steel producers would

[21] Edmund Faltermayer, "The Hyperinflation in Plant Construction" *Fortune* 92 (November 1975), 107.

[22] *Statistical Abstract of the United States* (1976), p. 786, table 1337.

go along, profits could be increased eightfold with another 20 percent price increase, and so on. Eventually, of course, steel substitutes would begin to cut seriously into sales, but the profit opportunities before this would happen are enormous. The proviso that the Japanese and European producers go along is not unrealistic. Experience shows that they usually do, and that when they do not, they soon receive a stern warning from no less than the President of the United States.[23] The profits that powerful labor unions could obtain for their members if they really went all out are frequently even more fantastic. If the Teamsters Union were willing to shut down virtually the whole transportation system of the nation, which it has within its power to do, would there be any limitation on what employers and the public would pay to start things moving again? But obviously, pricing institutions rarely choose to exert their full powers. They voluntarily restrain themselves for one or more of the reasons described in Chapter 3.

The Special Difficulties Encountered in Applying the Principle to Pay Rates

As we will see presently, pay increases cause indeterminate inflation more than do price increases of other kinds. Yet neither the employer nor the employee typically approaches a pay rate decision with profit-maximizing in mind, whether or not the decision also involves a labor union as a participant. The basic reason is that jobs are too important. For the employer it is typically very important whom he can get and hold for the job—whether the employee is honest, industrious, intelligent, loyal, and so on. For the employee it is typically very important what the job is, whether it is likely to lead to better jobs with the same or other employers, whether he can expect to keep it for as long as he likes, and so on. The employer is therefore unlikely to think that keeping the pay rate as low as

[23] See opinion in Consumers Union of U.S., Inc. v. Rogers, 352 Fed. Supp. 319 (1973).

possible is the goal he ought to put before all else, and the employee is unlikely to think that raising the pay rate as high as possible is the goal he ought to put before all else. Neither studies of what employees want or value highly in their jobs, nor studies of what makes their work most satisfactory from the point of view of their employers generally conclude that pay is the most important factor.[24] Of course employees normally would be pleased to be making more, and of course they usually indicate their desire to make more if they have the opportunity, but the same could be said about better working conditions, more recognition or appreciation from their employers and fellow employees, job security, more interesting or otherwise satisfying work, and a host of other aspects of the employment situation. Profits in the economic sense are being pursued, but they are not being maximized.

If employees were really maximizing their profits, or any of these other job aspects, they would be continually shopping around for new job opportunities with other employers, and either continually changing jobs or using the opportunities they found as bargaining tools for obtaining more pay or other improvements from their present employers. Some of all this does go on, to be sure, but it includes only a small portion of all employees. Most people stay years with the same employer without looking elsewhere. Most people change jobs only when they move to another part of the country, when they change careers, or when they have no choice because their employer has discharged them.

People whose positions enable them to set their own rates of pay over a wide range also usually appear, at least, not to be maximizing profits. Physicians, for example, although they typically have very high incomes, could have higher incomes still if they would charge higher fees than they are currently charging. A physician with a specialty and an established reputation is almost sure to have a long waiting list of people who want his services. If he has a waiting list with his present fees,

[24] Albert Rees, *The Economics of Trade Unions* (Chicago: University of Chicago Press, 1962), pp. 27–28, 34–37; Peter F. Drucker, *The New Society* (New York: Harper and Row, 1950), pp. 47–48.

he surely could increase his fees and still have as many patients as he could handle. High-level executives in public-issue corporations also essentially set their own pay rates. Although they, too, are generally receiving high rates of pay, they could surely be receiving still higher rates if they chose. Every study of top-level executives of which I am aware has concluded that profit is not their primary motivation, still less their sole motivation, as the profit-maximization principle would require.[25]

If people's economic motivations could be summed up in a few words, it could be said that people make as much money as they can and feel is justified. A widespread and influential factor in the wage demands of organized labor, for example, is what on the Pay Board and Price Commission we came to know as "tandem relationships." Two unions representing workers in different industries each base their wage demands upon those of the other. What one gets the other demands as of right—or, sometimes, plus or minus some traditional or customary differential. "Tandem" is actually an inadequate word, because most of these relationships involve more than just two unions.[26] There are hundreds of local branches of the electricians' union, each representing electricians in a particular area, for example, and each bargaining separately with the employers in its area. But what any one of them gets affects what all of them will demand later. The same "tandem" effects occur among the locals of other construction unions

[25] For example, David Finn, *The Corporate Oligarch: An Analysis of the Men Who Head America's Largest Business Enterprises* (New York: Simon and Schuster, 1970), pp. 140, 153–54, 286–87, 289–93, and passim; Charles Perrow, *Complex Organizations: A Critical Essay* (Glenview, Ill.: Scott, Foresman, 1972), pp. 194–97.

[26] Rees, *Economics of Trade Unions,* pp. 54–57: Bok and Dunlop, *Labor and the American Community,* pp. 290–91; John Sheahan, *The Wage-Price Guideposts* (Washington, D.C.: Brookings Institution, 1967), p. 27; Adrian W. Throop, "The Union Nonunion Wage Differential and Cost-Push Inflation," *Amer. Econ. Rev.* 58 (1968), 79–80; Thomas Gale Moore, "Incomes Policy, Its Rationale and Development," in Phillip Cagan, Marten Estey, William Fellner, Charles E. McLure, Jr., and Thomas Gale Moore, *Economic Policy and Inflation in the Sixties* (Washington, D.C.: American Enterprise Institute for Public Policy Research, 1972), pp. 217–19.

and—plus or minus the traditional or customary differentials—among the different construction unions. The same occurs in most cities between the police and the firemen, even if, as is the case in most cities, neither the police nor the firemen are organized into labor unions. A bargaining agent for the National Education Association told me that essentially the same is true for teachers in different school districts. The same is true for the white-collar employees in different companies in the same or similar industries. Executives told me that the single most important factor in their salary determinations for their white-collar employees was the salaries that similarly positioned employees were being paid elsewhere.

All the foregoing pay relationships exist because the pay comparisons they permit provide such convenient and persuasive justifications. Both the employees and the employers feel justified in their wages if these are in what they consider to be the "right" relationship with the wages of the groups with which they consider themselves "in tandem." If one were to maintain that all of the possibly hundreds of different groups of employees that are in tandem with one another were profit-maximizing, one would be driven to maintain that their wages were all the result of the supply and demand for their services rising and falling at about the same time by the same relative amounts. This would be an unlikely set of coincidences.

Justification is also important among professionals who sell their services directly to the public. When the editors of *Medical Economics* conclude that it is time for physicians to raise their fees again, for example, which they seem to conclude regularly once a year, they publish both fee data and data on costs and cost changes, so that the physician-reader will know what fee increases are justified and what are the justifications.[27] When my research assistants interviewed physicians about how they set their fees, the answers they reported were always in terms of what the physicians said justified them in setting particular fees or in making particular fee increases.

[27] See, for example, *Medical Economics* 51 (January 1974).

CHAPTER 5

Competitive Inflation

Competitive inflation begins when people start increasing prices because other prices are, or have been, increasing. It cannot occur unless people have the power to increase prices, but we have seen that any one of the four conditions dealt with in the preceding chapters can give people this power. People usually decide to increase the prices that affect their incomes or profits when other price increases have meant that their real incomes or profits go down or, at least, go down relative to the incomes or profits of other people, creating a disparity that is not "right." Since it is generally not feasible to increase one's real income or profits by bringing another person's down, the reaction is to increase one's own prices—wages, salaries, or prices of other kinds. Price increasing for this reason, once begun, tends to spread and to proceed at an increasingly rapid rate. People whose prices are not controlled by pricing institutions form such institutions if they can. Those whose prices are controlled by pricing institutions use the institutions to increase their prices at more rapid rates. Thus, there is a *competition* that consists of trying to increase one's own prices at a more rapid rate than others' prices are increasing, so that one's own income or profits will rise in real terms, or at least not fall. Once such a competition gets underway it becomes nearly impossible to tell who is behind and who is ahead. Almost everyone can point to a time in the past when his income or profits, in real terms, seem to have been better than they are, or at least better in relation to the real incomes or profits of someone else. Traditional hierarchies of income or wealth become confused or disappear, and the resulting sense of drift encourages people to raise prices still more. The sources of inflation dealt with in Chapters 1 through 4 all converge to produce the kind of inflation just described. This, essentially, *is* the inflation that the United States and the other countries with modern economies now have.

The analysis of competitive inflation that follows makes more frequent reference to pricing institutions than to any of the other sources of pricing discretion that I have dealt with, but it would be wrong to draw the conclusion that the others are not important, too. The fact is, we can differentiate the sources of pricing discretion for analytical purposes alone; in reality they interact and contribute to one another, and they are generally all present at the same time. I explained in Chapter 3 why pricing institutions in many industries, especially the consumer-products industries, are made possible and practically inevitable by the industry's use of the nonprice forms of competition treated in Chapter 1 and by the buyers' uncertainties treated in Chapter 2. I explained in Chapter 4 why the sellers' uncertainties were aggravated by the presence of pricing institutions, by the use of nonprice forms of competition, and by buyers' uncertainties. And I explained in Chapter 2 how buyers' uncertainties are aggravated by the use of nonprice forms of competition. Moreover, the sources of pricing discretion are not cumulative in any straightforward, additive way. I advisedly call them sources rather than causes. They do not cause inflation, or even cause sellers to have pricing discretion, in any scientific way. They are rather influences on perceptions and attitudes, which like any influences on people's behavior are quite impossible to quantify. But although the other sources of pricing discretion contribute importantly to competitive inflation by contributing to the existence and effectiveness of pricing institutions, these institutions are the key for making competitive inflation possible. It is the individual pricing institution that generally constitutes the competitive actor—the competitor—for competitive inflation, just as it generally is the individual business enterprise that constitutes the competitive actor, or competitor, for economic competition of the traditional kind.

The "All-Specialists Economy"

But why doesn't price competition prevent such an inflation from getting underway or, at least, place limits on how high prices can rise before falling sales persuade the sellers and their institutions to stop? I have answered this question to some extent already, but an economist, at least, if not a general reader, may still harbor some doubts. It might still seem to him that if the federal government were wise and courageous enough not to keep increasing overall demand—wise and courageous enough to balance its budget and halt the expansion of the money supply—the price-increasing melee would come to a halt. It should halt, it would seem, when sellers finally realized that there was not enough purchasing power around to buy all the things they were trying to sell at prices higher than at present, and that this amount of purchasing power (that is, the demand) was not going to go any higher. Sellers, in other words, would be put to the choice between continuing to increase their prices and selling less and less, thereby causing more and more unemployment of people and resources, on the one hand; and on the other of stopping their price increasing and permitting people and resources to continue to work. The sellers, if they persisted in increasing their prices, would of course have to accept the fact that they and their own resources might soon be among the unemployed. What I have just outlined is the demand-pull theory of inflation or, speaking more precisely, its so-called "validation" variation. It constitutes the firm belief of most of the economists in the United States.[1]

But it is wrong. At least it is wrong if it contemplates that the inflation would stop any time short of a disastrous depression, and not start up again as soon as the depression was alleviated the slightest bit. Curing inflation this way, if it would work at all, would have the same drawback as curing a disease by killing the patient. To show why this is so I will have brief resort to some drastic simplifications designed to

[1] See Chapter 6.

emphasize certain truths. I will construct two imaginary "model" economies. In the first, the "all-specialists economy," I will imagine that there are no corporations, no labor unions, and so on, but only individuals, each selling just one thing, which is different from the things being sold by all the rest. Each individual, in other words, is a specialist and the only specialist of his kind. Moreover, the things that each specialist sells are assumed to be essential to the well-being of at least some other people, so that no matter how much he charges for them, other people will continue buying at least some of them as long as they have any money left. Finally, in order to facilitate some simple calculations that I make, I will assume that the economy consists of exactly one hundred such specialists. The reader should understand that these individual specialists, as I have defined them, are "perfect" pricing institutions. They have absolute control over their own prices, that is, their "price patterns." No individual will cheat on himself by undercutting his own prices.

If everyone in this economy sought to maximize his profits by charging what the traffic would bear, as traditional economics ordinarily assumes is the case, economic activity would quickly come to a halt. The first time a person became so hungry that he could no longer bear to go without food, for example, he would have to pay all the money he had to the lone farmer for however little food the farmer chose to give him. To a person who is starving, whatever he has, and all he has, is worth exchanging for even a little food. This person would then be unable to buy anything more from anyone else until someone paid him for his services, at which time he would presumably charge that person all he could bear, which would be all that person's money, for giving him his essential products or services. So it would go around the economy, each person working utter financial ruin on the next each time the next became desperate enough to pay all he had for the first person's products or services. A lesson that the members of this economy would presumably learn very early, therefore, is that life would hardly be worth living if each of them really charged all that the traffic would bear for his own products or services. A social ethic would presumably soon be formed that a person ought to charge only "fair" prices.

It could be, then, that under a social ethic of "fair" prices, life would proceed quite comfortably. Fairness could be judged by the skill or training that was required for the services and by the social prestige of the person who rendered them. A "fair" price would be a price that permitted the provider of the services to have an income consistent with the society's estimate of his skill, training, and prestige. The doctor might earn two or three times what the carpenter earned, and the carpenter might earn two or three times what the trash man earned, and so on.

Such an equilibrium would be difficult to reach, however, and even if it were reached it would be unstable. Suppose, for example, that just one person, the trash man, became dissatisfied with his place on the economic ladder and increased the prices for his services. Since some others, by hypothesis, needed his services, the higher prices that they had to pay for them would have the effect of reducing their real incomes. They would still be charging the same for their own goods or services and so making the same in monetary terms, but by having to spend more for trash-removal services they would have less left for everything else; their incomes would buy less than they did before, and so in real terms would be lowered. The response of most of the other people would therefore probably be to raise their prices, too, by as much as they thought necessary to restore their real incomes, that is, to restore their incomes' former purchasing powers. The trash man's price increase might also encourage others to raise their prices, even if they never had any trash to be removed and so were not directly injured by his higher prices. Their sense of propriety might be offended by the realization that the trash man was now earning as much or more as they, or that he was now earning even half as much as they. For any or all of these reasons, the trash man's price increase would be certain to trigger further price increases throughout the economy. These, in turn, for similar reasons, would trigger still more price increases, and the price equilibrium that had been somehow achieved initially would explode into a spiraling inflation.

I will dwell on this inflationary process for a moment more, because it is important to understand exactly why it works. Traditional economic theory teaches that when one person does not like the higher price another is charging, he refuses to buy. His refusal, plus the refusals of others who presumably feel the same way, cost the price increaser so much in lost sales that he supposedly rescinds his price increase. His expectation that this would occur normally inhibits him from trying to increase his prices in the first place. In the imaginary economy I have created, on the other hand, each person so badly needs what the others sell that he cannot refuse to buy from them, so long as he has any money left. When he finds that he has to pay more for what he needs because others are increasing the prices of what they sell to him, therefore, his only available recourse is to raise the prices on the things that he sells, too, so that he will have more money of his own with which to pay the higher prices others are charging. Thus a sort of competition occurs. Each individual tries to keep his own prices going up faster than the prices of the things he has to buy. Obviously, the faster anyone's prices go up, the faster others will try to raise theirs in order to keep their real incomes even. Once even one significant price increase occurs, it triggers others, and so causes inflation. Once the inflation begins, it proceeds at a faster and faster pace.

Except for the trash man, who started it all, every single participant in this inflation may be able to claim, correctly, that he is not to blame. All he may be doing is raising his prices enough to keep his real income the same, yet doing this is sufficient to create an accelerating inflation that will ultimately reach such a high rate as to destroy the economy. The only inherent restraint on this kind of inflation is the length of time it takes each person to respond to the price increases of the others by increasing his own prices. If people typically change their prices only once a year, say, the rate of inflation will probably not be very high. The rate of inflation itself, however, may encourage people who would not ordinarily increase their prices frequently to do so, in order to keep from losing too much real income before their next usual price increase. An inflation of this kind is thus likely eventually to break down its only inherent restraint.

What would happen if the government of this economy tried to fight the inflation by reducing demand, as our government invariably does? Suppose, for example, that the previous tax rate was 25 percent for everyone, and that the government previously spent all its tax money by providing police, defense, and other government services, but that in order to reduce demand, the government increased the tax rate to 40 percent without increasing what it spent for these services. Everyone's after-tax incomes of course would drop immediately, so the amounts of goods and services they bought from each other would also drop immediately. There would be a large increase in unemployment. Everyone except perhaps the farmer, whose products were the most essential, would sit idly by during a part of every workday. But the government's action would have given no one any incentive to slow down the pace at which he was raising his prices, let alone any incentive to reduce his prices. Since I have defined everyone as a specialist whose products or services are considered so desirable by the others that the others will continue to buy substantially the same amount of them whatever their price, a specialist would not sell appreciably more if he were to lower his prices. So, regardless of the government's drastic reduction of demand, the inflation would continue apace.

This point, too, is worth dwelling on, because I have found it difficult for many people to grasp. It seems to many that even the specialists, as I have defined them, must be able to sell more if they lower their prices, and that therefore they would lower them, and the government's demand reduction would work to quell the inflation after all. If prices are lowered, it would seem, everyone could buy more of everything with the money he had, so everyone, despite being a specialist, would sell more. This would indeed be the case if everyone or almost everyone lowered his prices, but the difficulty is that this economy or any similarly constituted economy would never reach this state because there is no *individual* incentive for any of its members to get there. If any one specialist were to lower his prices while the others did not, he would not sell appreciably more, so he would lose profits overall. The money people saved from his lower prices would be used to buy more—perhaps from him, but probably also from all the other specialists who had the things they considered essential, whether or not the other specialists had lowered their prices. A lone price-cutter would benefit everyone else more than he would benefit himself. Everyone else would get about the same increased sales, but only he would have reduced his prices.

On the average, in this imaginary economy where there are exactly one hundred members, a lone price-cutter would lose ninety-nine cents in profits for every dollar he cut his prices, while the others, who did not cut their prices, would gain a penny each. If two sellers happened to reduce their prices at about the same time, the arithmetic is such that each would lose about ninety-eight cents while everyone else would gain about two cents. Since average prices would be going down (very slightly) at the same time, however, we must also take this into account. The average price level would fall 1 percent for each dollar of price reduction a single seller put into effect. The arithmetic that takes everything into account is simple in principle but lengthy, so I will just state the result. The price-cutters would only begin to break even if fifty of them cut prices all together, and even then the additional real wealth they were creating (by reducing unemployment) would go entirely to the benefit of those who had not cut their prices. The conclusion is inescapable that a demand reduction by the government would not slow the pace of this inflation so long as people were left free to price as they chose. The government could slow the pace or stop it entirely if it were to *order* everyone to stop raising prices all at once—but the government could do this equally effectively without reducing demand.

The reader's reaction at this point is perhaps that all this may be true in the kind of economy I have imagined, but this only goes to show that it is a very peculiar economy. But in this respect, at least, this economy is not at all peculiar. What I have just described has already been noted in the economy of the United States in some sectors, although neither its presence outside these sectors nor its significance for inflation has yet been appreciated. The sectors in which it has been noted are the craft unions, especially the craft unions in the construction industry.[2] Each such union represents just one craft—electricians, plumbers, carpenters, and so on. Only a very small portion of the total cost of a typical building project is accounted for by the wages of one craft, and the amount of each craft's services that a typical building project requires is virtually independent on their cost. A building needs so much electrical wiring whether that wiring will cost a $100,000 or $110,000, for example. Thus, just as in my imaginary economy, if the United States government lowers demand and thereby reduces the number of building projects, no craft union has any individual incentive to reduce its members' wages. Since their wages constitute only a very small proportion of the total cost, the savings that would result to builders would not appreciably increase the number of buildings being built, and to the extent they did, the benefit would go *entirely* to the other workers, whose wages had not been lowered. I will not elaborate further, because it is all just as I explained in my imaginary economy. The reader should be able to see immediately that the situation just described is not unique to the craft unions in the construction industry, however. For example, the proportion of the total cost of an automobile that is accounted for by any one of its component parts or materials is generally extremely small.[3] A 10 percent increase in the price of steel would probably not increase the cost of a $6,000 automobile more than a few dollars. For a capital-intensive industry, the percentage of total costs that are accounted for by all wages together is small, so in such in-

[2] John Sheahan, *The Wage-Price Guideposts* (Washington, D.C.: Brookings Institution, 1967), pp. 39–40, 52–54.

[3] The term for this phenomenon in traditional economics is "derived demand." See, for example, Albert Rees, *The Economics of Trade Unions* (Chicago: University of Chicago Press, 1962), pp. 70–73.

dustries wages are likely to continue to rise despite very substantial drops in the demand for the industries' products, even when the workers are not organized by crafts. Peter Drucker noted this fact for the steel and automobile industries early in 1981.[4]

To return again to the imaginary economy, the result there of a demand reduction by the government is even worse than I have yet described. Since the demand reduction would cause everyone to sell less, that is to say, to be less employed, and since the specialists presumably gauge the propriety and fairness of their prices by the size of the incomes they provide, the effect of the demand reduction would presumably be to *increase* the pace of the inflation. People would try to gain back by price increases the income losses they had suffered from underemployment. This effect, too, is not just a quirk of a peculiarly defined, imaginary economy. Industries in the United States have indeed raised their prices in the face of falling demand and justified the increases by saying they needed them to maintain their profits.[5] Labor unions in the United States have indeed demanded wage increases for their members to compensate them for less employment or elimination of overtime suffered because of lowered demand.[6]

Of equal interest is the answer to the question, what would

[4] Peter F. Drucker, "The Danger of Excessive Labor Income," *Wall Street Journal,* January 6, 1981, p. 22.

[5] Leroy H. Mantell and Francis P. Sing, *Economics for Business Decisions* (New York: McGraw-Hill, 1972), pp. 239–48; Neil W. Chamberlain, *The Firm* (New York: McGraw-Hill, 1962), pp. 193–95; "Profit Pinch: Firms' Earnings Drop in 2nd Quarter Eased from 1st Period Slump," *Wall Street Journal,* August 1, 1975, p. 1; Ralph E. Winter, "Heading Higher: At Many Companies, the Order of the Day Is To Move Prices Up," *Wall Street Journal,* December 7, 1976, p. 1; Cynthia Saltzman, "Slump Forces Auto Renters To Raise Rates," *Wall Street Journal,* October 7, 1980, p. 29.

[6] This phenomenon has been better documented in England; see Dudley Jackson, H. A. Turner, and Frank Wilkinson, *Do Trade Unions Cause Inflation?* 2d. ed. (Cambridge: Cambridge University Press, 1974), pp. xiv–xv, 115–16, 199; Robert Lekachman, *Economists at Bay* (New York: McGraw-Hill, 1976), p. 35. But the phenomenon has been observed here too. See, for example, the experiences of the typographers, movie-production workers, longshoremen, coal miners, and merchant seaman referenced in Chapter 2.

happen if the government of this economy took *no* actions of the traditional kind, either to try to reduce the inflation or to increase it? The government, we will assume, continues doing with demand whatever it was doing before the inflation began. If it was keeping demand level, it continues to keep demand level. If it was increasing demand at a steady but moderate rate in order just to take into account the rate of growth of the real volume of goods and services being bought and sold in the economy, it continues increasing demand just at this rate. The answer, perhaps surprisingly, is that there will still be an increase in unemployment. Not as much as if the government had changed its previous policies in the direction of reducing demand, of course, but still some. As prices rise, it takes more money to purchase the same amount of goods and services. A measure of demand is the amount of money in circulation times the rapidity with which the money circulates.[7] If demand is not increased just as rapidly as prices are rising, therefore, the real rate at which goods and services are being purchased has to go down. There being fewer goods and services purchased, there must also be fewer sold, which is another way of saying that there must be more unemployment. If the government of this economy wishes to avoid an increase in unemployment, therefore, it must increase demand at least as rapidly as the rate of inflation!

Wage and price controls of the kind that the United States has had during wartime and, in 1971 and 1972, during peacetime are not effective to prevent or stop this kind of inflation. Such controls work by "freezing" all wages and prices at the levels they had on some "freeze date." Sometimes incremental increases are allowed thereafter, either in proportion to a seller's cost increases or on some across-the-board basis, such as allowing wages to increase a certain percent per year, but these are variations that do not affect the controls' essential character. The problem is, once competitive inflation has started, any freeze date is bound to work innumerable injustices by stopping the competitive process in mid-motion.

[7] Paul A. Samuelson, *Economics,* 9th ed. (New York: McGraw-Hill, 1973), pp. 284–87.

Some groups (labor unions, industries, professional groups, and so on) will have just received large price increases and so will be made very well off by the price structure on the freeze date. Others will not have received increases for long periods, and will perhaps have been just about to receive them, and so will be caught far behind and made (and thereafter kept) quite badly off. The justification sometimes offered for thus "freezing" wages and prices is that the freeze date is chosen as a time before the inflation had a chance to start, so the price structure on the date is fair to everyone, on the theory that it reflects what everyone was getting when the competitive market was working normally. But once competitive inflation has started, the competitive market is surely *never* thereafter working "normally," if it ever was. And by the 1980s, it has become impossibly disruptive to choose as a freeze date a time so long ago as to predate the inception of competitive inflation. Moreover, the injustices inflicted by "freezing" are likely to prove especially disruptive because it was the perception of precisely those injustices that fueled the competitive inflation in the first place.

The Economy Consisting of "Specialists" and Others

Let us now vary the imaginary illustration so as to make it more like a real economy. Imagine that there are still exactly one hundred specialists whose services or products are essential or nearly so for others, but that in addition there are large numbers of people who are all capable of doing about the same things and so compete with one another. None of them is capable of competing with any of the one hundred specialists, however. Note that none of the nonspecialists possess anything like the power that a specialist possesses to raise prices, because they are in competition with one another for whatever they sell. Let us assume that among these nonspecialists are clerks and general factory laborers. If a clerk demanded a higher price for his services than other people thought his services were worth, he would not be able to sell any of his services. The people who might otherwise have bought them would instead buy the services of another clerk, at a lower price. The specialists, however, would still have the same power to raise the prices of their services as they had before.

When a specialist in this slightly different kind of economy raises his price, does he thereby trigger a general inflation? The answer is, not necessarily. Whether he does depends upon the impact, economic or otherwise, of his price increase on the other specialists. The impact on the nonspecialists is irrelevant. They must accept his higher prices, and thus a reduction in the purchasing power of their own incomes, without effective protest, because they are essentially powerless to raise their own prices or incomes. If the particular specialist in question happens to sell his services almost entirely to nonspecialists, therefore, he can increase his own income as much as he wants by correspondingly reducing the purchasing power of theirs—that is, by correspondingly decreasing their real incomes—without necessarily triggering inflation. But to the extent that he sells services to other specialists, if his increases are large enough to be noticed by the other specialists they will probably trigger a general inflation of specialists' prices.

Moreover, even in the first case, in which the specialist sold almost all his services to nonspecialists, his price increase would probably trigger a general inflation of specialists' prices, too, because other specialists' sense of social or economic decency would be offended by the first specialist's earning more, relative to themselves, than they thought proper. They would respond by increasing their own prices. Note, however, that in any event the inflation, if it occurs, occurs only among the prices of the specialists. Their prices go up and up, and therefore their real incomes also go up and up—although their real incomes suffer some dilution from the inflation. The nonspecialist's prices, on the other hand, do not go up at all, but since the nonspecialists also feel the effects of the inflation, their real incomes go down and down. The specialists are the inflation's cause; the nonspecialists are its victims.

All that is necessary for inflation of this kind to begin and to continue is that there be persons in the economy who are "specialists" in the sense that I have used this term, and that the total of the incomes that each of them feels is appropriate for himself exceed the total share of the national income that is available for all of them together. What happens is that each person continually raises his own prices in order to make up for what he has lost in real income by reason of the price increases of the others. Everyone must continue doing this forever because, since the total income aspirations are greater than the total real income to go around, some people, at least, will always find themselves earning less than they feel they deserve.

What happens if the government tries to fight inflation in this kind of economy by reducing demand? The prices of the specialists would not be affected, for the reasons already stated: their prices and their incomes would continue to rise, perhaps even more rapidly. Just as before, however, the specialists would suffer more unemployment. Among the nonspecialists the effects would be different. The prices they charge for their services or products would generally be forced down. Since the demand for all services and products would be down by virtue of the government's actions, the demand for their services would have gone down too, and since they are in competition with one another a reduction in demand would generally decrease both their employment and their prices. A buyer of a clerk's services might say to the clerk, for example, "there are plenty of clerks looking for work, so unless you sell me your services for less, I will buy the same services from one of them, and they will be happy to sell them to me at a lower price." There would indeed be plenty of clerks looking for work, because the general demand reduction would have reduced the demand for clerks' services.

Thus, reducing demand does reduce the rate of inflation. It reduces it, however, very unfairly by not reducing the inflation in the specialist's prices—and possibly even increasing it—but by causing *de*flation among the prices that the nonspecialists charge; the bit of deflation added to the untouched or aggravated inflation works a net decrease in the rate of inflation. Again, the specialists are the causes of the government's measures to reduce demand, but the nonspecialists are its principal victims. One cannot say they are its sole victims, because the specialists have suffered some unemployment too. The lion's share of unemployment will probably have fallen on the nonspecialists, however, precisely because the services of the specialists are essential, or nearly so. People will tend to use larger shares of their decreased incomes in order to keep buying the services they consider essential, and so will cut down their purchases of nonessential services more than proportionately.

Moreover, although a demand reduction will reduce inflation in this kind of economy, albeit quite unfairly, the reduction will be only temporary. Eventually the government will have to cease reducing demand. Either the resulting unemployment will have reached intolerable levels, or it will have gone on intolerably long, or everyone's standard of living will have suffered too much from the failure of the economy to grow, or, possibly, the inflation will have been reduced sufficiently so that people think it has been beaten. When for any reason the government reverses its policies and begins again to increase demand, the nonspecialists' prices, which were the only prices to have been forced down, will come bounding back up again at least as rapidly as they were forced downward earlier. Economic theory and observation agree that to the extent prices are demand-responsive at all, they are almost always demand-responsive upward at least as much as they are demand-responsive downward. What economists have called "price stickiness"—the failure of prices to respond to demand—works nearly always more powerfully to keep prices up in the face of falling demand than to keep prices down despite demand rising.[8] *Thus, despite all the unemployment and*

[8] Gardiner C. Means, *Industrial Prices and Their Flexibility* (Washington, D.C.: U.S. Govt. Printing Office, 1935), p. 8; Gardiner C. Means, "The Administered Price Thesis Confirmed," *Amer. Econ. Rev.* 62 (June 1972), 292–306; John Kenneth Galbraith, *Money: Whence It Came, Where It Went* (New York: Houghton-Mifflin, 1957), p. 221.

other suffering it will have caused, a demand reduction in this kind of economy will have accomplished nothing enduring to curb inflation.

It also remains true in this kind of economy, as it was in the first kind of economy described, that unemployment will increase if the government fails to increase demand at least as rapidly as the rate of inflation, and for the same reasons. In fact, the relationship among the rates of inflation, of demand increase, and of unemployment remain exactly the same as they were in the first imaginary economy. All that is changed by imagining that the economy also includes some nonspecialists who compete is that, because of their presence, the rate of inflation will probably be lower; but the rate of increase in demand must still equal or exceed the rate of inflation or the difference will be made up by the rate of increase of unemployment. Everything said earlier about the ineffectiveness of wage and price controls for preventing or stopping competitive inflation in the all-specialists' economy also applies to this kind of economy.

Competitive Inflation in a Real Economy

The second imagined economy, which includes both specialists and nonspecialists, is similar in all relevant aspects to the economy of the United States. All that is necessary to convert it to a description of our actual economy is to replace its specialists with pricing institutions. A pricing institution is generally less effective in controlling its members' prices than the imagined specialists were in controlling theirs, but to the extent that pricing institutions are effective, their effects on each other and on the economy as a whole are precisely the same as the effects of the specialists. The differences are only in degree.

Our real economy also differs from the imagined one in not having a sharp line between its specialists and its nonspecialists, that is, between those who belong to pricing institutions and those who do not. In reality, almost all of us have the prices of what we sell controlled to some extent by pricing institutions, but the institutions vary widely in effectiveness. At the lower end of the scale they shade off either into having no effect, in which case the prices concerned are set entirely by competition; or into having a bad effect, in which case the prices are deliberately set to the persons' disadvantage. School teachers, nurses, and secretaries, for example, have traditionally had their pay set not by competition but by pricing institutions, but they have traditionally been underpaid nonetheless. The people in these occupations have traditionally been women, and the pricing institutions that set their pay rates have usually been controlled by men. But the difference between a shading-off and a sharp line in these respects makes no material difference in the process of competitive inflation.

The United States economy also differs from the second imaginary economy I pictured in having a higher proportion of its people in some kind of pricing institution than the proportion of specialists in the imagined economy. Virtually everyone in our economy has his income heavily influenced by a pricing institution of some kind. Almost no one, these days, is in a truly price-competitive situation for his income. As I mentioned in a preceding chapter, even stock brokers, who buy and sell stocks in a nearly perfectly competitive environment, have their own incomes set by a very rigid pricing institution, which sets their commissions. Their commissions provide their income, and they are payable at the same rates whether stock prices rise or fall. Thus, our economy in fact acts and responds more like the first imagined economy, in which everyone is a specialist, that is, everyone has his income controlled by a pricing institution, than like the second, in which a relatively large proportion of the working population is pictured as selling its services competitively.

I used individual specialists to stand for pricing institutions in my imagined economies in order to emphasize the two aspects of pricing institutions that are most important for competitive inflation. Like an individual with respect to his own prices, a pricing institution is capable of raising virtually all the prices of the goods its members sell at about the same time. The capability of simultaneity or near simultaneity enables it to raise prices by relatively large amounts. And like a specialist of the kind I defined, a pricing institution's members sell goods that at least a substantial number of other people find essential, so that even relatively large price increases will not materially reduce sales. The goods that the members of pricing institutions sell are generally felt by substantial numbers of other people to be essential simply because in a modern economy almost all goods are considered by substantial numbers of people to be essential, whether the goods are sold by members of pricing institutions or not. Goods in an actual economy are of course not typically regarded by people as absolutely essential to their well-being—people would not pay all their wealth or income to an electrician for his services, even if they were the only services of the kind to be had, for example. But such an extreme situation is not necessary for sellers to be able to raise prices substantially without appreciably reducing sales. And in an actual modern economy, almost all kinds of goods are regarded as essential to at least this extent. If, for example, the prices of automobiles were all to rise 5 percent, automobile sales would hardly suffer. Too many people have adopted ways of living for which they must have automobiles. When prices generally can be increased even 5 percent without materially decreasing sales, an inflation of almost any annual amount is possible, because prices can be raised indefinitely many times per year.

The course of competitive inflation as I have described it is also useful for understanding why economists have persisted so long in mistakenly ascribing all inflation, including competitive inflation, to excess demand. The actual causal chain, as I have described it, is this: competitive inflation has essentially nothing to do with demand. It results, rather, from the combination of people's inability to prevent other people from raising their prices and people's ability to raise their own prices (including their own wages or salaries, of course). The reasons for both the inability and the ability were set forth in Chapters 1 through 4, although for competitive inflation, pricing institutions are the single most important factor. As soon as *anyone* in the economy raises his prices, the resulting inflation causes at least some other people's real profits or incomes to fall. Having no way of preventing this inflation, the only way people have of preventing their real profits or incomes from falling is to raise their own prices, which causes more inflation. The process, once begun, never stops. The inflation of which it consists gets generally worse and worse. Among the effects of this inflation is that unemployment (of both people and resources) increases apace, unless the government increases aggregate demand. So, of course, the government does increase aggregate demand—not necessarily as promptly or by as much as it should, but enough at least to prevent unemployment from reaching politically intolerable levels.

The objective situation thereby created is quite misleading, and since most economists today insist upon using objective data exclusively, because it supposedly makes their observations more scientific, the situation is quite misleading to most contemporary economists. Viewed objectively, which is to say, viewed with regard only to what appears on the surface, inflation is accompanied by rising demand, and, if the government raises demand just rapidly enough to keep unemployment stable, the rate of inflation and the rate of rising demand can even be observed to be about the same. The conclusion *seems* inescapable: that the rising demand is causing the inflation—although the fact, of course, is exactly the other way around. Inflation is causing the rising demand through the intermediation of the government, which acts to avoid increasing unemployment. But hundreds, probably thousands, of economists have been satisfied not to look below the objective appearances. A truly immense amount of work has been carried on in academia and in institutions and foundations in the last two decades to gather the objective data that thus "prove" that rising demand has been the cause of our inflation.[9]

Although many have tried, objective data alone also cannot be used to determine who caused this kind of inflation on the basis of who gained the most from it.[10] The trash man in the example we imagined was clearly the cause, but there is no reason to expect that before the process had ended, or any time during the process, he would have gained either more or less from the price increase he gave himself than others gained from the price increases they obtained later. In a real economy, there is usually no way even of determining who caused the inflation by finding out who made the first price increase that upset the preexisting price equilibrium, because in a real economy, these days, there are usually no price equilibria. Inflation has become continuous. Finally, even if an equilibrium or a relative equilibrium does or did exist, and the persons whose price increases upset it can be found, they cannot on these grounds alone be blamed for their actions. The equilibrium may have been one under which their share of the total national income was unjustly small. Labor unions in our country surely would not be the force that they are, for example, if people generally did not believe that they constitute a means of raising workers' incomes, and that the workers' incomes, thus raised, are closer to a fair share of the total national income than they would otherwise be.

[9] For example, Allan H. Meltzner, "Money Growth and Inflation," *Wall Street Journal,* May 17, 1978, p. 18; Phillip Cagan, "Monetary Policy," in Phillip Cagan, Marten Estey, William Fellner, Charles E. McClure, Jr., and Thomas Gale Moore, *Economic Policy and Inflation in the Sixties* (Washington, D.C.: American Enterprise Institute for Public Policy Research, 1972), pp. 89–153; Sanford Rose, "The Agony of the Federal Reserve," *Fortune* 90 (July 1974), 91; John O'Riley, "Review of Current Trends in Business and Finance," *Wall Street Journal,* September 22, 1975, p. 1; Milton Friedman, "What Price Guideposts?" in George P. Shultz and Robert Z. Aliber, eds., *Guidelines: Informal Controls and the Market Place* (Chicago: University of Chicago Press, 1966), pp. 18, 25.

[10] See, for example, Jerry Flint, "Bending Wage Guidelines," *New York Times Economic Survey,* January 7, 1979, p. 11; Derek C. Bok and John T. Dunlop, *Labor and the American Community* (New York: Simon and Schuster, 1970), pp. 275–87.

The Origins of Competitive Inflation in the United States

In the imaginary "all-specialists economy," competitive inflation began as soon as a single price was increased. The imaginary economy that included nonspecialists was not so volatile, but even there competitive inflation was easily ignited, and the volatility of the actual economy of the United States, we concluded, was probably less than that of the first of these imaginary economies but more than that of the second. Yet, competitive inflation did not really begin in earnest in the United States until late in 1973, and the spark that ignited it—a quadrupling of world oil prices simultaneously with some sharp increases in food prices caused by shortages—seems to have been a much stronger stimulus than our reasoning predicted would have been necessary. One would have thought that one of the many lesser "economic sparks" that had occurred earlier, such as the Vietnam War, would have been enough. On the other hand, once competitive inflation began, it never disappeared. Our inflation rates have never gone back to where they were before 1973, and they seem to have a long-term upward trend. The events of late 1973 and 1974 must therefore have had two effects: to set off competitive inflation in the United States for the first time, and to make our economy so susceptible to competitive inflation that it has never since stopped, and promises to get generally worse and worse.

The explanation, I think, is that the events of 1973–1974 and the sharply increased inflation that immediately followed, which would otherwise have gradually disappeared, combined to work some fundamental alterations in people's knowledge and attitudes. Specifically, sellers learned the price-increasing techniques described in Chapters 1 through 4, and changed their attitudes about the sizes and frequencies of price increases they considered permissible; buyers began accepting larger increases before changing their buying habits. Although some sellers in the United States obviously knew of these techniques and practiced them before 1973, the knowledge was previously not widespread.

When OPEC first raised oil prices, some in the United States predicted that oil sales would decline sharply and that OPEC would break apart as a result. When this did not happen but, on the contrary, not only the OPEC countries but all the international oil companies made enormous profits, price setters in other industries were quick to pick the lesson up. Oil is *not* more essential than are the things that many other industries produce. Something is "essential" for the purposes of permitting its prices to be increased if enough people will continue to buy it even if its prices rise, and by this test probably most things are essential in the modern world. Certainly motor vehicles, basic foods, coal, electricity, college educations, television sets, liquor, tobacco, and the hundreds of different products and component products of the construction industry are essential by this test, for example. The example set by OPEC's success did not teach the price setters in other industries *how* to get their prices up, because OPEC is a kind of cartel that would be illegal under the laws of the United States, but there were industries that could serve as examples for techniques in raising prices here. The American steel industry had been an effective pricing institution since the fifties. The American automobile industry had been one since at least 1971. That was the first year that the Price Commission, which I served as general counsel, had to control the prices of this industry. The commission discovered that it could control them by controlling the prices of just General Motors' automobiles. The rest of the industry raised or lowered its prices to match. And surely there were many other pricing institutions whose existence prior to 1973 has never been documented. In addition, there were certainly many industries in which the members were already using the price-increasing techniques. Evidence that the success of OPEC did indeed teach the lessons here described is that many major American industries did form themselves into pricing institutions for the first time, or did otherwise change their sales strategies shortly after 1973, as was noted in Chapters 1 and 3. When the *Wall Street Journal* reported the liquor industry's abandonment of price competition in favor of modern sales methods in the middle seventies, the *Journal* commented that this was probably the *last* major consumer-products industry thus to convert.

The success of OPEC proved that sales were not nearly so price-elastic as had been widely supposed. Once competitive inflation began, sales were made even less price-elastic than they had previously been by the changes that the increased inflation wrought in people's attitudes. As we have seen, inflation requires a government to increase aggregate demand in order to avoid increasing unemployment. It must increase demand rapidly enough to avoid having sales go down. If sales do not go down, it means that most people find that, one way or another, they are able to buy as much despite the inflation as they could before. (Not everyone is able to, of course, but it logically has to be the case that people can do so, on the average, if demand is increased enough to avoid an increase in unemployment.) The inevitable result of this, in turn, is a changed attitude toward rising prices. People become more tolerant of them. Moreover, once people get used to inflation, price increases of more than the generally expected amounts can *increase* sales, by leading people to expect that the prices will soon go higher still, so that they should buy as much as they can afford now. These changed buyers' attitudes must have changed sellers' attitudes too. An industry whose prices were not being increased must have felt that it was losing out. That the prices of its products were not rising presumably did *not* appreciably increase its sales (see Chapter 3), and it was not obtaining the extra profits per unit of sales that higher prices would have provided. Once competitive inflation had begun, people undoubtedly also became more tolerant of other people's wage or salary increases. The attitude was adopted that others probably needed higher incomes to cope with inflation, too.

That the higher rates of inflation that began in 1973 became more or less permament was probably also due to sellers' having to learn price-increasing techniques to stay ahead of their rapidly rising costs. Once having learned them, they undoubtedly saw no reason not to continue using them, even after the emergency had subsided or disappeared. At least in the United States, rapid inflations prior to 1973 had never posed such an urgency, because they had always been demand-pull. Sellers not only have no difficulty in raising their prices in demand-pull inflations, they could hardly prevent their prices from rising if they wanted to. Demand-pull inflations occur because there is "too much money chasing too few goods." Any seller who does not anticipate the rising demand for his goods by raising his prices fast enough will find his goods being purchased more quickly than he can produce them or obtain them at wholesale. A seller under demand-pull conditions literally must keep raising his prices in order to avoid shortages. But at least before buyers' attitudes had had a chance to change, sellers in the period after 1973 would have encountered no less difficulty in raising their prices than they had previously. They nevertheless had to raise them, and raise them rapidly, to cover their suddenly rapidly rising costs—of oil and its many derivatives (gasoline, plastics, electricity, and so on) initially, and soon thereafter rising wage costs and the rising costs of whatever other goods had previously joined in the heightened inflation. Some sellers presumably learned the price-increasing techniques from observing the industries that were already using them—the steel industry and the automobile industry were already using the pricing-institution technique, for example. Others must simply have raised their prices and been surprised to learn that sales did not fall, or fell less than they had anticipated. For example, a seller in an inflationary market presumably had only to raise his prices in order to discover how profitable it was, provided only that he did not raise them too much more rapidly than his competitors were raising theirs.

Historical evidence of what people did not know is by nature hard to come by. The journalists and social scientists of the time are likely not to have known it either, and so probably failed to ask the right questions for the historical record. The failure of people to act as they presumably would have, had they known, is some evidence, but a mere failure to act in a certain way is usually susceptible to a variety of explanations. I have come across only two incidents that indicate the extent of the ignorance of price-increasing techniques prior to 1973. One of them is from my own experience. As a legal advisor to a company in an industry that traditionally announced its prices once a year, I sometimes sat in on the company's pricing discussions. In this industry there were a few firms, generally the same year after year, that tried to raise the level of the price pattern for the whole industry. My firm was not one of them. Since it is inherent in the workings of an industrial pricing institution that the price pattern will be set at the level that is desired by the firm that wants it set at the lowest level (unless this firm is too small to matter), these few firms always failed in their efforts. The reason that the executives of the firm that I advised did not go along with them was their belief that they were really aggressive price competitors and only wanted higher list prices in order to give themselves more room for price competition through secret discounting. Whether the executives' perceptions of the other firms' intentions were right or wrong, these facts are evidence of ignorance of the benefits that all the firms could have realized by operating cooperatively. If the few firms' intentions were as the executives of my company thought them to be, these firms were ignorant of the potential benefits. If the few firms' intentions were not thus, but really were to gain higher prices and higher profits for everyone by raising the price pattern, my firm's belief that their intentions were otherwise is evidence of ignorance of the benefits or, at least, ignorance of how best to go about trying to obtain them. Although I left the private practice of law well before the seventies, I have followed the price patterns of this industry since, and by the middle seventies its prices had risen very substantially. Its executives must have learned some things after I left.

The other incident is from a 1922 court opinion.[11] The man-

[11] Soule v. Bon Ami Co., 1922, 201 App. Div. 794, 195 N.Y.S. 574, aff'd. without opinion, 235 N.Y. 609, 139 N.E. 754.

ufacturers of Bon Ami cleanser received a letter offering to disclose to them a money-making idea if they would promise to share the profits equally with the writer. The company promised. The idea was that the price of the cleanser to grocers be increased just eight percent, which the writer estimated would not be enough to discourage grocers from buying the cleanser and also not enough to cause them to increase its retail price. So the company's profits would be increased at the grocers' expense. The company tried the idea and it worked, but never gave any of the profits to the writer. The writer sued but lost. The court held that nothing so obvious could constitute the consideration for a promise that would make it an enforceable contract. Such a simple pricing strategy does seem obvious today, but the Bon Ami Company presumably would not have had to be told about it if it had been truly obvious at the time. Before receiving the letter, the company, like almost everyone else, must have assumed that price increases invariably reduced sales, and usually substantially.

The learning and attitude-altering that proceeded so rapidly beginning in 1973 are unlikely ever to be reversed, except as they rest upon the expectation of continued inflation. To this extent they could be reversed, of course, if inflation were eliminated for a substantial period. But there is no other way. People are not so gullible as to be persuaded by a temporary wage and price freeze that inflation will not resume when the freeze is lifted, for example, and they would surely understand that the freeze would sooner or later have to be lifted. So there is no hope of eliminating inflation by eliminating the knowledge of price-increasing techniques or by changing buyers' and sellers' inflationary attitudes. The knowledge and the attitudes might change if inflation were eliminated for a long period, but it is unlikely that even then the knowledge of price-increasing techniques would be forgotten. The techniques would have become a part of economic history, always accessible to the curious. And the price-increasing techniques will undoubtedly still be used even in the absence of inflation, although on a reduced scale. Prices are generally changing even in a noninflationary economy, the absence of inflation meaning only that the "ups" do not overbalance the "downs." The heightened susceptibility of the American economy to outbreaks of competitive inflation has therefore probably become a condition as permanent as societal conditions ever are.

Inflationary Expectations and "Talking Inflation Down"

The description of competitive inflation makes it obvious that people's expectations of inflation influence the rate of inflation. The more inflation people expect, in general, the more there will be. This is not because buyers are willing to pay more in the expectation that if they wait they will have to pay still more. Competitive inflation has essentially nothing to do with what buyers are willing to pay. When prices are set by pricing institutions, buyers have little choice. But expectations of inflation induce sellers to feel justified in charging more, expecting that their costs will rise more and that they will need higher profits in order to keep their real incomes the same. Sellers' expectations affect competitive inflation because it is the sellers' pricing discretion that makes the inflation possible.

Competitive inflation can be "talked down" for similar reasons. If the administration in power can convince people that its anti-inflationary measures will work, they will, to some extent at least, simply because enough people expect them to, even if the measures themselves are quite useless. The nature of competitive inflation also makes it possible for an administration to "talk it down" in the sense of urging sellers to restrain their price increases. Corporation executives and labor leaders may respond affirmatively to such urgings out of patriotism or out of feelings of personal or political loyalty to the administration, and the pricing discretion that they possess will enable them to give their feelings effect. Voluntary wage and price programs are especially effective with the kinds of pricing institutions that consist of employers of unorganized employees, because it is in the employers' immediate monetary interests to comply. When President Carter asked that pay increases be kept to 7 percent or less in 1979,[12] employers all over the country were quick to express their intentions of doing so.

Both psychological methods can be employed simultaneously, and the success of either will contribute to the success of both. To the extent that inflation is successfully talked down, inflationary expectations are decreased. To the extent that inflationary expectations are decreased, people are more likely to comply with an administration's urgings to restrain price increases or to follow its voluntary wage and price guidelines. And the successes of both methods will be automatically augmented by reductions in the increases in the wages and prices that are indexed. Finally, if, as is likely today, psychological methods are accompanied by demand-reducing measures, the inflation will be reduced to the extent that these measures reduce the demands for goods (including labor) that are still subject to some significant amount of price competition despite the factors treated in Chapters 1 to 4, and these reductions, too, will contribute to the success of the psychological methods.

Nevertheless, there are drawbacks. The reductions in inflation are not likely to be fairly distributed. Unorganized employees are likely to have their wages and salaries decreased (in real terms), while organized employees and the self-employed will not. The especially patriotic and public-spirited will carry a higher burden in self-inflicted losses than will the rest of us. People who agreed to indexing arrangements will find that they have lost out to people who did not. This may or may not be unfair under the circumstances, but it is likely in any event to discourage indexing in the future. There is bound to be a good deal of unfairness from the unavoidable arbitrariness of the timing of the methods' application. Some groups will find themselves comfortably or extravagantly ahead, with years of large increases behind them. Others will

[12] "Wages & Prices: Carter's Gamble on Restraint," *Business Week*, November 6, 1978, pp. 60–62.

be caught short, with their opportunities to catch up restricted or denied. The unfairness, in turn, will make the reduction in inflation only temporary. The spiral will resume as soon as a few groups or a few large individual sellers or labor unions become dissatisfied with their relative positions and begin again to increase their prices substantially.

A third drawback is the risk that any temporary successes will be misinterpreted as successes of the anti-inflationary measures that accompanied or gave rise to the psychological effects that were the true causes. In the case of any accompanying demand-reducing measures, this risk is a virtual certainty. We have seen that it is actually inflation that causes demand to rise, not vice versa, by compelling the government to raise demand in order to avoid increasing unemployment. A reduction in the rate of inflation will likewise cause the rate of increase in demand to fall, by permitting the government to reduce the rate of increase without increasing unemployment. The inflation rate will actually have fallen for one or more of the psychological reasons just described, but the excess-demand theorists, of course, are almost certain to conclude, and so to claim, that their theories have (finally) been vindicated.

There would be no great harm in this, except that the false vindication is all too likely to mislead the country into thinking that the inflation could really be whipped, perhaps for good, if only demand could be, or had been, reduced even further; and there will be renewed efforts to do so, with all the attendant unemployment and other sufferings that such efforts cause. In short, the demand reductions will wrongly be given credit for what the psychological measures really brought about, and the country's ability to discern the true causes of inflation will be delayed for years.

CHAPTER 6

Demand-Pull / Cost-Push / Wage-Push

Demand-Pull Inflation and Demand-Pull Theories of Inflation

There is only one truly determinate kind of inflation, that which I call "classical demand-pull inflation." When demand throughout the entire economy ("aggregate demand") is rising so rapidly that producers throughout the economy cannot increase the supplies of goods ("aggregate supply") rapidly enough to keep pace, people in effect bid against one another to obtain the always scarce goods, and prices keep rising. People do not necessarily actually bid against one another, although in a very rapid demand-pull inflation this does happen. Ordinarily, sellers anticipate the rises in demand by raising prices before they put their goods on sale. The effect is the same, however, because only the people who are willing to pay the ever-higher prices get the goods. This kind of inflation is truly determinate because it is determined by the continuous gap between aggregate supply and demand. Anything done to try to eliminate it other than to eliminate this gap will have at best only temporary effects. A continuous gap between aggregate supply and aggregate demand can in theory appear for any number of reasons, but historically the reason has always been a government running large fiscal deficits, coining or printing money too rapidly, or otherwise too rapidly increasing aggregate demand.[1]

[1] Armen A. Alchian and William R. Allen, *University Economics*, 3rd ed. (Belmont, Ca: Wadsworth Pub. Co., 1971), pp. 701–704; Abba P. Lerner, *Flation: Not INflation of Prices, Not DEflation of Jobs: What You always Wanted to Know about Inflation, Depression, and the Dollar* (Harmondsworth: Pelican Books, 1973), pp. 23–29; Paul A. Samuelson, *Economics*, 9th ed. (New York: McGraw-Hill, 1973), pp. 242, 826–27.

Contemporary inflation, sometimes called "stagflation,"[2] occurs in the absence of a gap between aggregate supply and aggregate demand. Specifically, it occurs when there is *unused production capacity*—idle workers, idle machines, unplanted croplands, even crops and other goods already produced but stored or destroyed rather than sold. A large majority of the economists in the United States have nevertheless managed to maintain faith in the demand-pull theory as the correct explanation of contemporary inflation, although the theory has been changed. It has been divided into several different theories, connected with one another only by the historically continuous belief that the cause of all inflation, ultimately at least, is excess demand.

Many of the current versions of the demand-pull theory would hardly appear to be such to a layman, because they dispense with explanations. They merely assert causal correlations between inflation and some kind of aggregate demand. Nonexplanatory versions of the demand-pull theory are especially common among monetarists, who, as their name implies, assert a causal correlation between inflation and a particular kind of demand, either the money supply generally or a particular kind of money supply.[3] (So-called "M-2" is the kind of money most frequently blamed at the present time.)[4] All such correlations have two things in common: they are

[2] Graham Keith Shaw, *An Introduction to the Theory of Macro-Economic Policy,* 2d ed. (New York: Barnes and Noble, 1973), pp. 39–42; Howard S. Ellis, *Notes on Stagflation* (Washington, D.C.: American Enterprise Institute for Public Policy Research, 1978).

[3] For example, Milton Friedman et al., *Milton Friedman's Monetary Framework* (Chicago: University of Chicago Press, 1974); Milton Friedman, "Japan and Inflation," *Newsweek,* September 4, 1978, p. 75; William Fellner, "Introduction," in *Contemporary Economic Problems 1978* (Washington, D.C.: American Enterprise Institute for Public Policy Research, 1978); Lindley H. Clark, Jr., "Credit Squeeze," *Wall Street Journal,* November 13, 1978, p. 1. "To be sure, a theory of inflation that does not at some stage rely on the inflationary stimulus being originated in or accommodated by the money supply is fatuous." Michael L. Wachter and Oliver E. Williamson, "Obligational Markets and the Mechanics of Inflation," a paper prepared for delivery at the Law-Economics Workshop, University of California at Los Angeles, April 5, 1978, p. 1.

[4] See, for example, Friedman, "Japan and Inflation."

very rough,[5] and they beg the question of which of the things they correlate is the cause.[6] The roughness consists in an absence of any clear delineation either of how much demand or rate of demand increase is supposed to cause how much inflation, or of what length of time, if any, is supposed to elapse between the inflation and its asserted cause. Because of their question-begging, the theories overlook the possibility, which I showed in Chapter 5 to be the virtual certainty under normal conditions, that it is not the increasing demand which is causing the inflation, but the inflation which is causing the increasing demand. The roughness of the correlations constitutes additional evidence that this is the direction in which the cause and effect actually runs. The government action to increase demand is not caused in any mechanical sense by inflation, of course. The rising demand rather follows the inflation, or precedes it to the extent that the government perceives or anticipates a problem of rising unemployment or slowed growth, or both, and decides to act; and the rising demand varies in amount according to the force of the government's action. The correlation is also roughened by the fact that to the relatively small extent that prices in our economy are still responsive to rises and falls in aggregate demand, the cause and effect do work in the direction the theorists assert. This process, of course, is operative concurrently with the dominant process, which operates in the opposite direction. This too was explained in Chapter 5 (the "nonspecialists' prices").

When it wants to avoid increasing unemployment or slowing economic growth, the government of the United States increases aggregate demand in one or both of two ways. It runs a fiscal deficit or it expands the money supply. Both ways,

[5] See especially ibid., and Allan H. Meltzner, "Money Growth and Inflation," *Wall Street Journal,* May 17, 1978, p. 22.

[6] This particular question-begging is intrinsic to any theory that rests exclusively on time-and-place correlations between rates of inflation and rates of increase of (some kind of) aggregate demand. Being intrinsic, it can be observed in Friedman, *Friedman's Monetary Framework;* Friedman, "Japan and Inflation"; Fellner, "Introduction"; Clark, "Credit Squeeze"; Wachter and Williamson, "Obligational Markets"; and Meltzner, "Money Growth and Inflation."

when continued long enough, become integral parts of the functioning of the government, upon which widespread and politically powerful interests come to rely, and fiscal deficits and annual increases of the money supply have been regular parts of the functioning of the United States government since before the Second World War.[7] In the case of the money supply, even an increase in the established annual rate of increase is difficult to prevent. In the American banking system, monetary expansions are initiated by borrowers, who generally borrow in order to invest, directly or indirectly, in the maintenance or expansion of the country's production facilities. Such investment is the chief source of the country's increased employment and economic growth. So in order to slow or stop an increase in the rate of monetary expansion, the government must take affirmative steps that it knows will slow investment, and it knows that the slowing of investment will in turn increase unemployment and slow, stop, or reverse economic growth. Government decisions to increase demand, therefore, are in practice generally refusals or passive failures to slow ongoing processes that automatically increase demand; and the refusals or failures, for obvious reasons, are generally more politically popular than their opposites would be. It is small wonder that decisions to reduce the rate of increase of demand are rarely made and still more rarely carried out. It is small wonder, too, that so many of our more conservative economists, whose political beliefs make them suspicious of government anyway, have incorrectly concluded that the rapid expansions of aggregate demand are the principal cause of our inflation rather than the other way around.

Current versions of the demand-pull theory that include explanations are rare, and those explanations are not clear. I have had to compose the following explanation by inference from several sources.[8] The profit-maximization principle

[7] *Statistical Abstract of the United States* (1977), pp. 246–47, 518, 533; *Historical Statistics, Colonial Times to 1970,* series X (Washington, D.C.: U.S. Govt. Printing Office, 1975), pp. 410–17.

[8] Paul A. Samuelson, *Economics,* 9th ed. (New York: McGraw-Hill, 1973), pp. 826–31; John Sheahan, *The Wage-Price Guideposts* (Washing-

dictates that prices are generally at or near their profit-maximizing levels at all times. Once the percentage of capacity utilization gets high enough—say, 85 or 90 percent—marginal costs generally increase as capacity utilization increases. Since maximum profits are reached when marginal profits are zero, and marginal profits, by definition, equal marginal revenues less marginal costs, profit-maximizing levels for prices generally increase when capacity utilization increases, after capacity utilization has passed the point of 85 or 90 percent. An increase in aggregate demand increases capacity utilization if it occurs more rapidly than capacity is increasing—that is, more rapidly than new production facilities are being built. So if aggregate demand is increased rapidly enough to cause an increase in capacity utilization when capacity utilization is already as high as 85 or 90 percent, profit-maximizing price levels will generally rise, and actual prices will generally rise with them. There will be an inflation, and its cause will have been an excessively rapid rise in aggregate demand coming on top of an already high aggregate demand—"excess demand," in brief.

A refinement of this explanation is to concede that prices are not always set at precisely their profit-maximizing levels, but to insist that sellers are always trying to set them there. In particular, it is said, some sellers anticipate rising demand by setting their prices higher than their present profit-maximizing levels, in hopes that their timing will prove to be just right for "catching" demand on the way up with prices that will be profit-maximizing for the long term over which demand is expected to rise. This strategy is required, supposedly, by sellers whose prices cannot be changed quickly. It is supposedly used by labor unions, for example, whose members' wages are typically set by collective-bargaining contracts that typically last for two or three years and so freeze the wages for this length of time. When demand does rise as antic-

ton, D.C.: Brookings Institution, 1967), pp. 136–40; George Leland Bach, *The New Inflation: Causes, Effects, Cures* (Englewood Cliffs, N.J.: Prentice-Hall, 1973), pp. 39–48.

ipated, it is said to "validate" or "accommodate" these sellers' "expectations."[9] Rising demand is still the culprit, because if demand were not allowed to rise, supposedly, these price increasers would ultimately learn that their "expectations" of demand increase would not be "accommodated" or "validated," and they would stop increasing their prices.

A captivating aspect of these current versions of the demand-pull theory is their appearance of proving not just that excess demand can cause inflation, but that excess demand is *always* the cause of inflation, and its only cause. For if prices really are always at or near their profit-maximizing levels, give or take some time for anticipations or delays, it does indeed logically follow that the only reasonable explanation for their continuously rising is that aggregate demand is continuously rising more rapidly than aggregate supply. Any other explanation would contradict the profit-maximization principle. For many economists today, therefore, the problem of explaining a particular inflation reduces itself to finding the time or times in the past when the rate of demand increase was too high, and the problem of preventing inflation in the future reduces itself to devising a strategy of fiscal or monetary restraint, or both, that will prevent demand in the future

[9] Paul W. McCracken, "Is the U.S. now in Step?" *Wall Street Journal,* November 28, 1978, p. 22: Albert Rees, *The Economics of Trade Unions* (Chicago: University of Chicago Press, 1962), p. 101; Milton Friedman, "What Price Guideposts?" in George P. Shultz and Robert Z. Aliber, eds., *Guidelines: Informal Controls and the Market Place* (Chicago: University of Chicago Press, 1966), pp. 25–31; Jerry E. Pohlman, *Economics of Wage and Price Controls* (Columbus, Ohio: Grid, Inc., 1972), pp. 111–15; William Fellner, ed., *Contemporary Economic Problems* (Washington, D.C.: American Enterprise Institute for Public Policy Research, 1976), pp. 4–9; Anthony M. Santomero and John J. Seater, "The Inflation-Unemployment Trade-off: A Critique of the Literature," *Journal of Economic Literature* 16 (June 1978), 499–544; Michael L. Wachte and Susan M. Wachter, "Money Wage Inflation: The Endogeneity-Exogeneity Issues," in Sidney Weintraub, ed., *Modern Economic Thought* (Philadelphia: University of Pennsylvania Press, 1977), pp. 309–36; Phillip Cagan, "The Reduction in Inflation by Slack Demand," in Fellner, *Contemporary Economic Problems 1978,* pp. 13–45; Abba P. Lerner, "A Wage-Increase Permit Plan to Stop Inflation," in *Curing Chronic Inflation* (Washington, D.C.: Brookings Institution, 1978), pp. 255–69.

from increasing too fast.[10] Thus the theorists who have tried to provide explanations have tended to search for the same kinds of statistical correlations as have the nonexplanatory theorists, with the same lack of success.

A basic problem is that neither group of theorists knows what to look for. A theorist following the classical demand-pull theory would know exactly what to expect: evidence that, try as they might, producers were simply unable to increase production rapidly enough to keep pace with rising demand. A theorist following one of the nonexplanatory current versions of the theory, however, has nothing to guide him. He "simply looks." If he follows one of the explanatory current versions, he does not have much more to go on. One thing his theory tells him to look for is evidence that profit-maximizing prices are rising, but when there is inflation this will *always* be the case. Since inflation increases costs as well as prices, and profits are what is left after prices have been reduced by costs, inflation causes profit-maximizing prices to rise just as rapidly as actual prices rise. So the theorist's search in this respect will be circular. He will always find this supposed cause of inflation to be present, but as one of the inflation's effects. Another thing his theory tells him is that profit-maximizing prices are more likely to rise rapidly if capacity utilization is already high, so presumably he should look for evidence of high levels

[10] See Lindley H. Clark, Jr., "Makings of a Mess: The Present Inflation Traces Its Beginnings at Least back to 1946," *Wall Street Journal,* April 25, 1974, p. 1; George L. Perry, "Slowing the Wage-Price Spiral" in *Curing Chronic Inflation,* pp. 23–55; *Economic Report of the President* (February 1970), p. 6; Ezra Solomon, "How Can It Happen Here?" *Stanford Magazine* 2 (Spring/Summer 1974), 9, 13; Richard J. Levine, "U.S. Inflation Blamed on Attempts to Avoid Slumps," *Wall Street Journal,* June 19, 1971, pp. 1, 16; *Economic Report of the President,* Submitted to the Congress February 1971 (Washington, D.C.: U.S. Govt. Printing Office, 1971), p. 3; *Economic Report of the President,* Submitted to the Congress February 1975 (Washington, D.C.: U.S. Govt. Printing Office, 1974), pp. 19, 128–35; *Economic Report of the President,* Submitted to the Congress January 1976 (Washington, D.C.: U.S. Govt. Printing Office, 1976), pp. 20, 22; Friedman, "Japan and Inflation." This approach to the prevention of inflation is at least implicit in all demand-pull theorizing, but see especially McCracken, "Is the U.S. now in Step?" and Cagan, "The Reduction in Inflation."

of capacity utilization.[11] The facts, however, have time and again demonstrated that inflation occurs when capacity utilization is not high, and sometimes even increases when capacity utilization is already low and falling.[12]

Moreover, producers possess a large degree of control over the extent of their capacity utilization. They control the extent to which they will expand their facilities by making new investments in them, for example, and they control the extent to which they will work their employees overtime, hire new employees, or lay off some of their existing employees. An attempt to link inflation with changes in overall demand through capacity utilization, therefore, is likely to end by trying to "shoot shadows"—the illusive "shadows" of producers' and investors' subjective beliefs, expectations, commitments, and plans. When overall demand is rising, producers will expand their production facilities because they will be optimistic about future demand; and capacity utilization will fall if the rate of expansion is greater than the rate of rise. The same will happen even if overall demand is not rising but producers merely expect that it will. Or the opposite results will follow if demand is falling or not rising as rapidly as producers expected it would, or even if it is rising but producers expected it not to rise so rapidly, or to fall. Capacity utilization, in other words, is much too "soft" to serve as an objective determinant. It is too subject to influence by people's subjective hopes, fears, beliefs, commitments, and expectations to constitute a sound objective basis for analysis or prediction.[13]

Lacking any real guidance in what they ought to find,

[11] See, for example, Paul W. McCracken, "Our Unmysterious Inflation," *Wall Street Journal,* April 23, 1979, p. 18; Cagan, "The Reduction in Inflation." See also Sanford S. Parker, "Business Roundup, the Two-Trillion Dollar Economy," *Fortune* 96 (July 1977), 9–15; Ralph E. Winter, "Purchaser's Plight: More Executives Fear Potential Shortages if Economy Heats up," *Wall Street Journal,* August 6, 1976, p. 1.

[12] Cf. *Federal Reserve Bulletin* 56 (December 1970), A62 with *Statistical Abstract of the United States* (1978), p. 482 (inflation rates).

[13] See, for example, Ralph E. Winter, "Many Firms Step up Spending to Expand Productive Capacity," *Wall Street Journal,* June 11, 1979, pp. 1, 20.

today's demand-pull theorists, not surprisingly, have come up with widely varying results that they claim prove that the theory, or their version of the theory, is correct. Some have reached as far back as twenty-five years prior to an inflation for the excessive demand they claim to have been its initial cause.[14] Many write vaguely of inflationary "inertia" or "momentum" which, once begun, continues indefinitely,[15] or refer to excessive demand increases occurring anywhere from five years prior to or concurrently with the inflation they are supposed to have caused.[16] Still others produce graphs or statistical tables in which the time lapse that is supposed to be necessary or appropriate is entirely blurred: price levels are shown to have been generally increasing at the same time as some kind of demand (money supply, for example) has been generally increasing, both over a period of several years.[17] In no case of which I am aware has anyone succeeded in relating a demand increase with a price-level increase in an exact, quantitative way. Milton Friedman has at least quantified the rate of demand increase that he considers the most that can occur over the long run without creating an excessive demand, but he apparently has no way of proving this to be the case, and he does not venture to predict how much inflation will follow from how much of a demand increase in excess of that which he prescribes.[18] Thus the attempts to extend the demand-pull theory beyond its sound classical base have all ended by being circular. Inflation is blamed on excess demand, and excess demand is identified as whatever rate of de-

[14] Clark, "Makings of a Mess."

[15] Perry, "Slowing the Wage-Price Spiral"; *Economic Report of the President* (February 1970), p. 6; Solomon, "How Can It Happen Here?"; Levine, "U.S. Inflation Blamed."

[16] See, for example, *Economic Report of the President* (February 1971), p. 3; *Economic Report of the President* (February 1975), pp. 19, 128–35; *Economic Report of the President* (January 1976), pp. 20, 22.

[17] See, for example, Friedman, "Japan and Inflation." The years covered in this case are 1971 to 1978, which of course included the worldwide food shortage of 1974 and the quadrupling of world oil prices in 1973–74. Neither development was noted in this "proof" that excessive money supply is the cause of inflation.

[18] See ibid.

mand increase, at whatever time or times, preceded or accompanied any amount of inflation.

Most of the reasons why the explanatory current versions of the demand-pull theory are incorrect can be extracted from Chapters 1 to 5. These theories, remember, assume that actual prices are profit-maximizing prices, give or take some anticipations or delays. But actual prices in a modern economy are not profit-maximizing, as was explained in Chapter 4, primarily because they are so frequently set through pricing institutions, as was explained in Chapter 3. These theories also implicitly assume that all the actual prices in a market can be profit-maximizing and stable at the same time. Chapter 2 explained why this is no longer generally true. The theories also assume that price competition effectively keeps a lid on actual prices in the absence of excess demand, whereas Chapter 1 explained why the emergence of a variety of effective nonprice forms of competition has made this no longer generally true. An error in the validation, accommodation, and inflationary-expectations versions in particular is the assumption that sellers generally need an increase in demand in order to increase their profits by price increases. In fact, since most products and most kinds of labor today compose only small parts of much larger wholes, or are considered necessary by their purchasers almost without regard to price, most sellers' profits today can *always* be increased by increasing prices, whether or not there are concurrent or following increases in demand. This condition was explained and described in both Chapters 3 and 5.

Moreover, as was also explained in Chapters 3 and 5, the impact of a change in aggregate demand upon a seller in a modern economy is generally much less than it would have to be to have the disciplining effects that the demand-pull theories suppose. A reduction in aggregate demand reduces people's incomes and profits—the total amounts which they can spend. But the price-disciplining effects of demand, when they work at all, work almost entirely through the difference between what the individual demands for a seller's goods are at his present prices and what they would be at higher prices. These differences are hardly affected by changes in the aggregate demand level at all. If a seller would find a price increase profitable at one aggregate demand level, he would generally find the same increase just as profitable at a lower (or higher) aggregate demand level. So reductions in aggregate demand, contrary to the theories' suppositions, generally leave sellers just as likely to make price increases as they were before. Finally, the observed correlations between inflation and increasing demand that seem to support the demand-pull theories even today are actually evidence of a cause-and-effect relationship working for the most part, although not entirely, the other way, as was explained in Chapter 5. All in all, it is difficult to avoid concluding that the contemporary versions of the classical demand-pull theory either dispense with explanations or are unclear because, consciously or unconsciously, their designers fear that they are wrong.

Another way of seeing why the various demand-pull explanations of today's inflation are false is to see that they include what economists call the fallacy of overlooking the "free rider problem."[19] The free rider problem is what ordinarily inhibits the voluntary financing of a public good. A public good is something that benefits people without regard to whether they pay for it. Examples are public parks, highways, landscapes, radio and television broadcasting, and national defense. Suppose that a public radio station (that is, one that does not accept paid advertising) were to seek to support itself entirely from the voluntary contributions of its listeners. It would ordinarily fail, because too many listeners would figure that they could listen without paying—they would choose to be "free riders" on the payments made by others. Ordinarily, therefore, the station would not receive enough contributions to keep going. And if it did succeed, it would almost certainly have obtained them unfairly. Many people would be paying a

[19] Paul A. Samuelson, "The Pure Theory of Public Expenditure," *Review of Economics and Statistics* (1954), pp. 387–89.

lot more than others while receiving the same or even fewer benefits. The free rider problem leads to the conclusions that public goods ordinarily have to be financed by nonvoluntary means in order to be financed effectively, and that they should be financed nonvoluntarily in order that the burdens of their financing be distributed fairly.

A reduction in the inflation rate is a public good. It benefits everyone regardless of whether he has helped to pay for it by reducing his own rate of price (or wage) increasing. The demand-pull theories implicitly assume that the free rider problem can be overcome by reductions in aggregate demand, which, they assume, compel everyone to reduce his own rate of price increasing. A reduction in aggregate demand is thus supposedly like a tax on listening to a particular public radio station, a tax that a listener would have to pay whether or not he wanted to. But the assumption about the compelling effect of a reduction in aggregate demand is incorrect. For all the reasons set forth in Chapters 1 through 4, even when aggregate demand is reduced it generally remains profitable for sellers to continue increasing their prices. And for the reasons set forth in Chapter 5 (competitive inflation), it generally remains necessary for some sellers to continue increasing their prices merely to keep from incurring losses. The firms in an industry that have had to pay a large wage increase in order to avoid or terminate a strike, for example, may have to raise their prices merely in order to avoid incurring losses, regardless of whether the demand for their products has fallen. Indeed, the falling demand may make a price increase even more necessary, if by lowering capacity utilization it raises unit costs of production. Since the assumption that an aggregate demand reduction will compel everyone to reduce his rate of price increasing is incorrect, the demand-pull theories are left simply as observations that *if* everyone reduced his own rate of price increasing voluntarily, everyone would benefit from the reduced inflation. This is true; but not everyone will do this voluntarily—not by a long shot—because of the free rider problem, and in any event their doing it voluntarily is not made more likely by a decrease in aggregate demand.

The Public Harm Caused by Demand-Pull Theories

An incorrect theory of inflation is always harmful in that it stands in the way of controlling inflation, which the government presumably would do if it were guided by a correct theory. The current versions of the demand-pull theory have in addition inflicted the harms associated with chronically low levels of aggregate demand. With essentially only one brief exception—the two years when it was preparing to enlarge the Vietnam War—the United States government has deliberately kept aggregate demand too low since the end of the Korean War, in the belief that it was thereby preventing worse inflation. The result has been decades of slow and sometimes negative economic growth and generally increasing unemployment. Policies of low aggregate demand are made especially damaging by the elusiveness of the goal of low aggregate demand, which in practice usually means a low percentage of capacity utilization. However low the government manages to drive aggregate demand, investors, by declining to invest, can always drive production capacity still lower, so that the government's goal, if it is less than investors generally consider appropriate, will never be reached for any length of time.[20]

Suppose, for example, that the government aims for a percentage rate of 82, believing that anything above this is inflationary, but that investors decline to invest in new facilities so long as, say, only 85 percent of the existing capacity is being used. If the government then manages to reduce the rate below 85 in its attempt to reach its target of 82, investors' refusals to invest will reduce the amount of capacity just as rapidly as existing facilities wear out and are not replaced, so that the rate of utilization will then rise again unless the government reduces aggregate demand even further. Such a contest has no end short of the elimination of all production capacity,

[20] David P. Garino, "Cautious Companies; Firms Like Monsanto Give Capital Projects Tough Second Looks," *Wall Street Journal,* December 30, 1976, p. 1; Ralph E. Winter, "Playing It Safe: Capital Expenditures Pick up," *Wall Street Journal,* December 22, 1976, p. 1.

since the government has no means of compelling investors to invest if they do not choose to. In practice the contest has no end. Goaded by its advisers' never-proven belief that excess demand is the basic cause of all inflation, the federal government continually chases the receding target of a low utilization of production capacity, with the result that the national economy is continually maintained in recession or near-recession conditions.

Others besides private investors also act so as to reduce production capacity when the federal government lowers demand. State and local governments reduce the rates of investment in new production facilities of the utilities (electric power, natural gas, telephone) that they regulate and of the capital programs (roads, public buildings) that they administer, for the same reason that private investors reduce their rates of investment—the governments, too, foresee less demand. State and local governments have the additional reason for cutting back that they anticipate lower tax revenues as a result of the federal government's lowering of demand. Parts of the federal government itself are also likely to reduce production capacity. The Department of Agriculture is likely to reduce the supplies of crops when it has reason to expect a lower demand for them. Federal regulatory agencies are likely to reduce the investment rates of the utilities they regulate, just as the state and local regulatory agencies are likely to reduce theirs. Labor unions and professional organizations are likely to react to the lowering of aggregate demand by lowering the supplies of the kinds of labor they control. They can restrict new membership, charge high initial or recurring membership fees, and ration the available jobs on the basis of seniority.[21] Apprenticeship programs can be made long or arduous. The right to practice a trade or profession can be made conditional on being licensed, and licenses can be made difficult to obtain.[22] Professional organizations, if not labor unions, can use their influence to limit the numbers and sizes

[21] Rees, *Economics of Trade Unions,* pp. 121–29, 151–58.

[22] Walter Gellhorn and Clark Byse, *Administrative Law: Cases and Comments,* 6th ed. (St. Paul, Minn.: Foundation Press, 1974), pp. 707–709.

of the schools that educate their new members.[23] Finally, supplies of all the categories of labor that gain their skills principally from on-the-job-training—everything from corporation executive positions to slightly skilled farm, factory, or clerical jobs—can also be reduced as employers reduce the number of new employees they hire.

The end result of long-continued policies of low aggregate demand is thus to reduce the nation's productive capacity in every respect except unskilled labor, whose supply no organization or institution controls. Unskilled labor becomes relatively surplus to everything else, which is another way of saying that the unskilled become unemployed.[24] In the "Business Roundup" section of its July 1977 issue, *Fortune* magazine enthusiastically predicted that the national economy would "virtually . . . complete its full recovery over the next eighteen months." It went on to say that capacity utilization would be back up to the 1973 level (which was 86 percent, the highest in some time), real gross national product would have expanded by 8 percent, and unemployment would have fallen to about 6 percent, which *Fortune* characterized as "approaching full utilization of the nation's manpower."[25] It is worth noting in passing *Fortune*'s apparent inability to see people as other than a production resource, which, of course, makes their 94 percent utilization look pretty good. The principal point I want to make, however, is the gross imbalance between labor and physical resources that has come to exist in our economy. Our long-continued low-demand policies have gotten us into a position in which even if our physical resources are virtually fully utilized, about 6 percent of our labor force—even by the very conservative official measure,[26] which is what *Fortune* was using—are still unemployed.

[23] "Undergraduate Medical Education," *Journal of the American Medical Association,* December 27, 1976, p. 2961.

[24] Paul O. Flaim, "Discouraged Workers and Changes in Unemployment," *Monthly Labor Review* 96 (March 1973), 10–13; Bertram M. Gross and Stanley Moses, "Measuring the Real Work Force: 25 Million Unemployed," *Social Policy* 3 (September/October 1972), pp. 5–10.

[25] Parker, "Business Roundup"; and see Winter, "Purchaser's Plight."

[26] Laurie Cohen, "Missing Numbers in the Census," *Wall Street Journal,* August 31, 1976, p. 10; Robert Lekachman, *Economists at Bay: Why*

The final irony is that not even this chronic surplus of labor has any appreciable effect of holding down prices (the prices of labor, that is, wages). Because of its makeup, the pool of chronically unemployed does not offer real alternatives to most employers. This is most obvious in the case of the most highly skilled occupations. If there is a shortage of physicians, engineers, or high-level corporation managers, the chances are still slim that many new ones can be found by searching the unemployment rolls or by looking into the nation's skid rows and ghettoes. It is less obvious but still generally the case for far less skilled occupations. People who have not had dignified, useful work for a substantial period generally become unfit for any work that requires even a modicum of discipline and application. They tend to be badly deficient even in such simple matters as getting to work on time or working all the days of the week they are supposed to.[27]

There is no way of knowing how much potential wealth we have lost through the slowed growth that results from low rates of increase of demand, but it must be enormous. If, as *Fortune* says, 86 percent capacity utilization is about as high as the national average can be before true demand-pull inflation will start up, and the average over the years has been only about 82 percent in fact,[28] the difference compounded amounts to more than 250 percent in twenty-five years—an *annual* loss of more than two and a half times our present total production capacity! But this is the least that it must be. Had investors been able to rely upon a strong, steady rate of demand increase, instead of being continually at risk that an inflation scare would cause the administration in office to reduce the rate, investment would surely have been much more than it was. The additional investment would have provided addi-

the Experts Will Never Solve Your Problems (New York: McGraw-Hill, 1973), p. 73.

[27] Anthony M. Alfano, "A Scale to Measure Attitudes toward Working," *Journal of Vocational Behavior* 3 (July 1973), 329–33; Jack Feldman, "Race, Economic Class and the Intention to Work: Some Normative and Attitudinal Correlations," *Journal of Applied Psychology* 59 (1974), 179–86.

[28] *Statistical Abstract of the United States* (1977), pp. 794–95.

tional capacity, and an 86 percent utilization of a larger capacity would of course have been more than the 82 percent utilization of the lower capacity that existed in fact. On top of all this should be added the substantial annual increase in productivity that would have resulted had labor union leaders and working people generally not feared that increased productivity would cost them or their coworkers their jobs. One should also add the increased productivity that would have resulted from the work of people who are presently in the ranks of the chronically unemployed or underemployed, who by all indications would have applied themselves more industriously in school and elsewhere to become productive members of society had they had any reasonable hope of getting and keeping decent jobs.[29] Finally, our environment would be in much better condition than it is. A major obstacle in the way of requiring industry not to spoil the environment has been the worry that the additional expense would deter economic expansion and cost people their jobs.[30]

Federal administrations have sought to avoid the depressing effects on investment of low aggregate demand by offering special tax incentives. By what was originally called "the 7 percent investment credit," a business is given a credit against its federal income tax for investments in depreciable production facilities.[31] By the capital-gains provisions in the federal income tax code, investors of all kinds are given especially low rates for profits they make on sales of investments that have appreciated in value.[32] But these and many other tax incentives have little effect on investment that is low because investors do not foresee sufficient demand. A tax incen-

[29] Herbert G. Gutman, *The Black Family in Slavery and Freedom* (New York: Pantheon, 1976); Leonard Goodwin, *A Social-Psychological Study of Work Orientations* (Washington, D.C.: Brookings Institution, 1977). And see Alfano, "A Scale to Measure Attitudes"; Feldman, "Race, Economic Class and the Intention to Work."

[30] Eckardt C. Beck, "Ending Pollution Blackmail," *New York Times*, May 8, 1978, p. A-19.

[31] 26 U.S.C. 46, as amended, §2 (b), 76 Stat. 963 (1962).

[32] Louis Eisenstein, *The Ideologies of Taxation* (New York: Ronald Press Co., 1961), pp. 95–105.

tive is of no value unless there are profits to be taxed. Investors who foresee insufficient demand are likely to see a substantial risk that their new capacity will not provide any profits.[33]

Cost-Push and Wage-Push Theories of Inflation

The other distinct group of theories about contemporary inflation are generally referred to as "cost-push" or "wage-push." In their simplest forms they are essentially no more than observations that when prices that are also costs go up, the sellers whose costs have risen are encouraged or compelled to raise their prices. Hence, "cost-push." If it is also observed that the economically most important price that is also a cost is wages, the theory is likely to be called "wage-push."[34] The theories that go no further than this are hardly theories at all, since they really say no more than that inflation consists of some prices going up before others. The wage-push label, moreover, is unfair. It could just as logically be said that wage earners' costs go up—the costs of the things they buy, from groceries to automobiles to housing—and that this pushes wages up. The name for the theory that made this observation would presumably be "price-push," and it would, with equal unfairness, place the blame on farmers and businesses, and make wage earners appear to be the innocent victims.

The more sophisticated theories of this kind go on to place the blame for prices rising more than is justified by underlying cost increases on the sellers' monopoly powers. This is an unarguable but not very helpful conclusion, since monopoly power means the power to increase prices.[35] The theories that go on still further generally end by making essentially the

[33] Bob Arnold, "Taxing Debate: Investment Credit Rise Has Had Little Impact on Economy So Far," *Wall Street Journal*, August 11, 1976, p. 1. See also Garino, "Cautious Companies"; Winter, "Playing It Safe."

[34] John M. Blair, *The Roots of Inflation* (New York: Burt Franklin & Co., 1975); Bach, *The New Inflation*, pp. 7, 69; Pohlman, *Economics of Wage and Price Control*, pp. 111–15.

[35] Samuelson, *Economics*, p. 483.

same demand-pull "validation," "accommodation," or "expectations" arguments as were summarized earlier. An additional weakness in the "push" theories is their failure to confront the difficult issues posed by wage and price controls. To claim that wage and price controls are unnecessary, as some such theories do, is inconsistent with blaming monopoly power for inflation.[36] On the other hand, to urge the adoption of wage and price controls on a permanent basis, even just for portions of the economy, is not quite logical either, unless the theory goes on to explain how the controls could be made simultaneously fair, economically efficient, and administrable. Merely pointing out that they have worked in wartime is not sufficient.[37] The civilian part of the economy hardly changes during a war, so such controls are much easier to administer then, and war psychology makes people generally more tolerant of unfairness and inefficiency. Moreover, during a war it is only the efficiency of the defense sector of the economy that is of real importance.

A Demand-Pull Theory for Modern Use

The classical demand-pull theory of inflation is sound. The kind of inflation it describes is still a regular occurrence in some parts of the world, and is still possible everywhere. However, the problem of identifying true demand-pull inflation has been complicated by the omnipresence of indeterminate inflation in its many forms. A test to identify any true demand-pull inflation that might be present is to see whether, if prices were not rising so rapidly, there would be *severe, widespread, and enduring shortages.* If there would be, and only if there would be, must there be demand-pull inflation present, and it must be present in those sectors of the economy, and

[36] See, for example, Hendrik S. Houthakker, "A Positive Way to Fight Inflation." *Wall Street Journal,* July 30, 1974, p. 12.

[37] See "Phase IV," Hearings before the Committee on Banking, Housing and Urban Affairs, United States Senate, 93d Congress, 1st Session (1973), pp. 2–8 (testimony of John Kenneth Galbraith).

only in those sectors, in which the shortages of this nature would appear.

It might seem that even mild, occasional, or temporary shortages would suffice, but they would not, because sellers have practical ways, other than continually raising prices, of dealing with them, and it is only continually rising prices that constitute inflation. Mild, occasional, or temporary shortages are a normal part of a modern economy. Most retail furniture stores, for example, carry only one of any large item, for display. Some of them will sell the display item if a buyer wants it, but most buyers, of course, will not want precisely the color, the fabric, or the size of the display item, and they may want it in a set that includes more items than are displayed. It is routine in the retail furniture business to have a buyer order what he wants and then wait anywhere from a week to a year for the factory to produce it or to locate it in a centrally located warehouse and ship it to him. There is a "shortage" of the item, but this is not a reason for increasing its price. Similar "shortages" routinely exist in most manufacturers' supply industries—metals, chemicals, and so on. Buyers and sellers alike understand that for prompt, assured delivery, a buyer must ordinarily order well in advance. There is usually also a "spot" market for quick delivery, but its prices are ordinarily higher and are not considered to be the usual prices, and it usually cannot supply large orders.[38] There are also many situations in which shortages are not an ordinary part of the business but nevertheless do not occasion price increases, because they are expected to be only temporary. When a newsstand runs down to its last few copies of a newspaper or magazine, it does not ordinarily increase the price. When a theater sees that it is about to sell out for a performance, it does not ordinarily increase the prices of the remaining seats. Manufacturers' supply industries behave similarly. They usually deal with temporary shortages by allocating the available supplies to their good customers, but not by increasing the

[38] See, for example, Eleanore Carruth, "The Nervous Capital Boom in Chemicals," *Fortune* 93 (February 1976), 98; Lewis Beman, "Why Business Ran out of Capacity," *Fortune* 89 (May 1974), 262.

prices.[39] The sellers' motivations are presumably similar in all these cases. They calculate that they would lose more patronage from ill will, in the long run, by raising prices than the profits from the higher prices would be worth to them.

The shortages that would appear if prices were not rising so rapidly would have to be widespread if the inflation is to be characterized as demand-pull, because if they were not they could be made to disappear again (or prevented in the first place) merely by shifting resources to the sectors in which there is shortage from those in which goods were relatively plentiful or in which production capacity was not being fully utilized. This kind of resource shifting may require government help, especially if capacity is almost fully utilized throughout the economy as a whole, but it has been done successfully in other countries—in Sweden, for example.[40] If the shortages are not widespread but nevertheless resist elimination by shifting resources, the chances are that the sellers concerned are maintaining the shortages deliberately. Diamonds have been artifically kept in short supply for generations by an international cartel in order to maintain their prices, for example. The federal government had a suit against the American Medical Association alleging that the association had done the same, for the same reason, for physicians.[41] The high or rising prices that result from shortages such as these are impervious to reduction by reductions in the rate of increase of aggregate demand, because the sellers concerned can reduce the supply to match, as was explained earlier.[42]

[39] Carruth, "The Nervous Capital Boom," and Beman, "Why Business Ran out," refer to this kind of allocation. See also John Kenneth Galbraith, *A Theory of Price Control* (Cambridge: Harvard University Press, 1952), pp. 10–12. My own interviews with industry executives also confirmed this.

[40] Assar Lindbeck, *Swedish Economic Policy* (Berkeley and Los Angeles: University of California Press, 1974), pp. 77–81, 97–107, 156–57, 184–94.

[41] Cheryl M. Fields, "AMA Promises to 'Battle' for Accrediting Role," *Chronicle of Higher Education,* February 14, 1977, p. 9. See also Milton Friedman and Simon Kuznets, *Income From Independent Professional Practice* (New York: National Bureau of Economic Research, 1945).

[42] See Chapter 3 ("supply institutions").

Application of the proposed test to the United States yields the perhaps surprising conclusion that there has been *no* demand-pull inflation here since the Korean War. Even the shortages of the mid-sixties occasioned by the expansion for the Vietnam War were not widespread or more than temporary.[43] To the extent that excess demand was truly responsible for any price increases then, that responsibility soon passed, and if the sellers concerned had not had other means of raising and maintaining prices, their prices would have fallen—which, in general, they did not. The very few prices that did fall when demand fell after this period had presumably risen temporarily as a result of excess demand, but the small amount of inflation they then constituted was canceled by the deflation they constituted later. The long absence of demand-pull inflation has undoubtedly been a result of our long-standing low-demand economic policies, which have been much more than sufficient for avoiding true demand-pull inflation. Application of the test to Sweden, on the other hand, demonstrates the existence of some demand-pull inflation during the post-World War II period. Sweden did experience widespread, severe, and enduring shortages or threatened shortages of skilled labor in particular, and it experienced what its economists called "wage creep" or "wage drift." Sweden apparently incurred this kind and amount of demand-pull inflation deliberately, in order to benefit from the rapid growth and high employment that came with it.[44]

Not even Latin American inflations are as fully caused by demand-pull as we have assumed. After years of inflation rates in the neighborhood of 200 percent, Chile increased the efficiency of its tax collection system and decreased its governmental expenditures so as to achieve a nearly balanced budget. The result was a massive increase in unemployment and only a 50 percent decrease in inflation.[45] In 1976 Mexico abol-

[43] *Statistical Abstract of the United States* (1977), pp. 794–95.

[44] Lindbeck, *Swedish Economic Policy,* pp. 19–20, 151–56.

[45] Everett G. Martin, "Bitter Medicine: Despite the Suffering, Chile Induces a Slump to Cure High Inflation," *Wall Street Journal,* November 4, 1975, p. 1.

ished its official exchange rate for the peso and let it float. The value of the peso dropped about 40 percent, as expected, but quite unexpectedly merchants throughout Mexico raised their prices on the order of 50 to 100 percent, even when their goods were not imported and they had no other costs affected by the peso's exchange rate.[46] It seems reasonable to conclude that Mexico's previous inflation was not all caused by excess demand either.

Conclusion

The classical demand-pull theory is sound, and with slight modification fit for current use. It is needed as an "alert signal" against demand-pull inflation, which is still a possiblity, although the application of the test shows it to have been rare in modern economies in recent years. The current versions of the demand-pull theory and the various cost-push or wage-push theories, however, are of no use because they are basically wrong. They all rest, at some point, on the assumption that all inflation is caused—that all inflation is initiated, maintained, or at least "accommodated" or "validated"—by excessive demand; and this assumption is false. These current versions of the demand-pull theory have in fact been very harmful. They have led the United States, in particular, to adopt economic policies that have substantially increased unemployment and caused us to lose enormous sums of potential wealth.

[46] Richard A. Shaffer, "Mexico: More Troubles ahead," *Wall Street Journal,* November 23, 1976, p. 24; "Mexico Closes 500 Shops, Stores for Raising Prices," *Los Angeles Times,* September 8, 1976, p. 1.

PART II

The Need for a New Economics

I have already defined what I mean by economic determinism: the belief that economic behavior is determined by the objective conditions under which it occurs.[1] Traditional economists are practically all economic determinists, whether they are aware of it or not. They have to be, or they would not be economists, as economists think of themselves. Almost all economics literature, from the elementary textbooks to the most advanced works published in professional journals, speaks in terms of the determinants of economic behavior. This literature is concerned with little else than proposing, explaining, testing, or searching for laws, theories, or "models" that purport to describe how economic behavior is determined by the objective conditions under which it occurs. It is this most basic assumption of economics that underlies economists' inability to understand the new inflation; and, as I will show in this part, it is to blame for many other things that have gone wrong with economics in recent years. The fact is, economic behavior is not determined, and modern economic conditions have freed it so much from the factors that used to constrain it (although they never really determined it), that determinism

[1] See the Introduction. The evidence that economic determinism underlies traditional economics is overwhelming. It extends from Adam Smith (see Andrew S. Skinner, "Introduction" in Adam Smith, *The Wealth of Nations,* Books 1–3 [Harmondsworth: Penguin Books, 1974], p. 12), to the present day (see Paul A. Samuelson, *Economics,* 9th ed. [New York: McGraw-Hill, 1973], pp. 220, 234), and from the most orthodox (see Samuelson, *Economics,* pp. 220, 234), to the most innovative (see Alfred S. Eichner, ed., *A Guide to Post-Keynesian Economics* [White Plains, N.Y.: M. E. Sharpe, 1979], pp. 11–12, 14–15, 24–42, 51–60).

When economists today talk about economic determinism they generally use the term "science" or "economic science." See, for example, Robert Aaron Gordon, "Rigor and Relevance in a Changing Institutional Setting," *Amer. Econ. Rev.* 66 (March 1976), 1, 2, and passim; Paul A. Samuelson, "Milton Friedman," *Newsweek,* October 25, 1976, p. 89; Paul A. Samuelson, *Foundations of Economic Analysis* (New York: Atheneum, 1947), pp. 1–20, 257–58; and Gunnar Myrdal, *Against the Stream: Critical Essays on Economics* (New York: Vintage Books, 1975), pp. 1–16, 141–47.

has in recent decades ceased to be even a good approximation.

Part I showed the extent to which prices are not determined by market forces in our economy, and how this lack of determination permits the inflation we now have. Part II will identify the sources of economic determinism, both historical and ideological. It will describe the harm that economic determinism has inflicted and continues to inflict, in addition to preventing our understanding the new inflation. And it will give the outlines of a new, nondeterministic economics, into which our present economics ought to be transformed.

Economic determinism logically entails two other beliefs—economic materialism and economic positivism—that will also be treated in this part. Economic materialism is the belief that economic behavior consists entirely of material things or, at least, that it consists of material things in its operative parts. It is obvious, I think, why this belief and economic determinism are linked. The objective things that a determinist believes determine economic behavior are material. "Objective" means "material," as these terms are here used. And these things must determine the behavior if, as a materialist believes, the behavior consists of them and nothing else. Economic positivism is the belief that one can learn the truth about economic behavior by observing only its objective, or material, parts, and that the truth or falsity of the statements one makes are to be ascertained exclusively by objective tests. It is also obvious why economic positivism and economic determinism are linked. If economic behavior were indeed determined by objective things, of course one could learn the truth about it by observing just its objective parts, because these parts would include everything that determined it. And one's statements about it could be proven right or wrong by objective tests.[2] In the vocabulary of positivism, statements

[2] See, for example, Milton Friedman, "The Methodology of Positive Economics," in *Essays in Positive Economics* (Chicago: University of Chicago Press, 1953), pp. 3–43; Lawrence A. Boland, "A Critique of Friedman's Critics," *Journal of Economic Literature* 17 (June 1979), 503–22; Gordon, "Rigor and Relevance," pp. 1, 2, and passim. Since, as the text says, economic positivism is a logical corollary of economic determinism, the citations in note 1 above support the statement that traditional economics is positivistic.

are commonly classified as either "positive" or "normative,"[3] or as either "objective" or "subjective,"[4] with the first term in either pair meaning the kind of statement that is capable of objective test. A "normative" statement is not capable of objective test because it is an opinion about what ought to be. A "subjective" statement is not capable of objective test because it is just a person's opinion. It can be true that a person holds a certain opinion, of course, whether the opinion is true or not.

[3] Friedman, "Methodology," pp. 3–43.
[4] Boland, "A Critique," pp. 503–22.

CHAPTER 7

The Sources of Economic Determinism

If the determinism of our economics has prevented us from understanding indeterminate inflation, why haven't we rejected the determinism? If not a single accurate deterministic law of economics has been discovered despite some two hundred years of trying, why haven't we long since rejected the determinism? Our economics, it turns out, remains deterministic for essentially three reasons. It was founded this way by Adam Smith, and ideas that are basic to a discipline are very slow to change. Economic determinism has always been a part of a larger intellectual milieu in which each belief gives and gains support from the rest. And economic determinism has served some important personal, social, and political purposes—not the least of them the furthering of the scientific aspirations of economists themselves. This chapter will elaborate on these reasons, as well as describe the forces in opposition to economic determinism.

Intellectual Origins

Economics as we know it began in 1776 with the publication of Adam Smith's *An Inquiry into the Nature and Causes of the Wealth of Nations.* Economic determinism began at the same time.[1] Smith said in *The Wealth of Nations* that economic behavior is guided "as with an invisible hand." However, he had said in his *The Theory of Moral Sentiments,* first published in 1759, that *all* human behavior is guided "as with

[1] Peter Stein, "Adam Smith's Jurisprudence—Between Morality and Economics," *Cornell Law Rev.* 64 (1979), 621, 622.

an invisible hand."[2] He therefore apparently attached no special significance to the fact, as he saw it, that economic behavior was determined. He presumably would have attributed the Scots' regularly taking Saturday night baths to "an invisible hand," if this indeed is what they did at the time. The sense of accomplishment that is evident in *The Wealth of Nations* must have arisen from his having thought he had discovered the *means* by which the "invisible hand" worked in economic affairs, which is something he never claimed to have discovered for human affairs of other kinds. The means, of course, was the market.[3]

Smith was also a materialist and a positivist before he published *The Wealth of Nations.* The group of Scottish thinkers to which he belonged thought that virtually everything was objective. Pain, pleasure, happiness, and every other human sentiment were supposedly measurable, just as were physical things that had sizes, numbers, and weights.[4] So when he wrote in *The Wealth of Nations* of the supposedly universal desire for "gain" or "profit," for example, he must have assumed that this desire was objectively observable and quantitatively measurable as well.

Smith thus viewed economic behavior as essentially no different from other kinds of behavior. He was a determinist, a materialist, and a positivist with respect to them all. This uniformity of his views also answers the question that many intellectual historians have posed of how the Adam Smith, who drew the apparently materialistic and amoral conclusions of *The Wealth of Nations,* could have been the same man who wrote *The Theory of Moral Sentiments.*[5] The answer is that he

[2] Adam Smith, *An Inquiry into the Nature and Causes of the Wealth of Nations,* Book 4, pt. 3; *The Theory of Moral Sentiments,* Book 4, pt. 1.

[3] Smith, *Wealth of Nations;* and see Fred R. Glahe, ed., *Adam Smith and the Wealth of Nations—1776-1976—Bicentennial Essays* (Boulder: Colorado Associated Universities Press, 1978), pp. 114–18.

[4] Garry Wills, *Inventing America—Jefferson's Declaration of Independence* (Garden City: Doubleday & Co., 1978), pp. 132–48; E. S. Morgan, "The Heart of Jefferson," *New York Review of Books,* August 17, 1978, p. 38 (review of Wills, *Inventing America*).

[5] Stein, "Adam Smith's Jurisprudence."

saw no inconsistencies between what seem to us today to be quite different things.

The group of thinkers to which Smith belonged were presumably influenced in their determinism by their admiration for Isaac Newton[6] and by their agreement with Francis Bacon that the epistemological premises and methodologies that Newton had used so brilliantly for the study of inanimate things could be equally successfully applied to the study of society.[7] Smith was able to carry his admiration for Newton even into the terms he chose to describe how he thought economic behavior was determined. An "invisible hand" is a metaphor that connotes a physical force. Had Smith wished instead to describe a kind of determination that worked solely or primarily through the mind, he would presumably have chosen a quite different metaphor, such as an "interior voice" or, perhaps, a hand that could be seen to "point the way" instead of one that invisibly pushed. At another place in *The Wealth of Nations,* he described markets as "machines" and the economics that he was setting forth as like "an imaginary machine."[8] Economists today still talk in mechanistic terms and in terms of force.[9]

Empirical Origins

When Adam Smith described the market forces that supposedly determine economic behavior, the world he saw really did function much as he described it. Each of the conditions described in Chapters 1 to 4 that operate to free prices from determination by market forces either did not operate then, or only did so weakly. Sellers did not have any effective way of

[6] Isaiah Berlin, *Vico and Herder: Two Studies in the History of Ideas* (New York: Viking, 1976); see also Jack Beatty, "Intellectual Portraits," *Commentary* 62 (November 1976), 86–91.

[7] Andrew S. Skinner, "Introduction" in Smith, *The Wealth of Nations,* Books 1–3 (Harmondsworth: Penguin Books, 1974), p. 12.

[8] Ibid., p. 15.

[9] Frank H. Knight, *On the History and Methods of Economics* (Chicago: University of Chicago Press, 1956), p. 180.

competing with one another except by lowering their prices. There was no television, no radio, and no widely distributed newspapers or magazines with attractive colored advertisements. There were no large chains or franchised retail establishments. Most of the goods that most people purchased were simple and not available in a wide variety; the relative worths of most goods could be assessed closely enough by the people who purchased them that they could make the proper price comparisons before they bought. Sellers had not generally learned how to create and operate pricing institutions at the retail, wholesale, or manufacturing levels. Effective labor unions were rare. When they existed they still could not raise their members' wages without limit, because employers were severely limited in their ability to pass on wage increases by increasing prices. Government pricing institutions were also rare, and the goods and services they covered were not of large importance. There were no government agricultural price-support programs, for example. Tariffs on imported goods were not uncommon,[10] but these by themselves cannot constitute effective pricing institutions because they do nothing to prevent price competition among domestic producers.

The dictates of profit maximizing were generally easy to understand and easy to follow. Since businesses were small, the person who made the pricing decisions was usually also the person who stood to gain or lose from them, and he was also in a position to make them face-to-face with the individual buyer. Since the same person did not have any effective nonprice forms of competition available, did not have goods to sell whose worth his buyers did not understand, and was not a member of an effective pricing institution, he also did not have to take into account any of these complicating factors when setting his prices. Finally, since most people then lived much nearer the subsistence level than they do now, there was rarely any doubt that by lowering prices a seller, or a whole industry, could increase his, or its, sales. If the price of bread were lowered, for example, people would almost surely

[10] Smith, *Wealth of Nations,* Book 1, Ch. X, pt. 2.

buy more of it, because they were hungry. They usually limited their bread purchases to the amount they could afford, not to the amount that kept them satisfied.[11] So conditions in Smith's time did closely approximate the ideal conditions that would produce "market forces" that would operate the way traditional economics says they do.

Viewing economic behavior from the standpoint of a historian also seems to provide some factual confirmation for economic determinism in the eighteenth and nineteenth centuries. Economic histories of the United States show that objective events and conditions such as the opening of the West, the invention of steam-powered rail and water transportation, rises and declines in the world's stocks of gold, the discovery of gold and silver in the United States and Alaska, rises and declines in the supply of paper money, droughts, crop failures, and crop surpluses had clearly discernible economic consequences. A plausible case can even be made out that events and conditions of an objective nature such as these provide a complete explanation of the economic history of these centuries.[12]

It was not until the Great Depression of the 1930s that the world suffered a large-scale economic event that was both traumatic and seemingly without sufficient objective cause. The long depression at the end of the nineteenth century was in some respects as severe, and it too seemed without objective cause, but probably because most economies were still predominantly agricultural, it did not give rise to as much suffering and so was not seen as so sharply challenging the assumptions that economic conditions were always objectively caused.[13]

[11] Adolph Lowe, *On Economic Knowledge* (New York: Harper & Row, 1965), pp. 203–10.

[12] Milton Friedman and Anna J. Schwartz, *A Monetary History of the United States, 1867-1960* (Princeton: Princeton University Press, 1963); Fred Albert Shannon, *America's Economic Growth* (New York: Macmillan, 1940).

[13] Charles P. Kindleberger, *The World in Depression, 1929-1939* (Berkeley and Los Angeles: University of California Press, 1973), pp. 19–29; Arthur Nussbaum, *A History of the Dollar* (New York: Columbia University Press, 1957).

A minor incident of the Great Depression also illustrates the extent to which the economic world by then, but only by then, had ceased to be governed by objective factors. Economic theory of the time held that people valued paper money primarily because it was convertible to gold, silver, or something else that was objectively scarce and on that account highly valued. United States currency and many of the bonds issued by the United States government were then generally convertible into gold at the holder's option. The Great Depression was characterized by falling prices. It was felt that if prices could be made to rise again, the depression might be cured. So President Roosevelt gradually increased the dollar value of gold by paying gradually higher dollar prices for it, and eventually entirely terminated the convertibility of currency and bonds into gold. This was done in the belief that if people valued their money less, they would spend it more freely and prices would rise. But the President's actions had no discernible effects on prices, and the depression continued. Whatever may have been true previously, by the 1930s people in the United States had apparently come to value their money for nonobjective reasons.[14]

Economics as a Science

By science I mean natural science. This is what is commonly meant by the word, and this is what people in universities, where distinctions of this sort make an important difference, nearly always mean.[15] It would be thought odd in a university setting to refer to a sociologist as a scientist, for example, although there would be no doubt that he was a social scientist. But unless the adjective "social" is added, the word is nearly always meant to include only physicists, chemists, bi-

[14] John Kenneth Galbraith, *Money: Whence It Came, Where It Went* (New York: Houghton-Mifflin, 1975), pp. 209–13; Kindleberger, *The World in Depression*, p. 15.

[15] *The Oxford English Dictionary* (London: Oxford University Press, 1971). See the fourth and fifth meanings of "science," which are the modern ones.

ologists, and others who are natural scientists. Moreover, when economists have used the word to describe their own discipline, a closer examination of the context will almost invariably show that they have meant a natural science.[16]

A natural science is deterministic, and rightly so. It seeks to discover laws of nature that describe, usually in mathematical terms, chains of cause and effect. The meaning of cause and effect is the same as the meaning of determinant and phenomenon-that-is-determined. Science involves more than just determinism, but determinism is essential to it. The necessity was expressed by Alfred North Whitehead as "the inexpungable belief that every detailed occurence can be correlated with its antecedents in a perfectly definite manner, exemplifying general principles. Without this belief the incredible labours of scientists would be without hope. It is this instinctive conviction, vividly poised before the imagination, which is the motive power of research:—that there is a secret, a secret which can be unveiled."[17]

Many, perhaps most, social scientists do not accept a distinction on these grounds between a natural and social science. They think that *any* science is deterministic, and that the social sciences differ from the natural sciences only in having a different object of study—human affairs—and in not having "progressed" as far yet in discovering deterministic laws.[18] Thus economic determinism is supported by the desire that economics be a science, in the specially natural-science sense.

The natural sciences, of course, have gone on to greater triumphs since the days of Isaac Newton. And in the late nineteenth century, scientists began to be admired more than any other kind of academician or scholar, impelling others to associate themselves with science. Other attractions are also offered by the sciences: they satisfy curiosity, they unveil secrets, as Whitehead said; the general principles—laws of nature—that they unveil are beautiful to contemplate. Anyone who

[16] See text below at notes 20–24.

[17] Alfred North Whitehead, *Science and the Modern World,* 5th ed. (New York: Mentor, 1954), p. 13.

[18] Martin I. Hollis and Edward J. Nell, *Rational Economic Man* (Cambridge: Cambridge University Press, 1975), pp. 4–10.

has ever understood a science can testify to its esthetic power. Being a scientist also offers the satisfaction of doing good for mankind. Because it is "objective," that is, positivistic, science is generally unaffected by personal and political controversy. Being a scientist also gives a feeling of power. Dr. Frankenstein bringing his monster to life or the science-fiction hero pushing the buttons that carry his rocket ship past the speed of light are vulgarizations of this feeling, but the feeling is real. It seems to come both from the unveiling of secrets (secrets always seem to give power to those to whom they are disclosed), and from an awareness that scientific achievements have indeed often conveyed power. The development of computers capable of handling astronomical amounts of data has, since the 1950s, added to this sense of power for economists in particular. Economics has become highly "mathematized."[19]

The economists' desire to be scientists can also be seen in their disputes over the kind of science that their field ought to be, or on what its being a science ought to mean. The disputants, at least the more prominent ones, have never wavered from a belief that economics ought to be a science in the natural-science sense, whatever else they thought it ought, or ought not, to be. Neville Keynes, writing at the turn of the century, insisted that what he called "economic science" should be "a body of systematized knowledge . . . concerned purely with what *is* . . . the whole province of which is to establish economic laws of uniformities." He went on to distinguish this from what he called a "normative or regulative science: a body of systemized knowledge relating to criteria of what ought to be."[20] This is an even stronger emulation of natural-science than prevails in economics today or, indeed, than probably prevailed at the time. Economists have never hesitated to recommend to governments or to anyone what ought to be—nor should they, of course, whether they are natural scientists or not.

Neville Keynes' son, John Maynard Keynes, writing in

[19] Wassily Leontief, "Theoretical Assumptions and Nonobserved Facts," *Amer. Econ. Rev.* 61 (1971), 1–2.

[20] Phyllis Deane, *The Evolution of Economic Ideas* (Cambridge: Cambridge University Press, 1978), pp. 102–103.

1938, distinguished between what he called a "moral science" and a "natural science" of economics, and urged the former. A "natural science" he defined as one that sought to discover rigid, unchanging laws, like Newton's law of universal gravitation. A "moral science" he defined as one that emphasized people's psychological propensities and how people acted under conditions of uncertainty. Although a "moral science" as Keynes the younger defined it might sound nondeterministic, it is clear that he did not intend it to be so. In the first place, he never renounced, or apparently even thought that he was being inconsistent with, his life's greatest work, *The General Theory of Employment, Interest and Money,* in which he sought to demonstrate the determinants of aggregate income. And as he demonstrated them there, they are quite as rigid and unchanging as any of the determinants that "economic science," in his view, might postulate.[21] In any event, even a "moral science," as he conceived of it, would have been just as deterministic as a "natural science," as he conceived of it. If people's *individual* psychological propensities were taken into account, the deterministic character of economics would indeed have been undermined; but nothing in Keynes' work before or after he made these statements indicated that he was contemplating anything so radical. In *The General Theory,* for example, when he seeks to refute the opinion then current among economists that there was no such thing as involuntary employment because a worker could always find an employer who would employ him at less than the going rate, Keynes does not take what would seem to be the obvious step (especially in light of what he said about a "moral science") of asking unemployed workers or employers why they did not act as economists said they would. Instead he went through an elaborate (and, to my mind, unconvincing) "thought experiment" that is remarkable for not dealing with what workers or employers actually thought at any point.[22] The conditions of un-

[21] John Maynard Keynes, *The General Theory of Employment, Interest and Money* (New York: Harcourt, Brace, 1936); Deane, *Evolution of Economic Ideas,* pp. 102–103.

[22] Robert Lekachman, *The Age of Keynes* (New York: Vintage Books, 1966), pp. 87–88.

certainty that Keynes mentioned are also quite consistent with determinism. They require only that the predicted results of the laws be stated in terms of probabilities rather than certainties. Physics, the most rigidly deterministic natural science, has always included laws that state their results as probabilities.[23]

R. A. Gordon, in his presidential address to the members of the American Economics Association in 1976, criticized his profession for having come to stress "rigor" over "relevance." He argued that by reversing the emphasis, economics would again be made more like a science. In their current emphasis on rigor, he felt, his colleagues were ignoring facts in order to make the *assumed* conditions of economic behavior simple enough to permit the construction of elaborate, tightly reasoned theories. This is not scientific, at least not when it is carried as far as many economists currently were. A science must remain true to the facts before all else—even, or especially, if this requires a sacrifice in the elegance or "tightness" of its theories. It is clear that nothing in Mr. Gordon's address suggested a desire that economics be less like a science.[24]

Other Sciences of Human Behavior

The Wealth of Nations was an immense success. This success, together with the attractions of being scientists, impressed the practitioners and founders of other disciplines, and led to a rash of attempts to apply scientific premises and methods to the study of human behavior in other areas. These attempts have ultimately been seen as failures by most people, I think, but they continue to this day. A related result was to bring pressure on existing disciplines to make themselves more scientific—to transform themselves completely or, short of this, to open their doors to scientifically inclined subdisciplines or "schools." These pressures have been felt especially

[23] Leonard I. Schiff, *Quantum Mechanics,* 3rd ed. (New York: McGraw-Hill, 1968).

[24] Robert Aaron Gordon, "Rigor and Relevance in a Changed Institutional Setting," *Amer. Econ. Rev.* 66 (March 1976), 1, 2, and passim.

in universities. The names of subjects often reflect them. Political science is almost universally so called, for example, although one would have thought that politics would be the last study to be regarded as a science. At many universities the study of library administration is called library science. History has expanded to include "quantitive history" or, as it is sometimes called, "cliometrics"—the use of statistical analysis on historical material to uncover people's historical practices, attitudes, and so on. "Quantitative history" is also sometimes called "economic history," because it is economic data that its practitioners use more frequently than any other.[25] The study of law has also become more "scientific," largely by the infusion of economics but also by an increased use of statistics and other scientific methodologies.[26] All this contributes to the support of economic determinism by making it difficult for an economist to consider the possibility of making his discipline less scientific than the other disciplines within his university.

Surely the most widely known body of thinking about human behavior avowedly established on scientific, deterministic principles—other than economics itself—is Marxism, which happens also to be based on economic determinism. Marx claimed to have shown that economic forces were the determining factors of the whole course of history.[27] An outstanding American historian who believed the same, although he was not specifically a Marxist, was Charles Beard, who in his most well-known work tried to show that economic forces determined the contents of the Constitution of the United States.[28] Herbert Spencer was another historical determinist,

[25] David Hackett Fischer, *Historians' Fallacies* (New York: Harper & Row Torchbook, 1970), pp. 7, 16–21, 127–28.

[26] Frank Michelman, "Political Markets and Community Self-Determination: Competing Judicial Models of Local Government Legitimacy," *Indiana Law Journal* 53 (1977–1978), 145–46. See, for example, *The Journal of Legal Studies* and *The Journal of Law and Economics*, both published by the University of Chicago Law School.

[27] Deane, *Evolution of Economic Ideas*, pp. 102–103.

[28] Charles A. Beard, *An Economic Interpretation of the Constitution of the United States* (New York: Macmillan, 1913); Morton White, *Social Thought in America: The Revolt against Formalism* (Boston: Beacon Press, 1961), pp. 111–15.

although he thought the determining factor was evolutionary "natural selection" rather than economics.[29] Thorstein Veblen, Oliver Wendell Holmes, John Dewey, and James Harvey Robinson were at least deterministically inclined, although they emphasized the empiricist, positivistic aspect of determinism over its strictly determining aspects, and they thought that the economists of their day were too "formal," by which they meant too abstractly rational rather than empirical, in applying determinism in that field.[30] Sigmund Freud was a determinist in his beliefs about human behavior.[31] Most sociologists have always been determinists; the new field of sociobiology is deterministic; the psychologist B. F. Skinner is an outspoken determinist.[32]

All of the examples mentioned are or were at one time considered quite respectable by large numbers of people. Spencer's ideas were once immensely popular in the United States.[33] Marxism is still the official philosophy of half the people in the world (although this guarantees neither that they understand it nor that they really believe it). Sociobiology is a current fashion, obviously thought well of by some.[34] B. F. Skinner was a prominent member of the faculty of Harvard University and is still promulgating his ideas in books that sell extremely well for their kind.[35] Psychoanalysis and sociology are still widely accepted and respected disciplines. The historians and philosophers mentioned, although they did not all found disciplines, were all considered at one time not only re-

[29] Herbert Spencer, *Social Statics* (New York: D. Appleton, 1850).

[30] White, *Social Thought in America,* pp. 11–31.

[31] See, for example, James Strachey, trans., *The Standard Edition of the Complete Psychological Works of Sigmund Freud* 6 (Honolulu: Hogarth Press and the Institute of Psychoanalysis, 1960), xiii–xiv, 46, 240–54.

[32] David L. Sills, ed., *International Encyclopedia of the Social Sciences* 15 (New York: Macmillan and Free Press, 1968), pp. 1–23; Edward O. Wilson, *On Human Nature* (Cambridge: Harvard University Press, 1978), B. F. Skinner, *Beyond Freedom and Dignity* (New York: Bantam/Vintage, 1972).

[33] "Spencer, Herbert," in Sills, *International Encyclopedia,* 15:121–27.

[34] Stuart Hampshire, "The Illusion of Sociobiology," *New York Review,* October 12, 1978, pp. 64–69.

[35] "Brave New Behaviorism," *Newsweek,* September 20, 171, p. 95.

spectable, but outstanding, and are still very highly thought of.

Of course the practitioners of these disciplines do not think that they are mistaken in taking a scientific approach. Many of them do, however, admit that they have not progressed as rapidly along scientific lines as they or their predecessors might have hoped. In any event, none of these disciplines has produced a single law of human behavior that even remotely approaches in accuracy, precision, or significance the laws of behavior of unthinking organisms or of inanimate matter that have been produced in profusion by the physical sciences. One has to include significance in such an assessment, because it is always possible to produce a "law" that is trivial or obvious. A "law" of political science might be that presidents of the United States are men, for example. This "law" would be quite precise, and it would be accurate for every application so far, and would probably remain so for the near future; but it would add nothing to what is already obvious. But failure of the scientific approach in these disciplines has only led to the conclusion that economics is unique. Economics alone among the sciences of human behavior has supposedly been a success. Every other such science is by comparison "in its infancy."[36] Even so profound a thinker as Isaiah Berlin, whose principal thesis in a lifetime of writing has been that it is a mistake to apply deterministic premises to the study of human behavior, has made an exception for economics.[37]

Materialism

Since economic determinism includes economic materialism, it has also received support from the intellectual climate

[36] Tjalling C. Koopmans, "Economics among the Sciences," *Amer. Econ. Rev.* 69 (March 1979), 1; Gordon, "Rigor and Relevance"; Deane, *Evolution of Economic Ideas,* pp. 125–42.

[37] See especially Isaiah Berlin, *Four Essays on Liberty* (London: Oxford University Press, 1969), pp. x–xxxi and passim; Isaiah Berlin, *Concepts and Categories: Philosophical Essays* (New York: Viking Press, 1979), pp. 120–21.

of materialism, the beginnings of which can be traced to the Enlightenment, which preceded and included the life of Adam Smith. I am using materialism here not in its technical philosophical sense but in its popular sense, through which it influences the thoughts of all of us who are part of Western culture. Materialism is the belief that the world is composed exclusively of material things—things that a person can perceive by means of his senses. Whatever is not material supposedly does not exist. The immaterial partakes of reality only insofar as people believe in it, which is to say that only the beliefs themselves are real: a person's beliefs can be perceived by him through his own senses and by other people through their senses when the believer speaks or writes about them or acts in accordance with them. But the things believed are not themselves real if they cannot be perceived through the senses. God, justice, right and wrong, good and bad, beauty, ugliness, values of any kind are therefore not real, although one's belief in the existence or nonexistence of any of them is real, and one's belief or opinion that they are an attribute of a real thing is real. One's opinion that a particular work of art is beautiful is real, for example. But the beauty itself, either as an abstract entity or as it might exist in the work of art, is not real. It is not, because it is incapable of demonstration through the senses.[38] (The materialism of Adam Smith and the school of philosophers to which he belonged, which conceived of even such things as human sentiments as objectively real, did not survive for long.)

Although the first concern of materialism is with reality, its most important conclusion concerns truth. Nothing can be true, it is said, unless its truth can be demonstrated by material things. More precisely, there is no possible truth *or* falsity

[38] For a description of the Enlightenment philosophy that shows its materialism, see Isaiah Berlin, "Introduction" in *The Age of Enlightenment* (New York: Mentor, 1956), pp. 14–21. Of course a belief as widespread and fundamental as our contemporary materialism cannot be exemplified by any one person or any one work. However, a good if somewhat extreme expression is given by J. L. Mackie, *Ethics: Inventing Right and Wrong* (Harmondsworth: Penguin Books, 1977).

in a proposition whose truth or falsity cannot be demonstrated by material things. The reader will recognize this as the conclusion of positivism. Positivism derives from materialism, both historically and logically.[39] Statements that are not thus provable or disprovable are "subjective" or "normative," which is to say they merely express the speaker's feelings or someone's opinion about what ought to be.

There have been materialists as long as there have been philosophers, but materialism probably owes its dominance as a popular philosophy to the decline of religious belief and the emergence and success of science, two developments that are themselves related. Both this relationship and the ascendency of science itself are probably associated in most people's minds with the debate that began with Charles Darwin's *The Evolution of Species* about which was true, the evolutionary account of man's descent from other animals or the account in the Book of Genesis of his immediate creation by God. The debate ended, in most people's opinion, with a verdict for evolution in the Scopes trial in 1925.[40] Materialism was bound up with the same two developments in Europe, although the Scopes trial had no significance there, and in Europe it was also associated with radical political philosophies and hopes for political revolution.[41] It reached what was probably its extreme political form in Russia in the late nineteenth century, under the name of "nihilism"—"two plus two is four and all else is nonsense."[42] Materialism in its technical philosophical

[39] Rudolph Carnap, "Psychology in Physical Language," in Alfred J. Ayer, ed., *Logical Positivism* (New York: Free Press, 1959), p. 174.

[40] The influence of "Darwinism" in American intellectual thought is traced in White, *Social Thought in America,* pp. 6, 13, 64–65, 70, 81, 104, 111–12, 206. See also Arthur Weinberg, ed., *Attorney for the Damned* (New York: Simon and Schuster, 1957), pp. 174–228.

[41] Frederick Copleston, S.J., "The Revolution to Henri Bergson," in *A History of Philosophy* 9 (New York: Image Books, 1977), 59–153; Frederick Copleston, S.J., "British Empiricism and the Idealist Movement in Great Britain," in *A History of Philosophy* 8 (New York: Image Books, 1967), 113–43.

[42] James H. Billington, *Fire in the Minds of Men: Origins of the Revolutionary Faith* (New York: Basic Books, 1980), pp. 389–400 (the quotation is on p. 390).

sense became the dominant academic philosophy in England at the end of the nineteenth century and in the United States in the early years of this century. It has remained the dominant academic philosophy in both countries ever since.[43]

The association between materialism and science is so close that they can almost be said to be the same. Materialism is the more far-reaching, however, because it asserts not just that science is a way to truth, but that it is the only way. The success of science has meant that even if our culture had not also become materialist, all disciplines that could not plausibly claim to be sciences would have suffered by comparison. But materialism goes beyond elevating science; it destroys the legitimacy of everything else. Today, a discipline that is not a science, in the minds of most people in universities, deals with neither reality nor truth. It deals primarily with the imagination. It can be entertaining, it can be useful for training the mind, but it tells us nothing about the world except the little that it may convey incidentally. Reading Charles Dickens in a literature course may incidentally convey to the student some information about England in the nineteenth century, and it will probably entertain him and train him in the use of words, but he presumably could have obtained the information more directly in a history course, and the improved facility in the use of words in a speech or writing course. Only the entertainment value is possibly unique to the course on literature. Thus, whereas science, when it entered into universities, tended only to diminish the arts and humanities by comparison—to crowd them out, so to speak—materialism gutted them.

This state of affairs was described by C. P. Snow in 1960 as "two cultures." The dominant, superior culture, as he described it, included all the sciences, both natural and social. (He was one of those who made no distinction other than subject matter and success between disciplines that study inanimate things or plant or animal life and disciplines that

[43] Morton White, *The Age of Analysis* (New York: Houghton-Mifflin, 1955), pp. 17–18, 21–30, 81–82, 189–91, 225–26, 236–38.

study human society.) The inferior culture included everything else. Since Snow was describing not the whole world but only universities and other centers of learning, however, what he meant by everything else was the arts and humanities. I have already described the overwhelming dominance that sciences and pseudo sciences enjoy in universities today. Snow described all this, although it was not so overwhelming when he wrote, about twenty years ago. The growing difference is evidence that the forces that created the dominance of science are still powerful. Snow was primarily concerned with the lack of intellectual interchange between the two cultures. To correct it, he suggested that those in the arts and humanities should learn the rudiments of science. Judging by the published responses, the suggestion was not well received. The unenthusiastic response is understandable. Snow was not offering to recognize the worth of the arts and humanities. All he was really suggesting was that they should become more like sciences.[44]

Science, together with science's destructive effects on religious belief, was probably the principal cause of the rise of materialism, but industrialization, capitalism, and democracy were also important. Emile Durkheim suggested that industrialization encouraged materialism through specialization. Each special occupation, to some extent, has its own values, and increased specialization makes the relativity of some values increasingly apparent. This tends to depreciate all values.[45] This effect is aggravated in a capitalist society, where the members of a specialty are brought into competition. Competition depreciates the humane values by making every-

[44] C. P. Snow, *The Two Cultures: And a Second Look* (Cambridge: Cambridge University Press, 1964), pp. 22–40, 71–75. Snow himself describes the responses to *The Two Cultures* in a section added to a later edition. See ibid., pp. 53–100. Perhaps the most critical reputable responses from the "inferior culture" were from the Leavises. See F. R. Leavis, *Two Cultures? The Significance of C. P. Snow* (London: Chatto & Windus, 1962); F. R. Leavis and Q. D. Leavis, *Lectures in America* (New York: Pantheon Books, 1969).

[45] Copleston, "The Revolution to Henri Bergson," pp. 146–47.

one's well-being seem to depend upon his willingness and ability to injure others.

The connection between democracy and materialism is not so easily explained, although it has been noted.[46] I will attempt to explain it, because this connection, I think, serves more than any other to preserve the powerful hold of materialism on our minds. First, however, I will respond to a question that the reader may already have asked himself. Why, if democracy is so important for materialism, is materialism also the dominant philosophical outlook in nondemocratic societies such as the Soviet Union and the People's Republic of China? The answer, I think, is that it is the leveling aspects of democracy, which it shares with these kinds of nondemocratic governments (but not with other kinds), that provides the materialist bias. Before democracy was established in England and the United States, it was opposed on the grounds that most people were not capable of self-government.[47] The response was education—mandatory, publicly supported education. Education is indeed necessary for democracy. If people are to participate meaningfully in their own government, they must be educated to the level of being able to understand the issues that their government will have to resolve. But if education is to make everyone capable of self-government, it has to be able to do so even for the slowest and most weakly motivated. If democracy is to work, learning must be made easy. (Learning also has to be made easy in a communist so-

[46] For example, José Ortego y Gasset, *The Revolt of the Masses* (New York: Mentor, 1952), pp. 43–48; Alexis de Tocqueville, *Democracy in America* (New York: Vintage, 1956), pp. 264–66, 273–78. Neither Ortego y Gasset nor de Tocqueville use the term "materialism," but both observe traits and attitudes that are included under the term as I define it. See also Joyce Carol Oates, "A Taut Novel of Disorder," *New York Times Book Review,* April 3, 1977, pp. 3, 34–35; Paul Jonas, "Home Thoughts from Abroad," *Harper's* 254 (April 1977), 20–21: John Leonard, "Falling off the Train," *New York Times Book Review,* April 3, 1977, pp. 3, 31; Robert Nisbet, "Public Unions and the Decline of Public Trust," in A. Lawrence Chickering, ed., *Public Employee Unions* (San Francisco: Institute for Contemporary Studies, 1976), pp. 13–33.

[47] See, for example, James Madison, *The Federalist Papers,* No. 10.

ciety, although for the different reason that only easy learning can make even the slowest and most weakly motivated sufficiently amenable to mass thought control.)

Materialism has been a beneficiary of the necessity of making learning easy, because it teaches that the only truths are those that are objectively demonstrable. Objectively demonstrable truths are relatively easy to demonstrate, and the demonstrations, once made, tend to be quickly and thoroughly convincing. They depend on only two things: the evidence of the senses, and logic. The evidence of the senses is probably the first and most thoroughly learned aspect of thinking, and it is absolutely convincing. Almost everyone has obtained a good grasp of it even before he reaches school age. Logic is probably the next easiest and most convincing mental faculty. Piaget has shown that the elementary rules of logic are learned early, and that once they are learned, it is almost impossible for a person to deny them sincerely.[48]

Materialism also makes learning easy by seeming to eliminate the necessity of making judgments. Judging is one of the most difficult faculties to learn, and it is usually the last to be learned; many people never learn it. The mark of a person's having reached mental maturity is commonly said to be his possession of "good judgment." It is commonly understood that by this test many people achieve maturity only late in life, and some never achieve it. Judging is required in almost everything a person does, from driving an automobile to deciding the esthetic value of a piece of music. The kind most often required, probably, is the judging of how to deal with other people, especially those with whom one is in a close personal relationship. Any sensitive person realizes that this can be exceedingly difficult.

A materialist cannot accept the fact of judging because judgments cannot be made to fit his criterion of truth content—their correctness or incorrectness is not objectively test-

[48] Jean Piaget, *The Construction of Reality in the Child* (New York: Basic Books, 1954).

able.[49] Even when a judgment involves a prediction, the failure of events to confirm the prediction does not prove the incorrectness of the judgment. It still could have been the best that could have been done under the circumstances. A materialist is therefore compelled to trivialize judging by regarding it as merely the expression or acting out of subjective or normative opinions. Every judgment is supposedly as good or bad as every other. Judging supposedly requires no learning.

Practically the whole educational value of the arts and humanities, except for memorizing, consists in their judgmental aspects, so when these are removed, education is made much easier. Fewer student hours need to be devoted to the arts and humanities, and those that are are filled with less interesting versions of their subjects. History is left as a string of events with dates attached to them. Literature and the other arts become just entertainments. The social sciences become the same as the natural sciences except for subject matter. They are left without the drama that the unfolding of events in history can have even when history is taught objectively and without the entertainment value that the arts can have even when no attempt is made to convey their esthetic contents. So

[49] The observations and conclusions in the text about moral and political judgments and judgments of other kinds, except esthetic judgments, are largely my own, but I was stimulated into the thinking that led to them by reading the works of Hannah Arendt. Dr. Arendt had barely begun what was to be her work on judging in 1975 when she died. "Editor's Postface," in Hannah Arendt, *The Life of the Mind* 2 (New York: Harcourt, Brace, Jovanovich, 1978), p. 242. The fragment that she wrote is on pp. 255–72. Other observations about judging, mostly implicit, are scattered throughout her works.

Immanuel Kant also wrote of judging, of course, but he meant by the term only esthetic judging; see Immanuel Kant, *Critique of Judgment.* He thought that moral judgments were primarily a kind of reasoning: Immanuel Kant, *Foundations of the Metaphysics of Morals.* For a very understandable explanation of these matters in Kant, see Frederick Copleston, *A History of Philosophy,* 6, pt. 2 (New York: Image Books, 1964), 101–70. For references to Kant's conclusion that morality may be a matter of judging, too, see ibid., pp. 160–61. For a good treatment of the kind of judging in which a government policymaker, businessman, or other administrator must engage, see Geoffrey Vickers, *The Art of Judgment* (New York: Basic Books, 1965).

education is made still easier by being made less interesting. Those who are neither logically nor practically inclined, or who find just logic and technology no longer sufficiently challenging, become bored and coast through or leave early.

Materialism and the democratic ethic have also combined to make education easier by transforming its authority structure. It used to be that faculties, deans, boards of trustees, and others in authority made judgments about the courses that students were offered, and the students were given relatively little choice in the matter. At the college I attended in the fifties, for example, an entering student had no choice in what he took the first year, one or two very limited choices the second year, and a rather wide range of choices for his third and fourth years—which, however, were significantly restrained by the requirement that he group most of them in the subject that he chose as his "major." In the sixties this changed in most universities to permit even entering freshmen to choose from a wide variety of course offerings, and at the same time wider varieties of courses were offered. There has since been a slight movement back, but the student is still typically permitted a much wider choice than he typically had in the fifties. These changes have presumably had the effect of making education easier; given the opportunity, many students will choose easier courses. The effect of these changes has been aggravated by another practice, which has also become common, of allocating a school's funds among its departments on the basis of the student-hours a department teaches. In order to obtain the funds they need for paying their faculty members and hiring new ones, the departments have to attract students, and a seductively easy way of doing this is to give easy courses and to give high grades despite low demonstrated achievement. There has indeed been substantial "grade inflation" almost everywhere in higher learning centers since the fifties.[50]

[50] Alston Chase, "Skipping through College," *Atlantic Monthly* 242 (September 1978), 33.

There is no sure way of knowing what motivated universities to make these changes, but my conversations with other educators and the evident plausibility of the argument lead me to think that materialism has been influential by denying the worth of anyone's judgment about what courses students should be offered, and that the democratic ethic has been influential by prescribing that students should be given the maximum possible range of choices. They are seen as the citizens for whom the university ought to be run democratically. Freedom is rightly regarded as part of the democratic ethic, and for students to have a wide range of course choices is also seen as giving them more freedom.

Education in the United States has seemed to deteriorate in recent decades, which are the same decades in which materialism has become ascendent in higher education, but it would not be fair or accurate to leave the impression that education has deteriorated grossly or that the influence of materialism on educational quality has been as entirely negative as I have so far portrayed it. A higher proportion of Americans now goes on to higher education, which presumably has the effect of making more students in elementary and secondary schools eager to learn and to do well in the things that will prepare them for higher education and enable them to meet the qualifications for entry. Television seems to have the effect of stimulating the learning process in very young children, so that many of them achieve much more in the earliest years of schooling, and even learn much of what used to be taught in the first grade or two before they begin their formal schooling. The natural sciences and the mathematics that are now being taught in colleges and universities and in the better high schools are generally more advanced than they were twenty or thirty years go. This presumably is a result of materialism too, but a result in the direction of more learning, and of more difficult subject matter. There are probably other forces working to improve education, but the net effect, I think, has been a general, although perhaps only slight, decline in the difficulty of education and a very substantial increase in its materialist contents.

Democracy also supports materialism because materialism seems to eliminate all the difficult distinctions that would otherwise have to be drawn among persons and policies. Who should be elected to office and what policies the government should pursue are made mere matters of opinion, on which the majority view must always prevail, because no person's opinion is supposed to be worth any more than any other's. If the majority today is prevented from putting a person in jail without a trial or taking away his freedom of speech, this is only because the majority two hundred years ago chose to place prohibitions against such actions in the Constitution. The majority is legally and morally entitled to remove these prohibitions any time it chooses to. If the majority chooses to eliminate the wilderness, destroy beautiful old buildings, or stop educating children, it is also supposedly entitled to do these things.[51] Scholars of constitutional law generally regard the attempt to find some legitimate basis for a judge's power to hold a law or other government action unconstitutional as the crucial task of their discipline, precisely because materialism has seemingly eliminated the bases in morality, justice, natural law, or the rights of man that were formerly thought to exist.[52] Finally, materialism is also supported by democracy insofar as the latter comprises a democracy of consumers. Few desires seem to be more universal than the desire to have things. People seem to become materialistic in our society quite without regard to the contents of their formal training.[53]

Materialism also has at least one undemocratic basis of

[51] John Hart Ely, *Democracy and Distrust: A Theory of Judicial Review* (Cambridge: Harvard University Press, 1980), pp. 181–83.

[52] Philip Bobbit, "Constitutional Fate," *Texas Law Rev.* 58 (1980), 695, 698–700, 708–716.

[53] Many of the connections between materialism and the democratic ethic that I have sought to explain in the text are described without explanation in Ortega y Gasset, *Revolt of the Masses,* and in de Tocqueville, *Democracy in America,* especially the latter. For evidence of the unfortunate impact of materialism on the life and thought of a major contemporary scientist, see Alice K. Smith and Charles Weiner, eds., *Robert Oppenheimer: Letters and Recollections* (Cambridge: Harvard University Press, 1980); see also David Joravsky, "Sin and the Scientist," *New York Review of Books,* July 17, 1980, p. 6.

support. Scholars, by the nature of their work, must generally excel in the mental faculties of reasoning or memorizing, especially reasoning. Materialism enables them to feel superior by making it seem that these are the only faculties that matter. A law professor, for example, can feel himself superior to judges, legislators, and practicing lawyers, because he is probably superior to them in reasoning ability, and any other supposed faculties such as the making of legal, political, or psychological judgments, in which these other persons might seem to be superior, materialism holds to be nonexistent. A professor in the arts or humanities cannot so readily avail himself of this sense of superiority, but the arts and humanities are a small and declining part of most universities.

The scholar's sense of absolute superiority is rarely directly expressed. It generally takes the form of an assertion that superior reasoning is the *only* necessary means of achieving some insight, understanding, or goal. It is thus made clear that the scholar and others like him are the persons most capable of achieving it, or that it is they, at least, who should lead the way. For example, a recent book by a law professor asserts that in the ideal society the only principles of governance would be rationality, consistency, and neutrality, and it defines neutrality as treating everyone as equal to everyone else except where doing so would offend the principles of rationality or consistency.[54] Another recent book, by a law professor who is also an economist, asserts that every major doctrine in the common law can be understood as an expression of economic efficiency, and that this fact can be discerned by reasoning alone; no knowledge of history is necessary, for example.[55] A person of superior reasoning ability who agrees with the thesis of the first book has the satisfaction of knowing that in the ideal society he would be superior in the only skill that mattered. He would presumably be among the rulers. A person of superior reasoning ability who agrees with the thesis of

[54] Bruce Ackerman, *Social Justice in the Liberal State* (New Haven: Yale University Press, 1980).

[55] Richard A. Posner, *Economic Analysis of Law* (Boston: Little, Brown, 1977), pp. 10–14, 22–27.

the second book has the satisfaction of knowing that he understands the common law better than anyone else ever did who was not granted this particular insight—even if the other person was, or is, a legal historian.

I will recount a conversation over lunch in which I participated at my university, which must be atypical only in touching so many deterministic and materialistic points so quickly. One person described a paper that he had recently heard presented at a law-school symposium in the Chicago area. The paper had shown a statistical correlation between the number of students graduating from a state's law schools and the likelihood that a state would enact legislation requiring graduating law students to prove their competency before entering the practice of law. The higher the number of law graduates, the more likely it was that a state would enact such legislation. The conclusions the paper drew from these data were that the legislation was motivated solely by the practicing lawyers' desire to limit their competition, and that the legislation was contrary to the public interest. No attempt had been made to ascertain whether limiting competition was in fact the sole motivation of the state legislators or of the practicing lawyers, or even whether this was in fact a significant motivation of either of them. No attempt had been made to ascertain whether the legislation had been sponsored or even supported by the organizations that represented the practicing lawyers. No attempt had been made to evaluate the legislation on its merits—to ascertain, for example, whether the public interest might indeed be served by having incompetents screened out before they were permitted to pass themselves off on a public that had little if any ability to make individual judgments of a lawyer's competency. Any attempt to find the actual motives of anyone would have violated the profit-maximization principle. The practicing lawyers were presumed to be maximizing profits, so the motive of limiting their competition must have been their actual—and only—motive. Any attempt to have evaluated the legislation on its merits would have violated the tenet of positivism that only objective factors count.

I expressed my disgust, probably not very tactfully, and then asked why this kind of supposedly scholarly research was supposed to be worthwhile. The answers from around the table were that the question was not one that could properly be asked. Whatever a scholar chose to do with his time was legitimate, because there were no objective standards for making the kind of distinction my question implied. One person (an avowed materialist, to give the devil his due) then objected that by this logic scholars had a right to be paid for playing chess. After some facetious byplay about the fact that scholars are indeed being paid to play chess with computers, if not with each other, these days, the general conclusion was reached, myself dissenting, that university teachers were entitled to teach whatever students chose to be taught, even if this included scuba diving. The students' opinions, expressed through their course choices, were the only objective criterion there was, and it had the additional claim of being the democratically expressed choice of the persons whom the teachers were being paid to teach. This left the question that I had asked unanswered, which had been about scholarship, not teaching, but the conversation then turned to other things. I had not said, for fear of arousing even more antagonism, that this kind of supposed scholarship must be attractive because it is so easy. One can style oneself a scientist for having done something about as difficult as balancing a checking account.

I must add, in fairness, that all the participants in the conversation are conscientious teachers and scholars. They do not teach just what their students choose to be taught, and they choose their subjects of scholarly research with what they think is due regard for academic and public worth. But they were sincere in what they said. Their attitudes will surely have a corroding effect on the scholarship and teaching of younger people, and probably eventually on their own. And irresponsible and destructive as these attitudes are, they are probably not as bad as those to come. Giving students their free and "democratic" choices is not the logical stopping place it appears. The comparative worth of freedom and democracy, relative to their opposites, is just as incapable of objective demonstration as is the comparative worth of different subjects of scholarship or teaching. The only logical stopping place for a philosophy that refuses to make judgments about the relative values of anything is that might makes right. A truly consistent materialist has no basis for concluding that a free and democratic society is superior to a totalitarian one.

Social and Political Purposes

Economic determinism also prospered after Smith introduced it because it served two great social and political purposes. It served to justify the freeing of property, land in particular, from restraints on alienation (that is, on transfer), and it served to justify government in not subjecting businesses to close supervision. These can both fairly be called great purposes, because without their accomplishment the industrial revolution could not have proceeded so rapidly. The freeing of property from restraints on alienation facilitated the industrial revolution by permitting property to be put to its most productive uses. Keeping governments from closely supervising businesses facilitated the revolution by permitting business decisions to be made by those who could make them best, the managers of the businesses. The governments could not have made them as well, because there were far too many decisions to be made, and the considerations that entered into them were too particular for any reasonable number of officials far from the scene to have made wisely. Both purposes were served by devising and supporting arguments that were addressed to rulers and advisors to rulers.

The argument that economic determinism provided against restraints on alienation was that if the restraints were removed, property not just *could* be, but *would* be put to its most productive uses. Market forces would compel it. The argument against close government supervision was essentially the same. Market forces would ensure that business decisions would be made wisely if they were left in private hands, whereas they could provide no such assurance if the government were to make them, because the government, by its nature, is a monopolist.

Both arguments had to meet powerful counterpressures. The restraints on the alienation of property were generally of ancient origin, and so represented vested interests and the inertia of long-standing tradition. Governments presumably would want to control businesses as a part of their inherent desire to control as much as possible, or at least as a part of the inherent desire of their bureaucracies to do so. They would also want to control businesses because these were quickly becoming the principal centers of concentration of wealth and income, and governments always need revenue. On the other hand, both arguments also had powerful forces in their support. Those who would be most benefited by freeing property from restraints on its alienation were the landlords, who would be proclaimed its absolute owners. Landlords were already a very powerful political force. And since businesses were the new centers of wealth and income, they of course came to possess the political advantages these entail.

The process of freeing property from restraints on its alienation was sometimes as innocuous as allowing owners to ignore the rules of primogeniture. The laws were changed to permit people to leave their land when they died to persons other than their first-born sons or to sell it free and clear during their lifetimes. However, in the United Kingdom freeing property also meant the forcible expulsion of families. The "restraints" in this case were real people: the peasants who had occupied and worked the land for uncounted generations, from whom the land had to be "freed" before it could be mined or used for mills or factories or, most frequently, for grazing sheep.

The legal justification for the tenants' expulsion was that the lord owned his land and so could do with it as he liked, but the legal justification only begged the real question. Land in the United Kingdom, as on the Continent, had as yet not been wholly owned by anybody. Rather, a variety of persons and institutions owned duties and had corresponding rights with respect to it. Those who actually worked the land owed the duty of working it. In return, they had the right to a portion of the yield and to occupancy. Others of the same social rank had the same rights but worked as carpenters, stonemasons, and so on. The lord had the right to general control and to take a substantial portion of the yield, and he owed the duty, among others, of protecting the land and its occupants from robbers, invaders, and other perpetrators of violence or theft. The church ordinarily also had rights and duties, as did other nobility higher in the hierarchy than the lord; and so, of course, did the king. So if the land was to be put to its most productive uses, it was argued, all these rights against it except the right of just one person, the lord, had to be regarded as restraints on the lord's rights, and his rights had to be regarded as absolute. It is this complete set of rights that constitute what we today regard as ownership, and that were created during the eighteenth and nineteenth centuries. They had not previously existed. The persons whose rights were taken away were not compensated. Although the process of taking away everyone's rights except the lord's in order to create the absolute rights of ownership was well underway by the time *The Wealth of Nations* was published, it was far from complete. It might still have led to widespread violence or rebellion, or been substantially slowed by the consciences of the new owners or of the persons in power in government. Economic determinism calmed the consciences and confirmed the resolve to push the process through.[56]

The principal legal instruments in the United Kingdom for evicting those who had worked the land were the enclosure acts, which were regularly enacted by Parliament until late in the nineteenth century.[57] A description of the applications of

[56] R. H. Tawney, *Religion and the Rise of Capitalism* (New York: Harcourt, Brace and Co., 1926), pp. 135–93. And see Cecil Woodham-Smith, *The Great Hunger: Ireland, 1845–1849* (New York: Harper and Row, 1962), pp. 54, 72, 87, 106–107, 147–48, 161–63, 184–85, 285–86, 374–76, 410–11.

[57] *Encyclopaedia Britannica,* 11th ed., 6 (Cambridge: Cambridge University Press, 1910), 782–84.

one of the acts, this one in Ireland in the 1840s, is recorded in Cecil Woodham-Smith's *The Great Hunger:*

> Throughout these months, as famine, in Routh's words, was "steadily and gradually approaching," evictions were reported weekly. The potato failure endangered the payment of rents, a swarming population was likely to become unprofitable, and landlords were eager to clear their property of non-paying tenants.
>
> Evictions, however, were not confined to populations of paupers and squatters living in mud huts. The most notorious instance, was the eviction of 300 tenants by Mrs. Gerrard from the village of Ballinglass, County Galway, on March 13, 1846. A population reasonably prosperous, according to Irish standards, was evicted with the assistance of police and troops, in order that the holdings might be turned into a grazing farm.
>
> The village of Ballinglass consisted of 61 houses, solidly built and well-kept, with thick plastered walls. The inhabitants were not in arrear with their rent, and had, by their industry, reclaimed an area of about four hundred acres from a neighbouring bog. On the morning of the eviction a "large detachment of the 49th Infantry commanded by Captain Brown" and numerous police appeared with the Sheriff and his men. Taking part in evictions was disliked by troops; a little later, on April 9, at an eviction of nine families at Guitmore, County Tipperary, a detachment of the 72nd Highlanders "openly said they detested this duty and gave the people money".
>
> At Ballinglass, the people were officially called on to give up possession, and the houses were then demolished—roofs torn off, walls thrown down. The scene was frightful; women running wailing with pieces of their property and clinging to door-posts from which they had to be forcibly torn; men cursing, children screaming with fright. That night the people slept in the ruins; next day they were driven out, the foundations of the houses were torn up and razed, and no neighbour was allowed to take them in.

Turned from every door, it was common for the evicted to seek refuge in what was called a "scalp." A hole was dug in the earth, two to three feet deep, roofed over with sticks and pieces of turf, and in this burrow a family existed. Slightly superior was a "scalpeen", a rather larger hole often made within the ruins of a "tumbled" house. Both from "scalps" and "scalpeens" the evicted when discovered were remorsely hunted out.

The Ballinglass eviction caused a scandal and was "personally investigated" by Lord Londonderry, a great Ulster landlord and a staunch Tory. On March 30 he made the statement in the House of Lords. He was "deeply grieved", but there was no doubt the statements with regard to the eviction at Ballinglass were true: "76 families, comprising 300 individuals, had not only been turned out of their houses but had even—the unfortunate wretches—been mercilessly driven from the ditches to which they had betaken themselves for shelter and where they were attempting to get up a covering of some kind by means of sticks and mud . . . these unfortunate people had their rents actually ready. . . . If scenes like this occured", finished Lord Londonderry, ". . . was it to be wondered at . . . that deeds of outrage and violence should occasionally be attempted?"

Lord Brougham, however, a staunch supporter of *laissez faire,* held a different view. He said on March 23 in the House of Lords: "Undoubtedly it was the landlord's right to do as he pleased, and if he abstained he conferred a favour and was doing an act of kindness. If on the other hand, he chose to stand on his right, the tenants must be taught by the strong arm of the law that they had no power to oppose or resist . . . property would be valueless and capital would no longer be invested in cultivation of land if it were not acknowledged that it was the landlord's undoubted, indefeasible and most sacred right to deal with his property as he list".[58]

[58] Woodham-Smith, *The Great Hunger,* pp. 71–72; see also pp. 22–24.

The cruelty and evident unfairness of the operation of the enclosure acts made it imperative that the justification of the process at least seem to derive from lofty principles of Nature or God. This was the assurance that economic determinism could provide. The landlords could appear as the instruments of Nature or God—the invisible hand's visible manifestations. It was his sure faith in this that presumably enabled Lord Brougham to characterize the ownership of property as "the landlord's undoubted, indefeasible and *most sacred* right to deal with his property as he list."

Whereas an evicted tenant in England had at least the chance of finding a job in one of the mines or mills that were being established in the cities, there were no mines or mills or any other urban employment to speak of in Ireland. Even before the potato famine, eviction in Ireland meant death for every member of the evicted family by what observers called the "slow torture" of starvation.[59] It was Lord Brougham's rather than Lord Londonderry's statements in the House of Lords that carried the day. Evictions followed by starvation or, later, emigration or "transportation" (sentencing to go abroad for a minimum number of years as a punishment for crime) continued in Ireland as elsewhere in the United Kingdom. It was not until another half century had elapsed that the pendulum swung back enough so that human rights began to be recognized.

In the United States, the only claimants whose rights in property were restraints to be eliminated were the Indians, and they were not a political force of significance. The freeing of property from the restraints on its alienation had been fully accomplished both in the United Kingdom and the United States by the end of the nineteenth century.

There was always the possibility of new restraints, but if these were to be imposed they had to be imposed by government, so the use of economic determinism for the purposes of keeping property free from restraints merged into the second great purpose of keeping business free from government con-

[59] Ibid., pp. 32–33, 76.

trol. This was a purpose that would never fade. There are innumerable reasons of health, environmental protection, esthetics, national defense, prosperity, and revenue why governments will always want to control businesses. No timeless principle will or should ever entirely succeed in thwarting these generally legitimate needs. However, the need of business to be left alone is also legitimate. The principle that was constructed out of economic determinism to answer the needs of business in this respect was *laissez faire*. Virtually anything a government might do to control or influence business decisions was said to be an undesirable "interference," not because the businessmen's decisions were necessarily wiser, but because the businessmen's decisions were supposedly determined by the forces of the market.[60] A new use of the doctrine of *laissez faire,* which seems to have appeared only in the 1970s, is to argue that governments ought to reduce their "interferences" with business and their economic activities generally because these are causes of inflation.[61]

Laissez faire also served the selfish interest of the rich by permitting them to keep their wealth whether or not they had earned it. Neither the English nor the American governments ever made any serious attempts to tax wealth even at the owner's death until the twentieth century. Another argument that served to protect wealth was that it was needed to provide the investment capital without which the economy could not grow.[62] This argument also rested on economic determinism, although not directly. A government could tax away all large concentrations of wealth without lowering the amount of wealth available for investment if the government supplied the investment itself, but a government could not do this without violating the principle of *laissez faire*. Lord Brougham's words are again worth noting: "property would

[60] Morton J. Horwitz, *The Transformation of American Law, 1780–1860* (Cambridge: Harvard University Press, 1977), p. 64.

[61] For example, William E. Simon, *A Time for Truth* (Berkeley: Berkeley Publishing Corp., 1979); Orrin Hatch, "Inflation, Taxes, the Budget, and You," *Reader's Digest* (July 1980), pp. 71–75.

[62] Louis Eisenstein, *The Ideologies of Taxation* (New York: Ronald Press, 1961), pp. 93–104.

be valueless and capital would no longer be invested in cultivation if . . ."— if the government of the United Kingdom did not refrain from interfering with a landlord's business decisions.

The interests of business and of the rich in having governments leave them alone would presumably have been felt under any kind of government, but they must have been especially influential in the popular democracies that had been established both here and in England in the nineteenth and early twentieth centuries. There are essentially only two protections that a minority has against a majority in a democracy. It can seek to obtain political power out of proportion to its numbers by wealth, superior organization, or extraordinary zeal. Or it can find principles of law, economics, or morality that appeal to the majority, and can thus protect it. Business and the wealthy inherently possess the advantages of wealth and superior organization; and economic determinism, primarily through the doctrine of *laissez faire,* was a principle with widespread appeal that protected them against the growing desire of government in the early twentieth century to control business and tax incomes. Economic determinism also offered some protection by making businesses appear politically innocuous. As long as market forces were operative, wealth and business supposedly could not threaten to control government because they would be controlled themselves by market forces.[63]

The Wealth of Nations was published the same year as the American colonists issued the Declaration of Independence. The American federal government was substantially democratic from the start, and became more so until early in the twentieth century. George III, who ruled the United Kingdom during the American Revolution, turned out to be the last of the kings of England to have exercised major power at the expense of Parliament, and he exercised more of it than had

[63] See Brown Shoe Co. v. United States, 370 U.S. 294, 344 (1962); Phillip Areeda, *Antitrust Analysis,* 2d ed. (Boston: Little, Brown, 1974), p. 25; Mark J. Green et al., *The Closed Enterprise System* (New York: Grossman, 1972), pp. 17–21.

either of his two predecessors. After George III, Parliament became more powerful with each successive monarch, and at the same time more representative of all classes and eventually both sexes in the British population.[64] The United States Constitution was amended to require the direct popular election of Senators in 1913, to permit the imposition of an income tax in 1913, and to extend the suffrage to women in 1920. The Interstate Commerce Commission was established to regulate railroads and water transportation in 1887. The Sherman Anti-Trust Act was enacted in 1890. The Clayton Anti-Trust Act was enacted in 1914. The Federal Trade Commission was also established in 1914. State constitutions were widely amended during this same period to permit initiatives, referendums, and recalls—direct popular votes to remove elected officials from office and to bypass legislatures, governors, and constitutional conventions, and put laws immediately into effect.

One sign that there was indeed a connection between economic determinism and *laissez faire,* on the one hand, and the threat that business and wealth felt from popular government, on the other, is the fact that economic determinism and *laissez faire* reached their ascendency at about the same time as did popular government. The neoclassical period of economics, which was the most rigidly deterministic and pro-*laissez faire* that economics has ever passed through, reached its zenith early in the twentieth century.[65] It was early in this century—specifically, in 1914—that the proponents of *laissez faire* won out over the proponents of government regulation of business in persuading Congress to enact the Clayton Anti-Trust Act and the Federal Trade Commission Act instead of establishing broad new forms of regulation.[66] Early in this century, too, the United States Supreme Court interpreted the Due Process

[64] Eugene P. Chase, Robert Valeur, and Raymond Leslie Buell, *Democratic Governments in Europe* (Nashville, Tenn.: Thomas Nelson and Sons, 1977), pp. 20–62.

[65] Deane, *Evolution of Economic Ideas,* pp. 94–104, 143–74.

[66] Edwin Rozwenc, ed., *Roosevelt, Wilson and the Trusts* (New York: D. C. Heath, 1953), pp. v–ix and passim.

Clause practically to incorporate the doctrine of *laissez faire* as a constitutional principle.[67] The Court had not done this before, and it took quite another approach toward wealth and business later in the century. The zenith of economic determinism in the study of history is probably marked by the publication of Charles Beard's *An Economic History of the Constitution* early in this century. Finally, it was in the early years of this century that philosophy, here and in England, first set itself firmly on a materialistic course.[68] Economic determinism is currently undergoing its greatest resurgence since the early years of this century, in the administration of President Reagan. Its close ties with the protection of the privileges of wealth and business are again obvious.[69]

Conceptual Inertia

Probably as important as anything in supporting economic determinism, however, has been conceptual inertia. Thomas Kuhn has shown by an examination of the sciences over several centuries that the basic ideas of a science, to which he gives the name "paradigms," change very slowly. The great majority of scientists, like the great majority of people anywhere, are not creative geniuses. They work to confirm what is already known or to extend it by small increments in established directions. They are reluctant to see the worth of what they have done undermined by new discoveries. They are also reluctant to learn new rules of the game after they have mastered the old ones. When a paradigm in some field is successfully attacked, scientists in that field frequently retire or die still believing in the old paradigm. The new paradigm is ac-

[67] Lawrence H. Tribe, *American Constitutional Law* (St. Paul, Minn.: Foundation Press, 1978), pp. 427–455.

[68] White, *Age of Analysis.*

[69] Henry Allen, "George Gilder and the Capitalists' Creed: The World According to Gilder," *Washington Post,* February 18, 1981, p. B-1; "A Conversation with George Gilder: 'Welfare State Promotes What It Is Supposed to Cure,'" *U.S. News & World Report,* April 6, 1981, pp. 53–54.

cepted only by the younger scientists. Scientists who seek to challenge existing paradigms are boycotted. Their experimental methods are attacked on specious grounds, their logical arguments are ignored in the hope that they will be forgotten. Kuhn's conclusion was that scientific paradigms are almost never given up, even by younger scientists, until new paradigms have been offered to replace them.[70] What is true of a science is surely even more true of a field like economics, in which paradigms can not be objectively proven or disproven.

Sources of Opposition

The sources of opposition to economic determinism must have been weaker than the sources of its strength, or it would not still be the basic premise of the only economics that the United States and most other Western nations have ever had. The principal political source of opposition in the United States has always been the labor movement. The effort to organize workers for the purpose of obtaining higher wages would have made no sense if wages were thought to be determined by market forces. The socialist movement was also a source of opposition; although it was never an important one in the United States, it was, and is, on the Continent and in England. But the socialist movement has opposed economic determinism only insofar as it has supported the labor movement. Socialism as an idea has many of the same historical origins as communism, and communism, as we have seen, is not only deterministic—it is specifically economically deterministic. Moreover, socialism, insofar as it fixes on the private ownership of the means of production as the central economic and political evil to be overcome, is almost compelled to grant a deterministic effect to this ownership. But in the mind of the leading contemporary American socialist theorist, Michael Harrington, socialism is opposed to economic determinism.

[70] Thomas S. Kuhn, *The Structure of Scientific Revolutions,* 2d ed. (Chicago: University of Chicago Press, 1970).

Harrington has shifted the focus of his concern from public ownership of the means of production to public direction of the course of production (although he does not disavow the use of public ownership as a method of accomplishing the direction).[71] A similar shift in emphasis seems to have occurred in England.[72] But this shift has occurred both in England and in the United States too recently to have had a discernible effect on the broader intellectual climate.

A recent source of intellectual opposition to economic determinism has been inflation. People undoubtedly suffered more from the Great Depression than they have so far from inflation, but the depression did not undermine economic determinism because its effects did not seem to result from people's choices. Employers, labor unions, farmers, the government—everyone wanted employment to increase during the depression, but everyone seemed helpless to increase it. Employers could not hire more workers unless they could sell more goods. They could not sell more goods unless more people had substantial incomes from employment. No one understood how to break the vicious circle. Inflation, on the other hand, quite evidently results from people's choices, and the choices that are most inflationary are generally given wide publicity. Major strikes and wage increases are front-page items, and are announced and pictured on television. Price increases by major industries are given almost as much publicity. It is usually obvious, too, that the wage increases and the price increases are occurring despite substantial unemployment of both people and resources in the industries, and that both involve all the workers of one kind or all the firms in the industry. Most people have also had the experience of seeing the prices of goods raised that have been on a retailer's shelves since before the price increase, perhaps have even been on sale at especially low "sale" prices previously. Under any of these circumstances it takes a thorough education in ec-

[71] Michael Harrington, *Toward a Democratic Left* (Harmondsworth: Penguin Books, 1969), pp. 102–10, 277–83.

[72] Ernest Conine, "Where Politics Is *Really* Depressing," *Los Angeles Times,* October 6, 1980, pt. 2, p. 7.

onomics to continue to believe that the persons who are doing the price increasing are just the helpless pawns of market forces.

The principal intellectual source of opposition to economic determinism, however, has always been the belief in free will and in the reality of values. A belief in free will does not logically require a belief in the reality of values, but the two beliefs are usually associated, because a major reason for believing in free will is that it gives reality and importance to values. One cannot feel satisfaction for having done the right thing or guilt for having done the wrong thing unless one feels free to have made the choice between them. One cannot praise or blame others for their choices unless one believes that they were free to make them. A belief in free will is obviously inconsistent with economic determinism. It is also inconsistent with economic positivism in particular, because free will cannot be objectively demonstrated. Most people outside of centers of higher learning probably continue to believe in free will and the reality of values for the simple reason that life otherwise would make no sense to them.

CHAPTER 8

The Costs of Economic Determinism

Economic determinism has prevented us from understanding indeterminate inflation. This is reason enough for rejecting economic determinism and rebuilding economics on a new base; and there are other reasons. Economic determinism is wrong. It is simply not true that people's economic behavior is determined, that objective ("material") things are the only operative factors in economic phenomena, or that economic behavior can or should be studied exclusively by studying objective ("positive") things. None of these assumptions was ever true, and modern conditions have destroyed the bases for their being even good approximations. So until economic determinism is rejected, economics will not be a fit instrument for understanding a modern economy in *any* respect. Economic determinism has also imposed some significant noneconomic costs.

There are, of course, numerous economic laws and theories that are premised on economic determinism. It would be an extremely lengthy endeavor to show how the falsity of the premise undermines each one of them. It is also unnecessary. Economics, like most bodies of knowledge that are organized as sciences, has a relatively small number of basic laws upon which almost all the others rest. If the basic laws can be shown to be faulty, the others must be too. So with just a few exceptions, I will confine my criticisms to the basic laws of traditional economics, to show that they possess faults to which economic determinism gives rise, and that these faults are so serious as to make the laws inappropriate for any scientific use.

Concentrating on the basic laws will also enable the reader to understand my criticisms without first having to educate himself in advanced economics. The little education he may require in elementary economics, I will supply. One—only one—of the basic laws that I will criticize (Keynes' law of the determination of aggregate income) is complicated. The additional effort required to understand it is worthwhile, because it serves as the principal illustration of the fact that economic determinism falsifies economics by making its laws unnecessarily complicated. Concentrating on the basic laws also has the advantage of avoiding the vagueness that is much more characteristic of the nonbasic laws. The basic laws of economics, it turns out, are generally the clearest.

The Transformation of Economics into a Rationalism

The forces that led to economic determinism also led to the creation and maintenance of economics as a science, because a scientific economics is a deterministic economics, sciences by their nature being deterministic. However, even while these forces were at their strongest, economics was ceasing to be a science and becoming what I will call, following Alfred North Whitehead, a "rationalism."[1] A rationalism, as Whitehead defined it, is a systematic body of thought that does not proceed from acts and does not seek principles or propositions that can be tested against facts. Its practitioners believe that they can learn what they want to learn just through introspection. Medieval scholasticism, for example, was a rationalism.

A rationalism is rational, which is to say logical. Its premises lead logically to its conclusions. It therefore lends itself to being used as a pseudo science. The formal structure of premise leading to conclusion is so similar to the formal structure of

[1] The first significant interpreter of Adam Smith was David Ricardo, who was a younger contemporary of Smith's. Ricardo's laws and theories were already notably rationalistic, a fact that was evident even to economists in the early years of this century looking back at his work. *Encyclopedia Britannica,* 11th ed., 23 (Cambridge: Cambridge University Press, 1911), 286–87; Alfred North Whitehead, *Science and the Modern World* (New York: Macmillan, 1925), pp. 9–13, 19–20, 39–40.

cause leading to effect that the former can easily be given the appearance of the latter.

Economics presumably became a rationalism because its practitioners never found any true natural economic laws. Very few were even proposed in the course of two hundred years. At least one prominent contemporary economist, Gerhard Tintner, has explicitly agreed with this conclusion—with what he calls "perhaps" a single, insignificant exception.[2] I will prove that economic laws are not natural-science laws by showing that they are entirely rationalistic. They are incapable of being used to make predictions that could be tested against facts at all. Incredibly, with the exception just noted, economists have been quite unaware that their discipline is not a science and never has been. They almost unanimously speak as though it were, at least in essence.

Whether a body of knowledge is a science depends entirely on the attitudes and precepts of the persons who practice it. Its subject matter is relevant only in affecting whether it can be a successful science. Alchemy, for example, was a science, as practiced by some alchemists. They sought to discover the laws by which things would combine to form gold. They carried out experiments and kept records of the results. If they did not always confine their work to objective things, they at least usually did.[3] But as we now know, the attempt was bound to fail. There is no way of combining anything to form gold without forming new elements, and the means for doing this were not available until after alchemy had ceased being practiced. Parapsychology may be another field in which, although a scientific approach is honestly and competently used, the attempt is bound to fail. To the extent that alchemy involved the use of incantations, magic spells, and the like to facilitate the combinations of things, on the other hand, it was an example of a nonscientific approach to a subject that could

[2] Gerhard Tintner, "Methodology of Mathematical Economics and Econometrics," in Otto Neurath, ed., *International Encyclopedia of Unified Science* 2, no. 6 (Chicago: University of Chicago Press, 1968), 16.

[3] "Alchemy," in *The New Encyclopaedia Britannica,* 15th ed., 1 (Chicago: Encyclopaedia Britannica, 1976), 431–36.

have been successfully approached scientifically. Chemistry is of course the science today that deals with the combinations of things on the level that alchemy did, and many of the techniques of chemistry could have been employed centuries ago.

Rationalisms are not necessarily inferior to sciences. Mathematics and philosophy are largely rationalisms, for example. And a subject that is not amenable to successful pursuit as a science may be successfully pursued as a rationalism. Economic behavior, however, is not such a subject. Economic behavior importantly includes objective things, although it involves other kinds of things as well, so it cannot profitably be studied on the basis of principles that neither look to facts for their support nor seek to arrive at conclusions that can be tested against facts to ascertain their truth. The response to the difficulties that were encountered in treating economics as a science, therefore, namely, transforming it into a rationalism, was a regression—a return to a prescientific way of thinking about the objective parts of the world, as Whitehead described. Rationalisms have their rightful place, but they are not for describing the realities of either the natural or the social world.

One of the early products of economic rationalism was Say's Law, which remained a mainstay of economic theory until the 1930s. It decreed that if an economy were left alone, business cycles would be self-correcting. (The law's rationale actually leads to the conclusion that business cycles would never occur, but since they evidently did, logic was bent to allow it to be said that they would be self-correcting.) Thus, the law decreed, if economic activity slowed, the activity would quicken if the economy were left alone. If economic activity proceeded too rapidly, it would eventually slow down if the economy were left alone. Busts would always eventually turn into booms, booms into busts, or either would eventually turn into a normal rate of activity.[4]

[4] John Kenneth Galbraith, *Money: Whence It Came, Where It Went* (New York: Houghton-Mifflin, 1975), pp. 218–20.

But the law said nothing about how slow economic activity would become before it quickened again, or vice versa, or about how long the process of self-correction would take. The law was therefore quite untestable. If a bust seemed to be going on too long, the explanation could be that the economy's self-correcting propensities were simply taking longer than one might have hoped, but the law was still correct, because all it predicted was an eventual recovery. Similarly, if a bust seemed to be more severe than busts ought to be or had been in the past, all would eventually be well. A second way in which Say's Law was rendered factually untestable was by its qualification that the economy be left alone. Any bust that lingered too long or went too deep, or any speculative boom that proceeded too far, could be blamed on anything the government had done that violated the principle of *laissez faire.* And of course governments have to be economically active to some extent, even if they limit themselves to employing policemen and collecting taxes.

An example of economic rationalism that is still current is the law of supply and demand. The law is that supply and demand together determine price. The supply of a good is defined as the amount of it that producers will produce at a price. It is typically represented as an upward sloping curve on a graph on which price is represented as the vertical axis and the amount of the good as the horizontal axis. The higher the price, the more of the goods the producers will produce. The demand for a good is defined as the amount of it that buyers will buy at a price. It is typically represented as a downard sloping curve on the same graph. Where the supply curve intersects the demand curve, we see the price that will prevail, because at this price the producers will produce exactly as much as the buyers will buy. If the price were any higher, the producers would produce more than the buyers would buy, temporarily, until those concerned realized that inventories were being built up faster than they could expect to be sold. The price would then fall so that buyers would buy more, or so that the producers would reduce their production, or both, and the price would go back to its determined level again. The mechanism would act similarly if the price were temporarily any lower than this level.[5]

Textbooks typically state that the law of supply and demand applies only to perfectly competitive markets—markets in which there are so many sellers and the goods are so much alike no matter who is selling them that no seller has any control over price, which is then always the same for all, the "market price."[6] Under any other conditions, the law of supply and demand is replaced by the law that a profit-maximizing seller sets his price so as to make his marginal receipts exactly equal his marginal costs. My own opinion is that the two laws are essentially the same—the same chains of reasoning are applied to different assumed sets of facts. To the extent the different sellers' goods are not alike, different sellers face different demands, and each can affect his price by varying his individual supply. Thus there is typically a slightly different price for each seller instead of a single market price. But the essence remains the same: the producers, or sellers, supposedly have their productions (the supply) determined by the prices they can obtain; the buyers have the amounts they will buy (the demand) determined by the prices they will have to pay; and the two determinations together intersect to determine the price or prices that will prevail.[7] But whether the two laws are really the same or not, they are untestable and therefore rationalistic in the same respects.

The laws are untestable because they fit any and all facts. *Whatever* the supply, demand, and price for a good, the law can be said to predict and explain the situation. The actual price must be the price at which the producers will produce what they are producing, because they are producing this much at this price. This must also be the price at which the buyers will buy what they are buying, because they are buying

[5] Paul A. Samuelson, *Economics,* 9th ed. (New York: McGraw-Hill, 1973), pp. 377–90.

[6] See, for example, ibid, pp. 68–69.

[7] Ibid., p. 395.

this much at this price. This must be the price the theory predicts, because the supply and the demand are as they are, and this is in fact the price. Economic texts commonly try to make the law of supply and demand appear to be testable by postulating the existence of what they call "supply schedules" and "demand schedules"—empirical determinations of what producers would supply at various prices and of what buyers would buy at various prices.[8] The schedules could presumably be used for plotting the curves on the graph, and the curves' intersection would then predict the price that was in fact being charged. However, no such supply or demand schedules have ever been compiled, so far as I am aware. Except under very rare and special conditions, they could not be, even in principle.

If, under the conditions that ordinarily prevail in the real world, a producer were asked how much he would produce at various prices, he could not give an honest answer without first asking about a host of other factors. He would have to know his costs of production in detail, for example—how much they would be at each level of production, since costs generally do not vary uniformly with production or remain fixed without regard to production, at least not for long. He would also want to know how long he could expect the price to last, since there are sure to be one-time costs of expanding or curtailing production that he would want to take into account. And so on, practically *ad infinitum.* Moreover, if he were thoroughly honest, he would have to confess that even if he had all the facts he wanted about production costs he could still only hazard a guess. For no producer ever really knows exactly how all the facts will "mesh" until the time comes and goes—if he can know even then. What really happened, and why, is generally not knowable even after the fact, as any historian, policeman, or lawyer could testify.

Finally, since in the real world no producer only produces—he also sells—this producer would also have to take

[8] Ibid., pp. 52–53, 59–60, 381–86.

his prospective sales costs into account. This necessity alone is sufficient to make the compilation of a supply schedule impossible, because the things for which sales costs are incurred affect demand, and demand affects price, yet the price is supposedly being set hypothetically as the basis for ascertaining how much the producer would produce. The producer at this point would have to say that he could not predict how much he would produce at a particular price unless he were also told how much he would have to spend per product in order to create the demand that would permit him to get the price. He could not be told this unless he were told the amounts of demand that each of the many possible nonprice forms of competition described in Chapter 1 would produce for his goods, and the costs per unit of sales of each. Just one of the many difficulties in telling him this would be that sales costs are generally not incurred as costs per unit of sales. A given amount of advertising will generally spread its effects a long time into the future, for example, so its costs per unit of sales will depend on what sales are throughout this period, and this will always depend in part on factors other than the advertising.

Questions directed at buyers and potential buyers to determine a demand schedule would encounter similar difficulties. And any actual attempts to construct supply schedules or demand schedules would soon uncover still another reason why the law of supply and demand is untestable: its hidden premise that as the price varies, all other factors remain the same. This premise is present in the assumption that there is a particular level of production or purchase that corresponds to a particular price. If this assumption were not made, there would have to be separate curves for each factor other than price that would affect production or purchase at a particular price. And of course in real life all other factors do not remain the same, even if they are known, and they are rarely, if ever, all known.

The profit-maximization *assumption* operates to make economic laws rationalistic by providing a condition that can be said not to have been satisfied if the law's predictions prove to be inaccurate. The profit-maximization *principle* is a law of economics in itself, and in the way it is almost universally used it is also rationalistic. It is a law because it asserts something about economic behavior—that sellers (the principle is not generally applied to buyers) behave so as to maximize their profits. If the principle were really used this way, and if "profits" were defined narrowly enough to avoid making the principle tautological, the principle would not be rationalistic. One could test it against the facts by ascertaining what sellers' motivations in different situations really were. The almost universal way of using the principle, however, is simply to state it as an assumption and then to go on to use it without saying anything about how likely it is to be correct under any particular circumstances. The reader is thereby given the impression that almost all sellers must maximize profits in fact, because profit-maximization is the only motivation mentioned, and *all* the laws that the author goes on to use or derive that depend upon sellers' motivations rest on this assumption. What the author gets away with, so to speak, is to make an implicit assertion that sellers always maximize profits, but because the assertion is only implicit, he can always plausibly deny having made the assertion at all. This is the way that the leading economics textbook for college use in the United States uses the profit-maximization principle, for example.[9]

The profit-maximization assumption leads directly to another law of pricing theory that is as basic as the law of supply and demand, if it is not part of it: the law that a profit-maximizing seller sets his prices so that his marginal revenues from sales exactly equal his marginal costs of making the sales. Indeed, the law is nothing more than the assumption. The proof of the law consists in showing that by setting his prices at this

[9] Samuelson, *Economics*, uses the profit-maximization assumption, implicitly at least, as early as p. 62, expressly states it as early as pp. 453–54, and assumes it and nothing else, whenever sellers' behavior is involved, throughout. The book's length is 886 pages.

level a seller makes the most profits he possibly can.[10] This law is rationalistic for the same reasons as is the law of supply and demand, because, as we have seen, they are essentially the same laws.

We saw in Chapters 5 and 6 that the theory that inflation always results in the last analysis from excess demand is also a rationalistic law, although we did not so label it.[11] It too is factually untestable because it can be said to fit any facts. Like Say's Law, it says nothing about time or amount. As a result, any amount of inflation, at any time, can be said to have resulted from any amount of demand, at any time or times prior to or concurrent with the inflation, and the theory can always be said to have been confirmed. Different economists have blamed our present inflation on different demand-increasing activities of our government that have occurred at different times for the past twenty-five years.[12]

The laws just shown to be rationalistic, plus Keynes' law of the determination of aggregate income, compose the entire corpus of basic economics as it is presently generally taught in the United States.[13] I will demonstrate the rationalism of Keynes' law in the next chapter. Practically every other law of economics derives from these, and so is also rationalistic.

The laws of economics were made rationalistic first by making their terms tautological. Thus, supply and demand were defined as amounts supplied or demanded at various prices, from which it follows that the price that they supposedly determine is already included in their definitions. The laws were also made rationalistic by being subjected to conditions that could always be said to have been violated. A failure of the facts to come out as the law predicts can then always be excused because a condition of the laws's application

[10] Ibid., pp. 489–96.
[11] See Chapter 5 at notes 7–8 and Chapter 6 at notes 1–19.
[12] See Chapter 6 at notes 14–17.
[13] Samuelson, *Economics;* Armen A. Alchain and William R. Allen, *University Economics: Elements of Inquiry,* 3rd ed. (Belmont, Ca: Wadsworth Pub. Co., 1971).

has been violated. Say's Law exemplifies this method. The condition that an economy be left alone can be said to have been violated by practically anything a government does. The frequent use made of "ideal" or "perfect" states is an extreme form of this second method. The defining conditions in these cases are so strict, rather than so vague, that it can always be said that they were violated. As every reputable economics text admits, for example, no "perfectly competitive market" has ever existed.[14] The almost universal assumptions of profit-maximization, full information, and rational behavior are also examples of conditions that can always be said to have been violated, but this fact is not commonly admitted. This might not seem on the surface to be true of rationality, but as this assumption is used by economists it means much more than just sanity. It frequently means that the business firms or whatever other economic agents are involved are capable of thinking through logical chains of reasoning—and acting upon them in the hurly-burly of the business world—that take the economist authors themselves several pages of fine print to explain.[15]

Still another means by which economic laws were made rationalistic was by what I will call the false objectification of factors. The factors that enter into the law as determinants are too subjective, too value-laden or otherwise insufficiently objective to serve as determinants. Both the law of supply and demand and the excess-demand theory of inflation exemplify this method. I have already shown how subjective a supply schedule is. The subjectivity of the concept of excess demand is obvious. What seems excessive to one person could easily seem insufficient to another, or about right to a third—even if the concept were not defined tautologically as the amount of demand that precedes or accompanies whatever amount of inflation is supposedly caused by it.

[14] Samuelson, *Economics,* p. 69.

[15] See, for example, Richard Markovits, "Tie-ins, Reciprocity and the Leverage Theory, Part II: Tie-ins, Leverage and the American Antitrust Laws," *Yale Law Journal* 80 (1970), 195.

Economists' Actual Use of Economic Laws

However, except for Say's Law, all the economic laws just described *can* be used to make predictions, and they have been, many times. But when they are, they are first implicitly changed so as to make them neither rationalistic nor deterministic. They are transformed into generalizations about economic behavior, similar to the generalizations about other kinds of human behavior that we all frequently make and act upon. I have not encountered a single instance in which an economic law was used to make a prediction except in this manner.

Three kinds of changes are necessary. One, the factors identified as determinants must be considered instead as just influences. Two, any qualifying conditions must be eliminated or at least made less stringent. The second change ordinarily follows almost automatically from the first. Once a determinant as been redefined as just an influence, it is ordinarily no longer necessary to place strict conditions on its operation, because the operation of an influence is commonly understood to vary, depending on the conditions under which it is felt. Three, the factors identified as determinants—now thought of as just influences—and the factor that they supposedly determine must be redefined, if necessary, to eliminate their tautological character and their false objectivity.

For example, the law of supply and demand can be made usable for making predictions by being rephrased as the statement that sudden and substantial increases in the supply of a good are likely to cause the good's prices to fall, and vice versa. This statement says "are likely to cause," which, of course, is a way of saying "influence." The only conditions on the operation of the influence are that the changes in supply be sudden and substantial. These are not stringent conditions, and they are not precise, but they have a reasonably definite meaning in the kinds of contexts to which the statement is meant to apply. "Supply," as the word is used in this statement, is not to be thought of as a curve on a graph plotted from a supply schedule, which is a falsely objective way of thinking of it, but simply as the quantity of goods that the sellers are offering for sale. Rephrased in this way, the law of supply and demand is undoubtedly correct, and it is useful for understanding and predicting the probable price effects of sudden and substantial changes in supply.

Economic laws are also commonly used as standards. For example, on the assumption that if it could exist, a perfectly competitive market would determine the economic behavior of sellers and buyers in certain ways, which are thought to be good, the requirements of a perfectly competitive market are used as a standard for judging real markets, to assess how competitive they are. More competition is presumed to be better, less to be worse. Some parts of the antitrust laws make certain practices illegal if, and only if, they can be shown substantially to reduce competition in the markets in which they are employed. Other parts of the antitrust laws make certain practices illegal *per se,* on the assumption that they necessarily reduce competition by substantial amounts.[16] The first group of laws requires that someone apply the economic standard in each case. In the second group, Congress or the Supreme Court has applied the standard and come to a conclusion that it considers valid for every case. In none of these instances is an economic law being applied as a scientific law; it is not being used to predict behavior or anything else. The use of these "laws" is purely evaluative, to distinguish legal from illegal, good from bad. And the evaluations have turned out to be inescapably subjective, as will be shown.[17]

Using a law as a standard renders its determinism superfluous, but does the determinism then do any harm? There is no logical necessity that it will, but it is likely to, by making the standard inappropriate. The determinism assumes that to the extent that the facts satisfy the standard, the kind of behavior that the law predicts *will* follow. In reality, of course, this is not so. The antitrust laws rest on the assumption that the closer real markets conform to the standard of the perfectly

[16] Philip Areeda, *Antitrust Analysis,* 2d ed. (Boston: Little, Brown, 1974), pp. 11–12, 275–88, 530–68, 594–99, 657–840.
[17] See this chapter at notes 36–41 and thereafter.

competitive market, for example, the more the behavior of sellers and buyers in them will provide all the societal benefits that competition is supposed to provide. But as was explained in Part I, competition under modern conditions frequently does not provide such benefits *even when it is quantitatively strong.* The standard of the perfectly competitive market is no longer generally appropriate in the modern world. It should be replaced by standards that are more discriminative of the sorts of markets to which they are meant to apply.

If economic laws are never actually used deterministically, why do economists persist in phrasing them this way? The principal reason must surely be to maintain the appearance that economics is a science, as we saw in Chapter 7. Another reason, I think, is worth mentioning because it discloses still another way in which economic determinism does harm: it is easy to phrase a generalization about behavior in a deterministic way—so easy that it inhibits thinking. A deterministic approach is therefore likely to lead to only superficial results. If a determinist discovers *anything* that affects economic behavior, no matter how slightly, he is logically justified in calling it a determinant, because he can logically say that it will affect the behavior to some extent, at least, if all other things remain the same. Even the slightest influences have discernible effects if all other influences are removed—as they are, in imagination anyway, by the assumption that all other things remain the same. So the determinist need think no further. He has his law. Indeed, he is prohibited from thinking further if he wants to maintain the correctness of his law. The moment he relaxed his assumption that all other things remained the same and began to think about the real world, he would have to acknowledge that the factors that affect economic behavior never all remain the same but one, that their effects are never quantifiable, that they are never entirely separable from one another, that *all* of them are never known, and that they never determine the behavior anyway, since the behavior is always in the last analysis human behavior, which is in the end always governed by free will. Economists have sometimes sought to justify their practice of making unrealistic assumptions by saying that it simplifies their thinking. It certainly does.

The Falsifying of Economics

Economic determinism has falsified economics primarily by making it deterministic, of course, but it has also produced what might be called subsidiary falsifications—less basic but still important falsifications that follow as logical consequences of the primary one. Probably the most damaging of these for the accuracy of economics has been to impute motives that people or economic organizations do not necessarily have and that, in some circumstances, they almost certainly do not have. Economic determinism logically requires that a single motive be imputed to everyone in their economic behavior, because if it were to be admitted that motives might be different, behavior could not be considered determined by the objective conditions under which it occurs. Different motives can lead to different behavior under the same conditions. Economic determinism also requires that satisfaction of the motive be maximized. If it were to be admitted that a person did not continue to pursue just one goal no matter how much of it he had already achieved, his behavior, again, could not be considered determined. The same objective conditions might then lead him to different behavior, depending on how much of the goal he thought he had already achieved.

The commitment to determinism sufficiently explains, I think, the otherwise incredible persistence of economists in assuming maximizing behavior. The relatively few who have become dissatisfied with the profit-maximization assumption have still not dropped the assumption of maximizing behavior. They have gone on to propose that something else—sales receipts, satisfaction, and so on—is being maximized.[18] This

[18] For the use of an assumption that sales revenues are being maximized, see Alfred S. Eichner, ed., *A Guide to Post-Keynesian Economics*

persistence is otherwise incredible because it is so obvious to any intelligent and unbiased person that individuals and other economic agents such as corporations do not universally or invariably maximize anything. Even if one does not believe in free will one cannot think that they do, if one has any familiarity with psychology, sociology, organizational theory, or history, or if one has a spouse, child, or any other close personal relationship.

The positivism of economic determinism also works to falsify. Positivism forbids any consideration of people's actual motives, since these are invariably subjective, and sometimes they are also normative.[19] It dictates that economic behavior is to be observed through its objective manifestations alone. But this is impossible. Human behavior makes no sense unless motives, reasons, purposes, intentions, or something else that helps to explain *why* a person is acting as he is are known or at least inferred. Human behavior without motives or reasons is not even conceivable. The attempt to make economics positivistic has therefore never been thoroughly carried through. Reasons and motives have been imputed to replace the actual reasons and motives that are ignored, in order that the behavior that is only positivistically observed can be made to make sense. Whether under any particular circumstances the imputed reasons or motives are the actual ones is a question that is not considered relevant. All that matters, supposedly, is that the observed behavior, with the reasons or motives imputed to it, make at least some sense.[20]

(White Plains, N.Y.: M. E. Sharpe, Inc., 1978), pp. 34–42. For the use of an assumption that a person's "satisfaction" is being maximized, see R. H. Coase, "The Problem of Social Cost," *Journal of Law and Economics* 3 (1960), 1. For descriptions of and citations to assumptions of still other kinds, see Oliver E. Williamson, "Firms and Markets," in Sidney Weintraub, ed., *Modern Economic Thought* (Philadelphia: University of Pennsylvania Press, 1977), pp. 185, 187–89.

[19] See Introduction at notes 18–22.

[20] George J. Stigler, *The Theory of Price*, 3rd ed. (New York: Macmillan, 1966), p. 6. For a good survey of the current uses of this approach, see Williamson, "Firms and Markets."

The Biasing of Economics

Motives always involve values. It can almost be said, if not quite, that motives are simply values under other names. The profit-maximization motive, for example, obviously translates into a supreme value placed upon profits. Since it is the profits of the person himself that are assumed to be maximized, the profit-maximization motive also translates into a value of absolute selfishness—absolutely selfish greed. When economic theory assumes a certain motive, therefore, it is making a statement both about what actual motives probably are and, if it goes on to demonstrate benefits that are derived from the assumption, what actual motives ought to be. The theory is biased. Traditional economics, by its almost universal use of the profit-maximization assumption, is making a statement that people and economic organizations are in fact generally selfish and greedy and, since it goes on to demonstrate benefits that derive from this assumption, that they ought to be. The role that positivism plays in thus biasing traditional economics is ironic, because one of the principal justifications that economic positivists have put forward for their approach is that it insures that economics will be unbiased, or "value free."[21]

We saw in the preceding chapter that traditional economics is also biased in a political sense, in favor of business and the rich, and that this bias is also a result of its determinism. The doctrine that incorporates this bias is *laissez faire*.[22] Although not as strongly interpreted as it used to be, *laissez faire* is still integral to traditional economics because it has to be if economics is to be deterministic. Market forces cannot have their supposedly deterministic effects unless the government leaves private economic behavior alone. Keynes' law, for example, although it advocates government "interference" to the extent of raising or lowering aggregate demand, and so is less *laissez*

[21] Milton Friedman, *Essays in Positive Economics* (Chicago: University of Chicago Press, 1953), pp. 3–7.
[22] See Chapter 7 at note 55.

faire than Say's Law, still advocates no more government "interference" than this.

Economics is also biased in favor of the values of competition, and this too results from its determinism. Competition is supposed to be the generator of the market forces that do the determining. One does not need to deny the many values of competition to recognize that they are not all served equally in every situation, that they conflict in some situations, and that there are other values, not served by competition, that a society might want its economy also to serve. With appropriate legal supplement, economic means might be found for encouraging and maintaining beauty in the environment, for example. Job satisfaction is another value that economic factors might be made to serve but that is little served by competition, especially at the lower ends of the economic scale.

A biased economics is unfair to those against whom it is biased. In the United States this includes practically everyone who is neither a corporate executive or rich. The rest of us still share in the benefits that traditional ecoomics provides despite its biases, and no one denies that these have been considerable. But the biases deprive many of us of a fair share, and also work directly to our disadvantage. Working people undoubtedly did not obtain the benefits of labor unions until decades after they otherwise would have, for example, and they were forced to work under worse conditions than otherwise would have prevailed—unsafe and unhealthy work places, for example—because of these biases.[23] A biased economics is also not a fit instrument for fashioning the economic policies of a democratic government. It fails to be fairly representative of the whole.

[23] For a description of the class bias against labor unions in the United States early in this century, see Walter Lippmann, *Drift and Mastery* (New York: Mitchell Kennerley, 1914), pp. 77–100; Walter F. Dodd, *Administration of Workmen's Compensation* (New York: Commonwealth Fund, 1936), pp. 1–2.

The Denial of the Possibility of Fundamental Change

Scientific laws do not change. If they are correct, they are correct for all time. Electrons and protons attract each other with the same force today as they did decades ago, when the force was first measured, and as they presumably always did and always will. This fact has led economists to believe that their laws, too, once discovered should not change. The rationalistic laws that they have devised do indeed not need to be changed, since they fit any and all facts; but, as we have seen, the only way that economic laws are really ever used are as standards or generalizations. If there are changes in economic conditions or behavior, the standards may become inappropriate or the generalizations incorrect. This is no more than what a competent social scientist would expect. He would not expect the conclusions drawn from a study of small-town life in the United States before the First World War to remain valid today, for example. But the belief that their laws are different, are "truly" scientific, misleads economists into just such mistaken expectations all the time. As a result they continue to use standards that have ceased to be appropriate and generalizations that are no longer correct, and they neglect to do the occasional checking that a social scientist would, to see whether their standards are still appropriate and their generalizations are still correct.

Thus, for example, one of the leading textbooks on antitrust law, in use as I write this in 1980, cites a leading economic textbook, published in 1970, for the proposition that oligopoly prices are "sticky."[24] The data upon which this conclusion rests date from 1901 to 1916 and from 1922 to 1933.[25] An oligopoly is an industry composed of only a few firms, selling a uniform set of products. "Sticky" means that the prices tend to remain the same for long periods. "Stickiness" is a kind of price behavior, and the conditions defined as oligopoly are

[24] Areeda, *Antitust Analysis,* citing Edwin Manfield, *Microeconomics* (New York: Norton, 1970), p. 311.

[25] Areeda, *Antitrust Analysis,* p. 15.

supposedly the determinants of it. In fact, however, oligopoly prices have not been "sticky" for decades. The prices of the steel industry have been volatile since the 1950s. The prices of practically all American oligopolies have been volatile since the middle 1970s.

The principal accomplishment for which Milton Friedman received the Nobel Prize in economics in 1976 was his discovery that people tend to save the same proportion of their incomes when their incomes increase, although the proportions change temporarily during the transition period.[26] But there is no more reason to think that this supposedly determinative relationship will remain true indefinitely than the supposedly determinative relationshp between oligopoly and price "stickiness."

The current economic theories of government regulation of business all posit supposedly determinative relationships between a government's supposedly inherent (and therefore timeless) goals of regulation and the effects of that regulation. These theories were formulated in the 1950s and 1960s. Events in the late 1970s and in 1980 have already disproved them.[27]

The so-called "Phillips Curve," named after its discoverer, A. W. Phillips, is either a law or a generalization, depending on how one phrases it.[28] It predicts that as the rate of unemployment goes up, the rate of wage inflation goes down, and vice versa. Stated this way it is just a generalization. But as its

[26] "Friedman Doubts Employment Goal in Nobel Lecture," *Los Angeles Times,* December 14, 1976, pt. 1, p. 1; Professor Friedman's publications in this respect are many. Most of them, with comments, can be found in Robert J. Gordon, ed., *Milton Friedman's Monetary Framework: A Debate with his Critics* (Chicago: University of Chicago Press, 1974), pp. ix–x, 180.

[27] Michael Levine, "Revisionism Revised? Airline Deregulation and the Public Interest," *Law and Contemporary Problems* 44 (1981), 179.

[28] A. W. Phillips, "The Relation between Unemployment and the Rate of Change of Money Wage Rates in the United Kingdon, 1861–1957," *Economica* 25 (new series) (November 1958), 283–99; reprinted in Max G. Mueller, ed., *Readings in Macroeconomics* (New York: Holt, Rinehart & Winstom, 1966) and in Robert James Ball and Peter Doyle, eds., *Inflation–Selected Readings* (New York: Penguin Modern Economics, 1969).

discoverer stated it and as many other economists have continued to repeat it, it is a law, because they state it as establishing particular mathematical relationships between these two rates for particular countries. But the "curve" began to be inaccurate, even as a generality, shortly after it was first published in 1958. It has taken some very fancy statistical work and the postulating of "short term," "long term," and "middle term" Phillips Curves, all supposedly interacting, to produce any close fits with reality ever since.[29]

The Defenses of Economics as a Science

Economists have brought forth a variety of arguments to defend their natural-science approach. Probably the most common is to define science in a way that makes anything else self-evidently wrong. For example, a "scientific" economics has been defined as an economics that refuses to disregard or contradict objective evidence or as an unbiased economics.[30] Of course no one wants an economics that illogically disregards relevant evidence or that is biased. These arguments miss the point. The only aspect of science that is at issue is its determinism, which as we saw earlier is quite acceptable, indeed inherent and unavoidable in the true natural sciences. The real issue is whether determinism ought also to be assumed for the behavior of thinking human beings and the organizations they control.

The scientific approach to economics has also been defended as identical to the activity of natural scientists, who, it is said, also treat idealized conditions knowing full well that they are only approximations of the truth. The factors that economic laws ignore are compared with friction, for exam-

[29] See, for example, Graham Keith Shaw, *An Introduction to the Theory of Macro-Economic Policy,* 2d ed. (New York; Harper and Row, 1973), pp. 75–79; Anthony M. Santomero and John J. Seater, "The Inflation-Unemployment Trade-Off: A Critique of the Literature," *Journal of Economic Literature* 16 (1978), 499–544.

[30] See, for example, Friedman, *Essays in Positive Economics,* pp. 3–6; Robert Aaron Gordon, "Rigor and Relevance in a Changing Institutional Setting," *Amer. Econ. Rev.* 66 (1976), 1–2.

ple, which physicists, in their laws, supposedly also ignore.[31] But the laws of physics do not ignore friction. Friction is a force that the laws of physics take into account in the same manner as other forces. When particular applications of the laws of physics ignore friction, the justification is always given that experiment or theory, or both, demonstrate that the effects of friction under the circumstances are negligible. Neither of these precautions is commonly observed in economics. It is in the laws of economics, not just in some of their applications, that relevant factors are omitted. And economists have no way of ascertaining whether the omission of any factor or factors will or will not make a negligible difference under the circumstances, because their laws ignore the other factors.

The scientific approach to economics has also been defended as a logical use of probabilities.[32] Since probabilistic predictions possess a greater tendency to be accurate as they are applied to larger numbers of instances—that is, the actual results are more likely to be "bunched" closer to the predicted results when there are more of them—another way of stating this same defense is that the scientific approach to economics is capable of producing useful results after all, so long as the laws of economics are applied only to large numbers. The laws of economics supposedly find their validity not in any certainties about how individuals will react to particular objective events or conditions, but in habits, customs, or traditions that people *generally* follow in their economic behavior. The habits, customs, and so on that form the basis for economic laws, according to this argument, are commonly referred to as "societal uniformities."

This is a plausible argument, and it is the one that could justify taking a deterministic approach to any social science. The first thing to be noted about it, however, is that as a justification for traditional economics, at least, it misses the mark. The laws that traditional economics has generated are not

[31] See, for example, Samuelson, *Economics,* pp. 69–70, 630.

[32] Friedman, *Essays in Positive Economics,* p. 5 n. 3; Stigler, *Theory of Price,* pp. 5–10.

probabilistic, they are rationalistic, and rationalistic laws are incapable of having scientifically calculated probabilities attached to their predicted outcomes, because they do not predict outcomes. The economists who have made the probabilistic defense seem to be unaware of this fact. George Stigler, for example, makes the defense in the early pages of his well-known book on price theory,[33] presumably as a justification for the laws and theories he is about to illustrate, but the book contains not a single law or theory that predicts outcomes in a way that would permit scientifically calculated probabilities to be attached to them. They are *all* rationalistic.

Moreover, the rationalistic aspects of economic laws do not lose their influence as the laws are applied to larger numbers. The reader need only review these deficiencies to see that this is so. Tautologies remain tautologies no matter how many instances of behavior they are applied to. Definitions of conditions that enable it to be said afterwards that the conditions were violated if the facts do not turn out as predicted maintain this capability without regard to the numbers of instances. Factors that are objective only in appearance possess no tendency to become objective in fact when applied to larger numbers. For example, the ascertainment of when an economy's aggregate demand becomes "excessive" for the purpose of causing inflation does not become any less subjective when applied to the aggregate demand of a large economy.

However, the principal error in the probabilistic defense of economics as a science is that the kinds of laws that it prescribes—laws that can be used to predict outcomes to which scientifically calculated probabilities may be attached—are impossible. Not only have none been found to date, none ever will be, no matter how long economists persist in the attempt. Such laws would be impossible even if there were no free will. They are certainly no less impossible if the existence of free will is granted. These are important conclusions, not least because they apply to all the social sciences. They require some explaining. I will begin by discussing the basis upon which

[33] Stigler, *Theory of Price,* p. 6.

probabilistic laws are derived in the sciences that do not concern the behavior of thinking beings—the true natural sciences.

The probabilistic defense must be taken to assume that the probabilities of which it speaks will be scientifically calculated, which is to say they will have a sound basis in logic or observation. This must be so because otherwise the defense would not constitute a defense of a *scientific* economics. Anyone can attach an unscientific probability to anything. I could right now attach a probability of 10 percent to the Dodgers winning the National League pennant next year, although I know little more about the Dodgers than that it would be wrong to predict their winning the pennant in the American League. In order for probabilities to be scientifically calculated, there must be a set of conditions upon which the probabilities can be based. For example, the probabilities of the various possible outcomes of a spin of a roulette wheel are calculated on the basis of the wheel and how it is spun. For an ordinary roulette wheel, the conditions upon which the probabilities would be based are that the wheel has numbers 1 to 32 plus one or two zeros on which only the house wins, that the numbers are colored alternately red and black, that the slots in the wheel for the numbers are all of equal width, that the wheel is perfectly flat, so that the ball is no more likely to roll into some slots than into the others, that no one interferes with the spin of the wheel or the roll of the ball after the wheel has been spun, and so on. If any of these conditions is violated the calculated probabilities of the outcomes of a spin will not be correct.

The scientist working in a true natural science can assure himself that all these conditions are met simply by specifying them. He specifies them as the conditions under which any experiment testing his probabilistic laws is to be run. Experiments that do not meet the conditions are not true tests. If, for example, some of the numbers in the roulette wheel that are normally black were painted red, red would presumably come up more often than black; this would not invalidate the probabilistic laws that had been calculated because the repainting would have violated one of the specified conditions, and the spins of the wheel would not have been true tests. But the social scientist has no way of specifying conditions, in most cases, because he does not know what the conditions are. All he has observed are the outcomes. He has observed that they have fallen into a particular pattern, but he does not know why. We mentioned earlier, for example, that Milton Friedman has observed that people's savings rates tend not to vary despite changes in their incomes, but he has not observed (or at least he has not reported) the underlying conditions from which these uniformities of conduct arise. Thus he has no way of scientifically calculating the probabilities that their conduct will continue. It is as though the scientist working with the roulette wheel never saw the wheel or even knew what it looked like, but observed only the outcomes—red numbers coming up about as often as black numbers, even numbers about as often as odd numbers, and so on. He could not specify the conditions that the wheel not be changed or interfered with, because he would not know what the wheel was or even that it was a wheel.

But it might seem that the social scientist could, in principle at least, dig deeper into his data or gather more data and discover what the underlying conditions were, and then he could scientifically calculate the probabilities of the outcomes. Friedman or some other researchers might ascertain why people's savings rates tended to remain the same during the periods that Friedman studied them, and having ascertained the reasons could then calculate the probabilities that the tendency would continue into the future—and at the same time, presumably, the probabilities that it would change in one way or another as time went by. This would not be possible either, however. If the underlying conditions were discovered, there would still be no way of *effectively* requiring that they not change, as the natural scientist can for his experimental conditions. Society cannot be controlled for experimental purposes the way a roulette wheel can.

A basis for the scientific calculation of probabilities could be achieved only if one could predict the probabilities that the underlying conditions would remain the same, and this would require the discovery of another set of conditions underlying the first set. But whether these underlying conditions would remain the same would also have to be predicted, which would require the discovery of a set of still more basic conditions, and so on, *ad infinitum.* The only stopping place would be the whole world—all the facts in the whole world, including the states of mind of every person in it, since people's actions are controlled by their states of mind, and people's actions are an integral part of any set of societal conditions or their continuance. This would be the only logical stopping place, because only at this point could it finally be said that nothing unexpected could happen to change what had been observed, since everything would have been observed.

But of course no law can possibly take every fact in the world into account. This is *in practice* impossible even if one does not grant the existence of free will. If one grants the existence of free will, it becomes *logically* impossible as well. For then, even if all the facts in the world could be taken into account, including the states of everyone's mind, someone could still change his mind in a way that would affect the outcomes, although this change had not been foreseeable on the basis of the facts that were observed. It is no wonder that economists implicitly gave up the attempt to make their discipline scientific and instead made it rationalistic, and that no other social science has ever derived a truly scientific law of probabilities, either. The whole endeavor is impossible.

Paul Samuelson has tried to save the scientific status of economics (he calls it the meaningfulness of economic theorems) by placing economic laws on what he calls a "qualitative" basis. He would give up the attempt to predict how much one objective variable would be affected by particular amounts of variation in the objective variables that supposedly determine it. He would be content to predict only whether, if the determining variables were increased or decreased, the determined variable would increase or decrease, without knowing the amounts of variation in either case. In mathematical terms, increases can be represented by positive signs, decreases by negative signs. So what Samuelson has suggested can be phrased as making economic laws sufficient only to predict the signs of the changes of the dependent variables when the signs of the changes in the independent (that is, the determining) variables are known. Thus, we would give up the attempt to deal with quantitative changes in order, supposedly, to deal accurately with "qualitative" changes, which is the term that Samuelson chose for changes that are characterized only by their signs. He first made his suggestion in the 1930s, but it was not published until 1945.[34]

Laws that are rationalistic can not even be used to make qualitative predictions, however, and as we have seen, all the basic laws of economics are still rationalistic, some forty years after the suggestion that they might be used qualitatively was first made. Various attempts were made to devise qualitative economic laws, but they all failed, so far as I have been able to ascertain.[35] It is a simple matter to show why the suggestion was bound to fail, although the demonstration requires some elementary mathematics.

A law of economics, if it is to be usable for making *quantitative* predictions, must like any scientific law be expressible in what is called "functional form." This means that the thing that the law predicts can be expressed as a mathematical symbol and placed on one side of an equal sign, and the things that determine it can be expressed as mathematical symbols and inserted into a function that is then placed on the other side of the equal sign. A function is some set of mathematical operations—addition, subtraction, multiplication, and so on. Thus, for example, if w is the symbol for the thing being pre-

[34] Paul A. Samuelson, *Foundations of Economic Analysis* (New York: Atheneum, 1965), pp. 1–20 and passim.

[35] For example, G. C. Archibald, "Chamberlin *versus* Chicago," *Review of Economic Studies* 29 (1961), 2–28; G. C. Archibland, "Profit-Maximising and Non-Price Competition," *Economica* 31 (1964), 13–22.

dicted, and x, y, and z are the symbols for the three things that are supposed to determine it, the law that states the prediction can be stated as:

$$w = f(x,y,z)$$

A small change in a variable is commonly signified by placing the letter d before the variable. Thus, a small change in w would be signified as dw. If one is willing to confine his interest to changes that are small enough, the changes in the dependent variable (w in the example) can always be expressed as simply the sum of the changes in the independent variables (x, y, and z in the example), each multiplied by a constant. This form of expression is called a "first-order differential form." It is a particular functional form. Thus, for small enough changes, one can always write,

$$dw = A\,dx + B\,dy + C\,dz$$

where A, B, and C are constants.

Samuelson's suggestion can now be seen as a suggestion that although we may not be able to discover economic laws that have either the functional form first shown above or the first-order differential form just shown, we can at least hope to find laws that will tell us just the sign of dw if we know the signs of dx, dy, and dz. The problem is that this does not work either. The reader should be able to see for himself that the sign of dw will not depend just upon the signs of the other three variables. It will also depend upon the sizes of the constants. But if we knew these, we would know the entire quantitative differential equation, and we would not have to be content with just qualitative results. Samuelson's suggestion works no simplification at all!

It might seem that it would, however, in the simplified case in which every independent variable but one was assumed to remain the same. If, for example, we were to assume that x were the only independent variable that changed, we could write,

$$dw = A\,dx$$

Now, it would seem, all we would have to know about A is its sign. If it were positive, positive changes in x would produce positive changes in w, and negative changes in x would produce negative changes in w, and vice versa.

But even this would not work. In real life, for every possible dependent variable (for every possible w) there are a very large number of possible independent variables—many more than just three. There are, in fact, as many as *might* change the behavior of the dependent variable *in any way*. This number is presumably without ascertainable limit, which is another way of saying that it is presumably infinite. So we can never accurately assume that all of the independent variables except one will not change. The best we can realistically hope for—and even this, it should be emphasized, is only rarely a realistic hope—is that only one of the things that might affect w will undergo any changes that are large when compared with the change in x. And even this would not be enough. For we would also have to know the *sizes* of the constants associated with all these other variables, relative to the size of the constant associated with x. We would have to know this, because if a relatively large constant is associated with it, even a small change in an independent variable can work a change in the dependent variable that is large enough to change its sign from what it would be if only x were changed.

At some points in his exposition Samuelson seems to assume that an economist could realistically expect that no independent variables but one would change in those cases in which the government, the seller, or some other actor in the situation had *all* the independent variables under his control. This would indeed be a safe assumption, but there probably are no such situations in the real world, and there is certainly no way of knowing in advance that there are. This assumption is just the assumption, under another name, that the social scientist can realistically specify the experimental conditions under which his laws are to be tested. The impossibility of making such a specification effective was explained when we discussed the difficulties in attempting to make probabilistic economic laws.

External Evidence That Economics Is Not a Science

If economics really were a science, there would not be the different schools of opinion within the subject that there are and always have been. Schools of opinion are common in the arts and humanities. But they are almost unknown in the true sciences because differences of opinion in a true science are always at least ultimately resolvable by resort to objective facts. Of course resort to the particular objective facts that would resolve a difference of opinion in a science may not be feasible at the moment—no one may yet have devised an experiment that could be carried out with the equipment presently available—but the knowledge that facts will eventually decide the issue tends to prevent any schools from arising even during a period of irresolution. The scientists on both sides of a controversy will cooperate in an attempt to devise experiments to resolve their differences.

Schools of opinion differing sharply on all sorts of issues not only abound in economics, but the issues on which they differ frequently have political connotations, which would be utterly impossible in a true science. One cannot imagine physicists, for example, dividing on an issue of physics along the lines of whether they were politically liberal or conservative. The most prominent division of opinion in economics today in the United States is that between the so-called "Chicago School" and the rest of the profession, which is politically more liberal. (The members of the Chicago School are concentrated at the University of California at Los Angeles, the University of Southern California, the University of Virginia, and the University of Miami, as well as at the University of Chicago.)

In 1950 Congress signaled to the Supreme Court that it wanted a more vigorous enforcement of the antitrust laws, especially against what Congress perceived to be a trend toward mergers that was threatening to bring about a substantial increase in domestic business concentration. The Court responded. Practically every antitrust doctrine, both as expressed in the statutes and as articulated by the Court in its judicial opinions, soon came to be couched in terms of a "lessening of competition" or words of a similar meaning.[36] Business practices that "lessened" or "tended to lessen" competition were prohibited. The Court applied the economics that it had to decide what lessened or tended to lessen competition, and looked forward to advances in economics to enable it to make such decisions more accurately and over broader areas of business conduct in the future.[37] But the expected advances never came. Competition, it turned out, is incapable of measurement. Conditions that influence competition—the number of firms in an industry, for example—can be measured, but there is no way, and there is not even the beginnings of a consensus on a way, of combining such conditions so as to formulate a legally significant factor of competition.[38]

In 1963, in *United States* v. *Philadelphia National Bank,* the Court announced that in default of adequate objective criteria it was laying down criteria of its own for certain kinds of mergers, which it admitted were to some extent arbitrary.[39] In 1973, in *United States* v. *Falstaff Brewing Co.,* a case that involved a different kind of merger, the Court split on whether avowedly subjective criteria were to be admitted into evidence or not and, if so, how much weight they were to be given.[40] Meanwhile, legal developments in other areas of application of the antitrust laws were similarly retarded and confused for lack of objective criteria.[41] It is fair to say, I think, that there

[36] Areeda, *Antitrust Analysis,* pp. 4–5, 37–40, 697–702.

[37] See, for example, Standard Oil Co. of California v. United States, 337 U.S. 293, 306–14, 322 (1949).

[38] Areeda, *Antitrust Analysis,* pp. 658–91 (treating a wide variety of factors that can affect competition, of which the effects of not even one are measurable).

[39] 374 U.S. 321 (1963), pp. 362–63.

[40] United States *v.* Fallstaff Brewing Corp., 410 U.S. 526 (1973), pp. 548 and passim.

[41] See, for example, Continental T.V., Inc. v. GTE Sylvania, Inc., 97 S. Ct. 2549 (1977), overruling its earlier decision, then only ten years old, on the subject of restrictions imposed on franchises; and see Fortner Enterprises, Inc. v. United States Steel Corp., 394 U.S. 495 (1969), and 429 U.S. 610 (1977), a case that the Court had to hear twice and on which it decided quite differently the second time, on so-called "tying arrangements."

has not been a single advance in economic theory since 1951 that has found application in the antitrust laws, as the Court had apparently expected there would. Competition is no nearer objective measurement today than it was in the 1950s.

Why Economics Can Never Successfully Be Studied as a Science

Economics has made some valuable contributions to human knowledge, but not through economists' attempts to study it as a science. We are now in a position to understand why. A science has to be deterministic. A physicist, for example, has to be able to assume that the behavior of the electrons he studies will be determined by the objective conditions in which he finds or places them; if they could make up their own minds which way to go and what other particles to combine with, their behavior could not be accurately described by scientific laws. In economics, however, as in any social science, the behavior being studied is *always* human behavior. Corporations, labor unions, government agencies, and so on are not human beings, it is true, but it is human beings and only human beings who always decide what they will do, that is, how they will behave. And even if one does not believe in free will, one has to accept the fact that if there are objective determinants of human behavior, *none* of them has as yet been found—neither by economics nor by any other science.

Positivism is a logical correlative of determinism, as we have seen. One can come to the same conclusion by reasoning from the positivist side of determinism. The positivist claims that the only truth there is can found, if it can be found at all, by the observation and analysis of objective things. The way he defines objective is by contrasting it with subjective and normative, the latter meaning essentially people's opinions of what is, ought to be, or should be done. But for the same reasons, economic behavior is also always subjective or normative, at least in the last analysis. It is always the behavior of some person or persons *choosing* what to do. An economic positivist who scrupulously followed his own prescriptions would have nothing to study. Subjective and normative kinds of behavior are the only kinds there are.

The probabilistic and qualitative approaches to economics are essentially strategies to get around these difficulties. The probabilistic approach tries to make human behavior seem to be determined (or seem to be explainable in "positive" terms) by searching for so-called societal uniformities—behavioral patterns that appear when large numbers of instances of behavior are statistically observed. Then, on the assumption that these are determined, it searches, usually also by statistical analysis, for what these determinants are. Societal uniformities do exist, but their existence does not prove that the behavior of which they are composed is determined. It is not even evidence that the behavior is determined, because behavior that is governed by free will should also produce patterns of uniformity when large numbers of instances are observed. People do not generally behave arbitrarily. They have reasons for what they do. People confronted with similar conditions are likely to draw similar conclusions about what they should do. People living in the same society are likely to have similar habits and customs and to be governed by the same or similar laws (laws of a legislative or judicial kind).

But, it might be asked, cannot societal uniformities be studied as though they were objectively determined, although we know that they are not? They can be, of course, but the study will never reach any really important results. If the behavior is uniform because it is in conformity with the same or similar habits, customs, or laws, the study of it is just unnecessarily complicated by a deterministic assumption, since the uniformity is readily explainable by the existence of the habits, customs, or laws. For example, that most Americans drive on the right side of the road is a fact that is obviously explained by the existence of customs and laws. It would be absurd to assume that there must be an objective determinant of this kind of driving. Moreover, for economics at least, the only truly interesting behavior is that which concerns choices that are not governed by habits, customs, or laws. A corporation executive does not decide what prices his corporation will charge by unthinkingly following a habit, custom, or law. Nor does a labor leader so decide what wages to demand or whether to call a strike.

Even to the extent that economically interesting behavior does concern choices that are governed by habits or customs (although not laws), the behavior will cease to be so governed if the people involved are confronted with anything that they consider important enough to make them stop and think. And it is precisely such important occasions or conditions that economics needs to understand if it is to be of any use. There would not have been a Great Depression if people had not changed their economic habits or customs in some respects. There could have been no cure for the Great Depression unless some ways could have been found for encouraging or requiring people to change their behavior again. Obviously, something had worked a change in people's habitual or customary ways, and something had to be found that would make them change again. It is difficult to see how a study of unchanging behavior would ever have led to the discovery of what the basis for either kind of change was or could be.

Samuelson's qualitative approach comes at the matter from the other side. Whereas the probabilistic approach seeks to harden the facts, so to speak, by considering only large numbers of them, the qualitative approach seeks to soften the theory. The attempt is to devise a "qualitative" mathematics that would be capable of dealing with "subjective-like" facts. (Samuelson never admitted that the basic economic facts are not objective. He never asked why the quantitative approach had failed. He just assumed that it had.)[42] But as we have seen, mathematics is not amenable to being softened in this way. One would need to know nearly as much about the economic reality in order to construct a qualitative theory as one would to construct a truly scientific, quantitative theory. Moreover, once the inevitably subjective and normative character of economic behavior is acknowledged, it follows that not even its

[42] Samuelson, *Foundations of Economic Analysis,* pp. 3–6.

direction, or mathematical sign, can be predicted solely on the basis of objective facts. Economists using the qualitative approach have produced exactly as many scientific laws as economists using the probabilistic approach—none.

The basic determinants of economic behavior posited by economics are subjective, but this fact is hidden by their objective-sounding names. There are just three such basic determinants: supply, demand, and profit—although profit, in different contexts, is given different names. Demand is people's willingness and ability to buy something at a particular price. Willingness is obviously a component of subjective choice. So is ability in this context, because it means financial ability, which involves willingness to forego other expenses in order to spend on the particular thing—willingness to forego saving, to dip into savings, to go into debt, and so on. Supply is people's willingness to produce and/or sell something at a particular price. This constitutes subjective choice for the same reasons as demand does, plus the subjective considerations described earlier in this chapter for "supply schedules." Profit, as the word is used in the profit-maximization principle or the profit-maximization assumption, is subjective in all the meanings that are commonly given to it except possibly the narrowest one, of monetary profits immediately realized from a sale—and even these are definable only with the help of accounting principles, the application of which to particular cases is inescapably subjective to a very large extent. In its broader meanings, profits include anything that the profit-seeker considers pleasurable or desirable. Pleasure and desire are of course components of subjective choice. Utility and satisfaction are essentially just other names for profits. They are also commonly treated as objective factors in economic theory, to be maximized. They are also subjective, for essentially the same reasons as are profits, broadly defined.

Such things as prices, net receipts, gross receipts, tons, volumes, and so on are not subjective, or at least there are common kinds of situations in which they can reasonably be given objective meanings, but economic laws are never composed of these kinds of things alone. So far as I can ascertain, the laws *all* also include some of the intrinsically subjective factors under objective-sounding names. They have to, because it is these factors that constitute the motives without which people would not act. Without the subjective factors, there would be no behavior; no one would "move."

It would be confusing enough, as well as inconsistent with being a science, if economics were merely to use these subjective motivational concepts as though they were objective. The confusion is compounded by the invariable practice of using them in what are commonly called their "marginal" forms. A "margin" is a very small change. The explanation of Samuelson's suggestive qualitative approach used marginal terms, for example—the variables preceded by *d.* The law that a profit-maximizing seller will price so as to make his marginal receipts equal his marginal costs is also, obviously, in marginal terms. What it means is that such a seller will price so that the *change* in his total profits resulting from one more sale will equal the *change* in his total costs resulting from the same sale. We went into some detail in Chapter 4 to show that the marginal profit is generally much more difficult to reduce to objective terms than the total profit. This is true in general if the total thing being studied is itself incapable of being objectively defined. It would be difficult enough for a corporation executive to predict the sales of a particular product if the product were priced at, say, ten dollars. It would surely be much more difficult for him to predict just how many more he would sell if the price were decreased by, say, ten cents. This prediction would involve marginal demand. Marginal costs, marginal supply, and so on all pose difficulties of essentially the same kind.

Post-Keynesian Economics

Throughout the book I have used the term "traditional economics" to mean the mainstream of that economics. The mainstream has always been composed of many currents, the differences among which are not important for our purposes;

and of course there have always also been some tributaries, the differences between which and the mainstream have also not been important for our purposes. The mainstream is currently commonly called the "neoclassical synthesis." There is really only one tributary of note at the moment, which is commonly called "post-Keynesian economics." The post-Keynesians constitute only a very small proportion of the economics community,[43] but as their name indicates they are especially concerned with macroeconomics, the branch of economics that is most concerned with inflation.

I agree with the post-Keynesians on practically all the issues upon which they disagree with the neoclassicists, and I have drawn upon the works of many of them in my treatment of the industrial pricing institution in Chapter 3. However, they and the neoclassicists agree on the fundamental concepts with which we are concerned in this chapter, so with respect to these concepts I of course disagree with them. In particular, post-Keynesians are determinists, and they evidence essentially the same errors and biases that I have tried to show result from economic determinism. A recent book by a group of prominent post-Keynesians written as a guide to their economics provides a vehicle for demonstrating this.[44]

Post-Keynesians continue to use the language of determinism. For example, in the introduction to the book, in describing the first of what he maintains are the five essential elements of post-Keynesian economics, the author says, "First, post-Keynesian theory offers an explanation of economic growth and income distribution—with the two viewed as being directly linked to one another. The key determinant is the same for both. This is the rate of investment. . . ."[45] There are many other examples, not quite so explicit,[46] and so far as can be ascertained from the book, which of course cannot go into detail on everything it describes, all the analyses take a deterministic approach.

[43] Eichner, *Guide to Post-Keynesian Economics,* p. vii.
[44] Eichner, *Guide to Post-Keynesian Economics.*
[45] Ibid., pp. 11–12.
[46] See, for example, ibid., pp. vii, 11–12, 14–15, 24–30, 51–60.

Prices are still assumed to be held down by competition except within what the post-Keynesians call an economy's "industrial core," which is the part of an economy that is composed of "multinational corporations and the somewhat less powerful national trade unions."[47] Even within this "core" prices are supposedly determined, although not by competition in the traditional sense. Prices are supposedly determined there by a maximizing motivation—specifically, a maximizing of the "growth in sales revenue over time, subject to a minimum profit constraint"—working in a context of an ability to vary supplies over a wide range in order to avoid price cuts, and a need of each firm to generate most of its growth capital out of its own sales revenues.[48] Thus, post-Keynesians still feel compelled to use a maximizing assumption for economic behavior, although they do not use the profit-maximization assumption, at least for explaining economic behavior within the "industrial core."

The post-Keynesians agree with me to the extent of concluding that contemporary inflation cannot be controlled exclusively through the traditional instruments of fiscal and monetary policy.[49] But they continue to believe that inflation is substantially affected by high levels of aggregate demand. They apparently still believe that even to the extent that inflation is not caused by high levels of demand, the conditions that cause it could be eliminated by eliminating the "multinational corporations" and "powerful national trade unions" that compose the "industrial core" (although they do not recommend this approach). They fail to see, or at least fail to agree with, what I regard as the most basic point of all for contemporary inflation: that the new forms of competition since about the mid-point of this century fail to determine prices enough to prevent inflation, whether the business enterprises are large or small and whether the employees are organized into unions or not. Finally, they fail to appreciate the volatility of what I call competitive inflation. They think that if an

[47] Ibid., p. 15.
[48] Ibid., pp. 34–42.
[49] Ibid., p. 17.

economy is essentially left alone, and no serious external pressures are applied, its inflation will not rise above tolerable levels.[50]

However, it would not be fair to leave the impression that post-Keynesian and neoclassicist economics are just variations of the same theme. The post-Keynesians are immeasurably superior, as a group, in their sense of relevance—in their instinct for what economics is really about. They have pushed their investigations squarely into the areas that existing theories least fit, as good scientists should, instead of using unrealistic assumptions to get rid of troublesome facts. Their description of the maximizing motivation supposedly at work at the industrial "core" is an example. It is not really a maximizing motivation, since it includes a constraint. Economists who were more concerned with the elegance of their theories would never have phrased it this way, but the post-Keynesians did, presumably because they were more concerned with being true to the facts.

The Costs of Trying to Prevent Economics from Being Just a Rationalism

Economists have not been unaware of the tendency of their discipline to turn into a rationalism, even though they have underestimated it. Their statements about the need to avoid tautological laws are evidence of their awareness. Additional evidence is the occasional enthusiasm they show for a new law that promises not to be rationalistic, but to say something definite, and the exaggerated importance they attach to such a law, although the law, when analyzed dispassionately, can be seen to be trivial or obvious.

A reportedly "controversial new theory called rational expectations" was put forth in 1976 and is still current.[51] The

[50] Ibid., p. 181–184.

[51] "How Expectations Defeat Economic Policy," *Business Week*, November 8, 1976, pp. 74–76; Mark Willes, "The Rational Expectations Model," *Wall Street Journal*, April 2, 1979, p. 26.

gist of it is that government economic policies can do little or nothing to achieve their aims because people anticipate them and take actions to avoid or evade them, which defeats the policies' purposes. For example, if the government contemplates imposing wage and price controls to prevent inflation, sellers, when they get wind of the intention, will raise their prices immediately in an attempt to "get under the wire." They will thereby cause more inflation immediately and in part, at least, also defeat the government's longer-range purpose if the controls are imposed. Thus, people acting "rationally" on their "expectations" of government policy can defeat, in part at least, the purposes of the policy. One would have thought that this fact was obvious for every kind of government policy. There would be no need of police if people were not always partially defeating the policies of the criminal law, for example.

Another economic theory that has gained a large following over the last few decades predicts nothing more than that the decisions that groups of people make through democratic processes are affected by the processes, and that there is no objective way of saying for sure that one process will provide a more accurate determination of the people's real wishes than another.[52] Again, one would have thought that this was obvious. Would the months of effort that the founders of our constitutional government put into designing the constitutional processes of lawmaking have made any sense to them had they not expected that the processes would make a difference? Would they have debated as long as they did or devoted so much argument to persuading the states to adopt the constitution had they thought that there was an objective measure of

[52] Kenneth J. Arrow, *Social Choice and Individual Values,* 2d ed. (New York: John Wiley and Sons, 1963); Charles Plott, "Axiomatic Social Choice Theory: An Overview," *American Journal of Political Science* 20 (1976), 511–96 and references at pp. 580–96; Peter C. Fishburn, *The Theory of Social Choice* (Princeton: Princeton University Press, 1973); Amartya K. Sen, *Collective Choice and Social Welfare* (San Francisco: Holden-Day, 1970). For a recent application of the Arrow theorem, see Michael E. Levine and Charles R. Plott, "Agenda Influence and Its Implications," *Virginia Law Rev.* 63 (1977), 561.

proving for certain that their design was or was not the fairest? This theory is also notable as another instance of false objectification. It posits that there are objectively existent wishes of people, capable of being measured, in order to make its point that no particular voting process can be said for sure to be capable of ascertaining how the wishes of the individuals composing a group should be combined.

The Personal and Social Costs of Economic Determinism

It is understandable if not always fortunate that science imparts a feeling of power and assurance. It "unveils secrets," as Whitehead said.[53] It has enormously increased the power at a society's disposal. And it has permitted such accomplishments as building the Panama Canal and taking men to the moon, from which everyone can at least vicariously derive a sense of power and accomplishment. Economics has occasionally imparted the same feeling. The writings of John Maynard Keynes reflect a strong sense of self-assurance, presumably arising from his belief that he had unveiled the secret of the business cycle and provided a sure means of controlling it. Walter Heller appeared elated for a few years in the sixties, after he had participated importantly in the Kennedy and Johnson administrations' apparently successful application of Keynes's principles to the American economy.[54] Milton Friedman's writings and other public activities reflect a similar sense, which presumably arises from his belief that his monetary theories hold the secret of controlling inflation. But the vast majority of economists, judging from their public utterances, have become timid and dispirited.

A *Wall Street Journal* reporter a few years ago character-

[53] See Chapter 7 at note 17.

[54] Walter W. Heller, *New Dimensions of Political Economy* (Cambridge: Harvard University Press, 1966).

ized economists as suffering from "future fear."[55] It is not just that they do not understand what to do. People have always been faced by difficulties that they don't know how to handle. This fear seems to be deeper, however, and to come from a combination of not knowing and believing that the economic events that concern them are in some fundamental sense beyond anyone's control. Some economists have expressed their belief that the determinant of contemporary inflation is democracy.[56] They suppose that elected officials have no choice if they wish to be reelected but to cause the government to act in ways that cause inflation. Others have expressed the belief that the determinant of inflation is prosperity, so that inflation will be a fact as long as prosperity lasts.[57] What the "future fear" and these fatalistic attitudes have in common is the belief that economic events and conditions are beyond human control, like volcanic eruptions and earthquakes, and that the best we can hope for is to learn to live with them in their mild forms and pray that they do not become worse. This too has to be counted as a harm of economic determinism.

Worse than the attitude that nothing can be done is the attitude that people ought to change, or be changed, to conform to economic theory. The chairman of the Federal Reserve Board a few years ago scolded Americans for not shopping carefully enough, in his frustration that competition was not keeping prices down as theory says it should.[58] The chairman of the Council of Economic Advisors blamed inflation on people "demanding too much," like spoiled children, and

[55] James P. Gannon, "Future Fear, Is the Economy Sliding into Five or Ten Years of Stagnation, Unrest?" *Wall Street Journal,* May 15, 1975, pp. 1, 23.

[56] Paul Craig Roberts, "Political Economy, Instability, Cui Bono?" *Wall Street Journal,* February 15, 1979, p. 20; Robert J. Gordon, "The Demand for and Supply of Inflation," *Journal of Law & Economics* 18 (December 1975), 807 ff.; see also James M. Buchanan and Richard E. Wagner, *Democracy in Deficit: The Political Legacy of Lord Keynes* (New York: Academic Press, 1977).

[57] Robert Heilbroner, "Reflections: Inflationary Capitalism," *New Yorker,* October 8, 1979, pp. 121–41.

[58] Paul E. Steiger, "Consumers Urged to Battle Inflation," *Los Angeles Times,* May 27, 1974, p. 1 (quoting Arthur Burns).

called it "sentimentality, prejudice, and myopia" for people to get in the way of the economy's "efficient" functioning with their "tears" about unemployment and environmental damage. The rising unemployment rate was not much to be worried about, he said, because it consisted of a *higher* proportion of young people.[59] A prominent economist writing in the *New York Times Sunday Magazine* deplored the tendency of corporate executives to do things that they thought would be in the public interest, instead of maximizing profits.[60] Many articles in recent years have urged us to accept the fact of higher unemployment in order to beat inflation—as though we who are not unemployed have any moral right to accept this status for others.[61] Those who blame inflation on democracy would presumably see no choice but to eliminate democracy if inflation were to become intolerable. There has been a line of thinking that dates at least from the early forties that the "road to serfdom"—the road to totalitarianism is what is meant—is traveled to the extent that a government asserts control over economic activity.[62] The greater danger seems to be from those who would sacrifice people to economic theory.[63]

Economic determinism, of course, cannot be given the entire blame for the materialism and alienation of the modern

[59] "Stein Blames Public for Inflation, Urges Self-Discipline in Spending," *Los Angeles Times,* July 8, 1974, p. 7.

[60] Milton Friedman, "The Social Responsibility of Business Is To Increase its Profits,"*New York Times Sunday Magazine,* September 13, 1970, p. 32.

[61] For example, Sanford Rose, "We've Learned How to Lick Inflation," *Fortune* 94 (September 1976), 100; "Friedman Doubts Employment Goal."

[62] Milton Friedman, *Capitalism and Freedom* (Chicago: University of Chicago Press, 1962), pp. 12–13; Friedrich A. Hayek, *The Road to Serfdom* (Chicago: University of Chicago Press, 1944), p. 70; Friedrich A. Hayek, *The Constitution of Liberty* (Chicago: University of Chicago Press, 1960). And see Christian Bay, "Hayek's Liberalism: The Constitution of Perpetual Privilege," *Political Science Reviewer* 1 (Fall 1971), 93, 112–13, 117–18.

[63] Hannah Arendt identified the willingness to sacrifice people to theory and to ignore facts that conflict with theory as a characteristic of totalitarianism. Hannah Arendt, *Origins of Totalitarianism* (New York: Harcourt, Brace, Jovanovich, 1973), pp. 348–51.

world, but it has contributed importantly. The determination of economic behavior has always been thought to occur through markets, and markets are deemed to work through competition. Competition is thus stressed to the practical exclusion of cooperation. Competition, moreover, is pictured as working, or at least working best, through the entirely selfish and entirely materialistic motivations of the persons who participate in it. This view of the world must inevitably have contributed to producing widespread alienation and materialism, and these are indeed attributes of American society that have been widely noted.[64] Economic determinism has also contributed to materialism in the larger sense through its own specific materialism, as was explained in the preceding chapter. Nothing is supposed to count economically except to the extent that it can be objectified, which is to say, to the extent that it can be measured. The natural way of measuring things in economics is by their monetary equivalent—by the cost, price, or dollar value. The psychological result has been to diminish the value of anything not measurable by money.

[64] Joyce Carol Oates, "A Taut Novel of Disorder,' *New York Times Book Review,* April 3, 1977, pp. 3, 34–35; Paul Jonas, "Home Thoughts from Abroad," *Harper's* 254 (April 1977), 20–21; John Leonard, "Falling off the Train," *New York Times Book Review,* April 3, 1977, pp. 3, 31; Robert Nisbet, "Public Unions and the Decline of Public Trust," in A. Lawrence Chickering, ed., *Public Employee Unions* (San Francisco: Institute for Contemporary Studies, 1976), pp. 13–33.

CHAPTER 9

The New Economics

Since economics cannot successfully be a natural science, it might be thought that the answer would be simply to transform it into a social science. The answer is not so simple, however. The social sciences have encountered the same problems in their attempts to model themselves after the natural sciences as economics has.[1] If they have not generally suffered so much, it is only because they have not generally sought so much. The right answer, I think, is that economics ought to be a social science, but not as the social sciences generally are now, but as they ought to be—essentially humanisms. A humanism is a study centering upon distinctly human interests and ideals. It does not deny the fact of free will, so it does not presuppose the conformity of human behavior to deterministic laws. The social sciences ought not to be like humanisms, however, in being removed from practical matters. Governments and individuals should continue to be able to look to the social sciences for understanding and advice.

Chapter 7 described the influences that support economic determinism. Influences can work both ways, of course. If economics ceases to be deterministic and becomes more humanistic, this development will influence the other social sciences and society at large, which will presumably be influenced away from materialism. The economics profession will benefit, not least from its vastly increased chances of success. Economists should start to gain the reputation, which they

[1] For a well-thought-out and well-known statement of the epistemological principles and methodologies that a social science ought to have (but which is much more positivistic than I would suggest), see Otto Neurath, *Foundations of the Social Sciences* 2, no. 1 (Chicago: University of Chicago Press, 1944). See also Martin I. Hollis and Edward J. Nell, *Rational Economic Man* (Cambridge: Cambridge University Press, 1975).

now lack, of really caring about people—about whether jobs are satisfying and interesting, for example, or whether housing is pleasant to live in, or whether cityscapes and landscapes are beautiful, or whether the environment is healthy and safe. All these things are importantly affected by economic activity. There is no reason that economics ought not to be as concerned with them as it presently is with profits and growth. Society would also benefit from an enhancement of the sense of free will. People who are taught to study themselves on the assumption that their behavior is objectively determined cannot help but come to believe that it is. The passivity, the fatalistic sense of helplessness when confronted with large problems that so many people in modern societies seem to have must surely be a result of these deterministic patterns of scholarly thought, at least in part. The social sciences should be leaders in making people aware of the wide scope of freedom they really have.

Economics as a Humanistic Social Science

In its empirical compass, the new economics would include everything that traditional economics does, and it would also include the nonobjective facts, which exist but cannot be demonstrated conclusively because they cannot be measured. For example, the new economics would take into account people's actual motives. Motives cannot be measured, and they are incapable of objective demonstration. At some point, the statements of the persons to whom the motives are attributed must be believed, or their motives must be inferred from a combination of what they say and what they do. Either way, the matter is never objectively without doubt. That it makes sense to take the actual motives into account despite their nonobjective nature is proven by the fact that all of us do so in our personal affairs. If we are aware of other people at all, we are continually asking or inferring their motives. Other social sciences have successfully taken actual motives into account; the works of David Riesman and C. Wright Mills in sociology are outstanding examples.[2]

In the significance it would attach to the facts within its empirical compass, however, the new economics would be more modest than traditional economics. Nothing would be regarded as a determinant of economic behavior because, in fact, nothing is. Things would be regarded as what they truly are, which is at most an influence. This would effect a tremendous simplification, which ought to more than offset the additional complication caused by including nonobjective facts. The law of supply and demand, for example, which with its many ramifications in perfect and imperfect markets, and so on, currently requires hundreds of textbook pages for its explanation, probably could be reduced to only a few pages, and those pages would be much simpler for the ordinary student to understand. Nothing of value would be lost, because the deterministic aspects are false.

The acceptance of the fact of free will would mean that there could be no attempt to make *scientific* predictions of human behavior, but this does not mean that economics would not be usable for the purpose of making predictions. It could still be the basis for the inexact, nonnumerical kinds of predictions that business persons, politicians, statesmen, and people of all sorts make every day. What are the chances that a new Arab-Israeli war will erupt within the next year? I doubt that even the most astute student of the affairs of that area of the world would care to assign a numerical probability to his answer to that question, yet every person who studies Middle Eastern affairs must have some notion of how likely such a war is. The estimate of how likely something is, in human affairs, is not usually spoken of as a prediction at all, but as a judgment. The new economics should provide a much better basis for making judgments about what the future holds than traditional economics does, because its acceptance of the

[2] David Reisman, *The Lonely Crowd* (New Haven: Yale University Press, 1961); C. Wright Mills, *White Collar* (London: Oxford University Press, 1953).

fact of free will and its inclusion of nonobjective facts will give it a much more accurate and complete view of human affairs. Its inability to make scientific predictions will not be a loss, because the old economics couldn't either. It merely tried.

I pointed out in Chapter 8 that the truths that could be found in economic laws after the determinism had been stripped away were just generalizations about human behavior, and that the supposed determinants were just influences. The new economics would speak directly in terms of generalizations and influences. This would be more honest and accurate, and it would also be much simpler. The judgments that economists would make about how likely something is would also more often be concerned with influences than with outcomes. This is the kind of judgment in human affairs that is usually the most useful, again because of free will. This time it is the free will not of the persons about whom a judgment is being made but of the persons who will act on the judgment. The making of a judgment (or prediction) about the outcome of something that people can affect by their actions is senseless unless some assumptions are made about their actions. And what such people are most interested in, usually, are judgments about how they can act most effectively to increase the chances of certain desired outcomes.

The only sensible kind of judgment, and the most useful kind in such a situation, is a judgment about what kinds of influences on people will induce them to act in such a way as to produce the desired outcomes. If the State Department expert on the Middle East were asked by the secretary of state what his opinion was of the chances of war there, if he answered frankly he would answer that much depended on what actions the United States took or did not take with respect to that area. Even then, of course, no certainties could be attached to any judgments, but one at least could then begin to talk sensibly. The secretary's next question—which in real life would presumably have been his first one—would be, what do you think we ought to do or avoid doing to decrease the chances of an Arab-Israeli war? The expert's answers could then be made sensibly, and he would begin talking about what could be done to *influence* the Arabs and the Israelis not to start a war with each other.

These are the essential differences between the new economics and the economics we now have, which will result from its being a social rather than a natural science. Some additional differences will result from these. The new economics will be conceptually simpler. In particular, it will have a different and simpler concept of equilibrium. It will put greater emphasis on empirical research. It will not strive to remain "value free," although it will of course try not to be biased. And it will have a freer, more lively spirit.

The Simplification and Accuracy Effected by Abandoning Determinism—Keynes' Law as an Illustration

Keynes' law of the determination of aggregate income is easily the most important economic law discovered within the last half-century. It would presumably have cured or prevented the Great Depression had governments applied the measures it would have dictated. It has permitted the world to avoid recurrences of deep or lasting depressions ever since. The law has been a success, however, only because it has been applied nondeterministically, in the manner that economic laws are always used if they are used at all. The law as explained by Keynes is of course quite deterministic. His explanation of it constitutes the largest part of his *The Theory of Employment, Interest and Money,* which is a work of monumental size.[3] The law as there explained was so difficult to understand that it was not generally understood in the United States until it was explained again in simpler terms by American economists, notably Alvin H. Hansen.[4] By now, some

[3] John Maynard Keynes, *The General Theory of Employment, Interest and Money* (New York: Harcourt, Brace and Co., 1936).

[4] John Kenneth Galbraith, *Money: Whence It Came, Where It Went* (New York: Houghton Mifflin Co., 1975); Alvin H. Hansen, *A Guide to Keynes* (New York: McGraw-Hill, 1953).

forty years later, still simpler explanations have been worked out.[5] The explanation that follows is taken from the clearest current explanation that I could find, which, not surprisingly, is that of Paul Samuelson in his elementary text for college economics. My explanation is only about a twentieth the length of his. It is shorter because my purpose is not to explain but to illustrate how a deterministic law is both unnecessarily complex and positively misleading. After explaining Keynes' law as briefly as possibly in the way Keynes framed it, as interpreted by Samuelson, I will show that everything in it that is correct can be explained much more briefly still, and much more understandably and less misleadingly. This simpler, more understandable, and more accurate form of Keynes' law would be the normal form in which all economic laws could be cast in the new economics.

Aggregate income is the sum of the incomes of all the economic units of which the aggregate is composed. The aggregate income of a nation is commonly called its national income. (I will hereafter call an economic unit a person, without distinguishing between natural persons, that is, individuals, and corporations and other kinds of artificial entities. "Person" is easier to understand and less awkward than "economic unit.") The amount of a person's income that he spends on consumption is called, simply, consumption. Consumption is measured in monetary units. The amount of a person's income that he does not spend on consumption is called savings. A person's income is never all spent instantly, of course, and on the other hand it is generally all spent after enough time has elapsed. The distinction between consumption and savings thus requires us to specify a time period—a year is a convenient choice. Then it can be said that income that is spent on things that are consumed within a year is spent on consumption, whereas income that is not thus spent is saved. The amount that is spent but not consumed is called invest-

[5] See, for example, Robert Lekachman, *The Age of Keynes* (New York: Vintage Books, 1966); Paul A. Samuelson, *Economics,* 9th ed. (New York: McGraw-Hill, 1973).

ment. The ultimate source of investment presumably has to be income, but for reasons not clear to me, at least, Keynes chose not to make this source explicit, as he did with savings and with consumption. The excess of what the government spends over what it takes in by way of taxes, fees, and other receipts is called the government deficit. Finally, whatever a person receives from another person's spending or from the government is counted as his income except to the extent that it counts as a cost, and a cost is counted as such only to the extent that it consists of transfers to other persons, which then count as income to them, or of transfers to the government.[6]

A conclusion that follows from all these definitions is that the government deficit plus aggregate investment plus aggregate consumption equals aggregate income. There are many ways of proving this, but the most straightforward is probably the following. Add aggregate costs to both sides of the equation. The right side is then aggregate income plus aggregate costs, which must equal aggregate *receipts*—a concept that Keynes did not employ, but that there is no reason for us not to employ if we want to. The left side then equals the government deficit plus aggregate investment plus aggregate consumption plus aggregate costs, which equals aggregate *spending*—again, a concept Keynes did not employ—for the simple reason that these are all the kinds of spending there are, as Keynes has defined them. Then one can see that the two sides are equal, because aggregate receipts must be equal to aggregate spending, there being no place for money to go when it is spent by one person or by the government except to add to the receipts of another person. (Government receipts are not counted in Keynes' scheme. Instead of counting government on both sides of the equation, as spending on one side and receiving on the other, as private persons are counted, Keynes put the government on only one side, as a *net* spender, that is, as the spender of a deficit.) Finally, since we have shown that the two sides of the equation are equal when aggregate costs

[6] Samuelson, *Economics,* pp. 205–33.

are added to both, they must still be equal when aggregate costs are subtracted out again from both, and they must have been equal to begin with.

Another conclusion that follows is that aggregate investment plus the government deficit equals aggregate savings. The amount of income that is not spent on consumption is, by definition, saved. Thus, income equals consumption plus savings. We know from the first conclusion that, skipping the adjective "aggregate" for the sake of brevity, the government deficit plus investment plus consumption equals income. Substitute into the first conclusion consumption plus savings for income, and you get the government deficit plus investment plus consumption equals consumption plus savings. Consumption now appears on both sides of the equation and so can be subtracted out from both sides, leaving the government deficit plus investment equals savings.

When investment falls, therefore, for whatever reason, and other things remain the same, savings must fall apace. It also follows that aggregate income must fall, also by exactly the same amount, *if* everything else remains the same. But as a matter of fact it is likely to be worse than this, because experience shows that when their incomes fall people try not to allow their savings to fall by as much—they try, on the average, which is to say in the aggregate, to keep their savings at about the same percentage of their incomes, no matter what their incomes are. The result is to make their incomes fall even farther. For example, suppose a person has an income of $10,000 a year out of which he saves $500. If his income falls to $9000, experience shows that if he is average he will try to maintain a savings rate of $450. He will *not* borrow ("dissave") $500 a year so as to maintain his consumption at its previous level. Nor will he reduce his savings to nothing. Rather, he will both save and consume one tenth less—his consumption will go down to $8850 and his savings to $450. So when aggregate savings fall because investment falls, aggregate income will also fall. The fall in aggregate income will cause still more of a fall in aggregate consumption, which will cause still more of a fall in aggregate income, which will cause still more of a fall in aggregate consumption, and so on. When will it all end? Only when people's incomes have fallen so far that despite their desire not to decrease their savings very much, their actual savings (which, remember, must be the same as aggregate investment plus the government deficit) will be just what they want to save out of their much-lowered incomes. Thus, a decline in investment has what is called a "multiplier effect" on income. It makes income fall by some multiple—rather, it will if the assumption is accurate that savings fall only proportionately when income falls.

When aggregate income falls, aggregate spending falls with it, and when aggregate spending falls, employment generally falls with it. So a decline in investment brings on both lower incomes and higher rates of unemployment. A rise in aggregate investment has the opposite effect, up to the point of 100 percent employment, after which, of course, employment cannot go any higher. If investment continues to rise past this point, there is demand-pull inflation. No more goods are produced, but the additional spending continually bids up the prices of those that are.

Keynes showed all this and then made the observation that secured his reputation. *All* the described effects of a shortfall in investment can be avoided or transformed into the effects of a rise in investment, or vice versa, by changes in the government deficit of the same amount in the opposite direction. Since changes in the government deficit exactly offset changes in investment, they also have a "multiplier effect" on aggregate income, at least to the extent that the assumptions about savings are accurate. If a government increases its spending sufficiently, or decreases its receipts sufficiently, or both, it can bring an economy out of even the deepest depression, at least in theory. If the government keeps abreast of short-term fluctuations in investment, it can keep its economy on an even course at an employment rate of just under zero—an even course of almost no unemployment and almost no inflation. This is in fact what the federal government of the United

States learned to do during the Kennedy administration and did quite successfully until indeterminate inflation began to spoil things in the early seventies.[7]

I have not stated here the entire law of the determination of aggregate income. In particular, I have not treated its monetary aspects—the extent to which changes in the money supply, brought on by either government actions or the actions of private bankers, can offset the effects of changes in investment, just as changes in the government deficit can. The law's monetary aspects can be omitted without distorting the law because, according to Keynes, they have exactly the same results on aggregate income as do changes in the government deficit. Whether a government should offset unwanted investment changes by changes in its deficit or by changes in the money supply ought to be decided, according to Keynes, on the basis of which method is subject to the more precise control, which will be more effective under the particular circumstances, and which has the more desirable or fewer undesirable side effects.[8] But with the addition of monetary aspects, the statement of the law made here constitutes its essence. This statement is vastly shorter than Keynes was able to manage, much shorter than Hansen was able to wrest from Keynes, and shorter by far even than the shortest statement in a current elementary economics text that I was able to find. The reason that it can be made shorter again and again is that almost all of it is unnecessary. Keynes' genius consisted in his ability to discern a few very simple truths through the forest of obscuring deterministic conceptions and biases that he had to work with in the 1930s, which still exist.

The fact is, *any* decrease in spending, whether by persons or by the government, will have exactly the same depressing effect on aggregate income as does a decrease in investment.

[7] See Walter W. Heller, *New Dimensions of Political Economy* (Cambridge: Harvard University Press, 1966).

[8] Lekachman, *Age of Keynes,* pp. 103–106. The debate between "fiscalists" and "monetarists" can get heated, however. See, for example, Milton Friedman and Walter W. Heller, *Monetary vs. Fiscal Policy: A Dialogue* (New York: W. W. Norton, 1969).

The fact is also that any increase in spending, whether by persons or by the government, will have the same offsetting effect as does an increase in the government deficit. All the divisions into which the pie of aggregate spending is divided and all the different ways of viewing the pie and its divisions (as income rather than as out-go or spending, for example) are quite superfluous to the only point worth making and the only point that the law has ever been used for—the management of employment and national income by variations in the money supply or in the government deficit. The reader can prove this for himself by tracing the effects of any increase or decrease in spending. Dollar for dollar, they all have the same effects, whatever their source, whatever their destination, whatever their purpose. Recently published statements of the law generally acknowledge this fact, but only after they have gone through the statement with all its subtle and complex definitions and their interrelations.[9] Why does anyone still feel compelled to include all this extraneous material in the law's statement? Why did Keynes feel he had to include it? One cannot know for sure, of course, but Keynes and his initial interpreters, at least, must not have understood that it was extraneous. They presumably were only able to find their way to the conclusions about government deficits and money supplies by passing through all these supposed objective determinants. Believing as they did that all economic behavior is determined by something objective, they must have felt that national income, like everything else, must have its determinants, so they must also have felt that the only way to discover how to cure or avoid depressions was to discover these determinants. Keynes' more recent interpreters must feel similarly, despite their increasing awareness that the law is capable of a simpler statement than Keynes or any of the earlier interpreters gave it.

The way that the United States government uses the law is simply to make a guess, based on experience, of how much the deficit and/or one or more of the different kinds of money

[9] Samuelson, *Economics,* p. 228.

supply should be increased or decreased to obtain the desired effects on employment and national income, and then to make these changes in these factors. The data on employment and national income are watched, to see if they are responding as the government wants them to. If they are not, the deficit and/or the money supplies are changed again, accordingly. No precise use is made of the data on savings, income, investment, or the other defined quantities. The changes that occur in employment and national income after changes have been made in the federal deficit or the money supplies may or may not occur because of these changes. They may occur for other reasons, or for no reason that the government policy makers are aware of. None of this really matters, because whatever the reasons for the changes in unemployment or income, the government deficit and/or the money supplies can, in theory at least, be changed again to retard or accelerate them.[10] Finally, changes in employment and in national income, these days, do not at all occur in tandem, as Keynes implicitly assumed they would, because indeterminate inflation has had the effect of requiring constant increases in national income merely in order to keep employment from falling—as we saw earlier.[11] The management of employment and national income by means of manipulating the deficit and the money supply becomes less exact as indeterminate inflation increases.

The quantities that Keynes felt it necessary to include in his law are what in the preceding chapter I called false objectifications. They only seem to be measurable. Take the purchase of an automobile, for example. The definition of consumption tells us that some portion of the automobile's dollar value should be counted as consumption, presumably the portion that is consumed—that is, used up—within a year of its purchase. But there is no objective way of ascertaining how much this is, either at the time of purchase or at the end of the year's period. The purchaser generally has no precise expectations,

[10] The description in the text is derived from a reading of the Council of Economics Advisers' annual *Economic Reports to the President* (Washington, D.C.: U.S. Govt. Printing Office) for the relevant years.

[11] See Chapter 5 at notes 6–7.

and even if he does, unforeseen events such as an accident or the introduction of a new model that makes his largely obsolete can defeat them. According to the law, people decrease their savings when their incomes fall, although only proportionately, but if they decide not to buy new automobiles but to keep their old ones awhile longer instead, they will probably thereby *increase* their savings—whether they actually do or not will depend on the amount deemed saved by the purchase of a new automobile and on the amount deemed saved by keeping the old one and not consumed by purchasing a new one. The amount deemed consumed or saved by the purchase of an automobile is also dependent on the method chosen for paying for it. The more cash that is paid, the more the savings; the more that the purchase is made on credit, the less the savings, since borrowing is a form of negative saving. The purchase of a durable good such as an automobile must also be counted as to some extent an investment, since it is a form of spending that is to some extent not for consumption. This too brings into play a host of subjective and otherwise difficult considerations.

The ascertainment of a person's income is also difficult and subjective, especially if the person is a business. It depends upon the accounting system he uses, among other things. Not even the government deficit can be objectively measured. Widely differing amounts can be obtained for the same fiscal period, depending on which accounting system is employed to obtain them.[12]

In seeking to answer the charges of other economists that some important economic magnitudes cannot be measured, the econometrician Gerhard Tintner said they could be, because they are quantitative. He pointed out that consumption of specific quantities is given in terms of pounds and numbers of items, production of various quantities is again given in terms of pounds and numbers of items, interest rates are in

[12] *Economic Report of the President,* Transmitted to the Congress February 1971 (Washington, D.C.: U.S. Govt. Printing Office, 1971), pp. 70–74; David J. Ott and Attiat F. Ott, *Federal Budget Policy* (Washington, D.C.: Brookings Institution, 1977), p. 159.

percentages, prices are in dollars, and so on.[13] Tintner's answer fails to satisfy the shortcomings just shown with respect to Keynes' law. The fact that the amount of consumption of a specific good can be measured in pounds or number of items does not help at all to determine what the amount is, which, as we saw, depends upon the ordinarily highly subjective intentions and value assessments of the persons who are doing (or not doing) the consuming, at least when the goods are durables. Tintner's answer is also naive in failing to consider the problems of aggregating different kinds of quantities. It does not make sense to add numbers or pounds of automobiles produced to the numbers or pounds of apples produced. One must, of course, first convert all the units to dollars. But conversion to dollars immediately raises the question of price, which is generally highly subjective. Should the dollar figure for automobile production be the aggregate of the prices that the automobile dealers pay the manufacturers, which would normally include the amounts that the manufacturers paid to railroads and trucking companies to transport the new automobiles to the dealers, but would not include the dealers' costs of operation or profits? Or should it include only what the manufacturers receive for the automobiles, which would not include what they paid the transportation companies—unless they charged the dealers for the whole thing and paid for the transportation themselves? How can the prices of different manufacturers be accurately added together if they follow different charging or billing practices in these respects? Or should the prices used to provide the aggregates be retail prices, which would include the dealers' costs of operation and profits? And in all these cases there remains the problem of including or not including the costs and prices of credit, which is almost always extended both by manufacturers to dealers and by dealers to retail purchasers, although whether it is managed through separate credit agencies or

[13] Gerhard Tintner, *Methodology of Mathematical Economics and Econometrics* (Chicago University of Chicago Press, 1968), pp. 19–20.

not varies both among manufacturers and among dealers. And so on.

All the aforementioned difficulties in Keynes' law are compounded by the fact that all the quantities the law employs are defined in terms of the others. Savings, for example, is defined as income that is not spent on consumption, and income is defined as the received spending of someone else or of the government, less costs. So any difficulties in ascertaining the amounts of these other factors will also create difficulties for ascertaining savings, and vice versa. This property of the law also means that the law is tautological, so the law is rationalistic on at least two grounds. Also, although not strictly speaking inaccurate in this respect, Keynes' law is misleading in making it seem that the multiplier effect depends upon the extent to which persons spend their money on consumption rather than save it. Actually, a person who spends his share of the additional money the government put into the economy to buy an automobile that he intended to use for five years, for example, would be raising other people's incomes and contributing to more employment to the whole extent of his purchase, not just to the extent of the value of the automobile he intended to consume in the first year, as the law's description makes it appear. That this is so is obvious, I think. The law's description is technically correct nevertheless, because the assumption has already been made that aggregate investment has fallen. So a person's purchase of a durable good or other form of investment (which is at the same time also a savings) has already been taken into account and so should not be counted again with respect to the multiplier effect.

An economist who was not a determinist could have reached all the useful conclusions that Keynes reached so indirectly and laboriously much more directly and easily. His first step would presumably have been to ask what it is about a depression that is undesirable. The answer surely would have been the same as the answer Keynes came to, because this is a question that is not dependent upon economics. The answer, of course, is high unemployment and low (aggregate) income.

The next step for the nondeterminist economist, however, would presumably have been much simpler, since he would have gone immediately to the question of what the government might do about it. He would not have assumed that there were determinants of employment and income that must be ascertained before it was sensible to ask what the government could do about them. The nondeterminist's answer for the income would have been obvious. People's incomes can be increased if the government gives them more money, which it can do, among other ways, by lowering their taxes; or the government can spend money on employing them, or on buying the goods they were producing or could thereby be encouraged to produce. The answer for income would presumably have led directly to the answer for employment. Spending money on employing people or on buying goods they are producing or could produce obviously increases employment, and so would giving them money, on the reasonable assumption that some of the money, at least, would be spent by them in employing other people or buying the goods produced by others. There would also be a multiplier effect, to the extent that the people who received additional money from the government spent it and thereby raised other persons' incomes and generated still more employment. And this description of the multiplier effect would not misleadingly be made to seem dependent on an absence of savings. A little more thought presumably would have led to the conclusions that peoples' incomes and employment could also be increased by the government lending them more money, or by its taking actions that would encourage banks and other private lending institutions to lend them more money. These conclusions would be the equivalent of the monetary measures for affecting aggregate income, whereas the first conclusions were the equivalent of the fiscal measures. The nondeterminist economist's last step, presumably, would have been to explore whether any or all of the ways of increasing employment and income would have good or bad side effects, and whether some would be preferable to others on this account.

This imaginary nondeterminist could therefore quickly have come to the following conclusions: what is bad and needs changing about a depression is that too many people are unemployed and too many people have insufficient incomes; both conditions can be changed for the better if the government gives people more money to spend or itself spends more money; people can be given more money to spend if the government taxes them less, if the government spends more on them, or, under some conditions, if the government makes it easier and less expensive for them to borrow; any of these things that the government might do to increase the volume of private spending will have a multiplier effect, because what one person spends he generally spends by paying it to another person, who then generally spends some part of it, at least, again, and so on.

This is *all* there truly is to Keynes' law! Like the only true parts of any economic law, they are just some generalizations about human behavior. They are so obvious that it seems incredible that it took a genius to discover them. Who could *not* have seen that people would spend more if they had more to spend, that in spending more they would employ more people and increase incomes, or that people would have more to spend if the government taxed them less, spent more on them, or made it easier or cheaper for them to borrow? Surely, it required a genius to discover these things only because, then as now, economic truths were obscured by determinism.

Had the economics of the time permitted him to think about economic behavior in nondeterministic terms, Keynes presumably not only would have come to his conclusions much more quickly but the conclusions probably would have been put to use much more quickly. It would not have taken years for other economists to understand them and decades until government leaders could be persuaded to try them. The aura of mysteriousness and abstruseness that has never quite left Keynes' teachings presumably would never have arisen, so the distrust of the teachings, which has never quite been dissipated, presumably would never have arisen either. The implementation of Keynes' law in the United States in the 1960s is still being blamed by some for our present inflation, for example.[14] And what is true for Keynes' law is true for economics generally. Without its determinism it would be immensely simpler. Everything that is presently included in the elementary college course, and more, could probably be taught in high school, and the average student would be able to understand and remember much more of it. Then, freed from the need to overcome artificial obstacles in order to reach obvious truths, advanced economics could grapple with the truly difficult problems that confront the world.

A Nondeterministic Concept of Equilibrium

One of the central mysteries that any economics has to solve is equilibrium. Why in ordinary times are prices, for example, not different every time we go to a store, or at least not different by more than very small amounts? Why is almost everyone able to go to the same place, meet the same people, and do about the same things every workday, confident that his activities will be needed and that he will be paid a certain amount for what he has done? The ordinary equilibrium of economic life is taken for granted by most people, but for the economist it is a mystery to be solved, for it is the central fact of economic experience in every society. It presumably hides within it the solutions of other more limited but still important mysteries. Equilibrium is also a central problem for any economics because it occasionally fails to hold and sometimes threatens to dissolve altogether. Means must be found for restoring

[14] In principle, *all* those who believe that contemporary inflation arises at least ultimately from excess demand must blame the inflation on the implementation of Keynes' policies. The fiscal and monetary measures advocated by Keynes for the purpose of maintaining high rates of growth and unemployment have these effects by virtue of maintaining high levels of demand. So if there is inflation, the excess-demand theorists must conclude that these demand levels are, or were, excessive. Frequently, Keynes is also blamed explicitly. See, for example, "To Set the Economy Right," *Time,* August 27, 1979, pp. 24–26 and passim.

it when this happens. Thus, after the industrial revolution had got underway, economic equilibrium was periodically disturbed by business cycles. Since the early seventies it has been increasingly disturbed by indeterminate inflation.

It has always seemed to economists that the fact of equilibrium could only be explained by a restorative tendency. When an economy gets out of line, some force, a compulsion of some kind, must push it back again—must restore the equilibrium of the whole economy by restoring the part that got out of line, or at least by putting other parts into places that will restore the equilibrium as a whole.[15] If we assume a price equilibrium of no inflation, for example, and assume that one seller tries to raise the price of his goods, the way that the equilibrium would probably be restored would be his own subsequent decision to lower his price again, after finding that at the higher price his sales had dropped so far that he was making lower profits overall. Thus, one of the beneficient functions performed by Smith's "invisible hand" of market forces was the maintenance of equilibrium.

Paul Samuelson has shown that although an equilibrium that is maintained by a restorative tendency is logically conceivable without any maximizing assumptions, it is only barely conceivable, and the much more natural way of conceiving of it is with such assumptions.[16] The thing being maximized does not have to be profits. It could be receipts from sales, the satisfaction of shareholders, or anything else, but something must be maximized, which means that it must possess all the artificial aspects that were shown in Chapter 4 to make the profit-maximization assumption inaccurate as a description of reality; and it will bias and falsify economics, as Chapter 7 showed any maximizing assumption does. Samuelson's proof was first published in 1947. It goes a long way toward explaining economists' persistence in applying the profit-maximizing principle, although of course they had al-

[15] Paul A. Samuelson, *Foundations of Economic Analysis* (New York: Atheneum, 1974), pp. 260–62 and generally the remainder of the book, 263–355.

[16] Ibid., pp. 21–29.

ready been applying it by that time for about one and a half centuries.

As we have seen, the necessity of a maximizing assumption also follows from economic determinism. Equilibria that are maintained by restorative tendencies are also an aspect of economic determinism. Something supposedly determines what the equilibrium is and maintains it by restoring it after deviations. A denial of economic determinism does not require a denial of the existence of equilibria with restorative tendencies, however. All it requires is a shift from thinking that economic equilibria are maintained entirely by restorative tendencies to thinking that, although restorative tendencies may exist and be important, they are never determinative and so can never be the whole explanation.

But what else could explain equilibria? The question phrased this way is much too broad, because equilibria exist everywhere in individuals, in society, and in nature. A stone is, among other things, molecules in equilibrium, for example. So is the water in a glass, and this, incidentally, is also an example of an equilibrium without a restorative tendency. If the water is spilled, it possesses no tendency to flow back into the glass. The question can be usefully narrowed, however, to what else can explain societal equilibria, because economic behavior is always societal behavior.

The essence of societal equilibria is repetition. People tend to be, to think, and to do the same things day after day, year after year, generation after generation. Sometimes this repetition results from restorative tendencies, sometimes not. The chief sources of societal repetition are habits, customs, traditions, institutions, and laws. And there are three chief sources of these. First, when satisfactory ways of doing things are found, there is a natural tendency to do them again and again because they have proven to be satisfactory. Second, repetition saves effort. Imagine, for example, the effort that would be involved every morning in choosing among all the possible foods one might eat and deciding whether to eat any food at all, if one did not ordinarily eat about the same things shortly after arising every day. Third, repetition avoids conflict. Each of us has made his peace, so to speak, with the hundreds or thousands of other persons with whom he will usually have at least some slight contact during the day, by conforming his activities to the same patterns that everyone else conforms to. The others also conform in general, and as a result the vast majority of interpersonal contacts occur without significant conflict. If we drive to work in a large city, for example, we probably pass hundreds of other automobiles being driven in the other direction on the same streets. There is generally no conflict for the simple reason that we all drive on the right side, stop for traffic lights, pass on the left, and so on, day after day. When we get to work, we do not bargain anew with our employers or fellow employees over what we will do or what we will be paid. These things are bargained for occasionally, of course, but only occasionally, among other reasons because the bargaining is likely to give rise to conflict.

None of these sources of repetition gives rise to a restorative tendency. Quite the contrary. When an old way is abandoned because a new way is found to be more satisfactory, the tendency to repeat is then applied to the new way. When for whatever reason a new way becomes a habit, a custom, a tradition, or an institution, more effort is saved and more conflict is avoided by following it thereafter than by trying to go back to the old habit or custom. A great deal of effort will have gone into the shift to the metric systems of measurement in the United States, for example, if indeed the shift is ever completed. But once the shift has been completed, if it is, there would surely be an immense savings of effort by continuing with it rather than going back again to pounds, quarts, fahrenheit degrees, yards, miles, and so on.

Economic equilibria are a kind of societal equilibria, because economic activity is a kind of societal activity. We should expect, therefore, that economic equilibria would have their sources in habit, custom, and so on, and not possess restorative tendencies, just as do most other kinds of societal equilibria. One needs to make only a few quick observations to confirm that this expectation is accurate. The contracts that labor unions negotiate with employers in the United States (so-called "collective bargaining contracts") commonly have terms of three years. The wages they provide and the other terms they set do not have to be renegotiated more often than this, barring extraordinary circumstances. This involves repetition on at least two levels: wages and working conditions remain the same or change only according to prearranged schedules day after day for three years; and the negotiated arrangements are made to last for three years at a time, decade after decade. All three sources of repetition—satisfaction, saving of effort, and avoidance of conflict—are obviously involved at both levels.

Many industries have a tradition of making price changes only once a year. The automobile industry is an example. Again, all three sources of societal repetition are involved. An even more fundamental kind of economic equilibrium that is not of the kind that involves a restorative tendency is the daily work pattern of the employee, which has already been mentioned. None of this means that restorative tendencies may not also be involved, although they certainly are not involved to the extent that economists have assumed, or there would not be indeterminate inflation. But it does mean that it is not necessary to assume, either logically or empirically, that economic equilibria are maintained exclusively by restorative tendencies. Thus it is not necessary to assume that there must be maximizing motivations of some kind at work in an economy. The new economics would have no such presuppositions. Logical analysis based upon empirical research would be used to decide what the sources of equilibria were in each kind of situation or, when unique circumstances were encountered, in each instance.

The reader may have seen the similarity between what I have here called societal repetition and the societal uniformities mentioned in Chapter 8, which are supposed to be the basis for the deterministic laws of a social science. I do not intend the meanings to be quite the same. As I conceive of it, societal repetition would include nonobjective facts, whereas societal uniformities of course do not. If the behavior being examined were people's saving, for example, an economist working with the new economics would include in his research questions about why people saved as much as they did and the manner in which they saved it—by insurance, by deposits in savings banks, by contributions to pension funds, by Social Security contributions, and so on. An economist today would be more likely to be content with gross statistical results, and he almost certainly would not consider it pertinent to ascertain people's reasons. Since he would ordinarily confine himself to statistics, there would be no feasible way for him to take people's reasons into account if he did. The nonobjective aspects of people's behavior are important, however, for giving the researcher some basis for judging how firmly entrenched the regularity is. If, for example, people are found to be saving at a particular rate because they believe that this will provide the minimum they will need for their security in their old age, they would probably be less likely to reduce this rate if their incomes were to fall than if their reason was to have enough to spend for a vacation. But despite this difference, the two concepts are much the same, and what I said in Chapter 8 about the fragility of most habitual or customary conduct, its susceptibility to change as soon as people confront something they consider more important, is true for patterns of societal repetition as well. Societal equilibria are not characteristically highly resistant to change. It would be a serious mistake to assume that they were.

Although the kinds of research into economic societal repetition that would be helpful for increasing our understanding of indeterminate inflation mostly remain to be done, we already know enough to make a few observations. To the extent that competitive inflation has not already become runaway, it is largely the societal sources of repetition rather than any restorative tendencies that deserve credit. The means by which the groups that compete against one another in competitive inflation raise their prices are described in Chapters 1 to 4. All of them involve either situations in which the restorative tendencies that arise from market forces have been largely eliminated by modern conditions (inflationary markets, for example) or situations in which the sellers have devised or been given means for overcoming them (pricing institutions, for example).

It might be thought that restorative tendencies were still present, although weakened, and it was their presence that was still preventing competitive inflation from being worse than it is. But if this were the case, competitive inflation would have appeared and almost immediately increased to whatever rate these restorative tendencies in their weakened state had permitted, after which it would have remained at that rate. This is not what happened. No rate has maintained itself for long. Rather, the rates have fluctuated within a general long-term tendency to rise. This is what one would expect from the societal, nonrestorative sources of repetition.

The analysis of price-increasing that was made earlier, especially the technique that I called institutional inflation (Chapter 3), also suggests that restorative tendencies are not present. Market forces have almost nothing to do with the size of a wage increase a powerful labor union will settle for, for example. The factors that do seem to influence such a decision are those that have to do with potential and actual conflict—the third source of societal repetition. The union takes into account how much conflict a particular wage demand will trigger—with the employers who will have to pay it; with the federal, state, or local governments, which may take legal or political action against it; with other labor unions, which may resent the first union's attempts to take too large a slice of the pie for its members; and with the general public.

One other observation is also already possible. We would be quite wrong to place much reliance on the ability of the sources of societal repetition to keep competitive inflation within bounds for long. The thing that comes to be repeated in competitive inflation is not price, but price increasing, and the repetition of price increasing possesses a tendency to disrupt the equilibrium that, for a time, it seems to constitute. The rate of inflation for the United States for the year prior to the time I write this, for example, was about 12 percent. But this 12 percent was an average of parts that had individual rates during the same year of anything from a negative number (although this was rare) to two or three times the national average. The average, therefore, consisted of parts that may have been getting farther and farther apart from each other. If one part, for example, consisted of transit workers in New York City getting a 25 percent increase, and another consisted of public school teachers in California getting no increase (but thankful to hold onto their jobs despite Proposition 13), the spread between these two groups was obviously widening. In the future the teachers would be sure to point to the transit workers, among others, as a reason why they ought to be allowed a very large wage increase to catch up. On the other hand, the parts that compose the 12 percent average may also have differed from one another because the discrepancies of the past were being rectified, in which case the 12 percent would represent something close to a true equilibrium—except to the extent that the groups that were being caught up with would on that account try to pull ahead again in the future. The point is, we do not know; and the mere fact that a particular rate of inflation has existed for a year or so is *not* a reasonable ground for thinking that the same rate will be repeated. Both analysis and experience, even limited experience, point to the opposite conclusion. Competitive inflation will probably ultimately destroy every kind of economic equilibrium if it is not stopped by something external to it. It possesses no inherent equilibrium of its own.

An Increased Emphasis on Empirical Research

Because the new economics would not be deterministic, it would not have to make unrealistic maximizing assumptions about human behavior, and it would be free to take into account peoples' and organizations' actual motives, reasons, purposes, attitudes, and so on. This would free it to be more accurate and honest in its descriptions, and it could be unbiased as to the values people hold and ought to hold, and as to the groups and classes that ought to benefit most from the workings of the economy. This greater freedom would also be a duty, because the long-standing failure of traditional economics to inquire into these areas has left all of us, and economists especially, largely in ignorance of them.

One of these neglected areas is job attitudes. It took a book published in 1974 and written by a man who is ordinarily a radio interviewer, Studs Terkel, to inform Americans that most of them hated their jobs.[17] Job attitudes and what might be done to improve them are important because most of us spend about half our waking hours at our jobs. Job attitudes presumably also influence the actions of the organizations in which the jobs exist, and organizations are the units that carry on almost all economic activity in a modern economy. Thus we will never know what the motives of a business organization are until we know the motives of the persons whose jobs are to represent them in dealings with other organizations, and we will never know these until we know, among other things, their attitudes toward their jobs.

Job attitudes are part of a larger neglected area, nonmarket behavior. A person in his job is generally not in a market, even if the organization in which he holds his job is. Nonmarket behavior includes more than just job attitudes, however. For one thing, a person's behavior in his job is not totally determined by his job attitudes. For another, business organizations also act under other than market conditions. They may be in regulated industries, or, more commonly, they may be in industries in which there are private pricing institutions. The behavior of the firms that compose a pricing institution is at the same time behavior in a market, but the presence of the pricing institution importantly influences the behavior, as we have seen. Traditional economics has not ignored nonmarket behavior entirely. There are some good studies on executive behavior inside firms,[18] for example, and there is a small liter-

[17] Studs Terkel, *Working: People Talk about What They Do All Day and How They Feel about What They Do* (New York: Pantheon, 1974).

[18] Neil W. Chamberlain, *The Firm: Micro Economic Planning and Action* (New York: McGraw-Hill, 1962); Arthur A. Thompson, Jr., *Economics of the Firm: Theory and Practice* (Englewood Cliffs, N.J.: Prentice-Hall, 1973).

ature on regulated industries, but the emphasis on market behavior has been overwhelming. Market behavior has been emphasized presumably because markets, and only markets, supposedly determine economic behavior.

Some of these new areas of emphasis ought to have an immediate importance for inflation. The research that would permit a truly informed judgment has not yet been done, but I would guess that a good deal of the continual demand for higher wages by the members of some labor unions comes from their dissatisfaction with their jobs. Strikes and continually higher wages are their means for getting back at the rest of us. I used to know an electrician who felt demeaned by his work because it was so easy, for example. His response was to become a union official, working full time to organize more workers. I also suspect that the opposite is the case with some occupations. Their members are willing to accept lower pay and other disadvantages because they find their jobs very satisfying. This is unfortunately often the case with teachers, ministers, and probably also farmers. It may turn out that the only way to control indeterminate inflation is to make all jobs at least minimally satisfying. At least this may turn out to be cheaper, more humane, and less socially disruptive than any other method. Studies of nonmarket behavior generally will be important for inflation because it is only through nonmarket means—usually combined with market means—that prices can be effectively controlled in a modern economy. Executives' behavior and job attitudes are also likely to be important for designing measures to increase productivity, which has not been rising nearly as rapidly as it used to in many of the world's developed economies and not as rapidly as it needs to, to overtake population increases in the undeveloped economies.[19] Increased productivity would be an important

[19] "Current Labor Statistics: Productivity," *Monthly Labor Review* 103 (July 1980), 104–105; "Business Brief: Whatever Happened to Productivity?" *The Economist,* August 25, 1979, pp. 60–61; Gunnar Myrdal, *The Challenge of World Poverty* (New York: Pantheon, 1970), pp. 30–45; "The Wealth—and Poverty—of Nations," *New York Times,* August 31, 1980, p. E-3.

benefit in its own right, and it would help to control inflation by making it less likely that one group's increases in income will be another's decreases.

Oddly, another neglected area of empirical study has been competition. Competition has been studied too narrowly, almost entirely theoretically rather than empirically, and almost entirely as a determining force—the force that supposedly keeps prices down, keeps profits reasonable, allocates resources efficiently, and so on—rather than as an energizing and motivating influence. If economists had really given much empirical study to competition, they could not have missed all the aspects of it that I described in Chapters 1 to 4, which characterize it in a modern economy. Virtually every economic text, from elementary to advanced, still treats competition as primarily, even exclusively, a matter of prices, when in fact it has more importantly concerned other things, in most industries, for almost a century. Traditional economics has emphasized the determining aspects of competition to the near exclusion of others because it is deterministic, of course, but also because of the profit-maximization principle.[20] If the profit-maximization principle is to be believed, sellers need no other source of motivation or stimulation. Indeed, they would be incapable of sustaining any other. They are supposedly already insatiably and monomaniacally motivated for profits. In reality, however, the stimulus and energy to work hard are provided by the pursuit of profits *and* by competition *and* by many other things, in all sorts of combinations and interrelations that could be profitably studied. The profit-maximization principle is wrong in this respect as in others.

It is common experience that an individual or firm that is already wealthy or that finds the making of profits already

[20] For example, Phillip Areeda, *Antitrust Analysis,* 2d. ed. (Boston: Little, Brown, 1974), devotes much more space to explaining the control aspects of competition (see pp. 12, 23–35) than its other aspects, and when he does treat the aspects that encourage industriousness, he treats them under the heading of "cost minimization," that is, as controls on costs (p. 20).

easy will generally not work so hard to make more. Competition therefore provides an incentive of its own for industriousness both by making it not so easy to make profits (since one's competitors are likely to make them instead, or to produce market conditions by their actions in which it is more difficult for everyone to make them) and by providing a competitive environment. It is also common experience that people try to do better at almost anything in a competitive environment. Golfers play better golf in matches than when playing alone. Children learn to spell more rapidly in spelling bees. Competition seems to have this effect in part because most people find it fun, if the stakes are not too high; and in part because competition permits people to release their aggressions in a socially acceptable manner, by striving to "beat" the opposition. Competition can discourage industriousness, however, when the stakes are too large, because most people then become overly cautious. When the margins for error are too small, competition can discourage experimentation.[21] Moreover, cooperation, the opposite of competition, is also a spur to industriousness. Most industrial tasks within a business organizaion are done much more in a spirit of cooperation than of competition. Team sports always function on a combination of cooperation and competition. Thus, too much competition or competition of the wrong kinds can also kill industriousness by interfering with cooperation, when the circumstances make cooperation necessary or desirable. It would seem that a great deal of empirical research will be required in order to make some sense out of all these sometimes mutually reinforcing, sometimes conflicting factors. A new economics will be freed to do it by not having to be so exclusively concerned with competition's supposedly determining "forces."

[21] Joseph A. Schumpeter, *Capitalism, Socialism and Democracy* (New York: Harper, 1943), chaps. 7, 8; Areeda, *Antitrust Analysis,* pp. 32–34. The clearest evidence in support of the statement in the text is probably from agriculture. Agriculture tends to be highly competitive. Farmers have developed practically none of the hybrids or other agricultural inventions of the last hundred years. Large seed companies or farm-equipment companies have developed some. The United States Department of Agriculture and university scientists have developed most of them.

An Acceptance of Society's Fundamental Values

We have seen that traditional economics is biased toward the values of selfishness and materialism and toward the rich and the businesses, and that these biases are related to its determinism. A nondeterministic economics would not be compelled to have these biases or any others, but it should nevertheless have values. Its values should be those that our society holds to be fundamental. (A bias differs from a value in the extent to which it is held in common. One ordinarily speaks of a bias in terms of the values of a part of a larger whole—a bias toward the values of the rich, for example, who compose only a part of a society.) Economics has always had the values of satisfaction of material wants and of efficiency. The new economics would add satisfaction of immaterial wants, satisfaction and enrichment from one's occupation, and economic justice.

There should be no embarrassment about accepting society's values. Every social science does, at least implicitly. Natural sciences do not, but only because such values are not relevant to the kinds of truth they are after. When a political scientist studies the governments of Nazi Germany or of Stalinist Russia, for example, among the important truths he wants to learn is how they suppressed freedom—what there was about them that eliminated freedom despite people's attempts to fight back, and what there was about them or the societies in which they existed that brought them to power and maintained them despite their suppression of freedom. The political scientist is rightly interested in this because he practices his profession in a society that has freedom as one of its fundamental values. A free society looks to its political scientists for guidance on how to preserve freedom. Thus, the attempts to make economics "value free" by making it a natural science have been mistaken: they have succeeded only in making it biased. They have also been hypocritical, although few governments, at least, have been fooled. Governments routinely choose as their economic advisers men and women who share their political biases.

Of course an economist ought not to use his discipline's values as an excuse for ignoring relevant information, any more than any other social scientist. The highest value of all, for any kind of scientist, is truth. But the open acceptance of values makes them less of a threat to factual honesty than they would be if they were hidden. Both the researcher and those who analyze his conclusions can be more alert for possible distortions. The open acceptance of values is also a protection against bias. A value overrides a conflicting bias in the same way that a more basic rule or principle overrides a conflicting subsidiary one. But there is no use pretending that economics any more than any other body of thinking will ever be entirely honest or unbiased. The best one can hope for is that it be conceptually organized so that its practitioners can consistently be honest and unbiased and that its practitioners will strive to keep it that way.

A New Spirit for Economics

Traditional economics has been called "the dismal science."[22] The characterization is apt. Not, however, because economics deals with the supposedly unavoidably dismal problems of allocating scarce resources, as its practitioners would have us believe.[23] Practically every social science, profession, or occupation deals with the problems of allocating scarce resources. A judge must decide which side will win the case; both sides cannot. Politicians must decide who among the many who want them will get the choice government jobs, and which districts and which people will receive more of the limited amounts of government spending. Physicians must allocate their time and the limited curative facilities at their disposal, and they must advise patients on alternatives among pain, expense, drug-induced stupor, and death. All sorts of

[22] The originator of the characterization was Thomas Carlyle. John Barlett, *Bartlett's Familiar Quotations,* 14th ed. (Boston: Little, Brown, 1968), p. 578.

[23] Samuelson, *Economics,* pp. 18–19, 23.

things besides those dealt with by economists have to be allocated because they are scarce.

Traditional economics has been dismal, rather, because its practitioners have so seldom allowed themselves to use their imaginations. Imagination is the play of intellect. In any serious intellectual endeavor, of course, the play is not entirely free; there are commonly accepted rules of logic, esthetics, or relevance by which it is constrained. All play has rules—the rules of the game, whether the game be chess or jump rope. The rules diminish the pleasure only when they are too restrictive, as they have been in economics. The rules for thinking in traditional economics forbid an economist to empathize with his subjects. He must think of them objectively, as "firms" or "economic agents." He must not speculate on people's reasons for acting. Rather, he must assume that they all seek to maximize something. He must not see that people's characteristic modes of economic action change, through learning, through the changing of attitudes or motives, or in any other way that cannot be explained as being determined by objective factors.

Traditional economics also lacks imagination, I think, because its deterministic premises deny that the objects of its study can be significantly affected by their imaginations (if they could be, their actions would not be determined). This impedes the investigator logically and psychologically, if it does not quite prevent him, from admitting a significant role for his own imagination. This negative feedback does not occur in the authentic natural sciences, because their objects of study are not people's conscious behavior. A physicist can quite consistently believe that the behavior of atoms is determined but that his own thoughts or behavior are not, for example. But an economist who is a determinist cannot make a similar assumption about his own thoughts or behavior, because he and his objects of study are the same.

A lack of imagination denies pleasure, and a lack of pleasure if persisted in long enough is perversely deepened and strengthened. Those who cannot or will not allow themselves pleasure in normal ways turn to getting what perverse pleasure they can from the act of denial itself: they become sadists or masochists. So economics is also dismal because it has come to be associated with the affirmation of the denial of pleasure or, what comes to the same thing, the insistence on the inevitability of want, scarcity, and pain. Probably the favorite aphorism of economists today is the statement attributed to Frank Knight, "there is no such thing as a free lunch." What this seems to mean to those who repeat it is that one ought never merely enjoy a pleasure or good in itself—every pleasure, every good, supposedly, will in some way, at least eventually, be paid for in pain. Traditional economics' most characteristic way of saying No to pleasure is to offer alternatives all but one of which is clearly unacceptable, and that one still painful. Thus, we have been told for years that we cannot have full employment unless we are willing to accept intolerably high rates of inflation along with it. Of course we have "chosen" continued high unemployment. We have also been told that we cannot have government economic controls to prevent inflation without giving up our freedom.[24] Economic determinism itself is a denial. It says that none of us can reasonably hope to have anything that objective factors have not determined for us.

The rationalization that economics has been dismal because it has to deal with scarce resources is also false. An economics that permitted itself to be imaginative could encompass immaterial resources, which are not inherently scarce. So far in the world's history, at least, the limits of how efficient, how capable, and how happy people can be made by improving their educations, their organizations, their governments, and their attitudes and practices have not even been approached. The average Japanese has hundreds of times more material resources at his disposal than does the average Indian, not because Japan's material resources are greater than India's, because they are not, but because the Japanese have made theirs

[24] See Chapter 8 at notes 61 and 62.

among the richest nations in the world in immaterial resources, and their material resources followed.[25] The material resources of the countries of Western Europe were almost annihilated by World War II. Yet after the war these countries rapidly regained and surpassed their previous material wealth. The reason was their people's ample possession of immaterial resources. They remembered how to produce things and how to establish efficient governments and social institutions, and they remained willing to engage in hard work. A new economics would be concerned with material *and* immaterial resources, and so would not have to deal only with resources that were inherently scarce.

The idea that economics is the study of the allocation of scarce resources is not even accurate any longer with respect to material resources in the developed economies. The principal economic problem of the developed economies, except for inflation, has long been unemployment, both of people and of physical resources. There have been too many people for the available jobs, especially for the decent jobs. There have been too many factories, mines, and acres of farm land for the amount of demand that has existed for what they could profitably produce. Of course there have been problems of scarcity, too. Factories during boom times might be hard pressed to find enough skilled hands; housing, especially housing affordable by poor people, and especially in urban areas, might be in short supply, and so on. But for the most part businessmen and occasionally government administrators—almost never economists—have dealt with problems of this sort. The problem of putting together scarce resources in the most efficient ways to produce products that are also, or would otherwise be, scarce is predominantly a business problem, not one of economics. Moreover, most such long-term scarcities could easily have been eliminated had economists found the answers to putting our large chronic surpluses of labor and productive

[25] *Information Please Almanac 1980* (New York: Simon and Schuster, 1980), pp. 194, 207; Edwin O. Reischauer, *The Japanese* (Cambridge: Belknap Press of Harvard University Press, 1977), pp. 4–5, 8, 16–31, 115–19.

resources fully to work. Thus, the definition that economists give of their own discipline, that it is the study of the allocation of scarce resources, reflects more their desire than the fact. There are all sorts of essentially unlimited resources to be produced and allocated, but to admit this would not serve the desire to be able to say No. One could not so frequently deny that there can be a free lunch.

An economics that took into account nonobjective facts, that openly adopted as its own the fundamental economic values of the society in which it existed, that acknowledged that these values would in some situations conflict, that recognized that some of the important things it dealt with were limited only by our choice of what we wanted most, and that was open to the play of the intellect, should be a pleasure. It would also be a more controversial economics. There would be few unanimous "economic answers." Economists would differ on issues of public importance in the same ways that other people do—not just on the means but also on the goals. This would also add to the pleasure, because the additional controversy would tend to be of the right kind. Controversy in which the differing goals of the contending sides are unexpressed tends to be acrimonious, because each side suspects the other of lying or of being ignorant of part of the truth. Controversy in which differing goals are openly acknowledged has the advantage of enlarging each side's understanding of the other even as they dispute. Controversies over sometimes conflicting values are therefore not only the conditon of a free society, they are the kinds of controversies that are least likely to tear a society apart. A new economics would contribute to making all public controversies this sort.

PART III

Controlling Inflation

Controlling inflation will be a large, complex, never-ending task. It will probably require an effort on the order of that which we presently put into the collection and enforcement of the federal income tax. The federal income tax makes a good comparison for other reasons, as well. Politics will be involved. Congress, the President, and the anti-inflation program administrator will be pressured to favor one group or another. There will be fraudulent evasion and honest avoidance. Even the best rules of the program will have to be continually changed or refined as people learn how to evade or avoid them, or as their unanticipated effects have to be countered. A specialized group of lawyers, accountants, and economists will emerge, to make their careers out of helping sellers deal with the program or to serve in the program itself.

But if the costs of preventing inflation will be heavy, the benefits will also be great. They will extend beyond the prevention of inflation. One extra benefit will be increased economic justice. As we have seen, indeterminate inflation quickly becomes competitive inflation. The transformation has already occurred practically everywhere. Competitive inflation is a war of group against group for shares of the aggregate real income. Some groups (labor unions, industries, professions, whatever) raise their prices in order to get larger shares, which causes inflation and thereby reduces the shares of other groups. The latter then raise their prices too, in order to restore their shares or to make them larger, which causes more inflation. This causes the first groups to raise their prices again, causing still more inflation, and so it goes in a never-ending spiral. This spiral has to be stopped if inflation is to be stopped. But as a practical matter, it will not be stopped, at least not for long, unless the overwhelming majority of the groups involved are made to feel that the share of real income that they are left with, relative to the shares that other groups are left with, is just. Moreover, the pattern of income distribution that the anti-inflation controls provide will have to be widely perceived as *more* just than the pattern of income distribution that preceded it, because the preceding pattern induced competitive inflation. And a pattern of income distribution, in order to be widely perceived as just, will have to be actually just, at least in the long run.

Another factor that we can reasonably count on to provide increased economic justice is the inherent desire of the men and women who will be required to make the judgments about income distribution to do a good job. Experience shows that the authority to make important judgments is generally taken very seriously by those who possess it. Good men generally become better when they become judges. Bad men sometimes become good. The judging that would occur in an anti-inflation program would not ordinarily occur in a court, but the aspects of the situation that conduce toward good judging are not dependent on this. They derive rather from the sense of responsibility, the prestige, and the public accountability that go with the authority to make important judgments, or at least can be made to go with it if the authority is well designed.[1]

The best evidence of this is the Anglo-American so-called "common" law. This is the law that was made by judges in the course of their judging here and in England since its beginnings in England in the thirteenth century. When the kings of England began sending out judges to settle disputes among the citizenry, the "writs" they issued to describe the kinds of disputes that the judges were to settle offered almost no guidance as to how the judges were to settle them. The judges had to make the law themselves. The kings were not even very interested in what the law would be. Their interest was in reducing the high incidence of domestic violence that was then present by offering a peaceful alternative for settling disputes and a peaceful means of punishing those who persisted in

[1] Henry M. Hart, Jr., "The Supreme Court 1958 Term, Forward: The Time Chart of the Justices," *Harvard Law Review* 73 (1959), 94–125.

violence.[2] The Anglo-American common law is still in existence in almost all English-speaking countries and many other places too, and it is highly respected for, among other things, its justice. We can reasonably expect a similar "common law" of income distribution to develop from the efforts of appropriately organized officials making judgments about groups' incomes, and we can also reasonably expect this law to be a just one.

There should also be other benefits. Competitive inflation is costly, in addition to imposing the costs of inflation. Strikes are especially costly, not only to the employers and employees directly involved but to everyone who is dependent upon the products or services that the employers and employees would otherwise produce. Also, inflation interferes with business planning, and it encourages the government to keep aggregate demand low in an attempt to alleviate it, which increases unemployment and slows or reverses economic growth. An economy in which inflation had been largely eliminated ought therefore to be more efficient. It would produce its goods at less cost and grow more rapidly. The prevention of inflation is also likely to require that jobs that are presently demeaning or otherwise unpleasant be improved in these respects. Those who work in them are unlikely to accept reasonable limits on their wages if they are not. It even seems reasonable to hope that all jobs will eventually be designed so as not to detract from the dignity of those who hold them and to provide at least a minimal satisfaction. Experience indicates that where these standards have not been met, wages—no matter how high—will not suffice to keep people working steadily.

Part III may come as a jolt. It is as narrow and practical as Part II was broad and theoretical. It nevertheless forms the necessary conclusion to a book on the new inflation, and it logically follows Part II. It is not enough just to understand the

[2] Edward Pollock and Frederic W. Maitland, *The History of English Law* (Cambridge: Cambridge University Press, 1909), 84–110, 136–225; Frederic W. Maitland, *Selected Historical Essays of F. W. Maitland* (Cambridge: Cambridge University Press, 1957), pp. 97–134.

new inflation. One also needs to know how to control it. Part III tries to show how. The measures that are suggested are the kinds that a new, nondeterministic economics could propose, and that the traditional, deterministic economics could not. A traditional economist would not propose them even if he did not agree with most of his colleagues that the ultimate cause of the new inflation is excess demand, because he would consider them to interfere with market forces. Being a determinist, he would believe that market forces could, and should, be the sole means of control for inflation, just as they could be and should be the sole means of control for all aspects of economic behavior. So neither the measures that I propose nor the reasons why I propose them could be properly understood without first having understood the theses about the inadequacy of traditional economics and the need for a new economics that I presented in Part II.

Part III may also come as unwelcome news. The proposed measures for controlling inflation will involve the law. The law, of course, will have to be administered and enforced. There will have to be a bureaucracy. There are profound reasons why no government, and especially no government of a free and democratic country, should use a bureaucracy to administer a large part of its people's economic affairs. Economic affairs have to be controlled—no modern economy ever has or ever could function chaotically—but the principal means of control should be the competitive market. Thoroughly socialist countries such as the Soviet Union that have done otherwise have suffered enormous economic losses, and there are good reasons for concluding that their attempts to get along without markets have contributed to their suppressions of freedom and democracy.[3] A reader who understands this may have hoped that the measures that I would propose would somehow not involve the government in economic affairs any more than it is already, even though he un-

[3] Charles Edward Lindblom, *Politics and Markets* (New York: Basic Books, 1977).

derstands, from Parts I and II, that market forces are not *and cannot be* sufficient to prevent inflation in a modern economy.

The only assurance I can offer this reader is that I share his concerns about bureaucratic economic controls, and I think he will find that the proposed measures would require a surprisingly small bureaucracy. They would leave sellers almost entirely free from government control in all respects except those that were described in Part I as means of increasing prices. And I have drawn upon my expertise as a former practicing lawyer and present law teacher, and my experience as general counsel to the Price Commission, to suggest a design for a bureaucracy that would be efficient and fair. Nevertheless, there remain some hard choices. If inflation is to be prevented, we will have to accept an increase in government economic control.

CHAPTER 10

The Shape of the Program

The conditions that permit indeterminate inflation are inherent in a modern economy, so a program against indeterminate inflation has to be permanent. This is the salient fact about any such program, which would differentiate it from every other anti-inflation program the United States has ever had. A program to prevent indeterminate inflation also cannot be on again–off again. It has to be on all the time.

The 1971 Economic Stabilization Program system of wage and price controls was both temporary and intermittent, and both these aspects caused harm. To the extent that those who planned the program had any notion of what they were doing, their purpose was to provide a "lid" on prices that would last long enough to eliminate "inflationary expectations," which to their mind threatened to send inflation sharply up just when the economy seemed to be pulling out of its slump and inflation seemed to be coming down.[1] "Inflationary expectations" were thought to cause inflation by self-fulfilling prophecy: people would raise prices in the expectation that other prices would soon be rising, and then, of course, prices would rise. The idea is not incorrect. It is a superficial form of the same concept I call competitive inflation. But it was oversimplified to the point of incorrectness in assuming that merely holding prices down for a while would eliminate people's inflationary expectations, and that when it did, their expecta-

[1] Arnold R. Weber, *In Pursuit of Price Stability: The Wage-Price Freeze of 1971* (Washington, D.C.: Brookings Institution, 1973), pp. 17, 130; W. David Slawson, book review of same in *Southern California Law Rev.* 47 (1974), 1255; *Historical Working Papers on the Economic Stabilization Program, August 15, 1971 to April 30, 1974* (Washington, D.C.: U.S. Treasury Department, 1974), pp. 12–17.

tions would stay noninflationary for an appreciable period after the controls had been lifted. If people had been expecting prices to rise before the program, why were they to think that prices would not rise again after the program ended?

Indeed, it became apparent soon after the program was underway that its widely known and officially emphasized temporary character was causing inflationary expectations to increase. The longer the program went on, the bigger the price explosion people expected when it ended. The name we in the program gave this situation was "the bubble." We thought of our controls as holding prices down against an increasingly powerful upward pressure, which would cause prices to "burst" when the controls were lifted. Inflation did take a sharp jump in early 1973 when Phase 2 of the program was ended (this really ended the program—Phase 3 was all talk and no action). The government's attempt the following summer to quell the inflationary expectations by putting controls back on again (Phase 4) was a failure. The precipitate ending of Phase 2 had apparently shown sellers that the government had no intention of controlling prices a moment longer than it thought it could get away with, so they knew they needed only bide their time before resuming their price increasing. In dismantling the program after the termination of Phase 2, practically all enforcement was cut off, even with respect to violators and suspected violators against whom enforcement or investigation was already underway, and the vast majority of the program's personnel were fired. The lesson could hardly have been lost on sellers: even if Phase 4 lasted as long as Phase 2 had, it was unlikely that they would ever be successfully prosecuted for violations, and everyone expected (correctly) that Phase 4 would be much shorter than Phase 2. The firing of personnel meant that the program had to start from the ground up again for Phase 4. The widespread public awareness that anyone hired would probably soon be fired, probably even sooner this time, made it very difficult—from what I saw, I would say impossible—to hire many first-class people for the newly expanded program.

Despite the harm inflicted by its temporary and intermittent aspects, the 1971 program's first two phases did effectively hold down prices while they were in effect. Whether on the whole the program did or would have done more good than harm in the long run, or vice versa, will probably never be known. The Arab nations' oil price increases and the worldwide food shortage, which both occurred soon thereafter, so scrambled economic events that discerning the program's long-term effects became hopeless.

The necessity of permanence makes it especially important to avoid the evils that characterized the anti-inflation programs we have had in the past. For one thing, the program should not be costly. Anything as large and burdensome to comply with on a permanent basis as the World War II program would be intolerable. Second, the program should not stand in the way of prosperity. The World War II and Korean War programs did not, but had they been continued past the cessation of hostilities they would have because their rules were obstructive and unwieldy. The fiscal and monetary measures we have used since the end of World War II have enormously impeded our ability to achieve prosperity. We owe to them our steady decline in per capita income relative to other countries and our growing pool of permanently and partially unemployed.[2] Finally, the program should not infringe constitutional liberties. The two former wartime programs and the 1971 Economic Stabilization Program each transgressed in this respect.[3] The 1971 ESP held people to account on the basis of rules for which proper notice was not given, and failed to offer appropriate hearings. Moreover, the 1971 ESP and the two wartime programs were free of judicial

[2] Lester Thurow, "The Myth of the American Economy," *Newsweek*, February 14, 1977, p. 11. See also Alfred L. Malabre, Jr., "Easing Squeeze after Steep Decline, Public's Buying Power Is Seen Increasing," *Wall Street Journal*, May 22, 1975, p. 1.

[3] See, for example, Shapiro v. United States, 335 U.S. 1 (1948) (immunity statute narrowly construed and self-incrimination privilege restricted for price-control records); Bowles v. Willingham, 321 U.S. 503 (1944) (certain rights to hearing denied under rent controls).

checks and restraints to an extent that our courts would never tolerate except in an emergency.[4]

A permanent program could easily meet each of these requirements if it were kept very small, but a program could not be kept small *in application* and still be effective. Indeterminate inflation can occur almost anywhere, and if it is allowed to continue it is likely to spread. In this respect indeterminate inflation is even more difficult to control than crime. To a substantial extent, crime can be defined away in some areas and the forces for fighting it concentrated in the areas that are left. A state could, for example, change its laws so as to make it no longer a crime for adults to gamble, to engage in prostitution, or to engage in homosexual acts. The police, freed from having to enforce these laws, could be employed to enforce the laws against activities that were still defined as criminal. But there is no way of defining away the inflationary impact of a price increase. If a legislature were to say that the wages or salaries of certain classes of people were not to be counted as inflationary and so were not to be controlled, although others were, the exempted wages or salaries would eventually have exactly the same inflationary effects. But to say that an effective program cannot easily be kept small is not to say that no attention can profitably be paid to its size. Its size, in numbers of people employed, can be kept reasonably small by, among other means, keeping its rules simple and few, even if their application is broad.

Of course the program, like any part of government, would seek voluntary cooperation with its rules and regulations. No laws are ever effective unless the vast majority of persons to whom they apply obey them voluntarily. But it would be unjust and ineffective to try to make compliance only voluntary. It would be unjust because sacrifices incurred voluntarily are almost never incurred equally. It would be ineffective because the sacrifices required, at least initially, would be more than

[4] See, for example, the restrictions of appeals to a "Special Emergency Court of Appeals" in Washington, D.C., P.L. 92–210, §211, 85 Stat. 744 (1971). This is discussed in the text later in the present chapter.

many people would be willing to incur voluntarily, especially when, as would undoubtedly be the case, they saw that others were not voluntarily incurring them. One suspects that the real motives of those who call for all-voluntary programs are to make the program less effective. An all-voluntary program has to be limited to modest targets, in order to gain sufficient voluntary acceptance. It especially has to be limited in its application to the economically or politically powerful, because their voluntary acceptance of its goals is of principal importance. The weak are likely to go along anyway, in the knowledge that if they do not the program could rather easily be changed to make their compliance mandatory. In any event, their failure to go along is not generally so visible. It is to the credit of the American labor movement that its leaders for some years now have not been urging the adoption of all-voluntary wage and price controls.[5]

With these few observations I have said almost all there is to say about the requirements of a program. What follows are mostly suggestions. In the present chapter are suggestions for the program's general rules, for its administrative structure, and for its relationships with other parts of government and with our constitutional principles. More specific suggestions for what the program should do for particular sectors of the economy are taken up in the next, and last, chapter. In both these chapters but especially the present one, I will be drawing to a large extent on my experience as general counsel to the Price Commission during Phase 2 of the 1971 Economic Stabilization Program. It would only be distracting to have footnotes to nothing more than a statement of this fact again and again, so there are no such notes.

Organization, Authority, and Placement

Since the powers of an effective program would necessarily be very broad, it is best to recognize this fact at the start. Rec-

[5] "As a New Leader Views Future of the AFL-CIO," *U.S. News & World Report,* November 19, 1979, pp. 82–83.

ognition is an essential step toward building a set of safeguards. The major safeguard would be a requirement of full justification and full public disclosure, neither of which any of our past wage and price control programs has ever had. By full justification I mean a requirement that *nothing* the program does to members of the public without the latter's consent be enforceable if, upon challenge, the program cannot justify it to the satisfaction of a court as both within the scope of the program's legal authority and reasonably designed to serve the program's goals. The laws of the United States already include such requirements for every government action, in theory. But for a program as powerful and as broadly applicable as this one would be, the requirement ought to be made real. By full public disclosure I mean that all hearings be open to the public and that, except in special individual cases, all the information that provides the legal justification for the program's action be available to the public. Full public disclosure and a requirement for full justification would help immeasurably to keep the program sensible and honest by exposing it to maximum public, congressional, and presidential control. Why this is so will be explained shortly.

The program would be more efficient and more effective if it were headed by a single individual rather than by a multimembered commission. The wage and price programs for the Second World War and the Korean War were headed by single individuals. The 1971 ESP was headed by a multimember commission called the "Cost of Living Council." It had, in addition, commissions subordinate to the council for prices (the Price Commission), for wages (the Pay Board), for prices and wages just in the construction industry (the Construction Industry Stabilization Council), for rents (the Rent Advisory Board), for medical services (the Committee on the Health Services Industry), and for state and local governments (the Committee on State and Local Government Cooperation).[6] Commissions are acknowledged to be less efficient and less effective than individuals. Their justification is that they pro-

[6] *Historical Working Papers*, p. 1000.

vide representation for different interests and spokesmen for the different interests' views. But an effective program would affect too many interests for either of these purposes to be fulfilled with a manageable number of commission members, and when not all interests are represented or spoken for, there is a danger of bias against those that are left out. Such biases were present in the 1971 ESP. No one represented small business on the Price Commission, and small businesses generally bore an especially heavy burden under the commission's rules. Unorganized labor was not represented on the Pay Board. So far as I was able to ascertain, unorganized people received not a single pay increase in excess of the board's guidelines. The dozens, perhaps hundreds, of such pay increases received by organized labor are a matter of public record.

The burden of inefficiency imposed upon the 1971 ESP by its complicated commission structure, on the other hand, was substantial. The Rent Board was so torn by factions that there never were workable rent regulations. The Internal Revenue Service, which was charged with enforcing them, complained that landlords, renters, and its own field personnel could not understand the ones that were issued. My office had the ultimate responsibility for interpreting them, but was never able to understand them either. They were too much the product of disagreements among the Rent Board's members "papered over" with meaningless phrases. The Construction Industry Stabilization Council went its own way in secret, so whether it helped or hindered the rest of the program was never known to anyone except its members, if even they knew. The chairman of the council considered secrecy to be important for his dealings with the lords and princes of the construction unions for the same reasons that secrecy is important in high-level diplomacy. The Pay Board and the Price Commission honestly tried to cooperate, but there was little they could do without the Cost of Living Council's approval, and that council met rarely and decided little of importance when it did. Its main concern was to look important despite the fact that the executive order from the President under which the program operated left it little to do. It was the titular head of the program, and its membership consisted of men and women of cabinet rank, but it was so starved for significant problems that one of its members, writing about the experience, later described as among its "major policy issues" whether the Girl Scouts of North Carolina could collect a dues increase and whether sales of honey came under the program's control before the honey had been "drained or strained."[7] The workings of the Price Commission's staff were materially retarded by the necessity of presenting to the commission itself all the problems that were regarded as important enough for its decisions, whenever it met, which was ordinarily one day a week. The chairman of the commission, who was also the day-to-day director of the commission's staff, was an able man who could easily have run the operation without the other members' help. All these conflicts and inefficiencies were especially unfortunate, because the members of the public who had been gathered to serve on these commissions, boards, and so on, were generally capable and dedicated.

I will henceforth speak of the single individual who would head the proposed program as its "administrator." The administrator should have cabinet rank, at least. In fact, if not in status, he should be superior to the secretaries for labor, for commerce, for housing and urban development, and for agriculture wherever their respective jurisdictions and his overlapped. Prices anywhere affect prices everywhere. Most of what these other secretaries are responsible for, on the other hand, could be accomplished at least as effectively if they were ultimately subject to someone else's authority with respect to prices. The Federal Reserve System should be brought within the program, and its functions made subject to the authority and general supervision of the administrator. All the federal regulatory agencies—the Interstate Commerce Commission, the Federal Power Commission, and so on—should continue as they are, except that they should be placed under the administrator's authority and supervision. All such state and

[7] Weber, *In Pursuit of Price Stability,* pp. 29, 33, 48, 49.

local agencies, of course, should also be placed under his authority and supervision. If all this sounds like a breathtakingly broad grant of power, it should be noted that it is no more than has been granted to every wage and price control program this nation has ever established.

It should also be noted that the amount of a program, agency, or department's power is only partly determined by the breadth of its application. It is also determined by the range of things the program can direct people to do and by the higher authorities to which the program is subject. In both these respects the anti-inflation program would not be powerful. The only thing it could control would be prices (including wages, of course), and it would be, or at least should be, subject to the higher authorities of the president, Congress, and the federal judiciary. Programs and agencies that are supreme over all the rest of the government (except possibly the president, Congress, and the judiciary) for the single narrow function that is their specialty are actually quite common. The Justice Department argues cases in court, generally, for all the rest of the federal government. A single part of the Justice Department, the Federal Bureau of Investigation, is the sole enforcer of most federal criminal laws, and all federal government agencies and departments, *including* presidents, members of Congress, and judges, are as subject to these laws as are the rest of us. The General Accounting Office has authority over all the rest of the federal government (again, except for the president, Congress, and the judiciary) for matters of accounting and expenditure. And so on. The breadth of power that the anti-inflation program ought to have would not make it unique among federal agencies.

The internal workings of the program and such external matters as the sanctions it can impose for violations of its rules ought not to be specified in advance, except in the very broadest terms. Every wage and price control program we have had in the past has been unnecessarily burdened by narrow or limited provisions of this kind, prescribed by Congress before there was any experience to test whether they would be appropriate and workable. I can speak from personal experience in saying that provisions of this kind for the 1971 ESP were not only a burden, they came close to killing the program. The only sanctions that we had been allowed by Congress turned out to be unworkable except through court procedures too lengthy to have reached their conclusion until long after the program was expected to end. We only barely saved the program by substituting measures that we designed ourselves, for which there was no specific authorization in our statutes.[8] We gambled that before the question of their legal authorization could be settled, the program would have ended, and we won—but the race against time was close, and the doubtful character of our legal authority frequently hurt us.

On the other hand, the program ought not to be given the privileged legal status in relation to review of its actions by courts that all wage and price control programs since the Second World War have enjoyed. The justification for these earlier programs was that they were intended to deal with emergencies and were to be dismantled when the emergency was over, which was expected to be within a few years. Although it may be that a program for combatting indeterminate inflation will not be established until after the situation has become an emergency, there could still be no reasonable expectation that the need for the program would disappear within a few years. Our liberties would be better protected if the program were made just as subject to judicial review as is every ordinary government department. The necessity of getting the program into action fast, to handle the emergency without undue interference from the courts, could safely be left to the courts' own feeling for the emergency. The past wage and price control programs were exempted from ordinary judicial review and made subject instead to review in what were called "Temporary Emergency Courts of Appeal" established for this purpose exclusively in Washington, D.C. The effect, presumably

[8] See Economic Stabilization Act of 1970, §§208, 209, 85 Stat. 744 (1971); Philip Shabecoff, "Price Panel Bars 1,500 Companies from Any Rises," *New York Times,* May 4, 1972, p. 9; Richard F. Janssen, "Many Middle-Sized Firms Ignoring Rules, Price Unit Aides Say," *Wall Street Journal,* May 18, 1972, p. 2.

intended, was to make judicial review especially expensive and difficult for a member of the public to obtain, and to make it likely that if he got it he would lose his case.

A Full-Justification Requirement

One will not find the term, "full-justification requirement," in any legal treatise, but any lawyer who has had appreciable contact with government administrative agencies will know immediately what I mean. Practically as soon as the Constitution of the United States was adopted it became apparent that Congress would never be capable of exercising "all legislative powers" for the federal government, as the Constitution provided it should. No single body could conceivably make all the laws that had to be made. Out of this realization was born the doctrine of delegation of lawmaking power. Government officials and, later, administrative agencies were authorized by statutes enacted by Congress (and signed by the president, of course) to make laws themselves. The laws made by the agencies were, and still are, commonly called rules or regulations, but with only a few exceptions they have every bit as much legal authority over a private person as a law enacted by Congress—which was, and still is, commonly called a statute.[9]

The statutes that authorize an agency to make law by rule or regulation were at first required to include definite guidelines as to what the agency's laws should be. The federal courts imposed this requirement and also policed the agencies' conformance with the guidelines. This requirement, plus Congress's constitutionally given power to override at any time any rule or regulation with which it disagreed, was thought to be sufficient to keep delegated lawmaking under congressional control. The requirement of definite guidelines was never more than nominal, however, because it immediately became apparent that in almost all those areas of the law in

[9] Stephen G. Breyer and Richard B. Stewart, *Administrative Law and Regulatory Policy* (Boston: Little, Brown, 1979), pp. 20–26, 37–43, 59–61.

which Congress found it necessary or convenient to delegate, no definite guidelines were to be found.[10] A major area of delegation has always been rate-making, for example. Commissions are authorized by statutes to set the rates to be charged by public utilities (telephone service, electric service, natural gas, railroad service, water transportation, and so on). No one to this day has been able to come up with definite guidelines that at the same time make economic sense for what a public utility should charge.

Crucial as it is to the preservation of democratic governance, the problem has still not been solved. What has evolved is a variety of measures for keeping agency lawmaking, together with other aspects of agency activities, within congressional, presidential, and judicial control. None by itself is enough, they are not always mutually consistent, and not even all together are sufficient, but they do constitute a valuable and sometimes effective means for accomplishing the task.[11] The single most effective such measure is the full-justification requirement, and it happens to be especially effective for the kind of lawmaking with which an anti-inflation program would be principally concerned, which is, of course, the setting of limits on prices. The requirement, as stated earlier, is that an agency's power to enforce its rules or regulations against a person be conditional on the agency's ability to demonstrate to the satisfaction of a court, if the person challenges the enforcement, that the rules or regulations and their application to him in this particular case are fully justified both by the factual evidence and by principles that demonstrate that the rules or regulations serve the public purposes that the agency is supposed to serve.[12] The agency itself can be the author of the principles, and in most cases has to be. Few principles or guidelines are of sufficient generality for Congress to enact. But although the principles created by an agency are usually much less widely applicable than the statutory guide-

[10] Ibid., pp. 59–61, 84–85.
[11] Ibid., pp. 37–102.
[12] For example, Citizens to Preserve Overton Park v. Volpe, 401 U.S. 402 (1971).

lines that Congress might have enacted, they are immensely valuable, because without them a court reviewing an agency's rules or regulations would have no ability to tell whether these were right. Without such principles, for example, what could a court sensibly make of an anti-inflation program's application of a rule to a particular supermarket that it not charge more than forty-nine cents a can for a particular size of can and brand of green beans? Without such principles, the court would obviously have no basis for assessing whether this price was too high, too low, or right. The principles, when the agency is required to create them, also provide Congress, the president, and the public with a means of controlling the agency and of assessing whether it is doing its job properly. Finally, the agency itself is provided with an essential means of doing and understanding its task. A large agency, at least, needs principles in order to organize, keep track of, and assess all the many things that are done by its subordinate parts.

I have stated the full-justification requirement as a willing and competent judge would enforce it. Not all judges always enforce it this way. In fact, if it were enforced this way against some agencies, the agencies would be stopped in their tracks. The Interstate Commerce Commission is responsible for literally billions of individual trucking rates, to which it gives its approval by a process that is meaningful for less than 1 percent, and even for these it lacks any clear principles. The Interstate Commerce Commission, as it presently operates, could not possibly meet a full-justification requirement for the vast majority of the trucking rates it sets. The result is that most trucking rates are not really regulated. The ostensible regulation, moreover, enables the truckers to set their rates *by agreement,* which the antitrust laws would otherwise prohibit, on the assumption that they are being regulated. The final result is therefore worse than no regulation at all. It is legalized price-fixing.[13] Moreover, no one—the truckers who are regu-

[13] See a dissertation by Joel Fishman, "Ratemaking and the I.C.C.: A Policy, Procedural, and Substantive Analysis of the Evolution and Implementation of Rate Proposals in the Trucking Industry" (Southern California, 1975). The dissertation is catalogued and kept at the Asa V. Call Law Library, The Law Center, University of Southern California, University Park, Los Angeles 90007.

lated, the commission, the president, Congress, or anyone else—has any way of knowing whether these prices are right, too high, or too low—except, of course, for the presumption that the truckers are not likely to be fixing them too low. The experience of the ICC demonstrates another important benefit to be expected from the application of a full-justification requirement to the anti-inflation program. The program would have to devise *effective* rules for preventing inflation. Rules that were not effective could not be shown to serve the public purposes the program was intended to serve. To the extent that the program could not come up with effective rules, it would be prevented by the requirement from having any rules at all. This would be preferable to sham rules, like the ICC's.

Full Public Disclosure

The Administrative Procedure Act[14] is sufficient to require all the public disclosure that ought to be required of an anti-inflation program, unless the act were overridden by a confidentiality requirement in the statute from which the program derived its powers. A confidentiality requirement is a legal requirement imposed upon a government agency, department, or program that any information it obtains from a person subject to its jurisdiction not be disclosed to the public or, expect for official purposes, to any other part of the government. A full-justification requirement is workable despite a confidentiality requirement, though only barely. But even apart from considerations of workability, an anti-inflation program ought not to have a confidentiality requirement, because it is in the nature of such a program that almost all the information that is needed to assess its performance is obtained from the persons subject to its jurisdiction. Without access to this information, Congress, the president, and the public would not be able to assess how the program is doing. The federal courts will generally need access to the same information to be able to assess whether the program is proceeding legally. The

[14] 60 Stat. 237 (1946), as amended, 5 U.S.C. 551 ff.

persons whose prices are being affected will need access to the information in order to know whether they are being treated equally with other persons similarly situated, and in order to prepare to argue their cases in the courts, if they think that the program is not treating them legally and fairly. Consumers and others who buy the things whose prices have been affected need access to the information in order to know whether they have been overcharged, and to call the attention of the program's enforcement arm if they have been.

Previous wage and price control programs in the United States have had confidentiality requirements.[15] I know from personal experience that at least the 1971 Economic Stabilization Program was thereby crippled. It succeeded in its mission anyway only because it was temporary. Phase 2 lasted only a little longer than a year, which was not long enough for the need for information to become urgent. Federal income taxes have always been collected under a rule of confidentiality. This may be justified for individuals. The taxes an individual pays can reasonably be regarded as no one's business except his and the government's. But the prices a person charges are always someone else's business. Others must pay them, and inflation affects the whole nation. Public utility rate-regulation programs, which are the only permanent kind of wage and price controls that the United States has yet had, do not operate under rules of confidentiality. The argument is sometimes made that a public utility can rightly be required to disclose to the public the same information as it discloses to its regulatory commission because it is a *public* utility, but it is a public utility only by virtue of having its rates regulated. One could equally logically characterize any business that had its prices affected by an anti-inflation program as a "public business."

So far as I knew, the men and women on the Price Commission and its staff were without exception well-meaning and honest, and they were generally far above average in intelligence. Nevertheless, except for the enforcement section for

[15] Economic Stabilization Act of 1970, §205, 85 Stat. 744 (1971).

big business, which was located in our Washington, D.C., headquarters, everywhere I looked the commission's rules were frequently applied unjustly or arbitrarily. The big business enforcement section was an exception for two reasons. Its chief and his immediate deputy were outstandingly capable public servants, among the very best I have ever encountered. Big businesses are generally capable of watching out for their own interests despite obstacles that would defeat smaller businesses and nonbusiness institutions (schools and hospitals, for example). The injustices elsewhere arose principally from undiscovered inequalities in treatment, which the rule of confidentiality rendered practically undiscoverable. One business might be required to accept lower profit margins than another, or it might be permitted higher profit margins than another. There was no way for anyone except the commission to know, because no one but the commission and the business concerned could see the data upon which the price limits, which determined the profit margins, were decided. The confidentiality requirements made it difficult for even the commission to make such comparisons, because they often depended upon varying interpretations of the data, of which only the staff members and the businesses immediately involved were cognizant. Moreover, the commission had every reason not to make such comparisons. Making them would have required a great deal of staff effort that, in the commission's opinion, could have been better spent on other matters. Any inequalities that were uncovered would have required more work to correct and would have hurt the commission's reputation for fairness and competence. The businesses themselves could not feasibly be called upon to help in the discovery of inequalities without violating the rule of confidentiality as it applied to other businesses' data. The confidentiality requirement permitted arbitrary treatment by preventing the accumulation of written precedents that accountants and lawyers could have referred to. It is generally impossible to state how rules were applied in a situation without disclosing the facts that entered into their interpretation.

Confidentiality also hinders enforcement. Enforcement officials receive fewer tips from the public than they otherwise might about possible violations, because the public has no way of knowing whether a price might be a violation. The inability to accumulate written precedents means that the rules remain vague, and it is difficult to prove a violation of a vague rule to the degree of certainty that our constitutional principles require, even in civil cases. Convictions in criminal cases are rendered almost impossible. Private enforcement, which is always civil, is also rendered practically impossible. Private enforcement of the rules of a price-control program generally proceeds through court actions brought by purchasers who claim to have been overcharged, seeking refunds plus any penalties they are entitled to. Under the 1971 Economic Stabilization Program, the penalties a purchaser could collect were twice again what he had been overcharged plus his attorneys' fees and costs of litigation. Not a single such action succeeded, however, and so far as I could ascertain only three were even initiated.[16] A purchaser had no way of knowing, let alone proving to the satisfaction of a court, that he had been overcharged.

The justifications commonly offered for confidentiality are privacy and injury to competition. A person's privacy is supposedly violated if others are permitted to know his finances. This justification has some force if the person is an individual and if the financial data are his personal financial data, but in a price-control program the persons are generally businesses, sometimes giant corporations, and the data are always those that relate to the person's business operations. How much money an individual may have been left by his father, how much he may be paying in alimony, and other things of a personal nature are almost never relevant, and so almost never need to be reported. When I discussed the possibility of eliminating the confidentiality requirement with businessmen and their lawyers and accountants, in my capacity as general counsel to the Price Commission, I never heard the privacy

[16] The number three is my own recollection. The official history of the 1971 ESP lists none; see *Historical Working Papers*, pp. 1045–1127.

justification persistently offered. It was sometimes offered initially, but after only a little argument on my part it was invariably retracted or forgotten. There are no good grounds for maintaining that a business, as such, has a right of privacy with respect to its financial affairs.

The justification of injury to competition, however, was argued strongly and persistently. The idea is that if a business's competitors could have access to its financial data, they could learn things that would enable them to compete against it unfairly. But I was never able to get a clear statement of what these things might be. I doubt that they exist. Real trade secrets—the secret ingredients of Coca-Cola, for example—are very unlikely to be discovered from the kind of financial data that would have to be made public for an anti-inflation program. The rule could be that if a business thought they would be, it could petition the program for special confidential treatment of the data. If the program denied the petition, the denial could be appealed to a court, just as would any other program decision. The justification of injury to competition also runs counter to the policy, recognized by the United States Supreme Court, that all aspects of a business except those specifically protected by act of Congress should be open to inspection and even imitation by competitors. Information about one's competitors and the ability to copy their successful products and methods generally enhances competition, and it generally benefits the public by spreading business efficiencies and superior products more widely. It does have the disadvantage of discouraging the making of profitable innovations, since the competitive advantage that they might offer will vanish if competitors can copy them immediately. But, the Court has ruled, it is for Congress, not the private businesses, to weigh the advantages against the disadvantages and to draw the lines between what can and cannot be made open to copying, and Congress had done so through the patent laws and the laws of copyright.[17] The absence of a confidentiality

[17] Fashion Originators' Guild of America v. Federal Trade Commission, 312 U.S. 457 (1941).

requirement could never offend either of these laws, because disclosure does not permit copying anything that is patented or copyrighted. Indeed, the laws permit nothing to be patented *unless* it is publicly disclosed, although a similar disclosure requirement for copyright has been eliminated.

Setting Individual Prices

The program would *not* generally set individual prices. There are literally billions of different prices charged every day in our economy. Trying to set them all through a program would be sure to lead to one of two results, either of which would render the program ineffective. Either the attempt would fail, and the prices would be set by the sellers substantially as they would have been without the program; or the prices would be set so inappropriately as to cause shortages, surpluses, plant shutdowns, unemployment, and other economic disturbances and injustices. There is no administrative method known, and none in sight, by which so many decisions could be made as frequently as they would have to be, and made wisely.

There is a small but well-established line of economic writing on the impossibility and inadvisability of wage and price controls of this nature. The argument is that they are impossible, essentially for the reasons just summarized; and, in addition, that the attempt to impose them is sure to lead to totalitarianism. In its frustration at not being able to make the controls work, the government supposedly would make the controls more and more rigid and more and more comprehensive of all the aspects of the economic life, and eventually of all the life, of the society. The argument concludes that there is no alternative to the market for controlling wages and prices, at least not for a free society. This argument is an hysterical extension of the argument alluded to in the introduction to this part, that massive bureaucratic displacements of the market are both inefficient and a threat to freedom and democracy.[18]

Only the first step in the argument is valid. Wage and price controls of the kinds that seek to set every individual price in a large economy are indeed impossible, but the attempt to impose them does not necessarily lead to totalitarianism. It is more likely to lead to ineffectuality, as it has in the case of the Interstate Commerce Commission. And it does not follow that there is no alternative to allowing wages and prices to be set by markets. There are other alternatives, some of which will be described in the next chapter.

The argument that wage and price controls lead inevitably to totalitarianism is really rather silly. Its only basis is the fact that most communist states do control their wages and prices. But other kinds of totalitarian governments have not and do not. In any event, it makes no sense to say that something that a government of a free society might do would inevitably lead to its becoming totalitarian because it is something that a totalitarian society does already. Totalitarian societies impose jail sentences. Are we therefore bound to become totalitarian if we impose jail sentences? Besides, the United States, England, and other free countries have all had such controls several times in their histories, both in wartime and in peacetime, over practically all aspects of their economies, and all these countries also now have portions of their economies continuously subject to such controls, and have had them so subject for generations. These portions are small compared to the economies as a whole, but still, in some cases, large enough to encounter the administrative problems that are supposed to lead to totalitarianism by way of frustration. Fi-

[18] Milton Friedman, *Capitalism and Freedom* (Chicago: University of Chicago Press, 1962), pp. 12–13; Friedrich A. Hayek, *The Road to Serfdom* (Chicago: University of Chicago Press, 1944), p. 70; Friedrich A. Hayek, *The Constitution of Liberty* (Chicago: University of Chicago Press, 1960). And see Christian Bay, "Hayek's Liberalism: The Constitution of Perpetual Privilege," *Political Science Reviewer* 1 (Fall 1971), 93, 112–13, 117–18. The argument is soberly and sensibly made in Charles Edward Lindblom, *Politics and Markets* (New York: Basic Books, 1977).

nally, the argument rests on the false premise that if the government does not exert controls, wages and prices will be sufficiently controlled by the market. In a modern economy, at least, this is not the case. There is instead continuous and probably, in the end, totally destructive inflation.

Comprehensive wage and price control programs that control individual prices have been imposed in the United States during every major war since the First World War. They always worked reasonably well to prevent inflation. And we remain a free society. But the programs, having been instituted in wartime, have avoided most of the administrative problems that would otherwise have made them impossible. They all used the "freeze" method. Wages and prices were not allowed to rise above the level they had been on some given date, or during some period before or concurrent with the time the controls were made effective. Sometimes, in what might be called a "modified freeze," they were allowed to rise above their "freeze date" levels only by amounts that reflected the sellers' increased costs. Thus, no government administrator had to decide what prices were appropriate for each of the billions of transactions that occurred daily. The existing prices were simply continued—subject, sometimes, to relatively small, cost-based adjustments.

This works, but it cannot work for long, because all prices eventually become obsolete, and merely adjusting for the increased costs incurred by sellers since the freeze is not a sufficient means of keeping them current. Such cost increases are difficult to measure and so are subject to a great deal of dispute. Each occasion can consume almost as much administrative time and effort as would be consumed by setting the price initially. Moreover, even if correctly measured, a cost increase does not necessarily measure the price increase that ought to be permitted. If prices are permitted to go up only in proportion to costs, profit rates are frozen. Profit rates obviously ought not to be frozen forever. They cannot be frozen for long without destroying the competition that is the heart of any privately directed economy. A freeze or modified freeze in wartime has avoided most of these difficulties because the wars have only lasted a few years, and during wars the civilian sectors of the economy, which are the only sectors to which the controls really apply, are prevented from changing as rapidly as they would in peacetime by the need to concentrate all possible economic efforts on building up and supporting the armed forces. Finally, although some competition and other economic incentives are destroyed, it does not matter so much during a war because for the time patriotism takes their place, and patriotism also helps those who suffer to bear the injustices of inappropriately set prices. Except for the concentration of economic efforts to build up and maintain the armed forces, the same considerations apply to *short* peacetime efforts during economic emergencies, such as the 1971 Economic Stabilization Program.

The United States, like every other major free country, has also had important segments of its economy subject to individual price controls for decades. In the United States, such controls commonly exist for the prices of services sold by the so-called "fixed utilities"—electricity, natural gas, and telephone—although other things such as trash removal and cable television are now also coming to be privately provided and to have their prices controlled on this basis. Such controls also exist in the United States for the transportation industries, except for airlines, which have only recently been largely deregulated. Fixed-utility rate regulation avoids most of the administrative problems that individual price regulation would otherwise encounter because the services are so nearly standard. Everyone who receives electricity, for example, is placed in one of only a few categories (residential user or industrial user, for example) and then charged according to the same rate schedule as everyone else in his category; and his "transactions" with the utility are automatically recorded and totaled by a meter. Thus, what in most other contexts would require millions of different pricing decisions requires only a few, which suffice for millions of buyers and billions of individual transactions. This sort of simplification is not generally possible for the transportation industries, however, and rate regulation for these industries has indeed largely failed. There is ample scholarly documentation of this failure,[19] and my own research has led me to conclude that the scholars have barely scratched the surface.

Nevertheless, the anti-inflation program ought to be given the authority to set or limit individual prices when and if necessary. There are times when nothing else would be sufficient, even without considering the eventuality of another all-out war. A very large natural catastrophe, a severe worldwide food shortage, or something like the actions of OPEC in 1973 and 1974 that concern a very important product or commodity might threaten to start off an inflationary spiral unless a price lid were clamped on immediately. Such a "lid" would presumably only need to be temporary. If the program administrator did try to keep it on longer than the president and Congress thought was necessary, of course they could override him and terminate it. There are also times when more limited severe economic dislocations would require individual price controls for some parts of the economy—just for oil or just for certain foods, for example. The administrators of commodities and securities exchanges generally possess the authority to suspend trading on their exchanges during periods of economic dislocation, either in general or for certain commodities or securities.[20] Trading could not feasibly be suspended in things like food or oil, but "freezing" the prices for a time would have substantially the same effect of calming people and of giving all concerned a breathing space within which to ascertain what the situation was and what of a more permanent nature might be done about it.

Hearing, Representation, and Competition

Like any government program, the anti-inflation program would have to conform to constitutional principles. Like any

[19] For example, Robert Fellmeth et al., *The Interstate Commerce Commission* (New York: Grossman, 1970) (the Nader Report on the ICC); Thomas Gale Moore, *Freight Transportation Regulation* (Washington, D.C.: American Enterprise Institute for Public Policy Research, 1972).

[20] 15 U.S.C. 781(k).

program not intended to be temporary, it would not be partially excused from these requirements on the grounds of national emergency.[21] The anti-inflation program, moreover, would be so comprehensive, and it would so importantly affect so many of us, that it ought to conform very carefully to constitutional principles. It should be designed with the same care as would be spent on the design of a new state or city government.

Two such principles that would apply with special force to a program of this nature are the right to a hearing and the right to representation. As the United States Supreme Court has worked them out, these rights are complementary. A person who is fairly represented in a body that makes a decision that affects him is not constitutionally entitled to a hearing on it; but if he is not fairly represented, he is. There is no constitutional prohibition of his being offered a hearing in the first case—just no constitutional entitlement to one.[22] This is the law, and it has been applied many times to government actions of an economic nature. For example, when the National Labor Relations Act was enacted in 1936, requiring employers and employees to submit to collective bargaining for wages and other working conditions, the act was upheld on the grounds, among others, that both employers and employees were guaranteed fair representation in the bodies that engaged in the bargaining.[23] A landlord's eventual right to a hearing on the amount of rent he could charge was recognized as his constitutional right even under the emergency conditions found to exist in the early stages of the World War II wage and price control program.[24]

It is not generally recognized, but it is the fact that compe-

[21] See, for example, Bowles v. Willingham, 321 U.S. 503 (1944), excusing the World War II wage and price control program from according certain constitutional rights, on the grounds of national emergency.

[22] Londoner v. Denver, 210 U.S. 373 (1908); Bi-Metallic Investment Co. v. State Board of Equalization of Colorado, 239 U.S. 441; 36 S. Ct. 141, 60 L. Ed. 372 (1915).

[23] 29 U.S.C. 151 et seq.; National Labor Relations Board v. Jones & Laughlin Steel Corporation, 301 U.S. 1, 57 S. Ct. 615, 81 L. Ed. 893, 108 A.L.R. 1352 (1937).

[24] See Bowles v. Willingham, 321 U.S. 503 (1944).

tition provides a third constitutional protection. A person, group, or class is not entitled either to a hearing or to representation on decisions that affect him or them if the control that competition provides—that is, the control provided by market forces—is deemed sufficient protection. No one, for example, is constitutionally entitled to a hearing on the prices of wheat, no matter what these prices are or how far they rise or fall, when the prices are controlled by a market. When prices are thus controlled, there is then no body of decision-makers that could hear complaints or in which one could be represented. A market makes its decisions and enforces them impersonally.

These legal principles are too well known to lawyers and of too little concern to others to be worth mentioning were it not for the presence of pricing institutions. With rare exceptions, the price-control program would not try to eliminate pricing institutions. Most of them are bound to be permanent features of any modern economy. In many cases the program's rules would, in fact, be designed to prevent inflation by using pricing institutions—to permit the program's officials to do only what the sellers could not do more intelligently and at less cost for themselves. There is a respectable although not conclusive argument that under these circumstances the pricing institutions would take upon themselves the mantle of "state action," a lawyer's term meaning that the institution becomes subject to the obligations and limitations that are the correlatives of other person's constitutional rights. Constitutional rights are rights only against the government. Private persons have no constitutional rights against other private persons. A private employer can constitutionally forbid his employees to speak out on certain issues, for example. However, there remains the question of what is the government against which the rights exist, and the answer the courts have given is that it is whatever or whoever engages in "state action." A sheriff certainly engages in "state action" when he makes an arrest, for example; but the concept has been stretched to include situations much further removed than this from ordinary government action. It might be stretched to include pricing institutions, especially if the anti-inflation program explicitly contemplates that an institution's powers be complementary to the powers of the program. In any event, the program itself might want to impose such obligations and limitations as a condition of permitting a pricing institution to retain the power it does; such a move would be consistent with the desire to observe especially carefully constitutional principles and principles of democratic governance.

Most kinds of pricing institutions already meet the obligation to provide fair representation. The representation of a member in almost any kind of seller's pricing institution is simply his ability to set his own prices and make public announcements about them. These actions constitute his "vote" on what the institution's price pattern will be and on the level at which it will be set.[25] Labor unions are required by law to afford fair representation to their members.[26] Most of them also provide hearings for certain kinds of grievances. Farmers are permitted to vote on the prices at which their crops will be supported by the Department of Agriculture in some situations.[27] Since in most cases it is the sellers themselves who organized and who operate their pricing institutions, it is not surprising that they are fairly represented in them. The only significant exceptions to the rule of fair representation that I have come upon are the pricing institutions that exist for the wages or salaries of persons who are not organized into labor unions and who, at the same time, are not sufficiently high in the employment hierarchy to be represented in the compensation-setting decisions by some of their own members. I will describe just a few of these situations for the light they shed on the importance of representation in a pricing institution.

I was interviewing a partner in a large downtown law firm in a large city on the setting of associates' salaries. Associates are the lawyers in a firm who have not yet been promoted to partner. Almost all lawyers are hired as associates and either

[25] See Chapter 3 at notes 22–30.

[26] 29 U.S.C. 411, Bill of Rights; constitution and bylaws of labor organizations.

[27] 49 U.S.C. 1911.

move up to become partners after several years or move out. The partners set their own pay out of the firm's receipts, and also the associates' pay. Except in some of the very largest firms, where they may work alone for long periods in back offices, associates spend much of their time working closely with one or more partners, doing most of the library research and other less skilled work, as well as learning the ins and outs of law practice. Since the partners generally work closely with the associates themselves and know that the associates of the present will produce the partners of the future, who will carry on the firm, I had expected before the interview to learn that in pay and in other matters the partners represented the associates quite well. Not as well as they represented themselves, of course, but substantially better than they represented the firm's secretaries and other nonlawyer employees. My expectations were confirmed.

Although his firm had long since stopped the practice, this partner told me, until a few years earlier most of the other large firms had sent one of their partners to an annual meeting among law firms in the area at which both associates' and secretaries' salaries were discussed. These annual meetings were still going on, but now only for secretaries' salaries. The discussion of associates' salaries had been dropped when it was decided that it probably violated the antitrust laws. Both the partner and I laughed when he said this, because it was obvious that the reason for stopping the discussion of associates' salaries applied equally to secretaries' salaries. The continuation of the discussion on secretaries was probably evidence that the firms cared enough about keeping secretaries' salaries down to continue meeting despite the legal risk, but did not care so much about setting the pay of associates.

Further conversation with the same partner revealed that either despite or because of the meetings, associates' starting salaries had for years (as far back as the early sixties, at least) probably, although not certainly, been higher than competition alone would have set them, whereas secretaries' salaries had clearly been less than competition alone would have set. The evidence was the supply in each case. Except for two or three years in the sixties, associates had always been in surplus, whereas, without exception, secretaries had always been in short supply. The reason why the conclusion is nevertheless doubtful in the associates' case is that the meetings had apparently served to keep the starting salaries of a relatively few associates down—those who had outstanding law school records and so could otherwise presumably have commanded large premiums—at the same time as they had apparently kept the rest up. But had the outstanding associates' starting salaries been allowed to rise, perhaps they would have drawn the others up too. In any event, the difference between associates and secretaries was clear. The secretaries, presumably because they are predominantly women and not in line to be promoted to partners, had not been well represented by the partners in matters of pay. On the contrary, they had been exploited. The associates, in comparison, at least, had been well represented and helped. The most valued secretaries with the most experience (twenty or thirty years) were making a little less than the least valued associates just hired. At least some of the secretaries were aware that they were being exploited. Legal secretaries with long experience in this city frequently "moonlighted," that is, secretly did legal work after hours for their own profit. "Moonlighting" by associates, on the other hand, if it occurred at all, was so rare as not to be rumored. In either case it is done secretly if it is done, because it diverts profits that might have been the firm's to the individual, and because, usually, the individual uses the firm's facilities without paying for them. The secretaries presumably would not have "moonlighted" had they not felt their firms were exploiting them.

A similar situation exists in the medical services industry. Pay scales there are generally decided by physicians, both for the physicians themselves and for the nurses and other help in the physicians' offices, and for the same groups in hospitals, special treatment centers, and so forth. The physicians generally control the latter, too, through being the dominant persons on the boards of the hospitals, the administrators of the hospitals, and the dominant persons in all the third-party payor plans such as Blue Cross.[28] The pay structure parallels that for the law, only with greater exaggeration. Physicians pay themselves extremely well, whereas nurses and virtually everyone else in the health establishments are poorly paid, often shockingly so. In Grand Rapids, Michigan, the men on the vehicles that carry medical equipment quickly to the scenes of emergencies and who give the first-aid treatment at the scene were paid only $2.50 an hour as recently as 1976.[29] Again, supplies demonstrate that the pay scales are far out of line with what competition alone, if it could have worked, would have set for them. Young men and women have been figuratively tearing down the walls trying to get into medical schools for years. There are almost three presumably *qualified* applicants for each place.[30] This is the case even though medical schooling is extremely long, expensive, and arduous. Nursing school programs, on the other hand, are generally not expensive, arduous, or long (two years is enough in some, with only a high-school degree required to enter), yet until recently places in many nursing schools were not filled, and nurses are still in short supply almost everywhere.[31] Positions below the rank of nurse are generally very badly paid and are often vacant, too, but reliable statistics are apparently not available for them.

Neither representation nor hearings can be fair in the con-

[28] See a research paper by Jane Stonecipher, "Medical Costs," September 16, 1975, which includes much additional information pertinent to third-party payor plans. The Stonecipher paper is on file at the Asa V. Call Law Library, The Law Center, University of Southern California, University Park, Los Angeles, California 90007. And see generally Rita Ricardo Campbell, *Economics of Health and Public Policy* (Washington, D.C.: American Enterprise Institute for Public Policy Research, 1971), pp. 27–39; Robert Stevens and Rosemary Stevens, *Welfare Medicine in America: A Case Study for Medicaid* (New York: Free Press, 1974); A. F. Ehrbar, "A Radical Prescription for Medical Care," *Fortune* 95 (February 1977), 164–72.

[29] Interview with a hospital worker.

[30] David E. Rogers, *American Medicine: Challenges for the 1980s* (Cambridge, Mass.: Ballinger Pub. Co., 1978).

[31] Joann S. Lublin, "Critical Condition: Severe Nurse Shortage Forces Some Hospitals To Close Beds or Units," *Wall Street Journal*, July 18, 1980, p. 1.

stitutional sense unless the persons concerned have access to all the information that is relevant to the decision that is to be made by the representative body or is the subject of the hearing. What this information will be depends upon the facts in each case and the nature of each decision. It can be said, however, that for the "freeze" type of wage and price controls the range of relevant information tends to be very narrow, and all of it usually relates only to the seller's own business. All that has to be known is the seller's own prices on the freeze date and, if there have been increased costs, what those increased costs are. What anyone else's prices, costs, or profits are is not relevant. But the anti-inflation program would not generally be a "freeze" type program, and it will, or should, always be concerned with economic justice, which includes equal treatment among similarly situated sellers. Moreover, some of the control methods it would use would make some sellers' financial data relevant in ascertaining permissible prices for other sellers. Fair hearings and fair representation under the anti-inflation program, therefore, almost certainly could not be provided unless there was full public disclosure, which is to say, among other things, no requirement of confidentiality. Hearing rights, although not rights to representation, are also connected with the full-justification requirement, although the necessity in this case runs in the other direction. It is at a hearing, and as our legal system operates only at a hearing, that the program's authority is challenged, thus requiring the program to provide the full justification in order to sustain its authority. The full-justification principle therefore requires the right to a hearing before the decision to which the hearing would apply becomes irrevocable.

Indexing

"Indexing" is the tying of a price or other financial obligation to the cost-of-living index or to some other standard that is expected to rise with inflation. When it applies to prices, as it almost always does at least indirectly, indexing always hurts the public because it contributes to inflation. It causes the indexed prices to rise higher and more rapidly than they presumably would have in its absence. Indexing is also both a public and a private benefit, however. It facilitates any long-range business commitment, including some that would not be made if indexing were not allowed. It enables the parties to long-range commitments to treat each other fairly. Without it, some persons' livelihoods could not be adequately protected, and some people would have practically no livelihoods at all. Pensioners probably need the protection of indexing the most, and many pension plans are indexed.[32] Indexing has also become common in collective-bargaining contracts.[33] It is practically universal in the contracts that public utilities make for their fuel supplies, which frequently run for terms as long as twenty years.[34]

Why not require everything to be indexed? Although indexing adds to inflation, what harm would this be if indexing were comprehensive enough to maintain every payment's real purchasing power? The answer is that comprehensive indexing must either not be enough to keep up with inflation, or it becomes impossible because the attempt to make it enough makes the inflation rise by ever-increasing increments. If everyone's pay check, pension check, and so on were indexed exactly to the rate of inflation, the indexing for each person would have to take into account the inflation that was being caused by the indexing for every other person. The mathematics is easy for a mathematician but too difficult for the general reader, so I will just state the result: such an indexing system would be stable only if the inflation rate without it would be

[32] A pension plan that entitles a pensioner to a share in an investment portfolio is considered by this definition to be indexed, for example. The assumption is that the value of the share will increase if the cost of living increases, and by about the same amount. See Internal Revenue Service Bulletin no. 1980-4, 42, *C.C.H. Pension Plan Guide* (current binder), §§17,095R and 25,327.

[33] Beth A. Levin, "Scheduled Wage Increases and Escalator Provisions in 1979," *Monthly Labor Rev.* 102 (January 1979), 20.

[34] See, for example, Tampa Electric Co. v. Nashville Coal Co., 365 U.S. 320 (1961).

zero, in which case, of course, it would not be necessary; in any other case the indexing itself would immediately produce an *infinite* inflation rate. So it is logically impossible for indexing to be both comprehensive and adequate—logically impossible that it both cover every payment obligation in the economy and fully maintain the real value of the payment. Anything short of full comprehensiveness and full adequacy is possible, but unless the indexing is considerably short of this, it will add very substantially to the economy's inflation rate. Thus if indexing is used very widely, the inflation rate is almost certain to accelerate. This, of course, makes things worse for everyone whose wages, salaries, and so on are not indexed, and it also makes it worse even for those whose wages are indexed, because a rising inflation rate makes indexing less adequate. Indexing can work only by reference to past inflation rates. If the rates are rising, the adjustments it makes are bound to be less than enough to match the current prices. Indexing is thus like a drug that can be beneficial if properly used in small doses, but that in large doses kills.

Israel has been using something close to fully comprehensive indexing for several years and is suffering the consequences. Practically all forms of payment obligations—wages, salaries, interest on savings deposits, interest on loans—are covered, from 80 percent to 100 percent. Everything is moved up semiannually in proportion to the inflation in the previous six-month period. The increases add to the inflation rate as soon as they are made, but each increase is not reflected in the indexing adjustments until the next semiannual adjustment date. For this and other reasons the inflation rate continually increases, and the annual adjustments are never enough. The rate increases have accumulated to the point that in late 1980 Israel had an annual inflation rate that was well over 100 percent and still climbing.[35]

Voluntary indexing in the United States is confined largely to very long-term business contracts, usually supply contracts,

[35] David B. Tinnin, "The Economic Sword over Israel," *Fortune 101,* (May 5, 1980), 244. "Israeli Inflation Soars to a World-Leading 134%," *Los Angeles Times,* September 17, 1980, p. 7.

collective-bargaining contracts, and pensions. The total is well short of enough to have the kind of inflationary consequences felt by Israel. The total should be watched, however. If it should grow to dangerous proportions, the category that ought first to be limited is probably collective-bargaining contracts. They do not have the same pressing need for indexing as do the other two categories, because they last for only a few years. By way of contrast, from the time that an employee first becomes a member of a pension plan until both he and his spouse have died can easily be fifty years. An additional reason why pensions need to be indexed is that when an employee becomes a pensioner, he is no longer in a position to help himself. He can no longer strike, or threaten to quit and work for a different employer. Moreover, the pensioner is generally dependent on his pension when he is receiving it, which means that he is dependent on its real value.

The indexing of all pensions being earned now, to be paid in the future, ought to be required by the rules of the anti-inflation program. The financial security of the elderly is a public responsibility. If part of it is to be left in the hands of private employers, the public has the right to demand that the security that they provide be real. This is only fair: there is no way except by a pension plan that persons of limited means can obtain financial security in their old age. An unindexed pension plan in inflationary times is simply a fraud on the participants. By extension, pensions presently being paid that are not indexed ought to be paid as though they had been indexed at the time the pensioner or his surviving spouse became entitled to them, from the day that the anti-inflation program becomes effective. The former employers cannot justly complain. They would be required to pay no more in real terms than they had agreed to pay, and they would still be allowed to keep the unearned and unexpected profits inflation had given them in the interim. The pensioners would thereby be given no more than they had once presumably honestly earned, although they would still be left without what inflation had taken from them in the interim. And the whole thing would last only as long as these relatively few pensioners or their spouses continued to live.

However, there are some cases in which the additional amount of pension provided by this newly required indexing would not be deserved. Although old-age financial security is often inadequate in the United States, it is sometimes more than adequate, and it sometimes reflects an unjust exploitation of the pension payer by the pensioner or by a group in his behalf. High-level corporate executives frequently have very generous pensions and pension plans. They made them for themselves out of monies that would otherwise have gone to their corporations' shareholders through profits or to the public through lower prices. Some public employees become entitled to substantial pensions after only a few years on the job, after which they can take other jobs, public or private, and become entitled to additional pensions without losing their rights to the first. High-ranking reserve officers in the armed forces sometimes get, or will be entitled to get, large pensions for which they will hardly ever have worked at all. If pensions like these were not indexed, the anti-inflation program ought not to require their indexing now. Probably the only protection the public has against them is to allow inflation gradually to diminish their real values, if they are not indexed. These pensions, when they are not indexed, could be distinguished from the pensions that ought to be indexed by making the mandatory indexing in all cases dependent upon the pensioner's showing of need. He ought not to be required to show a dire need, but he ought not to be entitled to mandatory indexing of a pension not indexed by itself except to the extent that, say, at today's prices, he would otherwise be receiving a total income of less than $15,000 a year. For a pensioner with a surviving spouse, of course, a different, higher figure would be appropriate. The legal principles that would permit distinctions to be made on this basis have already been developed. "Equity"—the traditional name for a court sitting to decide what a person morally deserves although no contract or other written law exists to give it to him—takes into account both past actions and present needs.[36]

[36] Henry Lacey McClintock, *McClintock on Equity*, 2d ed. (St. Paul, Minn: West Pub. Co., 1948), pp. 46–52, 59–69.

A plausible argument can be made that the indexing of pensions does not contribute to inflation because pensions are not included in the consumer price index. Pensions are not purchased by consumers. But they do contribute indirectly to inflation in at least two ways. They add to the payors' costs, and if the payors sell anything these are the costs of the things sold. Through pricing institutions and other means added costs tend to be reflected very quickly in higher prices, and even when price competition is dominant prices eventually reflect all costs. Second, since pension rights are universally recognized as an element in a person's compensation at the time that he obtains them, they contribute to competitive inflation in the ways that were described in Chapter 5. One labor union wants as good a pension plan for its members as another labor union has recently obtained for its members, and so on. Although pensions should generally be indexed, that their indexing does contribute to inflation should always be kept in mind.

A New Business Ethic

The difference between ethical and unethical conduct is frequently too subtle, too much a matter of motive and individual perception, for it to be effectively regulated by law, but laws can help. We have always had laws requiring ethical conduct, and they have sometimes been effectively enforced.[37] There is good reason to think that they help even where they are not legally enforced, if the standards they set are realistic. The persons to whom they apply who want to consider themselves ethical can point to them to support their actions. They can protect such persons against legal liability for actions that might otherwise be held to have violated some other legal duty. A lawyer can be held liable to his client for failing to act exclusively in the client's interests in the matters in which the

[37] George Gleason Bogert, *Bogert on Trusts,* 5th ed. (St. Paul, Minn.: West Pub. Co., 1973), pp. 343–54.

lawyer represents him, for example, except to the extent that so acting would violate other aspects of the lawyer's code of ethics.[38] A code of ethics can provide a focus for peer pressure against persons who do not want to act ethically, even where the code lacks legal sanction. Most professions have codes of ethical conduct, both with and without legal sanctions, and most have established institutions for formally enforcing them against their members, although not always with the support of the general law.[39] A few businesses that are not traditionally regarded as professions also have codes of ethics and have established enforcement mechanisms. The National Association of Securities Dealers does, for example.[40]

But business as such in the United States (and most other capitalist countries) has no formal code of ethics. Our more conservative economists believe that any ethic for business that went beyond simple honesty would be antithetical to the public interest because it would detract from the businessman's supposed duty to maximize his business's profits.[41] Traditional economic theory denies the need for business ethics beyond simple honesty, which is required to enable markets to work, on the grounds that markets best transform selfish greed into the benefit of all, so that any ethical requirements beyond simple honesty would only interfere. But a business ethic could not interfere with any market forces that are not there; if an anti-inflation program is needed to prevent inflation, market forces sufficient to prevent inflation do not exist. Market forces are insufficient to determine business conduct in many other respects too, of course, and even

[38] *The California State Bar Act and Rules of Professional Conduct* (Sacramento: State Bar of California, November 1979); *Model Code of Professional Responsibility and Code of Judicial Conduct* (Chicago: American Bar Association, February 1979).

[39] Ibid.; Judy Alsofrom, "New Ethical Principles for Nation's Physicians Voted by AMA House," *American Medical News,* August 1–8, 1980, pp. 1, 9.

[40] National Association of Securities Dealers, Inc., *Reprint of the Manual* (August 1969).

[41] For example, Milton Friedman, "The Social Responsibility of Business Is To Increase Its Profits," *New York Times Magazine,* September 13, 1970, p. 32.

when they are sufficient for some purposes it is difficult to see how they could really be impeded by a code of ethics.

One ethic that could replace the profit ethic for businessmen would be the duty to provide more and better products for lower prices.[42] The making of reasonable profits would be included, because reasonable profits are necessary to a business's survival. Especially good but not exorbitant profits could be considered one of the appropriate and proper rewards for providing especially good products. Something like this is in fact the ethic of every businessman I have ever personally known. Studies of business executives in the United States are unanimous, so far as I am aware, in reporting that most business executives both have a sense of ethical conduct and strive to follow it.[43] That this state of affairs has survived two hundred years of economics teaching to the contrary is testament to its rightness.

There are things that the federal government or the program administrator could do to help bring about a set of business ethics. The federal government could enact a law declaring it the duty of any person selling goods in interstate commerce or producing goods for such sale to sell or produce the goods only in ways he believed would benefit the public, for example. Such a law would be difficult to enforce in the usual sense, but it would have the important effect of freeing business executives from the worry that if they did make a decision to sacrifice profits for the public interest, their shareholders or superiors within the corporation could hold them liable for the lost profits or otherwise punish them for their actions. Such a law would probably not even be controversial. Most businessmen probably already consider themselves free to make such decisions, if not ethically required to. The secretary of commerce could be directed to establish a business

[42] See Richard H. Tawney, *The Acquisitive Society* (New York: Harcourt, Brace and Co., 1920), pp. 91–122.

[43] Edward S. Mason, ed., *The Corporation in Modern Society* (New York: Atheneum, 1967), p. 64; Charles Perrow, *Complex Organizations: A Critical Essay* (Glenview, Ill.: Scott, Foresman and Co., 1972). pp. 146–50; David Finn, *The Corporate Oligarch* (New York: Simon and Schuster, 1970), pp. 286–87, 289–93.

council, a standing committee of some sort, composed of business leaders and educators, to draft a code of business ethics and keep it current. The council could issue opinions on ethical problems of wide interest. If measures such as these were tried, I suspect that the common reaction would be that they ought to have been tried sooner. Most businessmen would probably welcome the enhanced esteem that a realistic code of ethics would provide them.

Although the good that a code of ethics for business would do would extend beyond the interests of an anti-inflation program, it would also help to control inflation. Controlling inflation presumably would be one of the public duties that the code would impose on a business person. To the extent that products and services were improved beyond the extent to which market forces alone would compel their improvement, they would be made less expensive, at least in the long run. Better products and services provide more value for the money. A more ethical business person presumably would voluntarily give more cooperation to the program, and his dealings with it, even when he disagreed, would be more open and honest.

Distinguishing Price Increases That Are Inflationary from Those That Are Not

Thc distinction suggested in the heading does not exist. All domestic increases are inflationary, if by inflationary we mean having a reasonable likelihood of contributing to inflation. My experience with the Price Commission convinced me that unless this principle is firmly established, which means announcing it prominently and enforcing it against everyone, an anti-inflation program will be subjected to numerous fruitless arguments with sellers about which kinds of price increases are inflationary. The usual basis of an argument that a price increase is not inflationary is that it cannot be shown to enter into the consumer price index, which is the commonly used measure of inflation. A labor union would argue, for example, that a wage increase for its members would not be inflationary because productivity in the industry in which they worked had risen enough to permit the wage increase without increasing overall unit costs. Even if what the industry produced was a consumer product, therefore, the cost of living index, it would be argued, would not rise. A corporate executive might make a similar argument on his own behalf or on behalf of his salaried employees, not necessarily because his or their productivities had increased but still on the grounds that some of the corporation's costs had gone down. Government employees, it was sometimes argued, could never receive an inflationary wage or salary increase, no matter how high the increase might be, because what they produced never entered into the price of anything at all. Pension increases were sometimes argued not to be inflationary because a pension is not a price. I also heard the argument made that a particular price increase should not be counted as inflationary because it was morally right. I heard this for price increases caused by the cost of new job-safety equipment and of equipment being purchased to reduce air or water pollution.

As my emphasis on the word *domestic* indicates, price increases on goods sold to persons outside the United States do not contribute to our inflation rate, at least not significantly enough to warrant treating them as though they always did. But with this sole exception, all price increases possess a reasonable likelihood of contributing to inflation in the United States, if for no other reason than that they are causes of competitive inflation. Competitive inflation is caused by *any* price increase or *any* increase in *anyone's* income, even if it is not commonly called a price (a pension, for example), that is visible to anyone else who possesses a power or who is a member of a group (ordinarily a pricing institution) that possesses a power to raise prices. That this is so is obvious, I think, from the way competitive inflation works. It might still be argued that the answer is to keep price increases secret, if this is the only way that they could contribute to inflation. But this would not be fair; it would undermine the credibility of the program; and it would not be possible in most cases, in any event. Most of the other kinds of price increases mentioned also contribute to inflation by increasing costs. Increased costs are generally reflected in increased prices very quickly where pricing institutions are involved. They are reflected in increased prices even under conditions of strong price competition, although it may take a longer time. It is obvious, too, I think, that a cost increase is a cost increase, whether or not other costs went down earlier or are going down at the same time. That the costs that enter into the calculations of employees' productivity are going down does not affect the fact that an increase in their wages will be an increased cost for their employers, for example.

CHAPTER 11

Some Specific Directions for the Program

My specific suggestions for an anti-inflation program are organized, by and large, by the kind of pricing institution that would be involved. Not surprisingly, it turns out that the kind of pricing institution that has developed in each sector is more indicative than anything else of the kind of wage and price controls that would be appropriate for it, and of whether wage and price controls would be appropriate at all. I do not suggest that some kind of wage and price controls be imposed on every part of the economy. But I consider every major part of the economy, and come to a judgment on whether controls of some kind are necessary there and, if so, what they should be. The actual anti-inflation program, when it is established, should do the same, and not limit itself to major sectors. It will have the ability, which of course I do not, of gathering the information necessary to an intelligent consideration of every part, major or not. This is important, because as I have said before, both fairness and effectiveness demand not only that inflation be stopped in every category of personal or business income, but, in addition, that the stopping place—the real incomes of everyone relative to everyone else—be widely perceived as fair. Perfect fairness will never be achieved, among other reasons because not everyone would ever agree on what it was, but good faith and a reasonable effort to achieve fairness would be enough, and this is something that the program could achieve.

Monetary and Fiscal Policy and the Money Pricing Institution

Monetary policy should be both made and implemented by the program. Fiscal policy, however, cannot be. A nation's fiscal policy consists of all the expenditures and receipts of all the nation's governments. So not even the central government can make its nation's fiscal policy alone. Fortunately for our ability to manage national fiscal policy, however, the expenditures and receipts of the federal government substantially exceed the expenditures and receipts of all state and local governments combined. So as a practical matter, our central government can, as a whole, largely if not completely control the fiscal policy of the nation. Although no single person or institution within the central government can make fiscal policy for it, unless that government is controlled by a dictator, Congress and the president together determine the expenditures and receipts for the federal government, so they together also unavoidably make its fiscal policy. They could not delegate their powers in this respect to the administrator of the anti-inflation program without stripping themselves of some of the most important powers they possess.

Back in the days when "fine tuning" of the economy through fiscal and monetary manipulation was still thought possible, proposals were made for giving the president power to raise or lower corporate and individual income taxes without the prior approval of Congress by up to some preset, small percentage. This is still a good idea, although events have dashed many of the unrealistic hopes we once had for it. It could alleviate a problem that could arise if one of the aims of a program against indeterminate inflation were successful—raising employment to close to 100 percent. To do so would require, among other things, a fiscal policy designed to keep demand high, so high that it might occasionally exceed the amount required to keep employment near 100 percent, and thus trigger some demand-pull inflation. Quick adjustments by small amounts might be necessary both to avert such excesses and, at other times, to avert sudden downturns that threatened to reduce employment. Although the quick adjustments that such a presidential power would make possible would not be enough for either purpose, because what the government spends or takes in is not, by any means, the sole "determinant" of demand, such quick adjustments would help. But even this relatively minor fiscal power could not properly be delegated to the program administrator. His role in its exercise should be to advise the president.

The power to make and implement monetary policy can be delegated, however; in fact, it already is. For all practical purposes it is presently being made and implemented by a group of federal agencies and departments headed by the Board of Governors of the Federal Reserve System. Since what the money pricing institution does with respect to both the prices of money (primarly interest rates) and the money supplies would be of great importance to the anti-inflation program, however, these powers should be placed under the general control of the program administrator. He should be able to set the target money prices and money supplies at which the money pricing institution would aim. However, the implementation of the banking, savings and loan, and other financial machinery that would be required to hit the targets should be left where it is, in the hands of the money pricing institution. The supervision of the nation's financial institutions is a large and complex task that serves many purposes in addition to influencing the prices and supplies of money. It would burden and confuse the anti-inflation program to make it responsible for this task too, and it would not be necessary in order to perform successfully its mission of preventing inflation.

The principal change in monetary policy should be to recognize that the prices of money are not essentially different from any other prices, which is to say, the principal concern should be to keep them stable and low. If high interest rates were felt to be desirable, temporarily or permanently, matters should be arranged so that the government rather than private lenders reaped the resulting unearned profits. A 2 percent increase above the level that had been established as providing fair profits to lenders, for example, might be implemented by imposing a 2 percent annual lending tax on all loans made or renewed during the period. This would have advantages in addition to that of avoiding undeserved income transfers from borrowers to lenders. It would be more flexible than raising interest rates directly, because it could be reversed at any time, and the reversal could be effective even for loans outstanding. It would simultaneously have fiscal effects, too, which would be in the same direction as the monetary.

Full Employment

One goal of the program should be to reach full employment rapidly. Full employment is important in its own right, and it also helps to reduce inflation. An economy functions more efficiently and more harmoniously when it is kept continuously at or near full employment. In particular, the labor-union militancy that composes the principal part of competitive inflation can never be sufficiently dampened unless people feel secure in their jobs.

But full employment does present special inflationary risks. Sweden, Japan, and West Germany have had decades of dealing with these risks. Their experience offers a guide that I have taken into account. We should expect our problems to be more difficult than theirs for at least a generation, however, because we have permitted long-standing unemployment to degrade a much larger proportion of our population than they ever did.

One group of special risks is, in fact, that which arises from approaching full employment from a position of having a large pool of long-term unemployed and partially employed. The new jobs that open up as the economy expands will not necessarily be in the areas where the unemployed live, and the unemployed will not necessarily have the skills required by the jobs. Unless the government intercedes well in advance to subsidize people's expenses both of relocation and of training, the new jobs will go begging for long periods. The vacancies will cause long-term (and therefore inflationary) shortages of goods, and the positions will eventually be filled only by the inducement of very high wages or salaries. Very high wages or salaries are an especially resistant source of inflation, because they are much less amenable to being brought down than are the prices of goods after they have once been raised. The recipients adjust their self-images and life styles upward. If the recipients had to be induced to move long distances or to give up other good jobs, they are likely also to have required assurances from their new employers that their wages and salaries would not be reduced after the labor shortages had been eliminated. So to avoid these inflationary risks, the federal government should maintain a large and diversified training and relocation program, presumably under the control of the Department of Labor.

There are additional reasons why the government should underwrite the costs of job training. One is simple fairness. Our governments already underwrite most of the cost of white-collar job training—that which occurs in schools, colleges, and universities, especially professional graduate schools. It is also unfair to expect employers to pay most of the costs of training, because they have no assurance that the people they take on will remain with them long enough to compensate them for the costs of training them. The situation is especially irksome, because if an employer undertakes a training program he is likely to lose his employees, after they have finished, to his competitors in the same line of business who have not incurred the expense of training them. And the competitors will try to take away the best employees and leave him with only those who were least successful in the program. The costs of training generally rise sharply if it is for only one or a few people. Placing training costs on employers, therefore, unavoidably imposes a special burden on small businesses. Experience shows that employers will not undertake sufficient training to meet the need for new, trained employees, presumably because of the difficulties just mentioned. Experience also shows that sufficient numbers of people will not—or can not—pay for their own training in advance. More of them presumably would if our economy were managed so as to give a reasonable assurance that there would be jobs available after the training was done, but it is doubtful that even then enough people would obtain training at their own expense.

People who lose their jobs because of technological advances should receive the retraining for which they qualify at no expense, and with a continuation of their former wages or salaries. People in training for the first time should also get a modest salary supplement, although we could get along well enough by not paying anything to young people. They could continue to have to rely on their parents' support. But I do not think that this would be fair, especially if others were given salary supplements even when they had other means of support—working spouses, for example. Especially during the first years of the program, when it will be necessary to overcome the cynicism of people who have seen too many government programs look promising but fade out, successful completion of any training program should guarantee either a job of the kind trained for or a wage or salary equal to that which a job of the kind would have paid. The guarantee could not go on indefinitely, but something like a one-to-one relationship would be about right. A six-month training course would carry a job or wage guarantee of six more months, a two-year course would carry a guarantee of two more years, and so on. Guarantees of this nature would also have the salutary effect of discouraging the government from continuing to offer training programs for which there were not sufficient jobs.

Shortages of goods would be less of a risk, but not so small a risk as to be safely ignored. The chief means of reducing such shortages would be information. All firms should be required to keep the program up to date on their current production volumes and future production plans and their current sales and inventories, in confidence if this proved to be necessary. The program would combine all this information and issue public warnings of spot shortages or surpluses that its information predicted would occur, far enough in advance for buyers and sellers to adjust to them or to avoid their occurrence. The handling of this much information for this purpose is feasible, with the computers now available. This is just the kind of thing that "input-output analysis" was designed for.[1] If it were to prove necessary to keep firms' estimates honest and complete, a penalty for incorrect reports and/or estimates could be imposed, analogous to the penalties that are already imposed by state governments on firms that contribute more than their share to the state's industrial accidents or unemployment.

A System for Concentrated Industries (Those Using the Industrial Pricing Institution)

This measure, which is complex enough to be called a "system," is by far the most complex I propose. I will first fully describe the system itself. The reader can confine his attention to this section if he likes, and still obtain a sufficient nontechnical understanding. I will then analyze its secondary economic effects (its effects other than to prevent inflation) and its special administrative aspects.

The System

The system that will be explained here is a result of my efforts to devise a system of regulation that would leave sellers free to set whatever prices they wish, that would maintain the incentives for efficiency and for pleasing buyers that competition presently provides, but that would nevertheless prevent inflation from being caused by the sellers to whom the system applied. The last qualification is necessary. No system could be proof against inflation caused by factors wholly external to it. For example, even if a perfect system for preventing inflation could be devised and applied to the entire economy of the

[1] Wassily Leontieff, *Input-Output Economics* (London: Oxford University Press, 1966).

United States, our economy would still be susceptible to inflation if OPEC increases world oil prices. I think that the system that I have devised achieves each of these goals. It may seem impossible to prevent inflation while still leaving sellers free to set whatever prices they wish, but this system does this in the same way that price competition does it in theory—and does it in fact, in the relatively few situations in which it works as in theory it should. Although sellers are left free to set prices as they wish, the *incentive* for increasing prices beyond certain limits, or under certain conditions, is eliminated or reversed. Under conditions of effective price competition, a seller is free to raise his prices any time he wishes, but he will lose substantial amounts of sales and so substantial profits if he raises them higher than the conditions of competition permit. So the conditions of competition eliminate or reverse the profit incentive for price increasing at or above a certain point. Similarly, under the system I have devised, although a seller would not necessarily lose sales if he were to increase his prices, in all cases he would at least not increase his profits, and in most cases he would reduce them, so his incentive to raise prices would always be eliminated, and in most cases it would be reversed.

The proposal is that the profits of whole industries be limited. An industry whose total profits exceeded a certain percentage of equity investment would be required annually to pay to the government all of the excess. The share of the payment that each member of the industry would make would be proportional to the member's share of sales in dollar volume during the period, regardless of its profits. For example, suppose in a given industry total sales were $15 billion, of which $1.5 billion were profits, representing a return of 15 percent on $10 billion of equity capital. If the "ceiling" average return had been set at 10 percent, the industry as a whole would be required to pay the extra 5 percent, or $.5 billion, to the government. Assuming that a particular member's share of sales was 25 percent, its share of the payment required would be 25 percent of $.5 billion, $125 million. (A company's share of sales would of course not necessarily be equal to its share of invested capital.) The net effect on the members of the industry, but for a short delay, would be the same as if the initial prices on all their products had been 3.3 percent ($125 million out of $15 billion) less than they were.

It will be shown presently that sellers would tend to price just low enough so as to make payments to the government unnecessary. If it were found that industries did not naturally price this low, a small penalty could be imposed—for example, payments might be made 110 percent rather than 100 percent of any excess. An industry pricing in the predicted manner could raise prices and still avoid payments only if costs increased. Since wages and excess profits of supplier industries would also be controlled, costs would rise only rarely, and in any industry for which the savings from technological advance exceeded the increases in these costs, prices would actually be forced down. The effect of implementing the system, therefore, would be to keep prices low and thus to prevent inflation.[2]

It would not be necessary to set every price within each industry; competition would continue to encourage managers to set prices rationally. For example, assume that an industry whose profits were limited sold products *A* through *Z* and that all of these products are priced to return costs plus 10 percent, except *B*, which is priced to return a profit of 20 percent. If the industry were even slightly price competitive, its members would be encouraged to produce more of *B* than of other products since its sale provides especially high profits. This increased production would automatically result in lower prices. Even if the members, through their pricing institution, were able to maintain the price of *B* at an artifically high level,

[2] If some industries did have to make payments to the government, the effect of lower prices could still be approximated by the government's returning any amounts collected from sellers to buyers (either ultimate consumers or industrial users) through income tax credits. For individual consumers, for example, these credits could be accorded in proportion to the amount of money that a family of a particular size and income level is likely to spend on consumption. These computations have already been made, for they form the basis for the tables on federal income tax forms for computing deductions for state and local sales tax.

they would probably not choose to do so. A firm that was not selling proportionately as much as *B* as were the other firms would be encouraged deliberately to lower its price relative to the prices of the other products. If it did not, the other firms would continue to take a disproportionately high share of the limited overall profits allowed the industry. Other firms would have to match this lower price or lose sales. If the product *B* were disproportionately low priced, the motivations and mechanics for raising its price to parity with the others would be essentially the same, though, of course, reversed.

Although there is a superficial similarity, the proposed system should be differentiated from an excess profits tax like that imposed during World War II.[3] The "tax" proposed here would take all or more than all of the excess profits, not simply a fraction of them. Less than 100 percent taxation would render the proposed system useless to combat inflation, for so long as an industry were allowed to retain any part of its excess profits, the member firms would still be motivated to raise prices in order to increase profits. The proposed system differs most importantly from an excess profits tax, however, in that it imposes its levy on the average profits of the entire industry rather than on the profits of each individual firm, and it requires each firm to remit to the government a sum in proportion to its sales rather than its profits. These differences have the important consequences of encouraging operational efficiency, allocating resources rationally, and facilitating enforcement.

This system would hardly be regulation at all, as we have come to know regulation for utilities, for example. Nor is it price control as we came to know it during the major wars and the 1971 Economic Stabilization Program. The overall limitation on profits would prevent *only* those price increases in which all the firms in the industry raise their prices in unison or nearly so in an attempt to make the industry's overall prof-

[3] See generally Randolph E. Paul, *Taxation for Posperity* (Indianapolis: Bobbs-Merrill, 1947), pp. 61–80; Roy Blough, "Measurement Problems in the Excess Profits Tax," *National Tax Journal* 1 (1948), 353.

its excessive. These are precisely the kinds of price increases that I described in Chapters 1 through 4 as having been made possible by the decline of price competition, and that constitute the core of indeterminate inflation. The system, moreover, would prevent these price increases by motivating firms through their individual profits, which is exactly the manner in which price competition would motivate them, and as I show in the section that follows, the motivation would be such as to allocate resources for both investment and production in exactly the manner by which price competition would allocate them. Finally, the system would *not* interfere with pricing behavior in any respect in which competition is adequately dealing with it.

Allocation of Resources and Profits

Limiting average profits would not lead to misallocation of profits within an industry. The firms that would have received the highest returns on sales in the absence of the limitation would continue to receive them in the same relatively greater amounts. Relative rates of return on equity investment could in theory change, but any such change would result in a better allocation of profits, for it would make the industry more price-competitive. Those firms that made the most profits under the system would generally be those that could use their resources most profitably without the crutch provided by excessive profits for all of them. Their higher profits under the system would reflect only the attributes of low costs and efficient operation, which a competitive system should reward.

Indeed, the allocation of profits among firms in the same industry would in some cases be made uncomfortably accurate. If an industry that was earning excess profits before the system was imposed contained a few firms whose equity investment constituted most of the equity investment of the entire industry, and if these large firms consistently made a much greater profit as a percentage of sales than the smaller firms, limiting the average profits of the industry could conceivably drive the weakest of the low-profit firms into bankruptcy.[4] The profits limitation would apply to every member of the industry, and since the weakest members are already making very little, their profits might well be turned into losses. The demise of these small firms would not result in a lessening of competition, for they are not viable competitors at present. The big high-profit firms now possess sufficient monopoly power to drive the weakest firms out if they so desire. They refrain because they wish to avoid the short-term reduction in profits that would result from the necessary price war; because they hope to make the industry appear competitive and thereby reduce the risk of antitrust suits or governmental regulation; because they consider cut-throat price competition unethical; or for other reasons. The profits-limitation system would expose the actual absence of competition in such industries, and the nation would be compelled to make the called-for choice in public policy: either antitrust actions could be brought to reduce the monopoly power of the strongest firms, or the weakest firms could be allowed to go under. It should of course be noted that any effective system of price controls would have this same adverse effect on weak firms in otherwise high-profit industries.

That the system properly allocated profits among different firms in the same industry is important as a matter of fairness. It is also important because in the long run allocations of profits influence allocations of resources. The firms that have made the most profits will most likely be the firms to expand the most rapidly. Whatever it was that they were doing better than the others, which resulted in their getting the most profits, will both encourage and enable them to expand more rapidly and make whatever they were doing better more typical

[4] The constitutionality of regulation that leaves inefficient firms with less return on their investment than more efficient firms in the same industry, even to the point of leaving some firms with "inadequate" returns, has been upheld by the United States Supreme Court. Permain Basin Area Rate Cases, 390 U.S. 747, 768–90 (1968). See also Aetna Ins. Co. v. Hyde, 275 U.S. 440, 447 (1928).

of the industry. Thus the industry as a whole is gradually made better by a proper allocation of profits among its members. The same process can occur among and between different industries, although in fact it rarely does to the extent it does within one industry, because of pricing institutions. Pricing institutions have the effect of raising or maintaining the profits of entire industries, although they do not ordinarily affect the relative profits of the firms within an industry. The rises and declines of entire industries relative to one another, in a modern economy, are more the results of buyers buying more or less of the different industries' products than of the industries' different profits levels.

The system would of course have some effect on the relative profit levels of different industries. In theory, the program administrator would have to set the maximum average rate of return on equity investment for each industry. If it were set lower for some industries than for others, of course the former industries would be relatively disfavored, and vice versa. Difficult as making such decisions might seem to be, they would still be infinitely easier to make, and therefore infinitely more likely to be made intelligently, than decisions about individual prices—which are the kinds of decisions that administrators have to make under the usual kinds of wage and price control programs. But the problem would in fact be even simpler than it appears. The system would set only a ceiling on average profits, not a floor, and would apply only to concentrated industries, not to the entire economy. Moreover, among the industries to which the system would apply, resources are already misallocated in a way that the system should alleviate. Unless the industry is expanding to fill shortages—and as we shall see, such industries could be exempted from coverage—an industry that makes consistently high profits year after year must be both keeping sales volume down and preventing new firms from entering the industry. Otherwise, sales volume would have risen and driven prices and profits down. Such an industry is therefore producing fewer products than the public would demand if its prices were set competitively, and too few resources are being allocated to such production. Forcing prices downward would force a reversal of the process, and thereby at least alleviate the underallocation, even if the price level were not forced down exactly the right amount to cure it. If the system were administered intelligently, the maximum rate of return would seldom be set so low as to cause products to be underpriced. Even if prices were set this low, and the administrator refused all appeals for adjustment, the system would eventually correct itself automatically. Very low rates of return would drive away investment capital regardless of how much the lower prices stimulated product demand, and the industry would become a "shortage" industry entitled to an exemption from coverage.

Details of Implementation

COVERAGE A limitation on average profits should be applied only to those industries whose members keep prices high enough to make excessively high profits. Industries that are nearly perfectly price-competitive should be exempted. Since any price increase in a perfectly competitive industry is caused by increased demand or costs, the prices are economically justified. They could not be prohibited without producing shortages, evasions, and, eventually, a breakdown of the prohibitions. Industries that are nearly perfectly competitive are exeedingly rare, and should be easy to identify. They usually have many members, none of whom is proportionately very large; their prices always (by definition) rise and fall as demand rises and falls; and they normally make only modest profits, which would make it unnecessary to cover them anyway.

Even an industry whose members were making what would seem to be excessively high profits should be exempted if the industry's products were in such rapidly increasing demand that production could not keep pace. Lowering the profits and hence, directly or indirectly, the prices of such an industry would increase the demand for its products still further and aggravate its difficulties in keeping pace. And lowering its profits would also lead to a misallocation of resources. The presumably high rate of return that an industry enjoys during a period of shortage may be necessary to attract large infusions of capital that will be needed if the industry is to expand rapidly enough to meet the rapidly rising demand. This is not to say that such an industry could not be making undue profits as well as the profits necessary for expansion. But choosing a proper rate of return would be close to impossible. Moreover, industries with such rapid rates of expansion are probably receiving the benefit of some invention or innovation; some degree of extraordinary profits is presumably necessary to encourage other industries similarly to progress. The characteristics of an industry deserving to be exempt from coverage for this reason ought to be easy to spot: a very high rate of expansion and virtually no unused capacity. These characteristics would be exceedingly difficult to fake. Although the members of an industry could in theory conspire to hold back on expansion in order to eliminate all unused capacity, to do so would present an almost irresistible temptation to the more efficient members to expand despite the conspiracy and capture the profitable new sales opportunities for themselves. Moreover, halting expansion would itself remove the industry from among those given an exemption.

Aside from these exemptions, whether the profit limitation should or should not apply to a particular industry would seldom be a critical question. The administrator could, if he so chose, apply the system initially only to a few industries, as a test. Even if the system were to prove feasible for all concentrated industries, it might be applied only to those considered potentially most inflationary, or to those to which it could most feasibly be applied. If the rate of return were well chosen, a noninflationary industry that was undeservedly covered would not be materially harmed. Except for the presumably light burden of filing reports, it could function exactly as it would if it had not been covered. Moreover, if it were understood that any industry that was not initially brought under its cover could, and normally would, be required to make whatever payments were necessary retroactively to the date of the system's inauguration, the system would effectively reduce inflation even if many potentially high-profit industries were not covered at first, or ever. An industry's only hope of remaining outside the system would then be to keep its prices and profits below the point at which, if it were covered, assessments would be required. All that would be necessary to make this retroactive application fair would be that the members of an industry be given notice of the accounting principles by which their profits would be defined and notice of the limit that those profits would have to exceed before payments would be required. The burden of paying excess profits would not differ materially from the burden of paying income taxes, which are not infrequently also levied retroactively.[5]

DETERMINING A RATE BASE AND A MAXIMUM RATE OF RETURN Determining a rate base and a maximum rate of return to be earned on the rate base for each industry would be the most difficult problem. It would first be a problem of measurement: firms in the same industry would have to adopt essentially similar principles of accounting, for this purpose at least.

If the administrator really had to set the rate of return for every industry, his task would indeed be difficult. But, as has already been explained, this would not be true. It is only the maximum rate of return that would ever need to be set, and even that would only need to be set for a relatively few, consistently high-profit industries. The maximum rate of return for these industries should presumably be a rate that would allow them to make about the same average rate of return as the industries that were not covered. (The maximum would of course have to be somewhat more than the average, because

[5] See "Setting Efffective Dates for Tax Legislation: A Rule of Prospectivity," *Harvard Law Rev.* 84 (1970), 436. See also W. David Slawson, "Constitutional and Legislative Considerations in Retroactive Lawmaking," *California Law Rev.* 48 (1960), 216, 232–33.

no industry could earn exactly the average each year.) Thus, the covered industries would be required to earn no more than the rest of American industry.

This method of determining the maximum should not apply to particularly risky industries. An industry that could prove that investment in its business was unusually uncertain should be entitled to a higher maximum rate to compensate for its higher risk. The proof of an unusually high degree of risk for an established industry should probably be a showing that, for some significantly extended period in the recent past, the earnings of the firms in the industry had in fact fluctuated substantially more than the earnings of American firms generally. A "banker's measure" of risk—the average interest rate an industry had to pay on its borrowings, for example—would not seem to be satisfactory. The risk that an industry presents to lenders would presumably be less if the industry had made very high profits; but the profits-limitation system proposes to eliminate precisely these excessive profits.

Whatever the difficulties to be encountered in choosing a proper maximum level for profits, they cannot logically be used as arguments against a profits-limitation system. *Any* system of price controls would encounter them. Since prices determine profits, prices cannot ever rationally be set without taking into account the profits they will allow. Moreover, since the industries to which a profits-limitation system would apply are those in which competition has proven insufficient to keep profits in line, applying the system would not create the difficulties of deliberate profit-setting but only shift them. The executives of the major firms, who now decide through the industry pricing institution what the prices will be for their entire industry, will simply find their discretion somewhat circumscribed in the public interest of preventing inflation.

ANTICIPATORY PRICING AND "SUCCESSIVE-YEAR AVERAGING"

A seller in an industry covered by the system would try to price just low enough so that his industry would not have to pay any excess profits to the government. Pricing higher would not benefit him or any other company in the industry.

In addition, pricing higher would impair good will, since customers would know that they had been charged more than enough for the industry to earn fair profits, and that their overcharges had been, in effect, a levy placed on them for the benefit of the tax-paying public. Pricing higher would also have the effect of reducing demand to whatever extent the demand was price-responsive, so that fewer goods might be sold. It would therefore work against the long-range interests of the members of the industry in having an expanding market. An expanding market would lead to expanding profits even under a profits-limitations system because it would support an expanding rate base. Further, expanding the markets and the size of an industry is often a prime goal of management even when higher profits do not result.

Assuming that the members of an industry would want to price just below the penalty point, the question remains whether they could plan their operations with sufficient precision to hit close to their target. Experience indicates that it would not be as difficult as might appear. Industrial pricing institutions set their prices based on profit projections. The record shows that industries' profits have thereby been kept relatively stable. Studies of several very large corporations have shown that they engage in what is called "target pricing." Management sets a rate of return on investment to be realized each year if possible, or in any event over the long run, and it sets the share of the fixed costs of the corporation that each product or group of related products should carry. Each product is then priced to return its proportionate share of the fixed costs, plus its own variable costs of manufacture and sale, plus its proportionate share of the target rate of return. Corporations that have followed these procedures have demonstrated that they can thereby hit close to their target rates of return year after year.[6]

[6] See, for example, Gardiner C. Means, "Pricing Power and the Public Interest," in *Administered Prices: A Compendium of Public Policy,* Senate Subcommittee on Antitrust and Monopoly of the Committee on the Judiciary, 88th Congress, 1st Session (Washington, D.C.: Comm. Print, 1963), pp. 213, 220–23.

In order to ensure that an industry did reduce its prices when necessary to stay within the profit limits, a small penalty might be imposed. For example, as I have suggested, the industry might be compelled to pay to the government 110 percent rather than 100 percent of any excess profits. Such a penalty could be made equitable even for those industries whose planning under the system proved inadequate for hitting the target consistently. For industries whose past performance demonstrated such planning difficulties, the limitation on profits could be set slightly higher than it would have been otherwise. The possibility of paying the penalty for misses on the high side would then be balanced by the possibility of keeping a small excess-profit reward for hitting right on target. The combination of penalty and reward could be considered as carrying neither moral opprobrium nor approval; together they would simply be an incentive for making compliance more automatic and the task of administration easier.

Industrywide target pricing, through the industry's pricing institution, could be made easier and the system generally more flexible if industries were allowed to skip payments in years in which the payments would be very small, so long as the accumulated net amount of payments skipped did not exceed a fixed percentage. Occasional narrow misses would then not necessitate the payment of excess profits to the government. For example, if the profit limit for an industry had been set at 10 percent and the allowed margin of error was 1 percent, the industry could in six successive years have average earnings of 11 percent, 10 percent, 10 percent, 9 percent, 10 percent, and 11 percent, respectively, and never have to pay the assessment. The overruns would not at any time have exceeded the accumulated underruns by more than one percent, the allowed margin of error.

Successive-year averaging would also somewhat reduce whatever risk might otherwise be present that the system would cause wide price fluctuations in industries that had both high fixed costs and widely fluctuating sales volumes. Their fixed costs would operate to reduce their profits per unit in the slack years, and they could set their prices correspondingly higher in those years to make up for the difference. Successive-year averaging would allow them to keep their prices uniform and make up in years of high demand for the relatively low profits their uniform prices provided when demand was slack.

DEFINING "INDUSTRY": THE CONSEQUENCES OF ERRORS OF INCLUSION AND EXCLUSION Since the proposed system would pit one company within what it defined as an industry against another, by making the higher-than-normal profits of one the necessarily lower-than-normal profits of the other, an industry ought to be defined for the purpose of limiting profits to include competitors and only competitors. Two firms should not be included within the same industry if they sold substantially different products or, unless one of them sold nationally, they were in different parts of the country. Single firms that sold substantially different products—"conglomerates"—would be simultaneously included within different industries. The definition would be similar to that already developed in antitrust law for determining whether firms sell within the same or different "relevant markets."[7]

When a single firm was placed for these purposes within different industries, it and the administrator would have to agree upon the principles for allocating its relatively fixed costs among the products it sold in each industry. That the principles be "correct" in some economic or accounting sense would be of less importance than that they be settled. An abstractly incorrect principle would increase the firm's profits in one industry and decrease them in another by the same amount. Unless the first industry was chronically low-profit, the long-term effect on the ability of the system to control general inflation would be nil. The greater danger would be the ability of a firm to juggle profits from one industry to another, to take advantage of temporary profit-keeping opportunities opened up by other firms in those industries temporarily

[7] See, for example, Tampa Elec. Co. v. Nashville Coal Co., 365 U.S. 320 (1961).

making higher or lower profits than usual. That danger would be effectively avoided by requiring that a firm have clear principles of allocation and abide by them, whatever they were.

The legal lines for bounding an "industry" could never be precise, but they would not need to be. Most errors would do little harm. For example, a failure to include companies whose total output represented only a small portion of the output of the industry in which they should have been included would inflict no discernible harm at all. Suppose ten companies produced all of a product that was sold competitively to purchasers on the eastern seaboard, but that the industry as defined by the program failed to include the two smallest, which together accounted for 10 percent of the total sales. The eight that were included would keep their prices below the relevant level to avoid being assessed for the excess. The two that were not included would be under no such legal obligation, but since they competed with the eight, they would have to meet their prices or lose most of their sales. The only error that failing to include the two companies would introduce would be to misstate the average profits of the industry by the amount by which the average profits of the two differed from the average profits of the eight, divided by a factor of ten, a probably insignificant amount. Indeed, the administrator might often intentionally fail to include the very smallest sellers in an industry, especially if there were many of them who did not, collectively, account for more than a small percentage of total industry sales. The distortion introduced would be trivial, and the omission would save a nontrivial amount of private bookkeeping and bureaucratic effort. Foreign producers might also be intentionally excluded, even if their domestic sales were substantial. The fact that their sales in this country were in competition with domestic producers would insure that their prices be kept down along with the prices of the domestic producers, and the failure to include their profits in the averaging process would not introduce an error at all, since it is only the profits of domestic companies that we could feasibly limit. Parallel reasoning would show that inclusion of some companies in an industry to which they did not properly belong would usually result in similarly insignificant changes in their profits and those of the industry.

AVOIDANCE, EVASION, AND DELAY A company intent on avoiding or evading the profit limitations would have to consider carefully how to do it. It would not help simply to charge a higher price, because prices *per se* would not be regulated. There would seem to be only two ways to break the law: either the company could hide all or part of the receipts from sales so that they would never show up as profits on the reports submitted to the program, or it could apply the legally prescribed accounting principles in a manner that would understate profits. The first way would constitute a fraud not only on the program, but on the tax authorities, on the shareholders or other owners of the company, and on the company itself. Thus the chances of detection would ordinarily be too great to warrant the risk.

Acknowledging receipts but attempting to characterize the financial operations of the company so as to understate profits would be similar to machinations for the purpose of reducing income taxes and, like them, could involve either fraud (factual misstatements) or legitimate avoidance (questionable legal characterizations). In either case, however, the inducement to make the attempt would be much less than for taxes, for a company that succeeded in understating its own profits would receive only a small part of the benefit of its success. A company whose sales totaled 10 percent of an industry's total, for example, and that succeeded in understating profits by $1 million, would benefit only to the extent of $100,000 itself, while its competitors would receive—at no legal risk to them—the benefit of the remaining $900,000. It would take either a very brave or a very generous company to undertake the risk of heavy civil, or even criminal, sanctions for such little selfish gain.

To avoid encouraging companies to contest payments merely for the purposes of delay, payments or portions of payments not made on the day upon which they would normally be due ought to carry interest charges at least equal to the rate the company concerned actually earned on its equity capital thereafter, instead of the standard federal tax penalty of only 6 percent. All the summary procedures available to the Internal Revenue Service in assessing, collecting, and appealing controversies involving the federal tax ought also to be made available to the program administering the limitations system.

Stimulating Price Competition by Helping Consumers Make Price Comparisons

We saw in Chapter 2 that a cause both of inflation and of higher stable prices is the inability of consumers to make meaningful price comparisons. This inability enables sellers to "creep" their prices up by small amounts, either directly, by simply raising the prices, or indirectly, by degrading the products. For the most part this condition is incurable. Price competition never will work very well on most products in a modern economy. But a measure that would probably eliminate enough of this condition to have a significant impact on inflation, and that would provide lower stable prices besides, would be to require that all expensive products (say, anything retailing for more than twenty or thirty dollars) carry strong and standard warranties.

Under the supervision of the program administrator and subject to his approval, representatives from each industry affected would work out standard warranties for the products of the industry, which each of the industry's products would have to carry. There might be only one warranty for each kind of product or there might be several, but each product of the kind would have to carry at least one, and this would be enough to guarantee reasonable product durability and performance. The least warranty permitted on any kitchen range might be full repair costs, including replacement parts, for five years, for example. The least permitted on automobiles might be five years, or 50,000 miles, whichever comes first—which the industry actually had on all its models for a short time in the sixties.[8]

Price comparisons would be facilitated in several ways. The product would not be degraded to a point that would be likely to produce an appreciable number of claims under the warranty. It is always more expensive, and usually much more expensive, to repair a product in the hands of the consumer than to make it good enough not to need repairing in the first place. Thus creeping inflation through product degradation would be made more difficult. The products would also be made more readily comparable. A consumer choosing between Brand *A* and Brand *B* would have fewer factors to compare, since the warranties, at least, would differ on fewer points. There would be only one or at most a few warranties to learn for each product, and experienced salesmen presumably would come to know and understand them all. This would also help a consumer to assess the worth of the product, because a product is generally worth what the manufacturer is willing to warrant it for, and little more.

In order to be effective, the requirement should be such that even the least warranty was a strong one. It has been argued that such a requirement would take away consumers' "freedom" to buy cheap products and to assume the risks of paying for repairs or of having to throw the products away quickly. There really is no such freedom, however, because consumers have no feasible way of knowing what degrees or kinds of risks they are assuming. With rare exceptions, manufacturers do not try to inform them, and usually do their best to mislead them into underestimating the risks. Purchasers of products with only ninety-day warranties on them, for example, surely do not expect the products *certainly* to become unusable on the ninety-first day. In fact, they have no idea what the odds are of anything in particular going wrong, within any particular lengths of time, or of what the risks are generally. Conceiv-

[8] Laurence G. O'Donnell, "GM Posts Biggest Price Rise in Years on '70 Models and Places Pressure on Ford over Reduced Warranty," *Wall Street Journal,* September 12, 1969, p. 3.

ably, manufacturers could be required to provide this information. A kitchen range might be required to state the results of the manufacturer's or the government's durability testing as follows, for example: "Tests show that there is a 40 percent chance that the oven will fail to go on because its thermocouple will burn out within two years; if this should happen, the cost of repair will be about $50. Tests also show that . . ." and so on, through the dozens or possibly hundreds of things that might conceivably go wrong within the time the product is likely to be used. Such statements could never be made fully understandable to the average consumer, however, and they would probably be more expensive and more irksome for most manufacturers than a standard warranty.

Most manufacturers, I think, would welcome a strong, standard warranty requirement, because it would help them against the kind of competition they most dislike—the competition from the products that are actually much worse in quality but only slightly cheaper in price, although most consumers do not know it. I think that most manufacturers would also welcome the requirement because it would enable them to take more pride in their products. Unethical competition degrades a whole industry. The manufacturers who would rather sell good products find that if they do not degrade, they will hardly sell any. Would the program have to employ strong measures to insure that manufacturers complied with their warranties? I think not. State courts have been moving rapidly in the direction of protecting consumers against defective products by awarding damage claims, quite high damages sometimes, for many years.[9] A consumer can collect on a warranty against a recalcitrant manufacturer quite readily in a small-claims court in most jurisdictions. Moreover, a pattern of failure to honor one's warranties is commercially noticeable. Retail salesmen are likely to hear of it and to warn potential buyers. Reputable retail stores will refuse to carry the

[9] William L. Prosser, *Law of Torts* (St. Paul, Minn.: West Pub. Co., 1971), pp. 656–65 (§§98–101).

products. The failure of manufacturers to honor their warranties has not been a major problem to date.

A warranty requirement would also combat inflation by combating planned obsolescence—the deliberate degrading of products, not in order to make them cheaper to manufacture but in order to insure that they will wear out quickly and require buyers to buy more soon. Planned obsolescence is the rule in the clothing industry, where it is not the clothes that wear out, but the styles that are made obsolete. Its extent in industries where style is not important is unknown. It has been suspected but, as far as I know, never proven. To conclude that it does not exist in other industries, however, would require one to believe the manufacturers of anything for which style is a factor are alone in their immorality, and this seems unlikely. Planned obsolescence is inflationary, because it is a form of product degradation and so is tantamount to a price increase.[10]

The federal government already controls labeling and packaging to an extent, to prevent it from being misleading.[11] This is an anti-inflationary measure because it helps the consumers to make meaningful price comparisons. For some products the controls go further, to impose affirmative requirements. A drug that has a generic name must carry a label that carries this name, for example, in addition to any brand name it may have.[12] Similar affirmative requirements should be extended to other kinds of products sold at retail. For example, government inspectors at the large urban centers where fresh produce comes in for distribution locally could assign each shipment an appropriate standard labeling. A carload of winesap apples might be assigned the label, "Winesaps, fresh as of (the date)—crisp, slightly sour." Whatever retailer sold apples from this carload would have to label

[10] For a well-thought-out plan for mandatory warranties of services, see "Guidelines for Extending Implied Warranties to Service Markets," *Univ. of Penn. Law Rev.* 125 (1976), pp. 365–414.

[11] 15 U.S.C. 1451–61.

[12] 21 U.S.C. 352 (e) (1).

them in this manner. Any food that was likely to lose flavor or other desirable qualities if refrigerated would have to be labeled as having been refrigerated if it had been. Similarly for any other kind of treatment that affected relevant qualities. If people could choose the products with the qualities they wanted, producers and sellers would be encouraged to produce and sell these products rather than others, and retailers would have more difficulty in charging higher prices than their competitors for what were obviously the same products. For meats, the requirements would have to apply both to preparation and to labeling. Retailers are presently free to mislead consumers by giving a cut of meat any name they wish, even if it is a cut that is generally known by some other name, and to cut meats differently merely in order to have something they can "honestly" name differently. These "different" cuts are frequently priced much higher even than the ordinary cuts with the ordinary names being sold by the same retailer.[13] The requirement as to preparation should be that no cuts other than those permitted be sold. The requirement as to labeling should be that every cut be given its standard, recognizable name on the package or counter label. Measures like these would of course somewhat restrict retailers' "freedom," but choice without the understanding to choose intelligently is not freedom, so consumers' freedom would not be restricted. And since choice without understanding leaves people open to exploitation, consumers would be less exploited.

Replacing Regulation with Planned Competition in the Transportation Industries

Utilities in the United States have traditionally been classified in two categories, those that are "fixed" and those that are not. The latter are generally but not invariably the transportation utilities. A utility is regarded as fixed if a substantial part

[13] John Keats, "Rip-off at the Supermarket," *Atlantic Monthly* 237 (March 1976), 27–34.

of the facilities by which it provides its services are literally or figuratively fixed to the land at or near the point where the services are provided. Examples of fixed utilities are those that provide telephone services, electricity, and natural gas, and the railroads. The fixed facilities of the first group are lines by which the services are delivered to the consumer. The fixed facilities of railroads are their tracks and terminals. There is generally no alternative to regulating the rates of a fixed utility. Once the facilities of one such utility are in place, that utility can easily underprice any other utility that might want to compete with it, because it is comparatively much more expensive for the second utility to install its own facilities. And often there is no space left for a second set of facilities.

Utilities that are not fixed, on the other hand, not only need not be regulated, they generally ought not to be, because they would function much more in the public interest under price competition. The federal government has already recognized this fact for airlines and has deregulated them.[14] In 1980 Congress enacted legislation to do likewise for trucking.[15] Most other forms of transportation could also be beneficially deregulated, and so should be. Even railroads could be, if the federal government would buy up their trackage and maintain it as "public railways," essentially as it already maintains public highways, although it should probably charge tolls for the public railways. Many railroad terminals are already public; those that are not could be made so. The only major transportation industry that is probably fixed unavoidably is intracity busing and railroads (subways). City buses and railroads need to have regular routes and regular schedules, and it is not generally feasible to have more than a very few operating on the same routes in a city.

Transportation industries that were deregulated might develop private pricing institutions, although they also might not. Transportation facilities are often available in very large numbers. There are millions of trucks currently being used

[14] Michael E. Levine, "Revisionism Revised? Airline Deregulation and the Public Interest," *Law and Contemporary Problems* 44 (1981), 179.

[15] Motor Carrier Act of 1980, P.L. 96–296, 94 Stat. 793 (1980).

commercially in the United States, for example. The prices of transportation services are also often not amenable to being set through pricing institutions because consumers find it relatively easy to make price comparisons. Provided they get themselves or their freight to where they want it to go safely and promptly, many people seem not to care much about anything else, and so will choose the cheapest services offered. Transportation may turn out to be like agriculture and labor in not being able to maintain effective pricing institutions unless the government helps. In any event, if pricing institutions do develop after deregulation in the transportation industries, it will almost have to be because they have been made feasible by the emergence of some very large firms that dominate the markets in which they exist, and this is the kind of situation that can be handled by the price-limitation system for concentrated industries. And the measures to be described in a moment, which should be applied immediately upon deregulation, ought to make the development of pricing institutions even more difficult than it otherwise would have been.

Price competition could be made more effective than it would otherwise be in a transportation industry in which consumers find it difficult to make price comparisons by the simple expedient of requiring every transportation facility to post its rates prominently in a readily understandable manner. This is commonly done already for taxis, although the competitive effect is nil, of course, if the rates are regulated. If all rates have to be posted this way, rate differences are immediately apparent, and the consumer can immediately compare them. If the trucking deregulation goes through as planned, for example, it might be conducive to the maintenance of price competition in that industry to require that all rates fit certain categories of weight and size of container, regardless of contents, except where special handling was necessitated (for example, if the contents are explosive, unusually fragile, have to be kept frozen, and so on). The program should have the authority to do this when it thought it would be helpful for any transportation industry large enough to have a significant impact on the national economy, and to require an appropriate local government to do it for local industries, such as taxis.

Improving the Regulation of the Fixed Utilities

There is no choice but to continue regulating the prices of the fixed utilities, because for them price competition is not feasible. Price competition requires at least four or five competitors to work well in any industry. The technological difficulties of having four or five fixed utilities serve the same area—four or five telephone companies, for example—are generally insurmountable. On the other hand, the fixed utilities do not generally pose the same difficulties for regulation as do, say, the transportation industries. We *can* reasonably hope to make regulation of fixed utilities work in the public interest. It does to a substantial extent already. What I offer here are only some suggestions for improvement.

Most fixed-utility regulation presently operates by reference to a utility's "base" of invested capital. The total cost of a utility's facilities, less depreciation, is its base. The prices of the services it sells are set by the regulatory commission so as to yield a "reasonable rate of return" on this base.[16] One difficulty with this scheme is its failure to differentiate among the different rates of return that are appropriate for different kinds of invested capital. A 10 percent rate of return, for example, would be too high for debt capital if the utility was able to sell its bonds at a rate of interest of only 8 percent, and at the same time be too low for the utility's equity capital. The utility might not be able to sell its shares of stock except at prices that would provide an expectation of a rate of return of, say, 12 percent. Schemes have been worked out that would make these distinctions, and thereby encourage utilities to capitalize themselves efficiently and permit the capital-cost savings to be passed on to consumers.[17] The program administrator should have the authority to require federal, state, and local regulatory commissions to move toward the adoption of these schemes as rapidly as their particular situations permit.

But the more serious source of inflation from fixed utilities

[16] William K. Jones, *Cases and Materials on Regulated Industries* (St. Paul, Minn.: Foundation Press, 1976).

[17] Robert L. Schlesinger, "Measuring Return on Equity," *Public Utilities Fortnightly*, May 26, 1977, pp. 19–22.

has been their rapidly rising costs, and these are likely to continue rising rapidly. Utilities rely to a larger extent than do most industries on borrowed capital, so their costs are especially affected by increases in interest rates, which over the last three decades have been increasing. Utilities are also especially susceptible to the higher costs imposed by environmental-protection measures. The electric and natural-gas utilities are especially susceptible to the costs of energy, which have also been rising and promise to continue rising. Fixed utilities are capital-intensive, and their capital consists in unusually large proportions of things fixed to the land: dams, reservoirs, buildings, large generators, pipes, lines, poles, and so on. The prices they pay for their facilities are therefore the prices charged by the construction industries, in unusually large proportion, and these prices have been rising extremely rapidly for years. Many, although not all, of the forces pushing these prices up would probably continue even after the establishment of an anti-inflation program, because they arise from natural causes such as the diminishing stocks of natural resources and the increasing ratio of population to land.[18] Existing regulatory schemes do hardly anything to encourage cost savings. On the contrary, they encourage increases in cost, especially capital cost, by making price increases dependent upon a showing of increased costs and by making profit increases dependent upon a showing of increased capital.

It ought to be possible to work out accounting practices that would identify and measure, at least roughly, the costs over which a utility has some control. An electric utility's costs of fuel oil for its generators would presumably not be such a cost, for example, whereas the operation, maintenance, and repair expenses of its generators presumably would be. A utility's employees should be permitted to keep some portion of any cost savings they are able to bring about by their own efforts, for a reasonable period of time (a few years), as an incentive

[18] Carol J. Loomis, "For the Utilities, It's a Fight for Survival," *Fortune* 91 (March 1975), 97 ff.; John R. Emshwiller, "Plunging Power: Big Financial Problems Hit Electric Utilities," *Wall Street Journal*, February 2, 1981, pp. 1, 12.

for effecting the savings. Employees should also be made financially secure against layoffs brought about by cost-reduction measures. This is only fair, and if it is not done, the effect of the financial incentives for cost reduction would be seriously undercut.

Unregulated Retail Industries

A retail industry that is highly concentrated—that is, has a few large firms that dominate the industry—could be regulated by the system for concentrated industries just as readily as could a wholesale industry with the same characteristics. But most retail industries are not highly concentrated, and it is they that I will treat in this subsection. Retail industries in the United States are typically highly competitive. They have low rates of profit as a return on sales and high failure rates, especially among their smaller members. Appearances to the contrary notwithstanding, however, they are not typically very price competitive. All the obstacles that a modern economy puts in the way of price competition, which were described in Chapters 1 and 2, are at their strongest at the retail level. As a result, retailers almost universally function within effective pricing institutions—institutions of the "markup" variety, described in Chapter 3. The pricing institutions, once established, also stand in the way of price competition.

Nevertheless, the program should essentially leave the retail industries alone, at least initially. They have not been significant sources of inflation in the past, and there is nothing to indicate that they will become such. They have served rather as conduits of inflation from the manufacturing level, inflation that may have originated there or further back—at the level of the labor union for the manufacturing industry, at a supply industry, or elsewhere. The markup tends to pass price increases along and to amplify them, but at the same time to keep prices down if they are kept down at the manufacturing level. This variety of pricing institution is thus likely to provide all the anti-inflation pressure that is needed on retailers.

Agricultural Products

Prices of most raw agricultural products are already controlled by the Department of Agriculture. The regulation sometimes works through controls on how much is planted, or how much is sent to market rather than stored, or how much is imported from other countries to be sold here; sometimes it is effected through tariffs on imported foods, through arranging sales to foreign purchasers or canceling or prohibiting such sales; and sometimes in still other ways. The methods are continually changing, but the fact of control has remained since the 1930s. It reflects political judgments with which an anti-inflation program ought not to interfere. Our agricultural policies have undoubtedly meant that food prices are higher than they otherwise would be, but the policies need not be and probably have not been a significant source of inflation. To the extent that they shield food prices from external shocks (crop failures, major changes in a foreign country's agricultural buying or selling policies, and so on), they help to prevent inflation by avoiding sudden upward bursts in food prices that might set off waves of competitive inflation. Food prices compose the most immediately and widely felt component of the cost of living for most people. The prices of many foods have risen even more rapidly than the general rate of inflation during the last few decades, but this fact reflects forces that would have had the same effects even if we had not had agricultural price supports. Meats have generally become more expensive in relation to other things, for example, because more people here and in other countries have reached income levels that permit them to eat more and better meat than their parents ate. Prices of foods of all kinds have felt the upward pressure exerted by a rising world population pressing against a more limited amount of arable land.[19]

The anti-inflation program ought therefore to have the authority to affect agricultural products in just two ways. It

[19] Stephen H. Schneider and Lynne E. Mesirow, *Climate and Global Survival* (New York: Plenum Press, 1976).

should be able to set the price targets at which the Department of Agriculture, by its various means, aims. It should be able to set the stockpiling targets, where storage is feasible, at which, again, the Department of Agriculture would aim; the Department would administer the actual stockpiling. Of course the program administrator should be advised by the department secretary on what the price targets ought to be, but the final authority should rest with the administrator. The secretary represents farmers, whereas the administrator would represent the country as a whole on matters of price. Storage could be a significant weapon against inflation by permitting the stockpiles to be sold off to avoid large temporary price increases resulting from crop failures and other unusual events. Stockpiling obviously could provide other benefits, too, in a world increasingly subject to famines.[20]

Agricultural Cooperatives

Agricultural cooperatives are the pricing institutions permitted to farmers by exemptions from the federal antitrust laws.[21] They do more for their members than ordinary pricing institutions do, however. They commonly operate marketing facilities and sometimes processing facilities, from which their members benefit in proportion to the volume of products that each sends to the cooperatives for sale. No legal limits exist for the size of a cooperative. As a result, many include practically all the domestic producers of the product concerned, and unless there is effective foreign competition or competition from similar products (different varieties of apples, for example), they control the price.

No cooperative should be permitted to be any larger than it has to be to obtain substantially all the potential efficiencies of joint marketing and processing facilities. If this size would be too large to permit enough cooperatives to provide a reason-

[20] Ibid.

[21] Practicing Law Institute, *Agricultural Cooperatives* (Corporate Law and Practice course handbook series, no. 151) (New York, 1974).

able amount of competition for a product, and if a reasonable amount of competition is not provided by other means (by foreign producers, for example), the farmers concerned should be offered a choice. Either they sacrifice the efficiencies to the point where there is sufficient competition, or their cooperatives will be regarded as fixed utilities and have their prices regulated essentially as such prices traditionally are. The progam administrator should seek the advice of one or both of the federal government's antitrust law enforcement arms (the Antitrust Division and the Federal Trade Commission) for judgments on the competition that this would require. When regulation was required, the program would presumably have to supply it itself.

The Pay of High-Level Executives

These are the men or women at the top of large organizations, usually business corporations, whose positions give them the power, if not always the appearance, of paying themselves. In some respects it might prove difficult for the program to limit their pay. Their positions give them extraordinary political power. Some of them, in fact, possess extraordinary skills, for which they presumably deserve extraordinary pay, and almost all of them can give the appearance of immense importance if they choose. Their positions allow them to give themselves impressive offices, hire highly competent public relations assistants, and so on. But, on balance, they are vulnerable. Their pay is often so high as to be unconscionable by any reasonable standard.

If at least the highest compensations of this kind were not brought substantially down, the whole program would be discredited. A program administrator could hardly expect to restrain the wages of the lower-paid workers in the nation if he were to allow the top two men at Ford and the top man at General Motors to continue each to take home more than a million a year in straight salary alone, for example.[22] I suspect that these compensations also lack support in the lower ranks of the same organizations, although for understandable reasons the men and women in the lower ranks have not publicly complained. These very high pay rates are typically much higher, often two or three times higher, than the pay rates in the same organizations at the next level down.[23] It is extremely unlikely that such a large jump in pay is needed to get the persons in the next lower rank who are chosen for promotion to accept. The prestige, power, and sense of accomplishment that the top positions offer would presumably be enough, even if no pay increase were involved.

These very high pay rates cannot be competitively justified, because if all salaries within the same industry were brought down, none would be needed to keep the occupants of the top positions from switching to other firms. The fact that only a relatively few industries pay such very high rates proves that they are not needed to induce competent people to take the jobs, because there is no evidence that the industries that pay them have had more competent leaders than the industries that do not. Finally, it cannot reasonably be argued that the recipients of the very high rates deserve them for their out-

[22] "Annual Survey of Executive Compensation: A New High for Pay at the Top," *Business Week,* May 14, 1979, pp. 79–107.

[23] Statistics on the pay of the next levels down are hard to come by, but the statement in the text is supported by analysis of the proxy information that the Securities and Exchange Commission requires companies with publicly traded stock to file. The SEC requires pay disclosures only at the very top of the corporation ladder, which typically includes only two or three positions, but even among them the differences are generally quite high—a 50 percent increase from the number three to the number one position is common, and some show larger gaps than this. And in some cases the top pay levels are so high that it would be incredible if the pay of the next level down were anything close. When, as was the case with Ford Motor Company in 1978, for example, the top two men were both getting well over 1 million dollars a year, it seems certain that the average vice president in that company was not getting anything close to this much. "Annual Survey of Executive Compensation" (1979); "Annual Survey of Executive Compensation," *Business Week,* May 12, 1980, pp. 56–84.

standing work, because there is no evidence that their work has been any better than the work of the leaders of other industries in which such high rates are not paid. Indeed, there is some evidence that points the other way. The pay rate of the top men in the steel industry and the automobile industry have both been among the highest in the nation, and both of these industries have performed notably poorly in recent years.[24]

The pay of the topmost persons in any organization should be limited to something like 25 percent more than the average pay of the next highest group of substantial size and importance within the organization, and the pay that anyone can take in total from all the organizations with which he is associated should be limited by some flat amount, say $300,000 a year. The first limitation would be difficult to enforce in some situations, because it would be difficult to ascertain the next highest group of substantial size and importance in the organization, so for these situations the second limitation would be of principal importance. The head of a conglomerate business organization would presumably be effectively limited only by the $300,000 limit, for example. But for a university president, a hospital administrator, or a labor union president, the first limitation ought to be workable, at least in the usual case. A university president's pay could be no more than 25 percent more than the average pay of his university's full professors. A hospital administrator's pay could be no more than 25 percent more than the average pay of his hospital's established full-time physicians. If the hospital had no full-time physicians, presumably full-time pay equivalents could be calculated on the basis of the fees for working part time. A labor union president's pay could be no more than 25 percent more than the average pay of the best-paid category of workers in his union.

[24] "Annual Survey of Executive Compensation" (1979, 1970); James Flanigan, "GM: A Giant Awakening to a Wider World," *Los Angeles times,* October 5, 1980, pp. 1, 26–28; Sease, "Testing Mettle"; Jeffrey Sheler, "Detroit Thinks Small: Will It Pay Off?" *U.S. News & World Report,* September 29, 1980, pp. 56–58.

And the chief executive of a reasonably tightly structured corporation—an automobile manufacturer, for example—even if it was a part of a larger conglomerate, could be effectively limited to no more than 25 percent more than the average pay of the corporation's vice presidents.

The limitations should apply even to a chief executive who owned all or part of the company. Since the limitations would not limit how much he paid himself through stock dividends and other ownership interests, he could, therefore, continue to pay himself in total as much as he does now (tax consequences aside). But the method of payment would at least be required to be a truer reflection of the pay's real basis. On the other hand, the limitations would not apply to people whose pay, though very high, was not from organizations that they effectively controlled. Thus, prize fighters, professional football players, movie stars, television news commentators, authors, inventors, and the like would not be covered. The limitations presumably would have an effect on the pay scales of the top-middle executives in the same organizations, however, although these positions would not actually be covered. The topmost executives whose pay would be covered ordinarily set the compensation of these lower positions. They presumably would set them somewhat lower, so as to maintain what they considered the appropriate differentials with their own lowered pay.

Of course the limitation should define "pay" to include pay of whatever kind that came from occupying the position in the organization. Contributions to a pension plan should be included; expense accounts that exceeded what was reasonably needed to carry out the person's business duties should be included to the extent of the excess; shares of stock and options should be included to the extent their market value exceeded the amount, if any, that the person was required to pay for them, and so on. That something need not be counted as income for tax purposes should be irrelevant to its being counted for the purposes of the anti-inflation program. The social, economic, and political purposes that are served by counting or not counting certain things as income for tax purposes bear no necessary relation to the purposes that would be served by an anti-inflation program.

Labor Unions

It should be made clear at the start, preferably by provision in the enabling act, that the program recognizes labor unions as a legitimate and desirable element of our national economic governance and will seek to make them more, not less, effective for protecting their members' legitimate interests. The labor union, where it exists, is the pricing institution of the working person's choice. A working person is at least as entitled to the protections of a pricing institution as is anyone else. Labor unions, moreover, perform many worthwhile functions in addition to helping to control their members' wages. They participate in governing the workplace, and they represent their members in that governance. For many of their members they give a sense of identity and a dignity not just in their dealings with their employers, but with the whole rest of the world.[25] In any event, labor unions are too well established for an anti-inflation program to be enacted over their members' determined opposition. Those who urge the abolition of labor unions seem to think that something like perfect wage competition would take their place.[26] But some kind of pricing institution for wages and salaries almost always exists. If it does not include a labor union, it is generally the management acting alone or in tacit agreement with other managements in the same industry. It would not be fair to compel working people

[25] Derek C. Bok and John T. Dunlop, *Labor and the American Community* (New York: Simon and Schuster, 1970), pp. 207–28; Albert Rees, *The Economics of Trade Unions* (Chicago: of Chicago Press, 1962), pp. 136–69.

[26] For example, Milton Friedman, *Capitalism and Freedom* (Chicago: University of Chicago Press, 1962), pp. 123–25; Gottfried Haberler, "Incomes Policies and Inflation," in Gottfried Haberler, Michael Parkin, and Henry Smith, *Inflation and the Unions* (London: Institute of Economic Affairs, 1972), pp. 45–50.

to be subject to a pricing institution in which they have no voice.

The basic concept for integrating labor unions into the anti-inflation program ought to be that they are a part of government. Together with employers they govern the workplace, and they represent the employees in this government. As a part of government they owe employees the same constitutional rights of representation and hearing as does any other part. As a part of government a labor union has no constitutional or moral right to lead or support its members in a strike against the wishes of its superiors in the government, and its members have no such rights either. Labor unions and their members would have to accept the program's decisions on wages and prices like everyone else. The right to strike should be abolished for all employees making at least the federal minimum wage for unhandicapped labor.

At the same time, the minimum should be kept high enough to provide a decent income, and either the program or the Department of Labor (including the National Labor Relations Board) should provide binding arbitration. Employers and employees alike would have to submit to this arbitration, even if they would rather jointly choose their own arbitrators. This is unfortunate, because some fine private labor arbitrators exist in the United States, who have developed good relationships with particular industries, but I see no alternative. Wages are not a private matter. In any event, private labor arbitration in our country does not generally include wages. It is concerned with job grievances. Job grievances are a sufficiently private matter to continue to be arbitrated privately. An employer could not give his employees who were union members a wage increase without going to arbitration, although if he and the labor union agreed, they could submit their agreement, together with a statement of facts and reasons showing why it was appropriate, to the arbitrator, seeking what lawyers call a consent judgment. Not even voluntary increases could be permitted to avoid arbitration, because arbitration would be the program's way of controlling wages.

Federal wage or salary arbitration, like federal price controls of any other nature, could constitutionally be imposed on state and local governments as well as on private employers. State and local government price increases contribute as much to the nation's inflation as any other. They therefore "affect interstate commerce," which is sufficient grounds for subjecting them to federal law if Congress chooses to do so,[27] and if these grounds were deemed insufficient, the Constitution also empowers Congress "to coin money" and "regulate the value thereof." Laws for reducing inflation would surely be deemed to be included under the power to regulate the value of money. However, Congress might decide not to exercise its powers to this extent over state and local governments, and if it did so decide, the program probably would not be harmed—so long as the law permitted states and local governments to come under the program's wage and salary provisions if they so chose. Some state and local governments have been effective, perhaps too effective, in holding down their employee's wages and salaries. Others have not been. The latter presumably would take the opportunity to come under the program, if they could.

Strikes had a rightful place in labor's armory until recently, and still do to the extent that society fails to offer a reasonable alternative. Arbitration would be the alternative. The arbitration would have to be fair for the alternative it offers to be reasonable. This is one of the many respects in which the program would have to provide economic justice if it were to be effective. But assuming that the arbitration is fair, strikes can no longer be considered rightful because they are costly, arbitrary (or worse), conducive of antisocial attitudes, and not generally effective. Strikes are costly, of course, to both employers and strikers. In a modern economy, strikes are almost always very costly to large numbers of people who have no connection with the labor disputes. There is nothing in the nature of a strike that ensures that the dispute behind it will be

[27] Laurence H. Tribe, *American Constitutional Law* (St. Paul, Minn.: Foundations Press, 1978), pp. 232–44, 307–18. But see National League of Cities v. Usery, 426 U.S. 833 (1976), limiting the reach of the commerce power over state and local governments.

settled justly. At best, the dispute will be settled arbitrarily. In fact, since it is generally settled on terms favorable to the stronger disputant, the issues giving rise to the strike are often settled worse than arbitrarily. The terms of the strong are imposed on the weak. Strikes are conducive of antisocial attitudes in that they create situations in which people are likely to become violent. The threat of a strike is a form of extortion.[28] The strike is a form of rebellion and, as such, justified only under the same sorts of circumstances as would justify other forms of rebellion. This is why it is consistent to admire the Polish workers' strike in Gdansk while at the same time support an abolition of the right to strike in this country, if it is replaced with an offer of fair arbitration. Finally, strikes are no longer generally effective for raising wages, because too many employers are now capable of passing on their increased wages as higher prices. Higher real wages for some therefore now generally mean lower real income for others, and the general level is not significantly changed.

At present, wages and working conditions and all the other usual subjects of collective bargaining are what lawyers call "nonjusticiable."[29] They are not fit subjects for judicial determination, because there are no generally accepted standards or principles to which a judge can refer for coming to a decision about them. Arbitration is essentially a judicial kind of determination, although it differs from actual judicial determination in being less formal. But whether the issues are considered "nonjusticiable" or not, arbitration of labor disputes has been occurring for some time, and it still represents a vast improvement over striking. But an arbitrator needs standards or principles just as much as a judge if he is not to decide subjectively or arbitrarily. And if the program were run properly, wages and the other provisions of collective bargaining contracts would in fact become justiciable. The general standard that would evolve would be equal pay for equal work. The

[28] *The Shorter Oxford English Dictionary* (1973) defines "extort" as "To wrest from a reluctant person by force, violence, torture, intimidation, or abuse of legal authority by importunity, argument or the like."

[29] Tribe, *American Constitutional Law,* p. 52–114.

issue for the arbitrator would be what kinds of work equaled others for pay purposes, and, if they were not equal, what wage differentials were justified by their inequality. In a full-employment economy, in which the aids to job training and job shifting that I have described were operative, this standard would not be subjective because the arbitrator would have before him (or could obtain) the evidence of what people generally thought. He would not have to rely exclusively on his or any other particular person's subjective assessments. Jobs at pay levels for which there were more qualified or qualifiable applicants than could be hired would evidently be paying more than they should. Jobs at pay levels for which not enough qualified or qualifiable people could be found would evidently be paying less than they should. For the best evidence of what people think is how they act. No amount of testimony or agreement to the contrary could gainsay the fact that a kind of job was not paying enough (or had inferior working conditions, and so on) if not enough people could be enticed to want it—or vice versa, if more than enough qualified or qualifiable people were applying for it. In some instances this kind of evidence is available already. Nurses have been in short supply in most parts of the country for years, despite the fact that entry into nursing training is not difficult.[30] So nurses' pay or nurses' working conditions are evidently inadequate. The same is the case for skilled secretaries.[31] On the other hand, there have usually been long waiting lists or large numbers of disappointed qualified applicants for the jobs of longshoremen, for most of the skilled construction trades, for the jobs of airline pilots, and for entry into medical schools for training to be physicians. So these jobs are probably being overpaid. But this kind of evidence is not yet *generally* reliable, because too many people are as yet unemployed or are unable to obtain the kinds of training for

[30] Joann S. Lublin, "Critical Condition: Severe Nurse Shortage Forces Some Hospitals To Close Beds or Units," *Wall Street Journal*, July 18, 1980, pp. 1, 20.

[31] See Chapter 10, section entitled "Hearings, Representation, and Competition."

which they are qualified. By this test, therefore, almost all jobs are at present overpaid—which is not true.

The effect of arbitration under the standard I have described, in a context of full employment, widely obtainable job training, and easy job shifting, would be to make pay differentials much closer to what they would be if they were really determined by competition than they are now. Now, almost the only competition that serves to determine pay differentials operates under conditions of *laissez faire*—the kind of competition that exists when the government does nothing. For pay, as also for most other kinds of price, *laissez faire* competition is generally ineffective for influencing prices. The arbitration process I have proposed would itself be a form of competition—planned competition—because the standard to be applied would refer the arbitrators to the effects of people freely choosing, that is, applying for the jobs or the job training they liked most. It would be a marked improvement over the present system, even as a form of competition.

Pay differentials based on status would be narrowed or reversed. The higher a job's status (to the extent that status is not related to skill), the *less* the job would have to pay to attract enough qualified applicants. The fact that much of a job's status today arises from the higher pay it provides, however, would mute this effect. Obviously, as the pay went down relative to the pay of other jobs, so would the status. Pay differentials based upon skills or special qualifications, on the other hand, would not necessarily be affected either way. Skills that are pleasurable to acquire or to exercise would have the effect of permitting the jobs that required them to attract sufficient applicants without higher pay. Many people find exercising their teaching skills pleasurable, for example.

The problem will eventually be posed, then, whether the program should reduce the presently too-high pay of some kinds of jobs or just hold them where they are until the rest of the economy's prices and pay levels inflate. If ony a small downward adjustment would be required, the second option seems preferable. It is much harder for most people to suffer a sudden, manifest pay reduction than it is for them to suffer the kind of gradual, hidden pay reduction that comes from gradual inflation. In some cases, too, the pay of a job that was so high as to be attracting too many applicants could be reduced only for beginners. The effect might be to discourage applicants sufficiently without imposing any hardships on those already in the jobs. But the really egregious instances of overpayment should be dealt with directly, because it would otherwise take much too much inflation for the rest of the economy to catch up. It probably would take something like 100 percent more inflation to bring pay rates and prices generally up to an appropriate level relative to the pay of senior airline pilots, for example. Moreover, to treat all pay levels, once achieved, as sacrosanct would encourage evasion and resistance to the program. Every slight gain won by whatever means would be converted into a vested advantage.

Appeals from an arbitrator's decision to a higher authority responsible to and presumably included within the program should be allowed for either party. And the program administrator should be able to "reach down" and bring up a decision for review even if neither party wishes. In this he would be representing the public interest. Once an industry has attained the power of passing on its higher costs from wage increases by raising its prices, its satisfaction with the amount of a wage increase cannot be permitted to be binding on the public. The satisfaction of an employer or group of employers with a wage increase has become especially suspect since the practice of proportionately matching the increase for all nonunion employees, including management, has become common. The fact is, however, that unless the vast majority of arbitrators' decisions are allowed to stand—that is, unless they are neither appealed nor taken up by order of the administrator, or, if they are, are disposed of by affirming the arbitrator's decision summarily—the labor union part of the program will not function effectively. Wage decisions are generally too highly particularized to permit their intelligent resolution by people far removed from the scene. Appeals, moreover, are time-consuming, and decisions on wages cannot generally be long delayed without detracting substantially from their value.

A device for both permitting appeals and administrator

"take ups" and at the same time alleviating, at least, the delays and difficulties of reviewing arbitrators' decisions far away from the particular circumstances that shaped them would be to permit appeals or "take ups" only on the issue of the size of the total pay package. This is generally all that the public has an interest in anyway, because this is generally all that determines the additional costs and higher prices of the employers, and this much could be intelligently and fairly reviewed, in most cases, at least, far from the particular locale. This much, in fact, might be *more* intelligently and fairly decided by someone removed from the scene. The appropriate size of the total pay package inevitably involves comparisons with other pay packages in other industries. Only a person or persons somewhat removed from any particular industry is likely both to be fully informed and to be unbiased about such comparisons.

The labor union part of the anti-inflation program would undoubtedly be the part most difficult and expensive to administer during the first decade or two of the program's existence, but it would be a mistake to assume that this high level of effort would necessarily continue. Once inflation has been largely eliminated, the necessity that every labor negotiation be an occasion for a substantial wage increase will be eliminated along with it. It ought not to take more than a decade or two for most of the large and unjustified inequalities in income to have been greatly lessened, if not eliminated. It does not seem unrealistic to expect that the focus of labor negotiations will then shift to matters other than wages. The focus will then presumably be the conditions that make jobs safe, enjoyable, and enriching. This is not likely to be easy, but it ought to be considerably less difficult to administer than the arbitration of large wage increases.

The countries of Western Europe that have experienced long periods of full employment have suffered from what is there called "wage creep" or "wage drift."[32] Labor unions in

[32] Arthur M. Ross, "Guideline Policy, Where We Are and How We Got There," in George P. Shultz and Robert Z. Aliber, eds., *Guidelines: Informal Controls and the Market Place* (Chicago: University of Chicago

their negotiations with employers in these economics ordinarily set only the minimum wages. The employers are left free to pay more to individual employees, and they commonly do: the majority of employees in most industries are paid more. The situation leads to wage drift because employers find it profitable to pay more in order to obtain or retain the employees who are more productive, but once they do, the less productive employees pressure their union to raise the minimum again. Once the minimum is raised the employers again find it profitable to raise the pay of the more productive employees, and the cycle repeats itself. Wage drift is thus a product of an unresolved conflict between social attitudes. These societies have not reached consensus on whether they want equal pay for all or equal pay for equal work. Equal pay for equal work implies higher pay for better work (and lower pay for worse work), and so conflicts with equal pay for all. If, as I expect, the anti-inflation program here leads to a clearer recognition of the principle of equal pay for equal work, which is already dominant in our society, wage drift here ought never to be a serious problem. The fact that labor unions in their negotiations with employers here commonly set the actual wages rather than just the minimums will also obviously work to prevent wage drift, assuming that this practice continues.

It would not do to be too sanguine about our immunity from wage drift, however. It is not unknown for labor unions here to push for wage equality rather than equal pay for equal work. Where wage differentials have thus been too thoroughly ironed out, and a peak of prosperity happens to reduce unemployment substantially in the sector concerned at the same time, something akin to wage drift has been noticed here, too.[33] But the government aids to job training and job shifting

Press, 1966), pp. 112–14; E. H. Phelps Brown, "Guidelines for Growth and for Incomes in the United Kingdom: Some Possible Lessons for the United States," ibid., pp. 147–50; Donald J. Robertson, *Factory Wage Structures and National Agreements* (Cambridge: Cambridge University Press, 1960).

[33] William Fellner, "Aiming for a Sustainable Second Best during the Recovery from the 1970 Recession," in Phillip Cagan, Marten Estey, William Fellner, Charles E. McLure, Jr., and Thomas Gale Moore, *Economic Policy and Inflation in the Sixties* (Washington, D.C.: American Enterprise Institute for Public Policy Research, 1972), pp. 241–47.

that I have proposed would serve to prevent this by eliminating labor shortages even at low levels of unemployment. And the arbitration I have proposed would also serve to prevent it *if* the standard of equal pay for equal work, which I also propose, were rigorously followed.

The implementation of this arbitration system would probably result in a large expansion of labor union membership. Employees who had not joined a union before because they would not have engaged in a strike would then have no reason not to join one. Employees who had not joined because they considered union membership beneath their class or because they disapproved of unions on political or economic grounds would then have less reason not to join. The arbitration system would give to labor unions a respect and an economic and political legitimacy they had never had before in the eyes of many, and it ought not to reduce their attractiveness in the eyes of anyone who had none of these reservations. If a labor leader might otherwise oppose the program, these facts might persuade him to support it. The increased respectability of union membership would probably also increase the pressure on employers whose employees remained unorganized to keep their pay scales comparable with those that were. In short, the effects of the arbitration system would be far more widespread than figures on 1980 labor union membership would make one suppose. Wages and, at the lower ends of the scales at least, salaries too, would practically *all* either be subjected to arbitration or set with an eye on what arbitration decided for others.

Medical Services

Medical services in the United States are distributed largely on a fee-for-service basis, with the fees largely or wholly paid by an insurance plan. Most insurance plans are paid for at least in part by an employer or by a state or the federal government.[34] The whole system is conducive to inflation. There

[34] 15 U.S.C. 781 (k).

is no way that the average patient can assess whether the fees he or his insurance plan is asked to pay are too high. Since he is not a medical expert himself, he does not even know if he needs the service. He must rely on his physican to make the choice for him. He must also rely on his physician to make the choice among different services, or different grades of services, for the same needs. And it is the same physician who then sets the prices of the services. He cannot compare different physicians' prices for the same services. He only learns what services he will need after he has consulted a physician, and by then he ordinarily already owes a part, at least, of the price. Moreover, what are purportedly the same services rendered by different physicians are frequently not really the same; their quality varies according to the physicians' skills. Even under a fee-for-service system without insurance, the physician would have a very large leeway within which to set the prices as he chose. Insurance makes the inflationary propensity worse by eliminating even the patient's blind resistance against paying too much.

The method that most medical insurance plans use for determining the fees that they will pay makes the situation still worse. Whatever fees a physician chooses to charge will be fully compensated, provided only that the fees are not within the top 30 percent or so that physicians in the area are charging. If they are in this top percent, they will be reimbursed only up to the amount of the highest fee that is not in the top percentage. The highest-charging physicans are therefore only partially reimbursed, but they characteristically have the wealthiest patients, or they would not be able to charge so much; and their wealthy patients offer little resistance to having to pay more than their insurance plans provide. All the other physicians are fully compensated whatever they charge, and so have every incentive to charge right up to the limit that they can.[35] As a result, fees go up by substantial amounts every year, the fee schedules that determine what insurance plans will pay go right up with them, and the prices of medical

[35] Ibid.

services are more inflationary than almost any other significant aspect of the American economy.[36] In 1977, the median physician's annual income from his practice, counting small-town and rural practices and counting physicians who had just left medical school, was $65,000.[37]

Another aspect of most existing insurance plans is to cover some therapies but not others—usually only the more expensive ones. Insurers tend to operate in this way because purchasers of insurance frequently think that they only need insurance for the most expensive contingencies, and that they can save money by taking the low-cost risks themselves. But the effect is that when an illness occurs, the physician is inclined to prescribe the more expensive therapies whether or not they are really better on a cost-benefit basis, or even if he knows they are worse for the health of the patient despite their higher costs. He knows that if he were to prescribe something not covered by the patient's insurance, the patient would have to pay, which is undesirable in itself, and in many cases the patient would not be able to pay. The patient, of course, is ordinarily quite willing to have the physician thus misprescribe, if it will permit him to come under his insurance coverage. Stories are legion of patients being kept in hospitals running up insurance-covered bills of $300 or so a day for weeks or months, when they could have been treated as well or better at home but at their own expense. Finally, the selective coverage of most insurance plans encourages people not to take the relatively cheap preventive measures that would increase their chances of remaining in good health, or to take the periodic examinations that would spot illnesses early enough to be treated at relatively low cost. The insurance does not cover the preventive measures or the examinations.

Fee-for-service pricing could be eliminated by the right kinds of third-party payor plans. The government could pay a

[36] *The Problem of Rising Health Care Costs,* Executive Office of the President, U.S. Council on Wage and Price Stability, Staff Report, April 1976 (Washington, D.C.: U.S. Govt. Printing Office, 1976). p. ii.

[37] Marianne Dekker Mattera, "Doctors Make Too Much Money? Baloney!" *Medical Economics,* June 11, 1979, pp. 77–79.

physician a fixed amount per year per patient regardless of the kinds of amounts of services the physician provides, for example, as is now done in England. But fee-for-service pricing could also be eliminated without bringing the government into the picture so overwhelmingly, and it is this approach that I suggest, for reasons that will become apparent. The most promising scheme is the privately owned and managed group practice. Group practices already exist, of course. They are sometimes called "health maintenance oganizations," or "HMOs."[38] But they are not yet as common or as effective as they could be.

A group-practice organization receives the same regular payment per patient whether the patient is sick or healthy, or whether he requires only routine preventive and diagnostic care or the most expensive major treatments available. The group receives its payments from the patients themselves, who agree to pay the regular amounts when they become members, or from the patients' employers, or from the government. It does not matter what the source or sources of payment are, so long as the payments do *not* vary according to a patient's need for services. This fact provides the group with the financial incentive to keep its patients as healthy as possible by the most economical means possible.

Group practices as they presently exist, however, generally have two drawbacks even when they are large enough to include the variety of services and facilities that is necessary for their efficiency. By reputation, at least, they do not presently include the most competent physicians. Their reputation is not that they include the worst, only that they include just the middling competent—younger physicians seeking experience to go out later on their own, and older physicians who cannot or do not want to work hard enough to have a lucrative solo or small-partnership practice. From one point of view, the quality of the physicians does not matter. If these physicians were

[38] See, for example, Marc J. Roberts and Ted Bogue, "The American Health Care System: Where Have All the Dollars Gone?" *Harvard Journal on Legis.* 13 (1976), 667–77.

not practicing in groups, they would still be practicing, and their being in groups improves their services. But society would gain more, proportionately, if even the best physicians could be attracted to group practices, because their services, too, could then be better utilized. The federal government, therefore, under the general supervision of the anti-inflation program administrator, ought to act to reverse the financial incentives that presently operate to keep the best physicians in solo or small-partnership practices. Group practices should be made relatively more lucrative. Financial penalties (through the tax laws, presumably) should be placed on solo or small-partnership practices in all areas of the country except those that are so sparsely settled as to make such otherwise inefficient forms of practice inevitable. Physicians who provide their services through qualified group-practice plans, on the other hand, should receive subsidies. To the extent that the federal government pays for medical services (as it does for patients age sixty-five or over, for example) it should limit its payments to what they would be if the patient were a member of a qualified group-practice plan.

This system of penalties and subsidies would have to be put into effect gradually and only after giving warning several years in advance, because both physicians and patients will need time to adjust. A very old person would be likely to have difficulty becoming a patient-member of a group practice plan today without having been a member for many years before, for example. A plan generally cannot afford to take high-risk patients at anything close to its usual monthly fees. Such a system of penalties and subsidies would be somewhat coercive of physicians, of course, but the coercion is justified. Modern medicine being as highly specialized and removed from the average person's understanding as it is, a physician has a moral obligation to offer his services in ways that enable them to be used efficiently, and that enable reasonable external controls on his competence and honesty. A physician's education is bound to have been paid for largely at public expense, even if he never received a scholarship of any kind. Medical school tuitions cover only a fraction of the costs of medical education.[39] A physician's practice after he has been educated is also already subsidized in numerous ways. The competitive markets that, despite their large imperfections, still work to limit the incomes of most people to some extent work hardly at all to limit physicians' fees. And anyone whose principal obligation is to help the dying and the sick ought to be especially ready to accept reasonable controls to ensure that he does not exploit them.

The hope would be that with the growth of group practices, fee-for-service arrangements would eventually die out, and with them the insurance plans that presently aggravate their inflationary and health-detrimental tendencies. The insurance plans that remained would be those that had made themselves appropriate to serve the group practices. But in the interim there are several steps the program should take to eliminate the worst effects of the existing insurance plans. No plan should be permitted to continue the present practice of paying one physician or one hospital more than another for providing the same service simply because the physician or the hospital chooses to charge more for it. This is surely the single most inflationary aspect of existing insurance plans; there is no excuse for it. Also, reimbursement schedules should be raised (or lowered) only when it is considered appropriate by the plan administrators to do so. The present system of allowing physicians and hospitals to set whatever fees they like and then matching them on the plan's schedules should be prohibited. A third-party payor plan should be required to cover all the reasonable alternative therapies for any illness it covers, including the "therapy" of allowing the patient to go home or to a nursing home to die, when this is the only reasonable alternative. Finally, no plan should be permitted to cover treatments of a major illness for which it does not also cover all reasonable diagnostic and preventive services. This would serve to encourage people to maintain their health economi-

[39] Seymour E. Harris, *A Statistical Portrait of Higher Education* (New York: McGraw-Hill, 1972), pp. 683, 688; Stephen Lewin, ed., *The Nation's Health* (New York: H. W. Wilson Co., 1971), p. 23.

cally by taking the steps that would spot a major illness early or prevent its occurring.

Inherited Wealth

Competitive inflation is a fight for increased real income, not a fight to choose one's ancestors. So it might seem that preventing indeterminate inflation had nothing to do with limiting inherited wealth. But wealth and income are much alike. Both are valued for the same reasons of prestige, self-respect, security, and provision of the ability to consume. Wealth is the accumulation of income that has not been given away or spent. Inherited wealth is wealth earned by someone else. If people's present earning abilities have to be limited to prevent inflation, therefore, and there is no doubt that they do, it would be quite unfair not at the same time to limit people's ability to inherit wealth. The distribution of wealth in the United States is already extremely unequal. More than a quarter is held by or for the wealthiest 1 percent.[40] This extreme inequality would surely be made even worse if incomes were limited but wealth from inheritance were not. Also, inherited wealth contributes to competitive inflation by setting standards or models of wealth that others try to match by raising their incomes.

The need to rectify unequal distributions of inherited wealth also exists apart from the need to prevent inflation. It is unfair that some people should start life with enormously more than almost everyone else, or that they should be able to consume enormously more throughout their lives without performing any useful work. Not even with all the unrealistic assumptions that economic theory has placed at their disposal

[40] Robert J. Lampman, *The Share of Top Wealth-Holders in National Wealth 1922-56* (Princeton: Princeton University Press, 1962), pp. 23–26, 191–95; John Keith Butters, Lawrence E. Thompson, and Lynn L. Bollinger, *Effects of Taxation: Investments by Individuals* (Boston: Division of Research, Graduate School of Business Administration, Harvard University, 1953), pp. 393–99.

has anyone been able to use economic theory to prove that competitive markets serve to equalize wealth or to make its distribution just.[41] The economic justifications of inherited wealth have had nothing to do with justice or with the working of competition, but rather with the supposed need of concentrations of wealth in order to provide the surplus for investment that an economy requires in order to grow. Without these concentrations, it is said, an economy would stagnate, and the only feasible means of providing them is to permit those that already exist to remain, which means not to interfere with the inheritance of wealth.[42]

It is true that concentrations of wealth are needed for investment purposes, but it is not true that they need to consist of inherited wealth. In fact, for at least fifty years in the United States and even longer in the United Kingdom, they have not.[43] Corporations have provided the necessary concentrations of wealth. There is no need for the wealth *represented by* a corporation—its bonds and shares of stock—to be concentrated in the hands of a few individuals in order for the corporation to provide an economically useful concentration *of* wealth. In fact, in the United States and the United Kingdom, corporations have been overwhelmingly not controlled by their shareholders but by the executives who administer them without holding large portions of their stock precisely because the corporations' stocks have not been concentrated in a few hands. (Even the people who own very large amounts of common stocks typically have stocks in relatively small amounts in large numbers of corporations.)

[41] For example, Paul Samuelson's elementary text describes income and wealth distribution in the United States and other countries, but offers no theories to explain them. Paul A. Samuelson, *Economics,* 9th ed. (New York: McGraw-Hill, 1973), pp. 79–99.

[42] For an excellent discussion of this and other rationales for unequal distribution of wealth, see Anthony Barnes Atkinson, *Unequal Shares: Wealth in Britain* (Harmondsworth: Penguin Books, 1972).

[43] Adolf A. Berle, Jr. and Gardiner C. Means, *The Modern Corporation and Private Property* (Chicago: Commerce Clearing House, 1932); Richard H. Tawney, *The Acquisitive Society* (New York: Harcourt, Brace and Co., 1920).

For investment purposes, corporations are actually much superior to wealthy individuals. Corporations never die. They never grow feeble or senile or too ill to make investment decisions. A corporation is much less likely to engage in abnormal behavior than is an individual, and if a corporation does behave abnormally, it is likely thereby to violate the laws that exist to insure that those who control others' wealth handle it honestly and with care.[44] Such laws have no application to persons handling their own wealth.

A variation on the foregoing argument is that large individual accumulations of wealth are necessary because they alone provide the funds that are invested in risky business ventures. However, no one has shown that individuals are more inclined toward risky investments than are corporations. What evidence there is on the issue points to the contrary. Most individual wealth in the United States is managed by so-called trust institutions—banks or trust companies. Their investment policies are notoriously conservative. The state laws under which they exist often require them to be.[45] *Large* risky ventures these days are invariably carried out by large corporate enterprises or by governments, rather than by individuals. The Alaskan pipeline, the development and operation of atomic power, the development and operation of communication satellites—these are just three of the better-known examples. In the early nineteenth century, before large business organizations had become common, it was often argued that the government ought to support private business ventures and protect them from loss, because people would *not* invest their own wealth in risky ventures.[46] The subsequent reversal of this argument makes it suspect in either form.

[44] George Gleason Bogert and George Taylor Bogert, *Handbook of the Law of Trusts* (St. Paul, Minn.: West Pub. Co., 1973), pp. 337–54; Harry G. Henn, *Handbook of the Law of Corporations and Other Business Enterprises* (St. Paul, Minn.: West Pub. Co., 1970), pp. 457–83.

[45] Bogert and Bogert, *Law of Trusts,* pp. 374–82.

[46] Morton J. Horwitz, *The Transformation of American Law, 1780-1860* (Cambridge: Harvard University Press, 1977), pp. 63–108, 109–11.

It is also argued that without the ability to pass on their wealth to their children substantially undiminished, people would not work to accumulate fortunes. A sufficient answer is that with the amount of wealth presently held by economic organizations, we no longer need individual fortunes; but the argument is also faulty in assuming that individuals generally work to benefit their children rather than themselves, after they have already accumulated enough to assure their children a decent upbringing. Such evidence as there is on this point is to the contrary.[47]

It is also argued that large accumulations of individual wealth are needed to provide the donations we need to support education and the arts. Obviously, the wealthy do contribute more than others for these purposes, but it is not clear that those who have inherited wealth do. There is some reason to think they do not, as least not as much as do those who earned their wealth. Those who inherited their wealth would not have it if it had been given for art or educational purposes instead. In any event, permitting large concentrations of inherited wealth to continue for this purpose is not essentially different from permitting monarchies to continue because of the royal dispensations kings and queens occasionally deign to give to commoners, and neither really has much to be said in its defense. There is no reason why governments cannot pay for the support of the arts and education, as of course they already do. More corporate giving for these purposes could also be encouraged by additional tax benefits, if this were thought to be preferable to direct government support.

The elimination of large accumulations of inherited wealth would provide many benefits, among them a step toward the validation of our claim to be a democracy. Of the ten men who have been president since I was born—Hoover, Roosevelt, Truman, Eisenhower, Kennedy, Johnson, Nixon, Ford, Carter and Reagan—only three, Truman, Eisenhower, and Nixon—

[47] See, for example, "H. L. Hunt Dies in Texas at 85; Billionaire was a Conservative," *New York Times,* November 30, 1974, p. 1.

were not millionaires before they became president. One of the exceptions, Truman, certainly never would have become president had he not been vice president when the former president died, and the other two, Eisenhower and Nixon, had many extremely wealthy backers. Great wealth is not quite so necessary to becoming a governor or a senator, but the record shows that for obtaining one of these offices too it provides enormous advantages.

It is also argued that despite all the possible advantages of a more equal distribution of wealth, wealth should be left where it is because taking it away from anyone or preventing him from inheriting it would be immoral. Wealth that a person has, the argument goes, belongs to him. He is therefore entitled to keep it or give it away to whomever he chooses, during his lifetime or upon his death, except in the relatively few cases where it could be proven that he gained it by illegitimate means.[48] This argument is fallacious on at least two counts. It begs a question and rests on a false premise. The false premise is that a government cannot rightly take what belongs to someone. If this were so, only thieves could be taxed. Of course a government can rightly take from any of us, provided only that there is a fair basis for determining who must pay how much. And what could be fairer than taxing on the basis of unearned wealth? The question that is begged is whether ownership of wealth should include the privilege of giving it undiminished to whomever one likes. Such a privilege does not attach to a job or any political authority that belongs to a person, for example. It ought not to attach to wealth, either, because like anything that is desired and scarce, it should be distributed equally except to the extent that a larger share has been earned.

It also follows that in our society, where a husband and wife typically share in the fruits of what each earns and has, that what a husband leaves to his wife upon his death, or vice

[48] Robert Nozick, *Anarchy, State, and Utopia* (New York: Basic Books, 1974).

versa, ought not to be taxed on that account. That our inheritance-tax laws were designed initially to tax such husband-wife transfers was a mistake that was in large part, although not completely, rectified by the amendment of the laws to include the so-called "marital deduction."[49] The laws ought to be amended to make such transfers not an occasion for tax at all. For similar reasons, the laws ought to be amended to make transfers of wealth to older members of one's family not an occasion for tax. A person who dies young ought to be able to die secure in the knowledge that he has left his surviving parents as much out of his earnings as he wants.

But gifts of wealth *down* the generations ought to be taxed, and heavily taxed. Their recipients have done nothing to justify receiving them. Their effect is to permit the recipients to consume without working, which is unfair. The principle therefore ought to be that, with the exceptions already noted, gifts of wealth, whether made during the giver's lifetime or at his death, be very heavily taxed. Amounts left to permit a recipient to live until he becomes an adult, to complete his education, and for other personal needs that can reasonably be expected while the person is still young should not be considered gifts of wealth, because they are not. They will be spent on the kind of things that people do to prepare themselves to be income-earning adults, whereas wealth, in the sense we are using it here, serves to permit consumption without work. There should also be exclusions for modest amounts of personal gifts—family furniture, the father's sporting equipment, the mother's jewelry, and so on—and special exclusions for gifts to meet the special needs of mentally or physically crippled children, gifts to charities, and so on, but the principle just stated should constitute the basic rule. American society would thereby be made more economically just and politically democratic, and a necessary condition for the fairness of the many limitations on income that will be required for preventing indeterminate inflation would have been met.

[49] 26 U.S.C. 2001; 26 U.S.C. 2056.

Land Speculation

I have chosen to treat land speculation last, not because of any importance of place but because it can be better understood if inheritance has been understood. In our economy, as in most economies in which land is privately held, land speculation is, next to inheritance, the principal source of unearned wealth that is not commonly regarded as income, and so not easily encompassed within a wage and price control program or other form of income policy. By land speculation I mean the profits that come from land ownership alone, apart from any improvements that are made on the land. Such profits are virtually automatic in a society with a growing population, because land is inherently scarce. They are also virtually automatic in a society that is undergoing modernization even if the population is not growing, because modernization generally brings with it greater land use. The profits from land speculation are both unearned and distributed so as to make a bad wealth distribution worse. They go only to those who are wealthy enough to own land already, and they go most to those who are already wealthy enough to own land in large amounts.

A sensible way of diverting these unearned profits to the public was proposed a century ago by Henry George.[50] He thought that the revenue thus yielded would be sufficient to permit the elimination of every other kind of tax, which may have been a correct estimate then. It surely no longer would be, but the revenues would be enormous, and other taxes surely could be substantially reduced. George's proposal was that land be assessed for tax purposes separately from the improvements, if any, on it, and the tax rate be maintained at a level that would make the land, again without regard to any improvements on it, essentially valueless. If the taxing authority wished to continue to tax improvements too, it of course could, but they would be separately assessed and taxed

[50] Henry George, "Our Land and Land Policy," *Works of Henry George* 9 (1898), 108–112.

at a different, lower rate. The George proposal has been reexamined occasionally over the years.[51] As far as can be ascertained, no sound argument has been raised against it yet. Presumably it has never been implemented in the United States on a large scale only because of the inertia of custom and the range of vested interests whose unearned profits it would reduce. Besides the landowners, the principal vested interests are the mortgage lenders. By keeping land values down the George proposal would reduce the need for mortgages. The money that landowners currently pay to lenders as interest would go to taxing authorities instead.

Implementation of the George proposal would contribute to eliminating inflation for the same reasons as would a stiff inheritance tax, and it would have essentially the same other social and economic benefits. If it were thought desirable to protect older people from higher taxes in their retirement years, the taxes that the proposal would impose on a residence owned and occupied by a person age sixty-five or over could be frozen when he or she reached sixty-five, until he or she died, moved out, or sold the residence. Equity would not require this, however. Such a person would be in no worse a position than a person who rented his or her residence without the limitation, and with the limitation he or she would be better off. Whether the proceeds from the George proposal should go to federal, state, or local governments would be a matter of indifference for purposes of controlling inflation. Since it is traditional that the proceeds from land taxes go to local governments, school boards, or other local taxing authorities, this tradition would presumably be continued. The role of the anti-inflation program administrator would only be to see that the proposal was implemented. The federal constitutional authority to do this would be the same as that which exists for controlling the wages and salaries of the employees of state and local governments.

[51] Donald G. Hagman, "The Single Tax and Land Use Planning: Henry George Updated," *U.C.L.A. Law Rev.* 12 (1965), 762.

Conclusion: The Need for National Economic Planning

The practical elimination of inflation and unemployment will not make our economy any more susceptible to conscious direction than it is now, but it will make planning more necessary. The practical elimination of unemployment will make the economy vastly more efficient. Many more people will be working, and no one who is working will feel the need to hold back in order to protect his or another's job. The practical elimination of inflation will permit investors to predict a steady expansion of demand more confidently, by eliminating the government's supposed need always to keep aggregate demand low and occasionally to restrict its growth sharply. The investors' confidence in steady expansion will then become a self-fulfilling prophecy. The economy will grow. Some of the measures that were proposed herein for reducing inflation would also increase economic efficiency directly, by their side effects. If the vastly greater production that all this will provide is not used intelligently, it will be an enormous waste. And it will not be used intelligently unless the federal government plans how it will be used, because our nation's economic needs are not such as can be met by people's individual choices of how to spend money in their own hands.

We need to pay for a decent retirement for the increasingly large proportion of our population that will have passed retirement age. The talk in recent years of whether the Social Security System is adequately funded for this eventuality is beside the point. When the nation as a whole is concerned, funding is just paper-shuffling. The monies that are being spent on older people are inevitably monies being earned but not being spent by younger people, whether there are some government bonds piled up in some storeroom in Washington or not. If we hope to pay the older people a decent amount without badly overburdening the younger people, the total amount that the economy produces must be substantially increased.

We also need to spend hundreds of billions, probably trillions of dollars on protecting our environment and cleaning up and otherwise restoring the parts of it that have been lost. Protection against air pollution alone will probably require the relocation of some major industries, the relocation of many urban airports, the installation of expensive air-cleaning devices, and the redesigning and manufacture of oil and coal burning engines of all sorts. We could also beneficially spend very large sums on improving our educational systems, especially in our large cities, where they have suffered serious decay. Just making them safe for the children in them would be a substantial improvement and would require large sums. Our judicial systems are generally badly overcrowded. Crime prevention needs to be improved and expanded to deal with rising rates of crime. We should vastly increase our spending overseas, to aid the undeveloped countries to limit their populations and to expand their economies. We need to do this if we hope to have a reasonably peaceful world for our children to live in. We need to continue to build and maintain defenses against nuclear, chemical, biological, and conventional terrorism and war.

We should use some of our increased economic potential for making jobs more satisfying and enriching, even when this might require a lessening of efficiency measured in terms of input and output alone. We should work out ways that would permit people to hold good jobs although they do not want to make the jobs their sole or their principal careers. Mothers, homemakers, or older people who would prefer to spend only a fraction of the workday outside their homes, artists who want to work on something besides their art only enough to keep themselves afloat, and those who would just prefer more leisure to more spending money ought to be given the opportunity to find good part-time work. Provision ought also to be made for people who would choose very different lifestyles, such as communes, to be able to do so without inordinate sacrifice of the standard of living they could expect.

All planning presupposes an attitude that we hold in common the nation's, even the world's, wealth. It is contrary to the traditional economic attitude that individuals are the owners of all wealth. Neither attitude is the whole truth. More planning will be a needed corrective to our long-standing overemphasis on the traditional view. To a much greater extent than we have yet been willing to admit, each of us depends on the others and on the things such as roads and the maintenance of public order that we provide in common for whatever wealth we might think our individual efforts alone have produced. Planning could give rebirth to the oldest, finest social principle of all: that life, liberty, and happiness are best pursued not by a fight of each against each, but by sympathy and understanding and mutual help.

INDEX

Administrative Procedure Act, 323
advertising: nonprice competition, 31–33, 39–41; product knowledge, 60
aggregate demand, *see* demand, aggregate
agricultural cooperatives: as pricing institutions, 68–69; regulation of, 382–384
alienation, economic determinism and, 210–216
allocation of resources and profits, 360–363
anti-inflation program (proposed), 20–24, 312–314; administration of, 315–320; agricultural cooperatives, 382–383; business ethic, 347; commission vs. individual control, 315–320; compliance, 313–314, 371–372; employment, 353–356; enforcement, 325–326; executive pay rates, 384–388; hearing and representation rights, 332–339; indexing, 339–344; individual price setting, 328–332; industrial pricing institutions, 356–372; inherited wealth, 403–408; justification requirement, 315, 320–323; labor unions, 388–397; land speculation, 409–410; medical services, 397–403; monetary and fiscal policy, 351–353; pricing institutions, 334–335; public disclosure, 315, 323–328. *See also* wage and price controls
antitrust laws, 12; industrial pricing institutions, 100–101
arbitration, 389–397
automobile industry: demand reduction, 8–9; pricing institutions, 102–103

behavior, economic, 185–187, 254–258, 264–266, 283; economic determinism, 237–238; market, 291–294; scientific study of, 193–196. *See also* buying behavior
bias: economic determinism and, 239–240; values and, 296–297
binding arbitration, 389–397
bureaucracy: commission vs. individual control of anti-inflation program (proposed), 315–320; economic controls, 308–309. *See also* anti-inflation program (proposed); government
businesses and corporations: confidentiality and wage and price controls, 325; conflict of interest, 114–119; ethics for, 344–347; government control of, 210–212, 215–219; laissez faire, 239–240; market forces, 217; pricing institutions, 102–103; profit maximization principle, 118–119
buyers' lack of understanding, as source of inflation, 46–64
buying behavior, 51, 53–54, 58–60; government attempts to inform, 64; product ignorance, 79; rising prices, 147–148; services and, 81–83. *See also* consumers

capacity utilization: as inflation indicator, 160–162; and low aggregate demand, 167–172; and price rises, 158–160
change, in economic theory, 241–243
commissions and panels, in wage and price control programs, 315–320
common stocks, as money pricing institution, 72
competition: in anti-inflation program (proposed), 334–339; confidentiality requirement, 326, 327; economic bias for, 240; economic determinism, 266; inflation and, 6–7, 10–11, 27; job training, 393; market forces and, 11–12, 15–16, 28–29; measurement of, 252–253; psychological effects of, 105–106; research on, 294–295. *See also* monopoly power; nonprice competition; price competition
competitive inflation, 13–15, 126–128; defining industry and, 369–371; full employment, 353–356; origins of in U.S., 146–152; and post-Keynesians, 260–261; and price increases, 348; pricing institutions and, 142–144; societal repetition, 289–291; specialist economy, 130–137. *See also* indeterminate inflation; inflation
competitive markets, 228, 369–371
compliance: avoidance of, 371–372; tax incentives for, 358, 365; voluntary, 313–314
confidentiality requirement, 323–328
conflict of interest, and profit maximization choice, 114–119
constitutional liberties, and anti-inflation programs, 312
construction industry, price cutting incentives for, 134–135
consumer price index, 347–349
consumer products, inflationary markets and, 56–57
consumers: government attempts to inform, 64; lack of understanding as source of inflation, 46–64. *See also* buying behavior
consumption, 272–275, 278, 280
contemporary inflation, *see* indeterminate inflation
cooperation, competition and, 295
cooperatives, pricing institutions and, 68–69, 150, 382–384
corporations, *see* businesses and corporations
cost of living, 88
cost-push theory of inflation, 14, 172–173. *See also* wage-push theory of inflation
costs: inflation and, 55; marginal, 112–113; price setting, 30–32, 88. *See also* prices; profits
craft unions, price cutting incentives for, 134–135
creeping inflation, 53, 55; and inflationary markets, 49–51; vs. institutional inflation, 76–77; and pricing institutions, 100; product degradation, 373

Darwin, Charles, and growth of materialism, 198
decisionmaking: subjectivity of, 19; price setting, 110–120
demand, *see* supply and demand
demand, aggregate: anti-inflation program (proposed), 357–360; competitive inflation, 348–349; inflation, 143; price increases and, 52, 164–165; shortages,

174. *See also* supply and demand
demand-pull inflation, 128, 155–172, 173; in U.S., 149, 176–177; investments and, 275; public harm, 167–172
democracy: inflation and, 264; materialism and, 201–202, 206
depression, 3; aggregate income theory, 271; economic determinism, 188–189
deregulation, in the transportation industry, 376–378. *See also* regulation
determinate inflation: demand-pull, 155. *See also* demand-pull inflation; indeterminate inflation
determinism, *see* economic determinism

economic behavior, *see* behavior, economic
economic determinism, 16–18, 181–183; and change, 241–243; economic laws as predictors, 235–236; failure to analyze inflation, 223–224; human behavior, 193–196; inflationary markets, 55–56; natural science, 190; personal and social costs of, 263–266; post-Keynesians, 258–261; shortcomings of, 223–267; sources of, 184–222
economic equilibrium, *see* equilibrium
economic forces, *see* market forces
economic justice, 21–22, 305–307
economic laws, 16, 181, 189–193, 196, 233–237
economic materialism, 182, 196–210
economic models, *see* economic laws
economic positivism, 6–9, 182, 198, 231–240
Economic Stabilization Program (1971), 310–314, 324
economics: bias of, 239–240; as science, 243–258; post-Keynesian, 258–261
education, and materialism, 202–205
employment and unemployment: anti-inflation program (proposed), 312, 353–356; chronic unemployment, 169–170; demand-pull theory, 144, 167–172; employer pricing institution, 82–83; government policies and inflation, 8, 136, 141, 157–158, 275, 278, 300; money supply, 277; Phillips Curve, 242; profit maximization decisions, 122–125; wage creep and full employment, 395–396
Enclosure Acts, 212–215
equilibrium: deterministic, 286; nondeterministic, 284–291; restorative tendency, 285–287, 290–291; societal, 286–288
evolution, science and materialism, 198
excess-demand theory of inflation, *see* demand-pull inflation
executives, and profit maximization principle, 114–119
executives' compensation, 83, 384–388

"fair" prices, 130
Federal Open Market Committee, as pricing institution, 69–73
Federal Reserve System: anti-inflation program (proposed), 317; monetary policy and, 352–353; as pricing institution, 69–73

fiscal policy, 70–73; of anti-inflation program (proposed), 351–353; government attempt to increase demand, 157–158. *See also* monetary policy
fixed utilities, 376–378; regulation of, 379–381; rate setting, 331
free markets, 3–4. *See also* market forces
free rider problem, 165–166
free will, and economic determinism, 15, 222, 248, 269, 298
"freezing": controlling prices, 330, 332; right to hearing, 339; wage and price controls, 136–137

government: business control, 210–212, 215–219; business ethic, 346–347; commission vs. individual control of anti-inflation programs, 315–320; economic controls of, 308–309; increase in aggregate demand, 144, 155, 157–158; laissez faire, 239–240; low capacity utilization goals, 167–169; as pricing institution, 73; reduction of demand, 132–136, 139–141, 176; restraining price increases, 91–92; setting individual prices, 328–332
government deficit, 273, 276–279. *See also* fiscal policy
government spending, 4, 5, 273, 277

health maintenance organizations, 400–403
hearings, right to in anti-inflation program (proposed), 333–339
hospitals, as pricing institutions, 74. *See also* medical services
humanism, economics and, 268–271

incentive programs, 41–42; price cutting, 132–135
income, theory of aggregate, 271–284
income distribution: anti-inflation program (proposed), 312; economic controls, 305–306; money pricing institution, 71–72
income policy: anti-inflation program (proposed), 388–389; inherited wealth, 403–408; land speculation, 409–410
indeterminate inflation: anti-inflation program (proposed), 310–314; anti-inflation proposal for industrial pricing institutions, 356–372; economic equilibrium, 285; failure of economic determinism, 223–234; full justification requirement for anti-inflation programs, 320–323; identifying demand-pull, 173; income and, 278; inherited wealth, 403–408; organizational structure for anti-inflation programs, 315–320; pay increases and, 122–125; pricing institutions and, 65–67; public disclosure requirement for anti-inflation programs, 323–328
indexing: anti-inflation programs, 339–344; competitive inflation, 14; of pensions, 342–344; and voluntary programs, 153
industrial pricing institutions, 75–78; anti-inflation programs, 356–372; nonunion employment, 82; price fixing, 100–101; profit maximization principle, 121
Industrial Revolution, and economic determinism, 210–212
industrialism, and materialism, 200

industry, defining for anti-inflation programs, 368–371
inflation: agricultural controls, 382–384; alleged causes of, 3–7; capacity utilization, 158–164; and competition, 27; economic positivism, 18–19; excess aggregate demand, 132–136, 139–141, 143–145, 156–157, 232; failure to explain, 223–224; full employment, 353–356; indexing for, 339–344; nonmarket behavior, 293–294; post-Keynesian thought, 260–261; psychological methods of control, 152–154; in specialist/nonspecialist economy, 138–141; stabilization of, 291. *See also* competitive inflation; cost-push theory of inflation; creeping inflation; demand-pull inflation, determinate inflation; indeterminate inflation; institutional inflation; wage-push theory of inflation
inflationary expectations, 9–10, 152–154, 310–311
inflationary markets: characteristics of, 46–49; economic determinism and, 55–56; price patterns in, 55, 76–77, 99; technological advance and, 56–60
inherited wealth, anti-inflation program (proposed) and, 403–408
institutional inflation, 76–77, 290
insurance: medical services and inflation, 397–403; as pricing institution, 74, 82
interest rates: anti-inflation program (proposed), 352; as money pricing institution, 72–73
investments: aggregate income, 273–275; capacity utilization, 167–169; economic growth of, 158; low aggregate demand, 170–172; money pricing institutions, 72–73; target pricing, 367; wealth protection, 216
"invisible hand," 184–186, 285

jobs: economic study of attitudes and, 292; labor shortage, 396–397; training programs, 354
judgments: economic laws as standards, 235–236; materialism and, 202–203; subjectivity of, 270
judicial review of anti-inflation program (proposed), 319
justification requirement, for anti-inflation program (proposed), 315, 320–323, 339

Keynes, John Maynard: post-Keynesian economics, 258–261; theory of business cycles, 3; theory of determination of aggregate income, 271–284

labor force, and low aggregate demand, 168–169
labor unions, 86, 168; anti-inflation programs, 388–397; competitive inflation and, 14–15; economic restraints on, 94; equilibrium, 290; opposition to economic determinism, 220–221; pay rate decisions of, 122–125, 135; as pricing institution, 74; profit maximization principle and, 117–119, 159; voluntary wage and price controls, 314
laissez faire: economic determinism and, 214–219, 239–240; pay

rates and, 393; Say's Law and, 226–227
land speculation, and anti-inflation program (proposed), 409–410
land transfer, and economic determinism, 210–216
lawmaking (by agencies), and full justification requirement, 320–323

manufacturers, price/nonprice competition, 38–39
market behavior, 291–294
market forces, 4, 5, 15–16; anti-inflation program (proposed), 21; business ethic, 345–346; and competition, 28–29; control of business, 217; equilibrium, 290; in Adam Smith's time, 186–188; laissez faire, 239–240; nonprice competition and, 32; pricing institutions and, 83–84; property utilization and, 210–216
market price, 33–34, 228; inflationary markets and, 49
marketing: choosing price/nonprice competition, 33–35; competitive inflation in the U.S., 146–148; nonprice competition, 39–45; selling techniques, 61–62. *See also* buying behavior
markets, 46; defining the boundaries of competitive, 369–371; inflationary, 46; as the source of the "invisible hand," 185–186
markup pricing institution, 78–81, 101, 121, 381–383
Marxism, 194
materialism, 196–210, 266
medical services: anti-inflation program (proposed), 397–403; as pricing institution, 73–74, 86; and profit maximization principle, 121
minimum wage: anti-inflation program (proposed), 389–390, 396; as pricing institution, 73
monetary policy: anti-inflation program (proposed), 351–353; as pricing institution, 69–73. *See also* fiscal policy
money pricing institution, 351–353
money supply: as measure of demand, 136, 157–158; inflation and, 4, 155, 156; investment level and, 276, 277–278; management of employment, 277–278; price of money, 71, 352–353
monopolistic market, 46–47, 51–52
monopoly power, 31, 47, 78; and anti-inflation programs, 361; cost-push theory, 172; pricing institutions, 67
motivation: competition as, 294–295; economic determinism, 237–238; economic study of, 268–269, 291–292; employee, 122–125; profit maximization, 110–114; values and, 239–240
multiplier effect, 275, 281–282

National Labor Relations Act, as facilitating the creation and effectiveness of labor pricing institutions, 85–86
necessity and satiety, 53–55, 96–98
nihilism, and materialism, 198
nonprice competition: forms of, 30–45; in the U.S., 146–147; predicting profitability of, 32; preference for, 35–39; preva-

lence of, 44–45; pricing institutions, 66; profit maximization decisions, 120. *See also* competition; price competition

Organization of Petroleum Exporting Countries (OPEC), 85, 147

pay rates, *see* wages and salaries
pensions, indexing for, 342–344
Phillips Curve, 242–243
planned obsolescence, 375
political considerations, restraints on price increases, 91–93
positivism, *see* economic positivism
post-Keynesian economics, 258–261
predictions: based on social science tools, 269–270; use of economic laws for, 234–237, 249–251
presidential power, setting taxes, 351–352
price competition, 30, 39, 142; anti-inflation program for industrial pricing institution, 357; business dislike for, 35–36, 103–104; creeping inflation and, 50–51; fixed utilities and, 379–381; in Adam Smith's time, 186–188; industrial price patterns and, 75–76; inflationary markets and, 99; limiting profits, 359–360, 363–365; negative aspects of, 102–103; nonunion employment, 82; prevention of competitive inflation, 128; price comparison, 372–376; pricing institutions, 65–66, 94, 98–100; reduced use of, 44–45; regulated industries, 6, 8, 377–378; in retail industry, 78–79, 381–383; services, 81; supply and demand and, 97–98; in transportation industry, 378; Interstate Commerce Commission, 85. *See also* competition; nonprice competition
price fixing, 78, 100–101, 322–323
price increase: anti-inflation program (proposed), 357–360; competitive inflation, 348–349; to offset employment loss, 135; and pricing institutions, 84–95; shortages, 174
price patterns, 75–76, 78–79, 93, 118, 120–122, 129–130
price setting, 18, 141–142, 147–152, 328–332
price stickiness, 78, 140
prices: anti-inflation program (proposed), 366–369; attitude toward rising, 147–148; buying behavior and, 59–60; capacity utilization, 158–160; choosing price/nonprice competition, 33–35; competition through comparison, 372–376; competitive inflation, 126–128, 348–349; cost-push theory, 172–173; equilibrium of, 284–291; "fair," 130; "freezing," 330, 332; indexing, 339–344; inflation and, 55, 56; inflationary, 347–349, in inflationary markets, 49–51; justifications for raising, 87–91; marginal costs/profits, 231–233; monopolistic market, 46–48; nature of, 15; nonprice competition, 30–32, 44; political restraints on increased, 91–93; pricing institutions, 85–95, 121–122, 142–143; product degradation, 62–64; profit maximization decisions, 109–114, 120; resale price maintenance, 36–37; retailers' markup, 78–79;

sales, 60–61; in specialist economy, 132–133; supply and demand, 83–84, 227–229; target, 367–368, 382–383; uncertainty about, 108–109; union incentives, 134–135; wage and price controls, 136–137. *See also* costs; profits; wage and price controls
pricing institutions: anti-inflation program (proposed), 334–335, 388–397; competitive inflation and, 126–128, 142–144; factors in price rises, 84–95; importance of, 95–106; market forces and, 83–84, 292–294; price competition and, 98–100; profit maximization decisions, 118, 120–122; restraints on, 91–95; role of in U.S., 147–152; in specialist economy, 129–130; types of, 67–84; voluntary wage and price controls, 152–154
privacy, and confidentiality requirement, 326
private pricing institutions, 121, 377–378
prize contest, 42
probabilities, economics as a science of, 244–248
product degradation, 48, 64, 373
product innovation, 41
productivity, behavior and job attitude, 293–294; low aggregate demand, 168–172
profit maximization principle, 52–53, 110–114, 231–232; bias of economic theory, 239–240; conflict of interest, 114–119; equilibrium, 285–286; excess demand, 158–160; in Adam Smith's time, 187–188; limitations of, 237–238; motivation and, 294–295; pay rate decisions, 122–125; post-Keynesian economics, 260–261; pricing behavior, 110–114, 119–122; pricing institutions, 84; retailers' markup, 79; in specialist economy, 129–130; supply and demand, 228; uncertainty, 108–110
profits, anti-inflation program (proposed), 357–363; capacity utilization, 158–160; competition and, 294–295; competitive inflation, 126–128; in "freeze" state, 330; inflationary market, 49–51; limitation of, 363–366, 369–371; marginal, 112–113, 158–160; monopolistic markets, 47–48; monopoly power, 31; predicting, 32; price increases, 55, 135; pricing institutions, 84–85; subjectivity of, 257–258; successive year averaging, 368–369. *See also* costs; prices
property, economic determinism and, 210–216
prosperity, anti-inflation program (proposed) and, 312
public disclosure, anti-inflation program (proposed), 315, 323–328
public utilities, 324
purchasing power, *see* supply and demand

rate base, determination of, 365–366
rate setting, fixed utility, 331. *See also* price setting
rationalism, and economics, 224–234, 261–263
recession, and low capacity utilization, 168
regulated industry: full justification requirement, 320–323; as pricing institution, 67–68; profit

maximization, 112. *See also* unregulated industry
regulation: agricultural cooperatives, 382–384; deregulation of the transportation industry, 376–378; economic determinism in business, 218–219; of fixed utilities, 331, 379–381; limitation of profits, 359–360; pricing institutions, 356–372; regulatory agencies, 317–318; of retail industry, 381–383
repetition, and equilibrium, 286–290
representation rights, in anti-inflation program (proposed), 333, 335–339
resale price maintenance, 36–37
retail industry: forms of competition, 37–39; profitability of inflation, 80; regulation of, 381–383; retailers' markup, 78–81, 94

salary, *see* wages and salaries
sales: competition and, 30–45; competitive inflation in U.S. and, 147–152; effect of price setting on, 60–61, 143; in inflationary markets, 49–51; in monopolistic markets, 46–48
satiety, *see* necessity and satiety
savings: aggregate income, 272–275; ascertaining, 281
Say's Law, 78, 226–227, 233
science: economics as a, 189–193, 224–226, 243–258; materialism and, 198–201; natural and moral, 192; and rationalism, 225–226
services, pricing institutions for, 81–83
shareholders, profit maximization decisions affecting, 116
shortages: demand-pull inflation, 173–175; and full employment, 353–355
Smith, Adam, development of economic determinism, 184–187
social science: economics as a, 268–271; and natural science, 190
socialism, opposition to economic determinism of, 220–221
specialist economy, 128–141
stagflation, 156
standards, economic laws as, 235–236
steel industry: as an industrial pricing institution, 76–77, 101–102; profit maximizing in, 121–122; providing price competition in, 102
stockpiling and inflation, 383
strikes, 20–21; anti-inflation program (proposed), 389–392; economic losses incurred, 94
successive year averaging, anti-inflation program (proposed), 366–369
supply and demand: ability to reduce inflation, 6–9; capacity utilization, 158–164; demand-pull inflation, 155–172; demand schedules, 229, 230; economic positivism, 18–19; economic rationalism, 227–229; excess aggregate demand, 4, 5, 7, 27–28, 143–144, 156–157, 166, 176, 232, 260; government reduction in demand, 132–136; 139–141; individual demand, 52; inflationary markets, 52–55; as influence not law, 269; justification for higher prices, 90–91, 164–165; monetary and fiscal policy, 70–136; necessity and satiety, 53–55; overall demand,

52; predictions, 19, 234–235; pricing institutions, 65, 66, 83–84, 95–97; productivity, 169; profit maximization, 158–164; psychological methods to control, 153; rationalistic, 232; subjectivity of, 233, 257–258; supply schedules, 229–230; temporary results of reduced demand, 7–10; unemployment, 167–172
supply-side economics, 7–8

tandem relationships, 124–125
taxation: of excess profits, 358–360; inflation and, 7–8; of inherited wealth, 408; investment credits as incentives, 171–172; presidential power to set rates of, 351–352; as pricing institution, 73; use of by government to lower demand, 168; wealth protection, 216
technological advance: inflation and, 12; inflationary markets and, 56–60
totalitarianism, government price setting and, 328, 329
transportation industry, regulation for competition, 376–378
truth, materialism and, 197–198
tying arrangements, 42

uncertainty, price setting and, 108–109
unemployment, *see* employment and unemployment
U.S. Controller of the Currency, as pricing institution, 69–73
U.S. Department of Agriculture, as pricing institution, 68–69, 85
U.S. Interstate Commerce Commission: full justification requirement, 322–323; as pricing institution, 85
unregulated industry, pricing institutions, 75–76. *See also* regulated industry

validation theory of inflation, 128
values: economic theory and, 296–297; motives and, 239–240
voluntarism, anti-inflation program compliance, 313–314

wage and price controls: commission vs. individual control, 315–320; confidentiality requirement, 324–328; cost-push theory, 173; Economic Stabilization Program (1971), 310–314; "freezing," 136–137; voluntary, 152–154. *See also* anti-inflation program (proposed)
wage creep or drift, 395–396
wage-push theory of inflation, 14, 86, 172–173. *See also* cost-push theory of inflation
wages and salaries: anti-inflation program (proposed), 389–397; controls, 136–137; equilibrium, 290; executives' pay rates, 384–388; indeterminate inflation, 122–125; justifications for higher, 87–91; market forces and, 16; profit maximization, 115–116; as source of inflation, 354
warranty requirement, 372–374
wealth, doctrine of laissez faire as protection of, 216, 403–408
workable competition, 12

Library of Congress Cataloging in Publication Data

Slawson, W. David, 1931–
The new inflation.

Includes bibliographical references and index.
1. Inflation (Finance) 2. Wage-price policy. 3. Competition. 4. Industrial organization (Economic theory) I. Title.
HG229.S58 332.4′1 81-13805
ISBN 0-691-04229-2 AACR2